The Fi... ...d the popular
imagin... ...using on
the live... ...may see... ...prehend what it
mea... ...endous shocks and demands of
...total w...

British Culture & the First World War:

- examines the war's impact on ideologies of race, class, gender and imperialism, the government's efforts to manage news and to promote patriotism, the role of the arts and sciences, and the commemoration of the war over the last century
- synthesizes key scholarship on the social and cultural history of the war
- reclaims a number of neglected or forgotten popular cultural sources such as films, cartoons, juvenile literature and best-selling novels.

Thoroughly revised and updated, the new edition of this accessible and refreshing text includes enhanced discussion of propaganda and debates over how the war ended, and places greater emphasis on the legacy and memory of the war.

George Robb is Professor of History at William Paterson Universtiy of New Jersey, USA.

Social History in Perspective series
General Editor: Jeremy Black

Social History in Perspective is a series of in-depth studies of the
many topics in social, cultural and religious history.

PUBLISHED

John Belchem   Popular Radicalism in Nineteenth-Century Britain
Andrew Brown   Church and Society in England, 1000–1500
Sue Bruley   Women in Britain Since 1900
Anthony Brundage   The English Poor Laws, 1700–1930
Simon Dentith   Society and Cultural Forms in Nineteenth-Century England
Joyce M. Ellis   The Georgian Town, 1680–1840
Paul A. Fideler   Social Welfare in Pre-Industrial England
Peter Fleming   Family and Household in Medieval England
Ian Gazeley   Poverty in Britain, 1900–1965
Kathryn Gleadle   British Women in the Nineteenth Century
Harry Goulbourne   Race Relations in Britain since 1945
Carl J. Griffin   Protest, Politics and Work in Rural England, 1700–1850
Anne Hardy   Health and Medicine in Britain since 1860
Tim Hitchcock   English Sexualities, 1700–1800
Sybil M. Jack   Towns in Tudor and Stuart Britain
Helen M. Jewell   Education in Early Modern England
Alan Kidd   State, Society and the Poor in Nineteenth-Century England
Peter Kirby   Child Labour in Britain, 1750–1870
Arthur J. McIvor   A History of Work in Britain, 1880–1950
Hugh McLeod   Religion and Society in England, 1850–1914
Donald M. MacRaild   The Irish Diaspora in Britain, 1750–1939, 2nd Edition
Donald M. MacRaild and David E. Martin   Labour in Britain, 1830–1914
Christopher Marsh   Popular Religion in the Sixteenth Century
Michael A. Mullett   Catholics in Britain and Ireland, 1558–1829
Christine Peters   Women in Early Modern Britain, 1450–1640
Richard Rex   The Lollards
George Robb   British Culture & the First World War, 2nd Edition
R. Malcolm Smuts   Culture and Power in England, 1585–1685
John Spurr   English Puritanism, 1603–1689
W. B. Stephens   Education in Britain, 1750–1914
Heather Swanson   Medieval British Towns
David Taylor   Crime, Policing and Punishment in England, 1750–1914
N. L. Tranter   British Population in the Twentieth Century
Ian D. Whyte   Migration and Society in Britain, 1550–1830
Ian D. Whyte   Scotland's Society and Economy in Transition, c.1500–c.1760
Andy Wood   Riot, Rebellion and Popular Politics in Early Modern England

Please note that a sister series, *British History in Perspective*, is available,
covering key topics in British political history.

Social History in Perspective
Series Standing Order ISBN 978–0–333–71694–6 hardcover
Series Standing Order ISBN 978–0–333–69336–0 paperback
(outside North America only)

You can receive future titles in this series as they are published by placing a standing order.
Please contact your bookseller or, in the case of difficulty, write to us at the address below with
your name and address, the title of the series and the ISBN quoted above.

Customer Services Department, Macmillan Distribution Ltd,
Houndmills, Basingstoke, Hampshire, RG21 6XS, UK

British Culture & the First World War

Second Edition

GEORGE ROBB

 palgrave

First edition published 2002
Second edition published 2015 by
PALGRAVE

Palgrave in the UK is an imprint of Macmillan Publishers Limited, registered in England, company number 785998, of 4 Crinan Street, London N1 9XW.

Palgrave Macmillan in the US is a division of St Martin's Press LLC, 175 Fifth Avenue, New York, NY 10010.

Palgrave is a global imprint of the above companies and is represented throughout the world.

Palgrave® and Macmillan® are registered trademarks in the United States, the United Kingdom, Europe and other countries

ISBN 978–1–137–30749–1   hardback
ISBN 978–1–137–30750–7   paperback

This book is printed on paper suitable for recycling and made from fully managed and sustained forest sources. Logging, pulping and manufacturing processes are expected to conform to the environmental regulations of the country of origin.

A catalogue record for this book is available from the British Library.

A catalog record for this book is available from the Library of Congress.

Typeset by MPS Limited, Chennai, India.

Printed in China

For William

Contents

List of Illustrations   viii

Acknowledgements   ix

Introduction   1

1   The Realities of Modern Warfare   7

2   Class, Labor, and State Control   30

3   Gender, Sex, and Sexuality   58

4   Nation, Race, and Empire   93

5   Propaganda and Censorship   119

6   Art and Literature   154

7   Popular Culture   182

8   Remembering and Memorializing the War   207

Notes   230

Further Reading   268

Index   280

List of Illustrations

5.1   Alfred Leete, 'Kitchener Wants You'   129
5.2   Savile Lumley, 'Daddy, what did YOU do in the Great War?'   130
5.3   Louis Raemaekers, 'Ain't I a lovable fellow?'   132
6.1   James Clark, *The Great Sacrifice*   164
6.2   C. R. W. Nevinson, *Paths of Glory*   167
6.3   Paul Nash, *The Menin Road*   168

Acknowledgements

I would like to acknowledge the assistance of the Librarians and Staff at the Imperial War Museum, the British Library, and the New York Public Library, Research Division. My research assistant, William Peniston, proved especially resourceful in tracking down numerous books and articles. I could never have completed this project without the enormous generosity of my colleagues and friends. Antoinette Burton kindly read and commented on various drafts of this manuscript. The book has also benefitted from conversations with Barbara Suess, Ted Cook and Jeremy Black. Lastly, I would like to thank my editor at Palgrave, Sonya Barker, and the press's anonymous reviewers for their many helpful comments and suggestions.

Every effort has been made to trace the copyright holders but if any have been inadvertently overlooked, the publishers will be pleased to make the necessary arrangement at the first opportunity.

Introduction

Britain's last surviving veteran of the Great War, Harry Patch, died in 2009 at the age of 111, and very few people now have firsthand memories of the war. Although the war is no longer a living memory, it continues to inspire passionate debate among Britons as to its meaning and legacy. A veritable flood of books about the war has continued unabated since the 1960s and will no doubt increase in intensity now that the centennial is upon us. Given the current outpouring of war books, there is a need for reliable surveys to navigate the vast historiography, synthesizing the most important recent work and evaluating the key debates.

This book is a brief, but comprehensive survey of British society and culture during the First World War. It looks not at military campaigns and battle strategies, but at the lives and experiences of ordinary Britons – how they responded to and were affected by the war, how they attempted to understand the war themselves and to explain it to others, how they dealt with the war's legacies, and how they have remembered the conflict in the decades afterwards. As literary scholar Samuel Hynes explained: 'The First World War was the great military and political event of its time; but it was also the great *imaginative* event. It altered the ways in which men and women thought not only about war but also about the world, and about culture and its expressions.'[1]

As a social and cultural history of the war this book explores both the objective reality of people's lives and the subjective representations of that reality. As social history it examines the material conditions of the nation at war – how people lived, worked, and interacted with others – as well as how the experience of war affected social structures like class and social behaviors like gender and sex. As cultural history, the book pays special attention to how Britons thought about the war and how they represented it in words and images. In all the chapters

I have combined a social and cultural approach. For example, when discussing women war workers, I examine both the realities of women's work (through employment statistics, labor agreements, and wage levels) and the representations of women war workers (in cartoons, newspaper reports, and novels).

Cultural evidence often gives a different perspective on the past than other, more conventional, historical sources and does not always agree with observed reality or measurable data. To continue with the example of women's work, British women definitely entered the labor force in increased numbers during the war. This fact, however, is not always apparent in literary and artistic representations of women during the war years. Many popular cultural sources, such as women's magazines and romance novels, ignored the growth of women's paid employment, instead focusing on their traditional roles as wives and mothers. This disjuncture between reality and representation suggests discomfort on the part of some commentators with women's new opportunities. By studying the tensions between social and cultural sources we can gain insights into contemporary debates about the war as well as continuing historical controversies.

Cultural representations of the Great War – in poetry, novels, films, and television – continue to shape collective historical memories of the conflict. In recent years there has been considerable discussion and debate about the accuracy of these representations. As some historians like Brian Bond and Gary Sheffield point out, the current understanding of the war as a tragedy is based more on the poetry of Wilfred Owen, the novels of Pat Barker, and on television series like *Blackadder Goes Forth* than on the most recent scholarly research. These historians dismiss most cultural representations of the war, which emphasize military bungling, deceitful propaganda, and a heartless waste of lives, as both lopsided and inaccurate. They point out that this view of the war as tragic and futile is contradicted by a great deal of historical evidence and was not shared by most people who experienced the war firsthand. Cultural studies of the First World War and its aftermath are thus crucial in understanding how our present-day attitudes toward the war have come about. Whether better historical knowledge of the war can displace or counteract the current pessimistic viewpoint remains to be seen.[2]

The following chapters will look at 'culture' in its broadest sense, not merely as art or 'the fine arts', but as the customs, ideas, and attitudes shared by a people or nation. This will include topics such as religious beliefs, fashion, and education, as well as ideologies of class and gender. Special attention will be paid to how such ideas and their attendant behavior were expressed through language (speech and print culture of all kinds) and other symbolic media such as painting, cinema, and music.

There are few general surveys like this one. Since the end of the First World War, the vast majority of books published on the subject have been military and diplomatic histories. For fifty years after the war historians examined the conflict almost entirely from the point of view of politicians, diplomats and generals. Although there was a publishing boom during the 1920s and 1930s of memoirs and other writings by former soldiers, nurses, and war workers, this literature made no impact on how professional historians discussed the war.[3] Of the tens of thousands of volumes on the Great War in the British Library or Imperial War Museum, most concern the political, strategic, or economic aspects of the war. Many popular histories on the war are still from the 'drum and trumpet' school of military studies, narrating the war's battles and campaigns with little reference to its larger social and cultural context.

Only since the 1960s have scholars seriously begun to redress this imbalance with social and cultural studies of the British home front, propaganda, and war art. Arthur Marwick's now classic work, *The Deluge* (1965), initiated a wave of pioneering work on the social history of the war. Another pioneering work, John Keegan's *Face of Battle* (1976), detailed the combat experiences of ordinary soldiers of the Great War based on letters and diaries found in the Imperial War Museum in London. Marwick's and Keegan's work was part of a growing field of history which sought to study society 'from the bottom up.' During the 1970s and 1980s, a great deal of important and original scholarship was published on such topics as women and the war, the war's impact on social welfare policy, and government-directed propaganda and censorship. In more recent years, this work has been supplemented by new studies of the arts, popular culture, and the construction of memory.

By the twenty-first century cultural history has almost supplanted social history among scholars of the war. Many of these cultural works draw inspiration from Paul Fussell's *The Great War and Modern Memory* (1975), an early and highly influential literary study of the First World War. This latest scholarship has begun to infiltrate general histories of the war, especially of the home front, but many of them continue to relegate cultural topics to a single chapter, usually at the end.[4] I reject such an approach, as every chapter in this book includes a great deal of material about art, literature, and other forms of cultural expression.

This volume synthesizes much of the best and most recent scholarship on the social and cultural history of the war. It also seeks to broaden the definition of wartime culture by reclaiming a great deal of neglected or forgotten work, especially popular cultural sources. This recovery is necessary because the overwhelming emphasis of cultural studies has been on the experience of the nation's most literate and articulate citizens. The memoirs, novels, and poetry of the cultural elite have historically been the most accessible works on the war, having survived in school curricula, libraries, and publishers' lists of books still in print. Wartime writings by women, the working classes, and common soldiers remain less well known, as do the many publications written for these populations or for juvenile readers. Yet a popular war novel, like Berta Ruck's romance, *The Land Girl's Love Story* (1918), had a much wider readership than the work of a 'serious' (critically respected) writer, such as H. G. Wells's *Mr Britling Sees It Through* (1916). Likewise, many Britons were more familiar with the now-forgotten patriotic poetry of Jessie Pope or John Oxenham than with the 'classic' anti-war poems of Siegfried Sassoon or Wilfred Owen. Much ephemeral literature and cultural production has been even less studied by historians: newspapers, magazines, posters, pamphlets, advertisements, sheet music, sermons, postcards, and films. These neglected sources are an invaluable means of enlarging and broadening our view of British society and culture during the war. For people not only experienced the war in vastly different ways depending on their military status, social class, sex, race, age, and geographic locale, but their personal characteristics also influenced what sources of information or what kinds of literature and art were available to them, as well as how they interpreted this material.

Much of the recent social and cultural history of the war has revolved around the question of whether or not the war represented a watershed in British culture. Some scholars of the First World War have credited it with a remarkable series of social and cultural changes, while others have argued that it changed little, or that those changes that did occur probably would have happened sooner or later anyway. The first view has been most eloquently expressed in Arthur Marwick's *The Deluge*, the very title of which imagines the war as a cataclysmic flood which swept away much of Victorian culture and inaugurated a more modern world.[5] More recently, revisionist histories have emphasized that the conservatism of British culture acted to constrain or absorb change. For example, in *Blighty* (1996), Gerard DeGroot concludes that 'War was tragic, in some cases catastrophic. But for most people it was an extraordinary event of limited duration which, as much as it brought change, also inspired a desire to reconstruct according to cherished patterns. If war is the locomotive of history, the rolling stock in this case was typically British: slow, outmoded, and prone to delay and cancellation.'[6]

Ultimately, the debate over whether the war promoted 'tradition' or 'modernity' is rather sterile. One could compile endless, rival lists illustrating wartime changes and continuities without gaining a deeper understanding of the conflict.[7] It is necessary to go beyond what is new or not new about the war and its aftermath and try to comprehend what it meant for an entire society to undergo the tremendous shocks and demands of total war. Whether or not the war originated trends or merely accelerated those already in operation, it dramatized for contemporaries the transition between two significantly different societies. One, marked by rigid segregation and inequalities between the classes and sexes, world economic supremacy, and imperial expansion; and another, more egalitarian and characterized by greater individual prosperity, but where industrial and imperial power were in serious decline.

More recently, historians have vigorously debated the purpose and legacy of the war, often challenging the prevailing popular view that it was a pointless waste of lives and that all combatant nations bore responsibility for the conflict. Brian Bond and Gary Sheffield make a strong case for German war guilt and contrast the values of a militarist Germany with those of a more open, tolerant and liberal Britain. They argue that the war was necessary, that the British fought it more effectively and competently than is generally realized, and that the Allied victory in 1918 was a desirable outcome that is still worth celebrating. In *The Unquiet Western Front* (2002), Bond especially challenges the pessimistic and cynical view of the war encapsulated in Fussell's *The Great War and Modern Memory* (1975). As the 2014 centennial of the First World War began, this academic debate has been taken up by politicians and the wider public, centering on the question of whether the war should be solemnly commemorated as a tragedy or celebrated as a British victory.

Chapter 1 of this book examines the implications of 'total war,' whereby combatant nations attempted to annihilate each other's military *and* incapacitate the civilian populations supplying the military. Modern science and industrial technology were called upon in unprecedented ways and left an ambiguous legacy. The technology of modern warfare could be variously imagined as the nation's savior and as the potential destroyer of the human race. The next three chapters of the book will consider the ways in which ideas and behaviors with regard to class, sex, and race influenced the course of the war and were themselves affected by the conflict. Colonized peoples, women, and the working classes all contributed to the war in significant, and often unexpected, ways, and they all imagined that their support for the British cause would improve their traditionally subordinate status. In some cases the war proved genuinely liberating, though in others it raised expectations only to dash them later. Chapter 5 examines the role of propaganda and censorship in the war, in particular the government's attempts to manage news and to maintain a high level of support for its policies. Chapters 6 and 7 explore connections between the war, the arts, and popular culture. Novelists, painters, composers, and filmmakers overwhelmingly supported the war, and their output represented a veritable 'militarization of culture.' Only after the war did a literature of disillusionment challenge these patriotic representations. The final chapter looks at the commemoration and popular memory of the war in Britain, as well as its enduring, and controversial, cultural legacy.

During the war, the historian A. V. Dicey looked forward to a future view of the conflict as 'it will be regarded by a fair-minded historian writing in AD 2000.'[8] Of course, Dicey confidently assumed that such a view would not differ significantly from his own patriotic and elitist version of events. The war itself has rendered such a history impossible. This book, with its emphasis on the lives and culture of ordinary Britons, can hardly be what Dicey envisioned, but is a logical consequence of the Great War's leveling tendencies. And given our own culture's skepticism about the possibility of writing 'objective' history, many would further reject Dicey's ideal as naïve and dated. This skepticism, need it be emphasized, itself owes much to the disillusionment wrought by the war and its undermining of society's uncritical faith in patriotism, science, and progress. As a would-be 'fair-minded historian' writing in the early twenty-first century, I can only celebrate this change.

Chapter 1: The Realities of Modern Warfare

In the First World War, modern science and industrial technology revealed their capacity for both awesome power and inhuman monstrosity. Machine guns, poison gas, explosives, submarines, airplanes, and tanks all contributed to the war's legacy of mass destruction and faceless violence. The massive scale of the conflict also required an enormous mobilization of Britain's industrial capacity. 'Total war' meant 'conscripting' millions of civilians to supply the military with weapons, uniforms, and food. It also meant attempting to destroy the enemy's ability to keep its own forces supplied and its civilian workforce in operation. Naval blockades, submarine attacks on merchant ships, and aerial bombings all sought to disrupt industrial capacity and to undermine civilian health and morale. In so doing, the belligerents blurred traditional distinctions between soldiers and non-combatants.

The war was a contest whose outcome increasingly hinged on scientific discovery and technological expertise. In 1915, a British physicist wrote: 'It is beyond any doubt that this war is a war of engineers and chemists quite as much as of soldiers.'[1] For the first time, nations mobilized thousands of scientists and engineers in support of the military. Geologists laid trench systems and tunnels, physicists designed acoustic devices, geographers drew artillery maps, biologists developed disinfectants, and psychologists treated shell-shock. The war accelerated the pace of scientific development. For instance, radio technology, chemistry, aeronautics, and clinical medicine all developed rapidly under the pressure of wartime needs. Popular interest in science was also stimulated by the experience of war, and propaganda made extravagant claims about the potential for later peacetime applications of military technology. Although the war did much to popularize and glorify science, there coexisted considerable ambivalence about the new technologies. Some observers clung to the utopian possibilities of science, while others saw wartime technology as the harbinger of Armageddon.

* * *

The nature of industrial society transformed warfare in ways little fore-seen by either generals or politicians. Wealthy and populous nations could raise and supply huge armies, and maintain them in the field for years on end. New military technologies such as explosives and long-range artillery gave entrenched troops a tremendous defensive advantage from which it proved nearly impossible to dislodge them. In September 1914, the Germans marching toward Paris reached the Aisne River and dug themselves in to face the approaching French and British Armies. The Allies, finding themselves unable to penetrate the defensive line, dug themselves in as well. The war of movement on the Western Front was over. The battle lines were not to alter significantly until 1918. Trenches protected by barbed wire and occupied on both sides by soldiers with machine guns and rapid-fire rifles were difficult to storm, and any attempts to do so were extraordinarily costly of lives. The technological advances in weaponry which had engendered this stalemate did not pro-vide any easy solutions to it.[2]

One of the war's most traumatic results was the massive death toll wrought by modern weaponry: 10 million soldiers killed, with over 700 000 British dead, rising to nearly a million when deaths of imperial forces were added. In a wartime address, Sir William Osler, professor of medicine at Oxford, considered the destructive capacity of modern science: 'It has made slaughter possible on a scale never dreamt of before, and it has enor-mously increased man's capacity to maim and to disable his fellow man.'[3] In less than a month from the war's beginning, more soldiers had died than in all the Napoleonic Wars a century earlier. Most deaths and injuries (60 percent) were caused by heavy artillery guns and exploding shells. Shrapnel shells each contained 250–350 lead balls and a charge of gun-powder timed to explode while the shell rose above its intended victims. Exploding shells would rain down hundreds of projectiles on heads below. Cloth caps offered British troops little protection, and new steel helmets were not issued until late in 1915. The new Lewis machine gun, which could fire 550 rounds per minute, also proved extremely costly of lives.[4]

Trench warfare created a logistical nightmare for which the military was utterly unprepared. Battlefields stretched for hundreds of miles, men could scarcely be distinguished from the ground, trenches were hidden from view, and generals were often far from the battle zone. Lord Kitchener, the War Minister, expressed the frustration of many military leaders when he confessed: 'I don't know what is to be done . . . this isn't war.'[5] It certainly was unlike any war with which the Army High Command was familiar. Educated in Napoleonic era cavalry charges and trained in operations against poorly armed Afghans and Zulus, most British commanders were bewildered by the unexpected 'stalemate' of the trenches. More recent lessons about modern firepower from the Franco-Prussian War or the American Civil War had not been learned. Nor had the Boer War's lesson about the ability of entrenched Afrikaners to hold off forces many times larger by using concentrated firepower.[6]

In the period 1900–14, the British Army had undergone profound modernization, but the process was incomplete at the outset of the war. It was developing from a small volunteer force appropriate to the defense of the Empire and fighting small colonial wars, toward a much larger force capable of waging continental war and proficient in modern weaponry. The British Expeditionary Force grew to such vast proportions in 1914–15 that there were insufficient numbers of experienced officers available. The nature of the officer class was also in transition from the gentlemanly ideal to a technically competent, professional ideal. The war took place amidst this transition, and many of its problems stemmed from a still largely traditional officer class trying to wage a modern technological war. Douglas Haig and many of Britain's other commanders trained at the Staff College in the 1880s and 1890s, where they were taught that the enemy was defeated by a decisive blow and that success depended on the morale of the army and the personal qualities of the commander-in-chief. Most of the Army's generals were veterans of colonial wars, with no experience of coordinating gigantic forces spread out over hundreds of miles. Many commanders also came from cavalry backgrounds and their continued faith in the value of cavalry is often cited as an example of their inability to grasp the realities of modern warfare.[7]

Most people on the General Staff and among the officer corps believed that modern weaponry could be overcome by psychological or human qualities, rather than by corresponding technological tactics. They were reluctant to think through the logical use of new weapons like the tank, but instead relegated them to peripheral roles. Military leaders were also reluctant to accept advice from scientific experts, who were usually their social inferiors and often came from the fringes of 'respectable' society. Instead of rethinking the basic ideas of modern, scientific warfare, there was a tendency among the military to reinforce old ideas of a structured battlefield and to yield to the 'more and more' syndrome, demanding more men, more artillery, and more explosives.[8]

A traditional emphasis on the need for warfare to be 'decisive' led to the massive offensives of 1916 and 1917 that aimed for decisive results. What happened at the Somme and elsewhere was the application of dated thinking to the technical reality of modern warfare. For weeks before the British advance at the Somme on 1 July 1916, the German trenches were saturated with heavy artillery fire. Around 700 000 men were assembled to clear a gap in the German lines, through which infantry divisions would then march heroically. Unfortunately, the preliminary bombardment had not destroyed the German's ability to defend their trenches, and in fact had alerted them to the coming assault, enabling them to call up reinforcements. When British troops went 'over the top' of their trenches on the morning of 1 July and began their march across 'no man's land', they were easy targets for German machine-gunners. As one German soldier later recalled: 'We were very surprised to see them walking, we had never seen that before . . . The officers were in front. I noticed one of them walked calmly, carrying a walking stick. When we started firing we just had to load and reload. They went down in their hundreds. You didn't have to aim, we just fired into them.' Despite horrendous British casualties on the disastrous first day, there was great reluctance to call off the battle after such lengthy and elaborate preparations. Strategy had become subservient to logistics.[9]

British commanders were also constrained by the realities of coalition warfare. Unlike the Germans, the British had to coordinate operations with several other nations. With French forces overextended on the Western Front and Russia on the verge of collapse in 1916, the smaller British forces were under tremendous pressure to take on a greater share of the fighting. The Somme offensive had to go forward, regardless of whether the British were adequately prepared. The vast resources that all sides committed to the war also made a compromise peace next to impossible. For the Allies to agree to a negotiated peace while German soldiers were still in France would have been an admission of defeat.[10]

Communications technology did not keep pace with weapons development and was to prove the Achilles' heel of military operations. Effective communications methods did not exist for the battlefield, and this was to prove a serious problem for commanders who needed to coordinate massive troop movements over vast territories. Radio transmitters were too unwieldy and unreliable, telephone wires broke under heavy bombardments, and optical signals could not be seen through the haze of battle. Armies frequently fell back on the oldest, low-tech methods: human runners and carrier pigeons. Commanders received sporadic reports from the front lines, sometimes long after the situation had changed, creating massive confusion and making effective responses impossible.[11]

As casualties mounted to an unprecedented level, staff officers began distancing themselves from the awful reality through the use of euphemistic metaphors of economics, such as 'no more money in the till.' They spoke of deficits, credits, and surpluses of troops and the need for 'further expenditure' of men. Some commentators have also accused Army commanders of distancing themselves physically from the horrors of frontline experience, but this was not usually the case. After all, some 60 British generals were killed during the war. Some commanders were doubtless insensitive to the human costs of the war, others were incompetent and unimaginative. Yet all the imagination in the world would not have brought a swift and painless victory. The weapons and resources available to both sides were such that no swift or easy resolution was possible.[12]

Why the war finally ended in 1918 with a German defeat is still a matter of historical debate. The traditional explanation is that the war was won through attrition and endurance. Ultimately, Britain and her allies were better able than the Central Powers to maintain mass armies in the field over several years and to keep up production of munitions and food. British naval superiority starved Germany of needed supplies and gave the Allies exclusive access to American industrial output, which was equivalent to that of the whole of Europe in 1914. Mass concentrations of men and munitions finally caused German resistance to crumble. Britain's industrial superiority in producing sheer numbers of weapons finally triumphed over either scientific sophistication or its capacity for strategic subtlety.[13]

In recent years military historians have challenged the belief in a war of attrition, by emphasizing the role played by new weapons technologies and new strategic innovations in finally breaking the stalemate on the Western Front. These historians argue that trench warfare was far from static and that significant scientific developments and tactical improvements were continually changing the face of battle. In this scenario, the British Army experienced a 'learning curve,' whereby commanders corrected their earlier mistakes and laid the groundwork for the Allied 'breakthrough' of 1918.[14]

* * *

The wealth that industrialism had made available to war making, as well as the nature of new military technology, ensured that no single masterstroke of strategy would swiftly end the struggle. In the meantime, all belligerent nations had to cope with the logistical nightmare of feeding and arming military forces that numbered in the millions. Many in

Britain feared that Germany was a more efficient and more 'scientific' nation, and that British industry might not be up to the contest.[15] Fears of national degeneration had been endemic since the late nineteenth century, engendered by Britain's economic depression and the military debacles of the Boer War. The experience of the first months of the war, when Britain struggled to raise a mass army and increase weapons production, seemed only to confirm the worst of these fears.

Britain had been almost totally dependent on Germany for many key industrial products, including pharmaceuticals, optical glass, precision instruments, and a whole range of chemicals needed to make explosives. Britain's dependence on the German chemical industry was especially dramatized by the fact that this was their only source of khaki dye for soldiers' uniforms and navy blue for sailors'. The war forced Britain to develop industries to replace German-produced goods. For the first time in history, the British government financed a company, British Dyestuffs, which manufactured a number of important chemicals and sponsored war-related research. The British were less successful in manufacturing the optical glass needed for rangefinders, telescopic gun sights, periscopes, and field glasses. The War Office was therefore forced to open secret negotiations with the German government for a supply of optical glass through a Swiss intermediary in return for supplying the Germans with rubber. For the most part, however, Britain succeeded in developing replacement industries. In the Autumn of 1918, an Exhibition of British Scientific Products was held at King's College, London, to display numerous domestically made commodities which had previously been imported from Germany.[16]

Overall levels of production also had to be increased, especially in the area of munitions. Attempts to blast away the enemy's defenses required an astronomical quantity of shells. Since heavy artillery lacked pinpoint accuracy, the military compensated by increasing the sheer volume of projectiles they fired. For example, in the Third Battle of Ypres, between 16 and 31 July, 1917, the British fired 4 300 000 shells. This represented the output of 55 000 workers for an entire year, and a cost of £22 million – nearly equal to the total costs of the home Army for 1914. Victory depended on supplying munitions on a massive scale and solving problems of industrial production.[17]

Industry struggled to meet the military's almost insatiable need for weaponry. A shell shortage developed in May 1915 and proved a great embarrassment for Prime Minister Asquith's government. In June, H. G. Wells and others publicly attacked the government for its reluctance to seek outside scientific expertise. Wells wrote to *The Times*, 'throughout almost the entire range of our belligerent activities we are to this day being conservative, imitative, and amateurish when victory can fall only to the most vigorous employment of the best scientific knowledge of all conceivable needs and materials.'[18]

In response to such criticism, the government created a new Ministry of Munitions under Lloyd George to better coordinate production. As a measure of its success, by 1916, 12 government factories and 16 private firms under Ministry contract were producing 1000 tons of the explosive TNT a week – 50 times the national output in 1914. Enhanced quantity, however, did not always translate into good quality. Some 30 percent of the 1.5 million shells fired in advance of the July 1916 Somme offensive failed to explode.[19] Ultimately, 61 percent of the total workforce was engaged in work directly related to the war, with the heaviest concentrations in the metals industry (90 percent) and chemicals (79 percent). Thus managing war production served to extend state control over the economy as a whole.[20]

The war hastened the adoption in Britain of principles of scientific management. American-style assembly lines and the use of interchangeable parts had been making inroads into British industry before the war, but from 1915 were applied on a gigantic scale to gun, airplane, and vehicle manufacture. The Ministry of Munitions, in particular, rationalized and modernized factory layout, power supply, and cost accounting at those establishments under its control. Time and motion studies were also extensively implemented in government-controlled factories. The war further encouraged and accelerated change from small-scale artisanal units to large-scale factory producers. This was especially apparent in the Birmingham metals industries, and elsewhere in clothing and shoe manufacturing. Fordism had arrived in Britain.[21]

British agriculture also became more highly modernized as a result of the war. Increased food production with fewer farm workers and horses necessitated greater mechanization, along lines that had long prevailed in the United States and Canada due to the massive size of farms. The government heavily subsidized the purchase of the most up-to-date farm machinery. Gaspower replaced horsepower, especially with the widespread introduction of the Fordson tractor from America. Small, lightweight, and cheap, the Fordsons proved to be 'the Model T's of the farmyard.'[22]

The vast needs of war revealed acute problems in British industry such as its amateurish management and its failure to keep abreast of the latest scientific advances, especially compared with Germany and the United States. The war encouraged much-needed industrial modernization, and the government often provided the capital necessary to upgrade facilities. Coal gave way to electricity and the internal combustion engine.

In new factories, 95 percent of the machinery was now powered by electricity, and the industrial capacity of electrical power stations more than doubled during the war. The reliance on gas-powered engines also became paramount during the war, for airplanes, tanks, armored cars, and a vast range of transport vehicles. The Army pool of motor vehicles grew from 1500 in 1914 to more than 120 000 by the Armistice. Wartime innovations served as a launching pad for Britain's new industries of the 1920s – chemicals, plastics, synthetic fibers, optics, and aeronautics.[23]

The British government and military eventually recruited a great number of scientists to assist in developing weaponry and the technology of warfare, though here, as elsewhere, they got off to a slow start. In 1914, the Royal Society convened a War Committee to 'organize assistance to the Government in conducting or suggesting scientific investigations in relation to the war', but the War Office responded coolly. Scientists frequently felt that their expert advice was ignored by civil servants, who resented their interference.[24] Only after the shell crisis and H. G. Wells's criticism of the government for its neglect of science did things start to change. The new Ministry of Munitions encouraged the application of science to warfare through its Trench Warfare, Explosives, and Munitions Inventions Departments created in the summer of 1915. The Admiralty also created its own Board of Inventions and Research in July 1915. In August 1916, the government created an Advisory Council for Science, and in December this was reorganized as a new Department of Scientific and Industrial Research (DSIR) to coordinate and sponsor scientific research in the national interest. The Department acted as a central clearing house for research problems, channeling questions to university laboratories and creating important precedents for contract research later. Academic scientists proved very successful in adapting themselves to war research, especially at 'red brick' universities such as Birmingham, Bristol, Leeds, and Manchester. The formation of the DSIR represented an important new commitment to state-sponsored research and development that was to continue throughout the twentieth century.[25]

A number of important research problems were encountered in the production of munitions. Very few explosives had been manufactured in Britain before the war and a number of their key chemical ingredients came from Germany. The Explosives Department under Lord Moulton embarked on experiments to find new ways to manufacture the toluene and glycerine necessary in making the old forms, and to invent new forms of explosives. For instance, the Department invented 'amatol' by combining precious TNT with the more abundant compound, ammonium nitrate. Chordite, which was used to propel shells, remained in short supply because of difficulties in making one of its crucial ingredients, acetone. This situation changed in 1915, when Chaim Weizmann, a chemist at the University of Manchester (later president of Israel), devised a fermentation method for producing acetone from starch. Chordite also required massive amounts of alcohol for its manufacture, which incidentally led to the restricted sale and higher costs of whiskey. Researchers struggled to streamline industrial production methods and meet the needs of the war machine.[26]

The cooperation under the Munitions Inventions Department (MID) of university, industrial, and government laboratories, military experimental grounds, and private workshops resulted in an unprecedented integration of previously separate scientific communities. A key function of the MID was to sift through the some 48 000 suggestions for new weaponry sent in by the general public between 1915 and 1919. Only about 200 of these ideas proved to have any potential use; the others included such bizarre schemes as using electricity to produce a deadly heat ray, or equipping balloons with magnets to snatch guns from German soldiers. The solicitation of public ideas reflected a faith in amateur inventors left over from Victorian times. The MID primarily refined existing devices or technologies which was typical of the scientific contribution to the war. Scientists did not change the face of battle and the conflict was mostly fought with technologies already in existence at its outset. The need to increase production of current technologies outweighed development of new ones.[27]

Science was also mobilized to deal with health issues, and a number of new medical techniques and skills were developed in response to war. As science became more ingenious in tearing people apart, it had to find new ways to put them back together. X-ray technology, pharmacology, neurosurgery, and plastic surgery all made significant advances during the war. Blood transfusion techniques were also improved, as blood storage became possible and the rudiments of blood-typing were understood. These developments helped doctors cope with wound shock and surgical shock resulting from the loss of blood. Shrapnel and high-velocity bullets caused an enormous number of bone fractures, which in turn concentrated resources on orthopedic care. The introduction during the war of a splint developed earlier by Hugh Owen Thomas revolutionized the treatment of wounded soldiers. The Thomas splint could be put on in a few minutes, before moving a soldier or even removing his clothing. It greatly decreased further injury during transport, and reduced mortality from fractures from 80 percent in 1916 to 20 percent in 1918. Altogether, 82 percent of wounded and 93 percent of 'sick and injured' British troops were returned to duty. The British Army Medical Service grew from a force of 20,000 doctors and nurses in 1914 to 160,000 in 1918.[28]

The First World War was the first war where more soldiers died from battle injuries than from disease or infection. The ratio of deaths from disease to deaths from injury was 0.67 to 1. In the Boer War, the ratio had been almost 2 to 1 and in the Crimean War, more than 5 to 1. This change is testimony both to the greater destructive capacity of modern weapons and to advances in modern medicine, especially in the realm of sanitation. During the war, further advances were made in antiseptic medicine. Wounds often became seriously infected due to bacteria which thrived in the well-manured fields of Flanders, and traditional disinfectants like carbolic acid often proved ineffective. Pathologists developed new hypochlorite germicides to cope with the problem. A team of researchers at Edinburgh University under Professor Lorrain Smith invented 'eusol' – a combination of bleaching powder and calcium borate which proved highly effective in treating septic wounds.[29]

The British pharmaceutical industry developed rapidly during the war and became more focused on medical research. Initially, there were acute shortages of drugs and anaesthetics due to British dependence on the German drug industry. Local anaesthetics like novocaine and beta-eucaine had previously been obtained solely from Germany. Stop-gap production was set up in new laboratories at St Andrews University under Professor James Irvine and at Sheffield University and Imperial College. The manufacture of new and pirated products, like the anti-syphilitic drug salvarsan, was also accelerated as a result of breaks with international trade agreements and product law.[30]

Another medical consequence of the war was the high number of mutilated and dismembered soldiers. The presence in wartime Britain of so many 'limbless heroes' altered people's perceptions of disability, which had formerly been an amalgam of pity and shame. One organization that helped 'cripples', The Guild of Brave Poor Things, changed its name during the war to the Guild of the Handicapped. More resources were directed to rehabilitation, and the development of better artificial limbs. The war also changed ideas about what kinds of work were appropriate to the disabled. No longer were they to be marginalized as street-corner vendors of pencils, but were to be retrained in all manner of industrial and clerical occupations. Under the terms of wartime propaganda, the disabled soldier was not less, but more of a man. After the war, unfortunately, disabled ex-servicemen lost much sympathy from both the public and the government. Another casualty of postwar economic retrenchment, they were largely forgotten, living on miserly veterans' benefits, grudgingly paid.[31]

* * *

Scientists and tacticians were unable to develop new offensive weapons or strategies to break through the war of stalemate, but their attempts to do so through poison gas, tanks, submarine warfare, and aerial bombing brought the war to new levels of technical complexity – or frightfulness, depending on one's point of view. The use of gas first brought to prominence a number of issues regarding the nature of 'civilized' warfare. Although tear-gas had been used by the French early in 1915, it was the use of chlorine by the Germans at Ypres on 22 April 1915 that grabbed headlines and was denounced as a violation of the 'laws of war.' Rudyard Kipling declared, 'we are dealing with animals who have scientifically and philosophically removed themselves inconceivably outside civilisation.'[32] Despite such denunciations, the British were quick to develop their own chemical weapons. On 18 May 1915, Lord Kitchener condemned gas as a 'diabolical' weapon, and in the next sentence announced 'His Majesty's Government feel that our troops must be adequately protected by the employment of similar methods.' As one Minister remembered: 'we agreed [Kitchener] should use anything he could get invented.' The Archbishop of Canterbury urged Britain not to use poison gas, but the King disagreed, arguing that 'the question is purely military, and that ethical considerations will not enter into it.' Although gas was widely used by Britain and its allies, in the public imagination it remained associated with German barbarism. For example, a cartoon in *London Opinion* in September 1916 showed the Kaiser urging his 'Professor of Frightfulness' to invent new weapons of cruelty. The professor's laboratory is filled with dastardly apparatus including liquid fire and poison gas.[33]

Britain took longer to emulate German chemical weaponry because of the inadequacy of its research and its inability to convert laboratory findings into industrial production. In an attempt to push things forward, in May 1915 the Royal Society asked chemistry professors throughout the Kingdom to furnish the Army with names and addresses of ex-students, and to encourage current students to join the Royal Engineers. One hundred soon volunteered, and formed the nucleus of a Special Brigade commanded by a young engineer, Major C. H. Foulkes. From then on, the British began to make their own contributions to chemical warfare. In 1916, for example, Captain W. H. Livens and his father, a civilian engineer, developed a method for projecting gas bombs, rather than simply releasing gas from canisters and waiting for it to drift across no man's land as the Germans did. Canister gas had proved an unpredictable weapon, depending on weather conditions and wind direction. The British first used gas projectiles near Arras on 4 April 1917. Their shell gas used chloropicrin – an asphyxiating and tearing gas, and the existing

German gas mask did not provide protection from it. The Germans then introduced mustard gas in July 1917, which caused temporary blindness and serious respiratory distress. By late 1917, gas bombs played a routine part in the war, undermining morale and keeping up nervous apprehension among frontline soldiers.[34]

By November 1918, 63 different kinds of poison gas had been tried by both sides. In no way did gas prove decisive; it lacked precision and was easily dispersed by wind and rain. Its psychological impact, however, remained significant. Artists and writers especially transformed a relatively feeble weapon into an object of extraordinary terror. John Singer Sargent's painting *Gassed* captured the terror of chemical weapons by depicting huge crowds of soldiers who had been blinded by mustard gas. Wilfred Owen's poem 'Dulce Et Decorum Est' includes a vivid evocation of the panic caused by a gas attack:

> Gas! Gas! Quick, boys! – An ecstasy of fumbling,
> Fitting the clumsy helmets just in time,
> But someone still was yelling out and stumbling
> And floundering like a man in fire or lime. –
> Dim through the misty panes and thick green light,
> As under a green sea, I saw him drowning.[35]

Gas injured and killed in unconventional ways which contemporaries found difficult to assimilate. It appeared to be taking war yet another stage away from a conflict where individual qualities of bravery, endurance, and honor mattered. 'War has nothing to do with chivalry anymore', lamented a German general, 'the higher civilization rises, the viler man becomes.' A science-fiction nightmare straight out of an H. G. Wells novel seemed to be coming true. Gas masks even stripped combatants of the last vestiges of their individuality, turning all alike into monstrous beings.[36]

While the British rejected poison gas as an example of German 'frightfulness', they welcomed their own new offensive weapon, the tank, as a miracle of scientific ingenuity. In October 1914, an army engineer, Lieutenant Colonel Ernest Swinton, wrote to Sir Maurice Hankey, Secretary of the War Council, about devising armored caterpillar tractors to penetrate the trench barrier. A number of prototypes were developed in 1915, with the military settling on the 'Mark 1', which was demonstrated to politicians and military commanders on 2 February 1916. Although Kitchener referred to it as 'a pretty toy', the War Office ordered 100 to be produced. Haig put the first 60 available tanks into battle at the Somme on 15 September 1916, without much success. This deployment was made against the wishes of Lloyd George and other tank enthusiasts who had wanted a massed attack later. Haig, however, was desperate for any success in the Somme campaign and revealed the 'secret weapon' before sufficient numbers could be made and utilized on appropriate terrain. The tank's unspectacular performance only confirmed the skepticism of the War Office, which mistrusted scientific innovation. The tank's potential was also lost on the Germans, who made no attempt to produce their own.[37]

The British public and press, however, were jubilant over the tank's premiere, newspapers dubbing the new weapon a 'land dreadnought', 'motor monster', 'giant toad', and a 'jabberwock with eyes of flame.' A vast range of miniature tank 'novelties' were commercially produced in china, metal, and wood, serving as pin cushions, jewelry boxes, watch holders, ink wells, cigarette lighters, savings banks, and paperweights. People were eager for signs of national inventiveness and the British public idolized the tank as a weapon of almost uncanny power. For too long, scientific initiative had seemed to lie with the Germans and their Zeppelins, submarines, and poison gas. By the last year of the war, the tank had proved more effective and played a role in pushing back the German lines.[38]

* * *

The air and sea war, like the war on land, developed in ways few had foreseen. Airplanes and submarines, for example, disrupted warfare on a two-dimensional plane with attacks from above and below. Navies and air forces also brought the war home to civilians. On 16 December 1914, German battle cruisers shelled three east coast towns, Scarborough, Whitby, and Hartlepool, causing heavy civilian casualties. For the first time since 1667, when the Dutch raided Sheerness, Britain itself became a theater of war. Both sides later bombed each other's cities, and each attempted to starve out the other's home front – the British through their naval blockade of German ports and the Germans through their submarine attacks on British merchant shipping.

Britannia ruled the waves, but the British Navy failed to win the decisive victory expected of it. It was assumed that naval battles would follow the pattern of setpiece encounters like the one that resulted in Nelson's victory at Trafalgar. Huge amounts of money had been spent on a naval race before the war, though the much-vaunted new class of battleship, the Dreadnought, turned out to play little role in the conflict. Great navies were now vulnerable to mines and torpedoes, and commanders on both sides were reluctant to risk their expensive investments. The Naval Commander, Lord Jellicoe, as Winston Churchill, then First Lord of the Admiralty, remarked, was the only man on either side who could lose the war in an afternoon. He could not win the war, for even the sinking of the German fleet would not do that. But the loss of Britain's fleet would doom the island nation.[39]

The German Navy never left port after the Battle of Jutland in May 1916, but its submarine fleet was busy revolutionizing the war at sea. The U-boat had proved less dangerous to battleships than had been feared, but it was able to sink merchant ships in large numbers at little risk to itself. Since Britain's food and oil supply came from overseas, the nation was in great danger of being starved out. During Germany's first submarine campaign in 1915, merchant ships were being sunk faster than Britain could provide replacements. Luckily, the nation was given a respite when Germany scaled back its attacks following the international outcry against the sinking of the passenger liner *Lusitania*. Germany resumed submarine warfare in February 1917 by targeting all allied and neutral shipping in the North Atlantic. Attacks were carried out without warning and with no regard to the safety of passengers or crew. Monthly shipping losses rose alarmingly, from 154,000 tons in January 1917 to 545,000 by April. A quarter of merchant ships leaving Britain were being sunk and food supplies fell dangerously low. Germany realized that its renewal of unrestricted submarine warfare would finally bring America into the war against the Central Powers, but it calculated (incorrectly) that German U-boats would starve Britain into submission before the United States could mobilize.[40]

British attempts to counter the submarine menace initially met with little success. The navy committed significant resources to a useless 'search-and-destroy' strategy. Technological research resulted in the ability to detect submarines with high-frequency sound waves and with 'hydrophones', but the vastness of the ocean made detection of such small objects difficult. Only the institution of 'convoys' during the summer of 1917 proved effective in reducing submarine attacks on shipping. Under the convoy system, a large number of merchant vessels sailed together accompanied by a protective naval escort. By October shipping losses fell to 270,000 tons, declining steadily to 170,000 tons in December. Convoys had been proposed much earlier, but naval conservatism proved difficult to overcome. According to Trevor Wilson, the Navy was 'imbued with a proud tradition, according to which going hunting for the enemy seemed a proper course and chugging along in support of merchantmen did not.'[41] The navy's ability to keep the sea lanes open secured Britain's access to crucial supplies of food and munitions from North America.

For contemporaries, the most disturbing aspect of the German submarine campaign was its attacks on vessels which had no way of defending themselves. Furthermore, U-boats could not provide accommodation to a destroyed ship's passengers and crew, to which international convention entitled them. The most a U-boat could do was to give those aboard a target vessel time to abandon ship before it was sunk. But this courtesy could force a U-boat to stay surfaced for 30 minutes – and risk being sunk itself by a British naval patrol. U-boat strategy thus entailed sinking passenger and merchant ships, killing civilians, and generally blurring the line between the people and commodities upon which it was or was not deemed legitimate to wage war. The British certainly condemned submarine warfare as yet another example of 'Hunnish beastliness', but the Germans countered that it was no worse than Britain's naval blockade of their own country, which aimed at the starvation of innocent people including women and children. A 'just' war proved incompatible with 'total' war – the principles of proportionality and discrimination between combatants and noncombatants could no longer be applied consistently.[42]

Nowhere was the war against civilians more apparent than in the air raids carried out first by Zeppelins and later by airplanes. In January and April 1915, Zeppelins raided the British coastline. At the end of May the first Zeppelin raid on London took place, killing 7 and injuring 35. Between June and October 1915, 9 more raids occurred, killing 127 and injuring 352. The raids occurred at night and caused much anxiety, and the inconvenience of protective blackouts. They did little to damage morale, but rather confirmed the popular image of Germans as ruthless killers of civilians. In the press, for example, Zeppelins were referred to as 'Baby Killers.' By 1916, improved British air defenses revealed the Zeppelins' weaknesses. They were slow moving, difficult to fly in high winds, and vulnerable to incendiary bullets since they were filled with highly explosive hydrogen gas.[43]

By 1917, the Germans had largely replaced the vulnerable Zeppelins with the new Gotha bomber plane, resulting in serious damage to British targets and new problems in British air defense. During June, 20 Gothas dropped 10 tons of bombs on London in broad daylight and escaped unharmed. In the worst raid, on 13 June 1917, 162 people were killed and 432 injured. Sixteen children were killed when their East End school was bombed. By 1918, London had developed an elaborate air defense of warning sirens, searchlights, anti-aircraft guns, and barrage balloons. There were regular night raids on Britain between September 1917 and May 1918, and some 300 000 Londoners nightly took refuge in Underground stations.[44]

During the course of the war, 1413 Britons were killed and 1972 wounded as a result of German air raids. Domestic casualties were negligible compared to those at the frontlines, but the bombings had a negative psychological impact out of all proportion to their numbers. Britain had remained geographically invulnerable since the Norman invasion of 1066. The new warfare threatened to blur the traditional distinction between soldier and civilian, front and home. Air raids made clear that the front was wherever the enemy chose to strike. This new sense of vulnerability deeply shocked and angered Britons and there were loud cries for reprisals. Sir Arthur Conan Doyle wrote to *The Times* at Christmas 1917 on 'the uses of hatred' in which he scorned 'platitudinous bishops' who had spoken against reprisal air raids and insisted that reprisals and a well-orchestrated campaign of hate against Germany were necessary. Likewise, the Reverend E. W. Brereton preached a sermon, reprinted in *John Bull*, in which he argued: 'We are fighting for dear life against enemies who are not Christian, not human beings, but reptiles. We claim the right to fight these fiends not with kid gloves. I scorn the humanitarians who object to reprisals.'[45]

Following the 1917 air raids on London, the South African politician Jan Smuts was appointed by the War Cabinet to investigate the coordination of air defenses. Since 1912, the Army and Navy had both maintained their own flying corps. Smuts now recommended the creation of a single, separate Royal Air Force (RAF), which came into being in April 1918. Smuts also envisioned that it would soon be possible for air forces to become 'the principal operations of war.' Retaliatory bombing raids on Germany began in October 1917. Between June and November 1918, the RAF carried out 242 raids on German airfields and cities. Just before the Armistice, the British were making plans for even more extensive bombing raids against Germany, in which they would utilize the new Handley Page aircraft that could carry a particularly heavy bomb load.[46]

The race for air supremacy produced astonishing technical developments in a short period of time. The fragile aircraft of the early part of the war could not carry heavy bombs or guns, and were mostly useful for reconnaissance. Air technology changed rapidly over the course of the war and it was vital to keep the fighting forces abreast of it. German Fokkers dominated the air war early in 1916, until they were bested by the new British planes, the FE-2b and DH-2, in the Spring. By Fall, the Germans were on top again with their Albatross, but in 1917 the British regained the advantage with their new Sopwith Strutter and Camel. To maintain the extraordinary momentum of flight technology demanded continuous and systematic research in order to produce aircraft that flew higher and faster, and had greater firepower. After 1917, the British state built national factories for the development and production of airplanes. In August 1916, Britain had 491 firms and 60 000 workers engaged in aircraft production. By October 1918, this commitment had grown to 1529 firms and 347 000 workers, or three times the production capacity of Germany's aircraft industry.[47]

By the end of the war, airpower had achieved a significance no one could have imagined in 1914. When the war began, Britain cobbled together an airforce by mobilizing private flight enthusiasts with their own machines. By 1918, Britain had the world's largest airforce, operating under a separate command and with important strategic functions. Aerial photographic mapping had become a key technique in assessing enemy strength and troop movements, and directing artillery barrages. Airplanes themselves also underwent a remarkable transformation. In 1914, British planes had a maximum speed of only 8 miles per hour, a rate of climb from the ground of 300–400 feet per minute, and the benefit of 60–100 horsepower engines. In 1918, the fastest planes could travel 140 miles per hour, their rate of climb was 2000 feet per minute, and they had 1000 horsepower engines. The maximum flying height had been raised from 5000 to 25 000 feet.[48]

Although the air war was highly dependent on modern scientific developments, it was often represented in the popular press in a rather romanticized manner. Aerial combat between fighter pilots was imagined as jousts between medieval knights, and flying aces like Albert Ball and William Bishop were celebrated as the new Lancelots and Galahads. Some fighter pilots even adopted a chivalric self-image. Cecil Lewis, who served in the Royal Flying Corps, recounted his experiences thus in his postwar memoir, *Sagittarius Rising* (1936): 'It was like the lists of the Middle Ages, the only sphere in modern warfare where a man saw his enemy and faced him in mortal combat, the only sphere where there was still chivalry and honour. If you won, it was your own bravery and skill; if you lost, it was because you had met a better man.'[49] The First World War's mass slaughter seemed to render the power of individual heroism insignificant. The air war was idealized because it was seen, however inaccurately, as resembling pre-industrial chivalric contests between heroic warriors.[50]

* * *

The highly impersonal and mechanistic nature of the First World War tended to efface the individual. Aerial bombing, submarine warfare, and long-range artillery all enabled troops to destroy 'targets' at considerable distance from themselves. As one observer noted: 'the artilleryman rarely sees the object of his fire; he has no personal contact with the enemy, but suddenly finds himself in a scorching fire, from a source which he cannot ascertain from an enemy he cannot see. It was like quarreling by telegraph.'[51] Likewise, in a story by Wyndham Lewis, a soldier remarked that he didn't know what killing meant, 'because I have never killed anyone I could see properly.'[52] Personal qualities counted for little in a war that seemed to be controlled by technology rather than by men, and where the individual was, at best, a cog in an industrial killing machine. In fact, many feared that the war would transform people themselves into machines. This idea was satirically expressed in the wartime cartoon 'The evolution of the fighting man', which depicted the transformation of a soldier from 1914 to 1919. For each year there is the addition of some device such as a steel helmet or gas mask so that by the last panel, the soldier is more machine than man.[53]

Ironically, a frequent response to the impersonality of 'modern warfare' was a retreat to the most primitive and irrational belief systems. Few frontline officers or soldiers were without amulets: lucky coins, religious medals, dried flowers, four-leaf clovers, and scripture verses worn in a bag around the neck. People looked desperately for signs of hope and loving providence in the midst of so much chaos and disorder. Some soldiers took refuge in such imagined manifestations of divine protection as the 'miraculous' suspension of the statue of the Virgin and Child on the spire of the bombed church in the French town of Albert. Widely circulated photographs also emphasized the survival of religious objects amid destruction, such as a cross or statue left standing in a ruined church. Eric Leed has shown that many soldiers became superstitious, even contrary to their temperaments, under the strains of battle: 'Magic, ritual, spell, and omen seemed to be an unavoidable response to the total loss of individual control over the conditions of life and death.'[54]

The profound sense of powerlessness that many soldiers experienced in the face of mechanized warfare also caused acute mental breakdowns and nervous disorders, which were generically termed 'shell-shock.' The strain of serving in the inhuman conditions of trench warfare, exhaustion from the inability to obtain sleep, and the witnessing of comrades' deaths and mutilations often proved too much to bear. By 1916, cases of shell-shock accounted for 40 percent of the casualties in some fighting zones. By the end of the war, 80 000 cases had been treated. Soldiers developed an especially rich vocabulary for insanity: loopy, tapped, dekko, doolally, touched, scatty, dippy. The enormous number of shell-shock cases forced the army to create a chain of treatment centers, ranging from clearing stations in France to mental hospitals in Britain. By 1918, there were six mental hospitals for officers and 13 for other ranks.[55]

The prevalence of mental illness among so many of the nation's 'heroes' encouraged a reconsideration of traditional views of insanity and helped break down old stigmas and prejudices. For instance, the rigid prewar distinction between the 'mad' and the sane now seemed less certain. A 1916 editorial from the *Lancet* argued that shell-shock cases should not be labeled as either sane or insane. There was in fact a medical 'no-man's land' which 'defied definition.' The experience of shell-shock also seemed to confirm Freud's view of neurosis as a flight from an intolerable reality through illness. Some British physicians even employed innovative psychodynamic techniques, similar to Freud's 'talking cure', in cases of shell-shock. Most famously, Dr W. H. R. Rivers at Craiglockhart Military Hospital in Scotland urged patients to overcome fears by confronting repressed memories and experiences. Rivers, who treated the war poets Siegfried Sassoon and Wilfred Owen, had his patients discuss traumatic wartime experiences and assisted them in redirecting 'energy, hitherto morbidly directed, into more healthy channels.'[56]

The psychiatric treatment of most working-class soldiers was usually less progressive than that officers received from the likes of Dr Rivers. A more common – and punitive – treatment was electric shock therapy, advocated by Dr Lewis Yealland, who operated a clinic in London. Yealland wrote *Hysterical Disorders of Warfare* (1918), in which he described his 'disciplinary' treatment of soldiers who had lost the ability to speak as a result of horrors witnessed in the trenches. Yealland 'ordered' his patients to get well. Most came from the ranks, and the blatant appeal to power and authority was part of the therapy. He then administered a series of strong electric shocks to the patient's throat until he began to make noises. If the patient recoiled from the shocks, he was reprimanded: 'Remember, you must behave as becomes the hero I expect you to be . . . A man who has gone through so many battles should have better control of himself.'[57]

Postwar attitudes toward mental illness were mixed. On the one hand, the war resulted in advances in psychiatric theory and practice. One of the first outpatient psychiatric clinics in Britain, the Tavistock Clinic, was established in 1920 as a result of Hugh Crichton-Miller's experiences treating shell-shocked soldiers. An official government *Report into Shell Shock* was issued in 1922, expressing considerable sympathy for soldiers affected, but also concluding that certain social or ethnic categories (Jews, the Irish, the working class in general) were more likely to crack under pressure. However, as the war receded into the distance, initial sympathy for the victims of war neurosis gave way to denial and insensitivity.

Soldiers suffering from war-related psychological disorders had access to little therapeutic assistance apart from institutionalization, and the Ministry of Pensions proved hostile to paying benefits to the victims of shell-shock. Peter Barham has documented the increasing neglect that the war's psychological casualties experienced at the hands of a state intent on economizing. Officials sought to reduce veteran's benefits by arguing that their mental illness resulted not from 'shell shock,' but from congenital conditions that predated the war. By the mid 1920s the government was rejecting more than 60 percent of claims for assistance by veterans suffering from psychological problems. The problems, however, refused to go away. More veterans were diagnosed with psychiatric illnesses in 1929 than in the four years immediately following the war.[58]

* * *

Profound scientific and technological wartime innovations meant that the British Army of 1918 was a far different fighting force from the Army of 1914. In recent years, a number of military historians have argued that new weaponry along with new battle tactics enabled the British to achieve a strategic breakthrough in 1918, ending the war of stalemate and finally defeating German forces.

Beginning in the 1960s, scholars like Correlli Barnett and John Terraine argued that the stalemate on the Western Front was far from static and that battle strategies were continually evolving and improving. During the 1980s and 90s military historians, such as Peter Simkins and Brian Bond, drew a more complex and nuanced picture of the British Army and its tactics, challenging old assumptions about unimaginative and inflexible military commanders wastefully sacrificing countless young men in a useless slaughter. This new military history of the Great War posited the notion of a 'learning curve,' whereby the military learned from the mistakes of 1916 and developed more subtle and ultimately successful battle strategies.[59]

The winning formula included better location and neutralization of enemy batteries through aerial reconnaissance, mapping, and sound ranging (using microphones to pinpoint artillery from the sound waves they generated when fired). Next, having knocked out enemy guns, there was better coordination of infantry and artillery through the employment of the 'creeping barrage,' whereby artillery fire fell just in front of advancing British troops, providing more effective cover against German gunfire. The Allied breakthrough was further assisted by the mass deployment of new weapons like tanks and more lightweight and portable machine guns and mortars. Finally, motorized supply columns vastly improved the resupply of advancing British troops.[60]

Military historians are right to emphasize the evolving nature of trench warfare and the re-education of the high command, but as some critics point out, it was a rather slow learning process. A year after the Somme offensive British commanders were still attempting massive infantry assaults against heavily fortified German positions. It remains difficult to establish how much the Allied victory owed to strategic innovations and how much to demographic and logistical advantages (attrition). German commanders also experienced a learning curve, but by 1918 Germany had exhausted its resources. In the end, the financial and industrial strength of the Central Powers was no match for the Allies. Allied GDP was more than three times that of the Central Powers. Britain and its allies easily outpaced Germany and Austria-Hungary in weapons production and they had far greater access to global resources of labor, food, and raw materials (oil, rubber, metals) due to their vast empires and command of the seas. The late entry of the U.S.A. into the war promised additional, and virtually unlimited, resources. By the summer of 1918 200,000 American soldiers a month were arriving in France.[61]

* * *

During the war, the nation became more science-conscious, and science achieved a stature and popularity it had never previously enjoyed. In 1916, the chemist G. C. Henderson argued that a positive effect of the war was that it aroused Britain from 'its state of apathy towards science' to a realization that its future happiness was 'ultimately dependent on the progress of science.' War made science a respectable occupation for a growing professional class and science assumed a more important place in the education system. People began looking to scientists, rather than politicians or generals, for signs of hope for winning the war, and they longed for some new 'secret weapon' to break through the stalemate.[62]

Popular scientific publications, such as *Inventions of the Great War* (1919) and *The New World of Science* (1920), tended to celebrate wartime innovations as evidence of British creative ingenuity. Newspapers and magazines increased their coverage of science and technology, and the public avidly read about the latest weaponry, tanks, and airplanes. 'Gadget' – a military slang term for any mechanical contrivance – was brought into general usage by the war.[63] The bizarre suggestions contributed to the Munitions Inventions Department were further evidence of a public obsessed with scientific gadgetry and schooled in the fantasies of Jules Verne and H. G. Wells. Some correspondents suggested filling shells with bubonic plague germs or freezing clouds so as to mount machine guns on them as an air defense. The cartoonist Heath Robinson published a whole series of comic war weapons, 'For the War Inventions Board.' They included such devices as 'The Armoured Corn-Presser for Crushing the

Enemy's Boot' – a giant armored tank, operated by five men who manipulate an enormous iron foot to stomp on the toes of German soldiers. Robinson drew humorous attention to Britons' wartime fascination with inventions.[64]

A number of popular war novels also involved science-fiction scenarios. For example, Arthur Benjamin Reeve's *The War Terror: Further Adventures with Craig Kennedy, Scientific Detective* (1915) was full of descriptions of scientific and technical gadgets, including an electromagnetic gun developed by a group of German assassins. Spy and detective novels were the perfect venue for elaborating the wartime fascination with gadgetry – code breaking, wire-tapping, explosives, among others. In Guy Thorne's *The Secret Sea-plane* (1915) the hero, John Gregor Lothian, invents a secret vehicle that can travel on land, sea, and air, and proceeds to use it to rescue his fiancée from German spies and destroy a fleet of Zeppelins sent to bomb London.

During the war many lamented that an elite education with an emphasis on the classics had left the British ill-prepared to wage a scientific war. On 2 February 1916, *The Times* published a letter signed by a large number of scientists who maintained that schools' neglect of science was a major cause of failures in the war. Shortages of qualified scientists and technicians led to calls for educational reform. A petition by leading scientists asked that science be given its proper place in education, and in May 1916 the Linnean Society formed a 'Neglect of Science' committee. An official Education Committee was also convened by the British government in 1916 to review the place of science in the school curriculum. Its 1918 report recommended a massive improvement in scientific education.[65]

While some Britons celebrated the wartime achievements of science, others saw only their legacy of mass death and destruction. For many people science and technology could no longer be viewed solely as benign agents of progress. The writer, Mrs St Clair Stobart, on hearing that in one trench 800 men had been killed within three minutes, responded bitterly: 'To this end has the wisdom of Man brought Man.' Reverend E. A. Burroughs, the Chaplain to the King, also concluded: 'The resources of man are at an end: civilisation, science, progress – all the things we trusted in – have failed the world in its greatest need.'[66] In a 1915 essay, 'Reflections Upon War and Death', Sigmund Freud further cast doubt on the presumed connection between technological achievement and moral improvement. The war, he argued, 'tarnished the lofty impartiality of our science, it revealed our instincts in all their nakedness and let loose the evil spirits within us which we thought had been tamed for ever by centuries of continuous education by the noblest minds.'[67]

In the postwar world, many were fearful and critical of the technologies of destruction that science had unleashed. In a 1919 lecture, Lord Moulton lamented the extent to which science had been subordinated to the needs of war. The historian A. F. Pollard likewise summarized 'our modern debt to science' as 'poison gases, Zeppelin bombs, floating mines and submarine torpedoes.' In 1929, Churchill wrote: 'Mankind has got into its hands for the first time the tools by which it can unfailingly accomplish its own extinction.'[68] The writer G. S. Street wondered 'if science, the great glory and boast of civilization in the nineteenth century, will destroy it in the twentieth.' Whatever scientific 'benefits' were produced by the war hardly seemed worth the cost. Street concluded: 'the evil wrought so far only in this war by certain inventions by far outweighs any good humanity may get out of them for centuries to come.'[69] Did millions of men need to die for the sake of improved disinfectants or streamlined factory production? A tiny fraction of the cost of the war applied to medical or technical research would doubtless have produced even better results.

Liberal thinkers struggled hard to make sense of the war and its mass death. H. G. Wells, thought the war a disaster, but a necessary one to convince people of the futility of war. Wells believed that the existence of weapons of mass destruction would actually deter future wars, as the consequences of their use would be too horrible to contemplate. The tank and airplane, especially, held out 'a prospect of limitless, senseless destruction' and would therefore promote 'an organized control of war.' When this vision failed to materialize, Wells began to lose hope for the future of humanity. His vision of scientific progress had no way to account for science's devastating side-effects.[70] George Bernard Shaw was also deeply disturbed by the war's barbarism. He grappled with its legacy in his play cycle *Back to Methuselah* (1921), where he fantasizes about humanity's ability to redirect evolution through force of will to achieve longevity and wisdom. Yet, in one of his possible scenarios, set in 3000 AD, the newly evolved humans are humorless automatons who advocate the extermination of the unfit. Perhaps humanity was indeed doomed after all. Even the normally optimistic writer Mrs Humphry Ward felt that the war's brutality had undermined traditional humanistic values. But in her last work, *Fields of Victory* (1919), she made a desperate plea for continued faith in progress: 'Germany has done things in this war which shame civilization, and seem to make a mockery of all ideas of human progress. But yet! – we must still believe in them; or the sun will go out in heaven.' Not everyone could muster such a resilient will to believe.[71]

Chapter 2: Class, Labor, and State Control

In a society as socially stratified and riven by class conflict as Edwardian Britain, national unity was not taken for granted. Leo Chiozza Money's *Riches and Poverty* (1905) had exposed the huge disparities in British society, whereby the wealthiest 12 percent of the population received half the nation's annual income and owned 93 percent of its capital. However, the outbreak of war in August 1914 was like pouring oil on troubled waters. National solidarity swiftly overrode ongoing industrial conflict, but the full extent of wartime social unity remains a matter of historical debate, as does the question of the war's lasting impact on the British class system. Individuals' attitudes toward the war, as well as their wartime experiences, were very much shaped by their class identities. Nonetheless, the sense of having participated in a great struggle to save the nation from destruction was almost universal, and this sentiment increased both citizens' attachment to the nation and their sense of entitlement to its gratitude. The proportion of the population drawn directly into the war effort was without precedent. By the Armistice, about 4 million men (24 percent of the adult male population) were under arms, and another 1.5 million women and men were engaged in munitions work.[1] Historians have traditionally emphasized the war's socially unifying aspects and its tendency to break down old class barriers symbolized by the extension of the franchise and social reforms.[2] More recent scholarship, however, has questioned the extent to which the First World War represented a move to a more open and egalitarian society. Revisionist historians have underscored the resilience of social hierarchy and pointed out that the gains of some groups promoted resentments in others, dramatized most notably by postwar industrial conflict and conservative retrenchment.[3]

At the time, all classes saw the war as a major watershed, believing that for those who lived through it, 'things would never be the same again.'[4] For the upper class, their world of gracious living, seemingly endless country house parties, low taxes, and cheap servants was no more. The war homogenized working-class experience and consolidated working-class confidence. Trade unions and the Labour Party grew in size and influence. The working class emerged from the war more cohesive, powerful, and ambitious than ever before. The middle class found new opportunities in the war, but also new uncertainties. Some were enriched, others experienced unprecedented hardships, and many lost faith in the old Victorian values of progress and self-reliance. Individualism, that much cherished ideal of nineteenth-century society, had clearly lost ground to collectivism. The circumstances of the war compelled the state to control almost every aspect of society, from industrial production, to food distribution, to the conscription of fighting men and the direction of civilian labor. This phenomenon occurred within the peculiar dynamics of Britain's class system, sometimes reinforcing long-standing class prejudices, other times promoting a more egalitarian vision of society.

* * *

In the years immediately preceding the war, there had been an escalation of class conflict in Britain on a massive scale. Most notably, strikes were occurring more frequently and over greater areas of the country than ever before. Caused by inflation and the consequent decline in real wages, slower industrial growth leaving fewer profits to be divided between capital and labor, and the greater determination of employers to curb the power of trade unions, strikes rose from 422 in 1909, to 521 in 1910, 872 in 1911, 834 in 1912, and 1 459 in 1913. Strikes were growing not only in number but also in size and duration. Total working days lost through strikes grew from 2 million in 1907 to an astounding 40 million by 1912. Many believed that a crippling general strike would have taken place in 1914 had not war intervened.[5] Growing Labour radicalism, with its rhetoric of an international brotherhood of workers, led many in the governing classes to doubt working-class loyalty should war break out. A number of people in the Labour movement, especially those with socialist beliefs, saw foreign policy as a conspiracy based on power politics, and war as an extension of those politics against the popular will. To the radical Independent Labour Party politician Keir Hardie, the Boer War had been 'a capitalist war' and the Labour Party's 1906 election manifesto had declared unambiguously, 'wars are fought to make the rich richer.' In 1912, the Labour Party Conference had agreed to investigate how far the threat of work stoppages could forestall the outbreak of hostilities, and on 2 August 1914, a huge anti-war rally was held in Trafalgar Square addressed by Keir Hardie and other Labour leaders.[6]

The German invasion of Belgium and Britain's entry into the war on 4 August brought about a radical change in attitudes. Socialist Internationalism was vanquished and many of its most prominent supporters turned warmonger, or were silenced. Hardie was shouted down by his own constituents and was forced to admit that once soldiers had 'gone forth to fight their country's battles', they must not be discouraged by dissension at home. Hardie was a broken man, and shortly before his death in 1915, sadly reflected: 'Ten million Socialist and Labour voters in Europe, without a trace or vestige of power to prevent war! . . . Our demonstrations and speeches and resolutions are all alike futile. We have no means of hitting the warmongers. We simply do not count.'[7] The whole Labour movement, with the exception of the small and marginal Independent Labour Party, united in support of the war. The Parliamentary Labour Party dropped its opposition to the war, causing Ramsay MacDonald to resign his leadership. He remained one of the war's most prominent and outspoken critics, was widely vilified, and lost his parliamentary seat in 1918. Arthur Henderson replaced MacDonald as party leader, and Labour joined the other political parties in declaring an electoral truce. On 24 August 1914, a joint meeting of the Labour Party, the Trades Union Congress, and the General Federation of Trade Unions urged employers and workers to abandon all strikes and lockouts for the duration and to reach amicable settlements of their differences.[8]

Most ordinary working-folk, unlike their union leaders, did not especially follow politics in the strife-ridden Balkans or elsewhere, so that news in August that the country was at war came as quite a surprise.[9] While many working-class communities responded enthusiastically, this attitude was by no means so nearly universal as it was among the middle and upper classes. Robert Roberts recalled that the declaration of war 'caused no great outburst of patriotic fervour' in the slums of Salford.[10] People generally supported the government, but there was also much uncertainty, fear and confusion. Not everyone rushed to enlist.[11]

Among the most impoverished there was an indifference to the war that reflected their alienation from society and lack of integration into the national community. The *Contemporary Review*, for instance, printed the comment of a working-class woman heard to say that: 'She did not see what difference it would make if the Germans did come and rule England. She had always been poor, and she didn't suppose she would be worse off with them than without them.'[12] Herbert Tremaine's wartime novel, *The Feet of the Young Men* (1917), also depicted the world of the urban poor, where the war was seen as the concern of their masters and bosses. Rural areas had the worst recruitment rates in the nation. Agricultural laborers were even less informed about national politics and international affairs than the urban proletariat. Authorities reported widespread ignorance and indifference about the war in the countryside.[13]

The initial tentativeness of some members of the working class probably had much to do with the extraordinary economic uncertainty, social dislocation, and political confusion of the war's early phase. Sylvia Pankhurst, Suffragette and socialist, spent the war years organizing relief in London's East End. Her memoirs of this period, *The Home Front*, feelingly portray the hardships war initially created for the very poor. Many workers in industries that exported primarily to Germany were thrown out of work, and separation allowances to soldiers' families were at first miserly and seldom paid on time. Pankhurst quotes one woman frustrated by an unfeeling bureaucracy that treated aid to soldiers' dependants as a charitable gift rather than a right: 'I think it a shame that the Government should be allowed to do such things just because you are poor . . . When they take your man . . . they don't care so long as they have him, what becomes of them left behind.'[14] Evelyn Sharp also wrote about the sufferings of poor people during the war in *The War of All the Ages* (1915). One chapter, 'The Casualty,' tells about a baby who died because of food shortages.

Many in the nation's elite doubted the working class's capacity to fight a major war, so that the resilience of civilian morale and the outpouring of working-class patriotism took them by surprise.[15] From early on, some cohorts of the working class, like miners, enlisted at extraordinarily high rates, so that 'the compatibility of class consciousness and patriotism could have no better illustration.'[16] Sylvia Pankhurst also made it clear that workers were quickly won over by war propaganda, much to her disgust and consternation. The need to defend Belgium from German tyranny had greater appeal than Pankhurst's discouraging notion of a capitalist war, and in frustration she wondered 'How could one make it plain to those whose untutored minds craved only for curt, net slogans?'[17]

The idea that workers only enlisted due to manipulative propaganda gained currency in the decades following the war, but has been seriously challenged by more recent scholarship. David Silbey examined records left by soldiers themselves – letters, diaries, memoirs, interviews, and oral histories – and concluded that working-class soldiers had a variety of motives for joining up. Some were spurred by economic concerns, seeing enlistment as a way to earn money for themselves and their families. For others the war promised adventure and escape from the dull routine of their lives. Patriotism also played a major role in working-class men's decisions to enlist. German shelling of British towns, massacres of Belgian civilians, and the sinking of the passenger liner *Lusitania* suggested a brutal war against civilians. Silbey concludes that working-class men no less than their middle- and upper-class counterparts wanted to protect their families, communities, and nation.[18] Ultimately working-class support for the war proved as enthusiastic and enduring as that of the elite. Scholars such as Gerard DeGroot and Catriona Pennell demonstrate that words like 'duty' and 'honour' occurred almost as often in working-class diaries and letters during the war years as in those from the middle class.[19]

Given the preponderance of the working class in the nation's population (over 70 percent), it should come as no surprise that much recruiting was specifically aimed at working men. Recruitment posters often employed dialect, as in those displayed on trams in Leeds: 'Nah then, John Willie, Ger Agate, Lad, an' Join t'Army.' An effective recruiting device among workers were the so-called 'Pals' Battalions' where young men from the same neighborhood or factory or sports club joined up together, appealing to the 'herd instinct' as one of the principal reasons for enlisting.[20] Recruiters also pointed out that the army provided 'meat every day!', which must have had an enormous appeal, given the meagerness of many working-class diets. Indeed, Army life could represent a significant improvement in the lives of the poor, at least before they went into combat. As Robert Roberts recalled, local recruits returning on leave astonished the neighbors. 'Pounds – sometimes stones – heavier, taller, confident, clean and straight, they were hardly recognizable as the men who went away.'[21]

The upper classes did not need to be tempted into the Army, given their martial traditions and close identity with the state. In fact, no social group greeted the war with more enthusiasm than the aristocracy. Great landlords aided the government in recruiting. Magnates like the Duke of Bedford or Lord Ancaster offered their tenants and employees generous terms for volunteering; they kept jobs open and allowed the families of volunteers to live rent free in their cottages. Society ladies joined in the general enthusiasm, converting their great houses into makeshift hospitals and organizing charity bazaars. The Duchess of Westminster established a Red Cross hospital in France and the Duchess of Sutherland organized an ambulance unit to serve in Belgium. Above all, the war gave aristocrats the opportunity to prove their worth. Since the 1880s, they had been the object of attacks by political radicals for their anachronistic hold on political power and their parasitic idleness. As David Cannadine has argued, here was a chance to show the country that they were not 'the redundant reactionaries of radical propaganda, but the patriotic class of knightly crusaders and chivalric heroes.'[22] The upper classes remained wedded to an outmoded view of warfare involving cavalry charges and combat between heroic individuals, though they were not the only ones to see the war through this distorted lens. Aristocratic soldiers and their families frequently adopted medieval language and conceits in their diaries, letters, and descriptions of the war. When Lord Lucas of the Royal Flying Corps died in 1916, he was memorialized as a 'Knight of the Round Table.' In a poem by Maurice Baring, he was lauded in Tennysonian terms:

> Surely you found companions meet for you
> In that high place
> You met them face to face
> Those you had never known, but whom you knew
> Knights of the Table Round
> And all the very brave, the very true
> With chivalry crowned.[23]

As casualties mounted and a war of stalemate set in, the romanticized view of war proved harder to maintain, though some always preferred it to the harsh reality. Others in the aristocracy sought solace in their customary pleasures. The upper classes continued their usual round of parties and lavish entertaining with few concessions to austerity. Colonel Charles à Court Repington recollected that 'Lady Ridley and I discussed what posterity would think of us in England. We agreed that we should be considered rather callous to go on with our usual life when we were reading of 3000 to 4000 casualties a day ... she supposed that things around us explained the French Revolution and the behaviour of the French nobility.'[24] Arnold Bennett's novel *The Pretty Lady* (1918) also gives a cynical picture of high society during the war and what passed for 'war work' among the more frivolous members of the upper classes.

Of course, it is important to realize that most characterizations of a frivolous aristocracy and foot-dragging proletariat came from the pens of the middle class. Most writers and novelists who commented on the war, both at the time and afterwards, were middle class, and they tended to characterize the contributions of their own class as typifying the best virtues of Britishness: steadiness, calm acceptance of whatever comes along, unself-conscious heroism. This ideal was lovingly portrayed by Anthony Bertram in his novel *The Sword Falls* (1929). Albert Robinson loses his home in a Zeppelin raid. Although old enough for military exemption, he goes to France where he bravely serves, is horribly wounded, and returns to London where he quietly goes back to work. The middle class evidently saw itself as the patriotic class par excellence. The enlistment rate for professionals and white-collar workers was twice as great as for manual workers.[25] Even after conscription was introduced, this disparity persisted since office workers were far less likely than factory workers to receive military exemptions for performing vital war work. As middle-class men rushed to the colors, their wives and daughters rolled bandages for the Red Cross, knitted socks for soldiers, and generally busied themselves in war-related charities.[26] And as the next chapter will show, a number of middle-class women were to enter the wartime workforce – a new and liberating experience for them.

But the great outpouring of middle-class patriotism was also accompanied by less noble gestures. Speculation in goods needed by the War Office became notorious in the early months of the war, as did hoarding by the 'selfish rich.' The president of the Board of Trade denounced in Parliament 'practices in many parts of the country that have led to great hardship, especially among the poorer classes, caused by the panic and greed of the better-to-do people, who have disgraced themselves by taking long queues of motor cars to stores and carrying away as many provisions as they could persuade the stores to part with.'[27] All classes sought to serve their nation in time of war, though none were free from charges of self-interest. And in a nation with long-standing social grievances, there were plenty of people ready to point the finger of blame across the class divide.

The reality of class solidarity was seldom as uncomplicated as the ubiquitous wartime slogans 'equality of sacrifice', 'the comradeship of the trenches', and 'all classes standing together' might suggest. The historian George Dangerfield's classic depiction of a growing working-class radicalism destroyed by the outbreak of war is not without its truth, but is much overstated.[28] Although the Labour movement supported the war, it did not approve of a war of conquest and continually sought a clear statement of progressive war aims. Nor were voices of opposition altogether silenced; Keir Hardie, Ramsay MacDonald, Sylvia Pankhurst, and others continued to denounce a war they saw as waged to benefit the rich and oppress the poor. At first their audience was small, but as casualties mounted and war weariness set in, more people listened. Even among those laborers who enthusiastically supported the war, there was a feeling that they were bearing a disproportionate share of the war burden and that their social betters were not doing enough. A soldier's wife from rural Shropshire wrote an angry letter to the *Shrewsbury Chronicle* in 1915, after feeling insulted at a local meeting where poor women were told that it was their patriotic duty to return to the land: 'I am prepared to go and help on any farm in the neighborhood at an honest wage, but not for wages that would not pay for the clothes I wore out at work . . . What about the farmers' wives and daughters? The one half of them are brought up to do nothing besides play the piano and dance the carpets . . . they can't soil their hands.'[29]

Many working-class women struggled to get by on the Army's separation allowances, and they felt the pinch of rising prices. Soaring food costs and escalating rents led to accusations that shopkeepers and landlords were 'profiteers.' Massive protests across the nation equated rack-renting landlords with Germans. Demonstrators at a Glasgow rent strike in October 1915, many of them women and children, held up signs that read: 'We Are Fighting Landlord Huns' and 'While My Father is a Prisoner in Germany the Landlord is Attacking Our Home.' An alarmed government fixed housing rents at their prewar levels.[30]

* * *

The war did not, contrary to patriotic expectations, suspend class conflict between capital and labor. When shell production lagged in early 1915, a deputation of employers told Lloyd George that worker drunkenness was largely to blame. He apparently accepted this charge as true, provoking an angry reply from Keir Hardie: 'In time of war one would have thought the rich classes would grovel on their knees before the working classes who are doing so much to pile up their wealth. Instead, the men who are working eighty-four hours a week are being libeled, maligned, and insulted.' Employers were pocketing record profits, but attempts by organized labor to secure a bigger piece of the economic pie were initially met with strong resistance and charges of disloyalty and defeatism. A cartoon in *Punch* showed the Kaiser giving Keir Hardie a bag of money, accompanied by the rhyme: 'Also the Nobel prize (though tardy), I now confer on Keir von Hardie.'[31] From their own standpoint, the Labour Party and trade unions merely wanted 'equal sacrifice.'[32]

As early as 1915, the term 'profiteer' was being used by workers to draw attention to the inequality of sacrifice. A cartoon in the *Workers' Dreadnought* showed a ragged working man holding a gun while two bloated capitalists sit behind him clutching money bags. The caption needled, 'Aren't They Worth Defending?' The war provided abundant growth opportunities for business as well as tremendous possibilities for jobbery and excess profits. Munitions contractors were making vast sums of money, in some cases for providing inferior goods, and there were plentiful opportunities for fraud and extortion, as in the case of a Scottish dealer who sold the government jute for sandbags at three times the normal price.[33] Many businesses continued to sell goods to Germany via neutral countries like Sweden or the Netherlands. For example, Dutch purchases of British cigarettes increased tenfold during the war, most of them making their way to Germany and German soldiers. Government returns from 1916 showed that coal, shipbuilding, iron, and engineering firms increased their profits by 32 percent over their prewar levels. Attempts to limit excess profits were easily evaded by making overgenerous allowances for depreciation and improvements.[34] Money was being made hand over fist, so that working-class demands for higher wages could hardly be met with serious cries of hardship.

Workers soon realized that the quest for increased production of weaponry and more recruits for the military made labor a scarce resource, and placed them in positions of considerable influence. The July 1915 strike by South Wales miners over a national pay settlement demonstrated the power of organized labor during time of war. Lloyd George's attempt to coerce miners back to work by declaring the coalfields a government-controlled establishment only encouraged miners elsewhere to threaten a national strike. The government, recognizing its weakness, immediately gave in. The war had made unions more powerful and increased workers' expectations. Many in the rank and file came to believe their leaders had sold their cooperation too cheaply, and a more radical leadership emerged in the form of the shop stewards movement.[35]

The most serious labor unrest of the war began in February 1915 as a small strike in Glasgow by members of the Amalgamated Society of Engineers for a wage increase of 2d. an hour. The strike was not approved by the official union leadership, but organized by shop stewards, the unpaid local workplace representatives of union members. The strike was settled for 1d. an hour, but the emboldened stewards went on to form the Clyde Workers' Committee (CWC) in October 1915. This organization caused so much trouble that the government eventually suppressed it, and imprisoned and exiled its leaders, among them the radical socialists William Gallacher and Arthur MacManus. The Committee aimed for nothing less than the abolition of the Munitions of War Act of May 1915, which had given the government almost complete control over industrial relations. The radicalism of the Glasgow movement saw the region dubbed 'Red Clydeside.' Early in 1916, the government suppressed Glasgow's socialist weeklies, *Forward*, *Vanguard*, and *The Worker*, and arrested their publishers. This action provoked strikes across Glasgow. In March 1916, the government arrested and deported to Edinburgh the main leaders of the Clyde Workers' Committee, threatened strikers with prosecution under wartime regulations, and actually imprisoned 30 of them. The CWC was effectively silenced, but a shop stewards' movement spread across Britain, sparked by rank and file disenchantment with the perceived moderation of union leaders, opposition to military conscription, and a general belief in the inequality of sacrifice.[36]

In November 1916, the call-up of a young Sheffield engineer, Leonard Hargreaves, provoked an unofficial strike and a nationwide campaign for his release from the army. The outcome was a spectacular victory for the shop stewards. Not only was Hargreaves released, but the government negotiated with the Amalgamated Society of Engineers a 'trade card' scheme of military exemption certificates which was operated by the union itself. When the continued bloody losses on the Western Front led the government to repudiate the trade card agreement in April 1917, it led to a massive wave of strikes across Britain, involving 200 000 engineers and shipbuilders in 48 towns. The outcome was an amended Schedule of Protected Organizations which kept even more engineers out of the Army. In June, the government appointed a series of Commissions of Inquiry to investigate industrial unrest in eight separate areas of Great Britain. Wartime labor actions convinced militant unionists that the government could not resist a resolute working class.[37]

The war sensitized workers to class inequalities and placed unions in a particularly strong bargaining position, but there were patriotic sentiments in working-class culture that set limits to social conflict. Strikes continued to take place, but at much lower rates than in peacetime. Working days lost by strikes had reached a record high of 41 million in 1912, 10 million in 1913, and 10 million in 1914 (mostly in the seven months before the war began). These numbers dropped precipitously to 3 million days lost in 1915 and 2.5 million in 1916. Only in 1918 did strike activity begin to approach the prewar level (with 6 million days lost), though during the period of military crisis in March 1918, strikes virtually disappeared.[38] Nor should strikes be interpreted as a challenge to the war's legitimacy. The vast majority of strikes were about pay and working conditions and were easily settled. Some members of the Clyde Workers Committee may have been Communists, but their followers had decidedly unrevolutionary aspirations. Nonetheless, the government was worried by the increase of strike activity in 1917–18, seeing it as a sign of war weariness and frustration at food shortages, the very issues that had precipitated revolution in Russia.

In wartime labor relations, the government intervened more drastically than ever before, both forcing employers to meet workers' demands and imprisoning strike leaders. The Defence of the Realm Acts gave the state almost unlimited supervisory and regulatory powers over industrial production and industrial relations. A major political shift began during the war, with the state taking on a new 'corporate' role in brokering compromises between organized labor and management.[39] The war thus represented an important transition from individualistic, competitive capitalism to a neo-capitalism based on less competitive industrial units more closely linked with the state.[40] During the war management and labor worked together to create mechanisms to accommodate their competing interests, such as the state-sponsored Whitley Councils, in which employers and workers met regularly to discuss wages and working conditions. The need for national efficiency also drove the government to adopt gradual measures of state control that would have been unthinkable during peacetime. Railways, shipping, and mines were drawn under government control, as were vital supplies of raw materials and food, while the government itself became an industrial employer on a massive scale.

* * *

During the war an increasingly familiar pattern developed, whereby early reliance on market forces gradually gave way to half-hearted state regulation and eventual state control. This pattern manifested itself in military recruitment, munitions production, labor supply, food distribution, and even propaganda. The initial hesitancy to regulate represented a Liberal reluctance to extend the powers of the state, combined with genuine governmental inexperience and outright hostility from business interests whose power was considerable. Furthermore, the decentralized nature of government kept many departments and branches from learning from each other's experience. Volunteerism remained in place in some areas into 1918, having been abandoned by others in 1915. The initial policy of Asquith's Liberal government was 'business as usual' – a slogan suggesting the war would require no great alteration of the economic structure or social fabric. Early military blunders and a serious shortage of artillery shells in the spring of 1915 thoroughly discredited the laissez-faire approach to the war. The Prime Minister himself seemed a relic of an earlier, more leisured era. Asquith continued to spend weekends at country house parties and to play bridge two hours every day, begrudging time spent on the War Committee. As Trevor Wilson put it: 'A growing section of the nation was coming to see his style of government as the cause for these misfortunes, and to yearn for a more decisive, ruthless, committed leadership.'[41]

In May 1915, Asquith was forced to form a Coalition government with the Conservatives and Labour, dedicated to a more efficient prosecution of the war. An important development was the setting up of the Ministry of Munitions in June under Lloyd George. The Ministry divided the country into ten munitions districts managed by business-men interested in the work. Consumer industries were forced to convert to weapons production, and the government guaranteed a steady sup-ply of raw materials, fuel, and labor. As long as munitions were made on time, the control of profits was not too strictly enforced. Workers in 'controlled' establishments could not take jobs elsewhere without their employers' written consent, which amounted to a badge of slavery to many in the labor movement. The imposition of military conscription in January 1916 further depleted the industrial workforce, necessitating greater government management of labor resources as well as the more vigorous recruitment of women workers. In December 1916, the more dynamic Lloyd George ousted Asquith as head of the coalition and insti-tuted a more streamlined executive in the form of a five-man inner War Cabinet: Lloyd George, the Conservative leader Bonar Law, the Labour leader Henderson, and two ruthless colonial administrators, Curzon and Milner. This government continued to strive for greater efficiency, which usually translated into more state control and less democracy.[42]

Laissez-faire Liberalism proved unable to cope with the pressures of mass war. Market forces were not sufficient to call up the massive mate-rial and weapons needed to supply an army of millions, any more than volunteerism was able to fill the ranks of such an army. The Liberal Party itself was dealt death blows by the strains of war. It had to abandon its principles of laissez-faire and free trade while policies that permitted censorship, conscription, price regulation, internment of enemy aliens, and ill treatment of conscientious objectors all flew in the face of the civil libertarian and individualistic traditions of Liberalism. The mod-ern trend toward big government also became a reality for the first time during the war. Public expenditure rose from 12 percent of GNP in 1913 to 52 percent in 1918, and after falling to 24 percent in 1929 rose to 35 percent in 1939, dramatizing the power of the state to intervene in the life of society. By the end of the war, the 20 clerks in the Contracts Department in August 1914 had grown to 65 000 officials in the Ministry of Munitions, which came to control two million workers in 250 govern-ment factories and mines, and another 1.4 million in 20 000 government-controlled establishments. Altogether, ten new government ministries and 160 boards and commissions were created during the war.[43]

Fabian Socialists like Beatrice and Sidney Webb saw this 'war social-ism' as the coming of a system they had long anticipated. In 1916 Sidney Webb and Arnold Freeman published *Great Britain After the War*, in which they predicted a more egalitarian society brought about through state intervention in the lives of the poor. The Britain of the future would be a finer country, they believed, because the 'war aroused us from our slothful acquiescence in the social iniquities that persist around us.' Whether or not the war promoted such utopianism, it certainly enhanced the power and reach of the state. In this respect the Great War made Britain more typically 'European' in terms of the large role the state bureaucracy now played in many aspects of people's lives.[44]

* * *

Over the course of the war, the government initiated numerous social welfare policies aimed at improving civilian health and morale. Out of this series of reforms emerged an important new principle – that basic welfare was a right of citizenship and not a charitable gift. Early in the war, controversy over separation allowances helped clarify this point. The dependents of military recruits were entitled to separation allowances, which in the first years of the war were administered by the Soldiers' and Sailors' Families Association (SSFA), a private philanthropic organization. Most of the field work was done by middle-class 'lady visitors,' who 'acted as the advocates, disciplinarians, troubleshooters, and morality police of soldiers' wives.' Many working-class women resented the officious and patronizing manner of some visitors, but the visitors defended their work, arguing that 'they were forging important links between the classes.' Labour leaders criticized the SSFA for treating payments as charity, to be given only if working-class women met their expectations of good behavior. Labour insisted the money was a right and should be administered by the state, a position that triumphed in 1916 when the Ministry of Pensions took over separation allowances. The traditional philanthropic ideal of moral reform was out of step with wartime democratic sentiment. Separation allowances ultimately cost the government almost half a billion pounds, nearly as much money as soldiers' pay. The unprecedented circumstances of the war had made such massive social spending possible.[45]

The 'one nation' psychology which was a prerequisite of the war effort encouraged many forms of social engineering. At the end of the war, the pioneering social investigator and industrialist, Seebohm Rowntree, argued that 'we have come to regard many conditions as intolerable which before had only seemed inevitable.'[46] Numerous social welfare policies favorable to the working class were implemented during the war. Their genesis was complex, stemming in part from patriotic paternalism, in part from fears of national degeneration, and in part from working-class demands. In August 1914, for example, persons active in the Labour movement set up the War Emergency Workers' National Committee 'to protect working-class interests during the war.' Under the leadership of Jim Middleton, Assistant Secretary of the Labour Party, the Committee pressed the government for numerous measures that were ultimately adopted: more adequate war pensions, better dependents' allowances for soldiers' families, government control of sugar, milk, and other foodstuffs, and protection against eviction by landlords of soldiers' families.[47] The government was not always quick to follow Labour's leadership, though it was spurred on by a growing realization of national weakness.

Most alarmingly, by late 1915 the army was rejecting almost 30 percent of volunteers as unfit for military service. During 1917–18, of the 2.5 million recruits examined, only 36 percent were passed as fit for full military service. Forty-one percent were graded as unable 'to undergo physical exertion' or 'totally or permanently unfit for military service.' Figures for the unfit were a serious indictment of the British class system. For example, the 210 18-year-olds from Lancashire and Cheshire placed in the lowest grade averaged 4 feet 9 inches in height, 84 pounds in weight, with 30 inch chests. By way of contrast, only 5 to 10 percent of middle and upper-class men were rejected as too short, underweight or unhealthy. Even more than the Boer War, the First World War showed the military consequences of so many people having been brought up in poverty.[48] In addition, the unprecedented carnage of the Western Front led many to fear that the best of the race was being destroyed, leaving only the weak and puny to reproduce. Leonard Darwin, president of the Eugenic Society and son of Charles Darwin, observed that 'our military systems seem to be devised with the object of ensuring that all who are definitely defective in mind or body shall be as far as possible exempt from all risk of being shot at, whilst those who are especially strong, courageous or patriotic shall be placed in positions of great danger.'[49] The intensification of these demographic and eugenic anxieties led to an expansion of the maternal and child welfare campaign in the hopes of increasing both the size and quality of the population.

The tremendous loss of life and the falling wartime birthrate led to pro-natalist policies designed to save the lives of as many children as possible. The government underwrote the expenses of new prenatal and child welfare clinics, and home visitors for expectant mothers. Milk prices were fixed and regular quotas reserved for families with young children. Official support for infant welfare was dramatized by the first 'Baby Week' in July 1917. A series of events was opened by Queen Mary on 3 July at Central Hall, Westminster, where the Queen was met by an 'honor guard' of 120 mothers and children drawn from 80 maternal and infant welfare centers in London. The Bishop of London later spoke at the Fulham Babies' Hospital, where he observed that 'the loss of life in this war had made every baby's life doubly precious.'[50] The link between high infant mortality and military weakness was underscored by the 1917 report by the Carnegie Trust on maternal and child welfare. The report calculated that if the 'wastage' of male infant life for the past 50 years had been no worse than at present, an additional 500 000 men would be available for the military.[51]

The accession of the Coalition government in May 1915 also generated various policies that eased hardship among the working class. In July the government limited the price of coal, which had been rising steeply, and in September it checked advances in meat prices. Most significantly, in November, following rent strikes and widespread agitation, the government pegged rents of working-class dwellings at their prewar levels. Considerably less popular, but no doubt a contributing factor to better health, was the government's reduction of the alcoholic content of beverages and restriction in licensing hours, first in munitions areas and then generally. In London in November 1915, opening times of establishments serving alcohol were limited to the hours from noon to 2:30 p.m. and between 6:30 and 9:30 p.m. The stated purpose of this regulation was to improve worker productivity, but it also meant that more money became available to spend on food and other necessities.[52]

No area of civilian health was more important than nutrition, though, here as elsewhere, the government formulated food policy in fits and starts and only imposed rationing in the last months of the war. Military camps put pounds on undernourished recruits and factory canteens often supplied low-cost meals, yet for most Britons, the war years presented real difficulties in obtaining enough food.[53] In the early years of the war, there was a strong Liberal resistance to regulating foodstuffs as constituting a restraint of trade, but this did not prevent the government from guaranteeing a minimum price for wheat as a sop to farmers.[54] Rationing also ran counter to the Liberal tradition of laissez-faire, and there was the additional fear that it would hurt civilian morale. Mandatory rationing was preceded by appeals for voluntary self-denial, meatless days, rules against 'flaunting' luxury foodstuffs, and even a Royal Proclamation on saving grain read in places of worship. In 1916, 'war bread' was introduced to stretch wheat reserves by adding barley, oats, and rye; later soy and potato flour were added. The resulting denser, darker bread may have been healthier, though certainly less appealing to contemporary tastes.[55]

Appeals for voluntary restraint were directed at the working classes through a series of bread posters, one example of which depicted a giant loaf floating above the Union Jack, beneath which 'Waste Not, Want Not!' and 'Save the Nation's Bread' were printed in bold letters. Another poster presented an imaginary monologue by 'Mr Slice o'Bread,' who

lamented that he was wasted every day by millions of Britons – the equivalent of 'two shiploads of good bread!' wasted every week. However, this
figure was arrived at, many working people found it insulting as they
were not in the habit of wasting food.[56] Likewise, the Board of Trade's
appeal to the public to eat less meat demonstrated an insensitivity to
the realities of working-class life. As spokespersons from the East End of
London were quick to point out, most working families were only able
to purchase meat once a week and their diets would admit no further
economies.[57] At times the hypocrisy of the upper classes was palpable, as
on 2 December 1915 when Asquith addressed a conference of organized
workers, urging economy and frugality, but then hastened off to attend
the lavish wedding festivities of his daughter. Of course, notions of 'frugality' were relative, as Sylvia Pankhurst discovered at a dinner party
given by Nancy and Waldorf Astor, where presiding over a table 'sumptu-
ous with abundant meats', the hostess declared her intended austerity.[58]

By the summer of 1916, the food situation was causing anxiety as the
German submarine campaign threatened supplies. In November the
Food Department was created at the Board of Trade with compulsory
powers under the Defence of the Realm Act (DORA); in December,
after the fall of the Asquith government, it was elevated to the status
of Ministry. Unfortunately, the first Food Controller, Lord Devonport,
proved ineffective, relying primarily on voluntary rationing. By the
spring of 1917, the food situation was dire: two million tons of food had
been lost in ship sinkings and the country had only a three- or four-week
food supply in stock. Devonport resigned in May amid mounting criticism. The Ministry of Food noted dramatic decreases in the availability
of certain key foodstuffs. National butter consumption, for instance, fell
by more than half between October 1917 and January 1918.[59]

Escalation of food prices and food shortages in 1917–18 did more than
anything to heighten working-class resentment and disenchantment with
the war effort, especially when this hardship was coupled with an awareness of social contrasts. Some in the government saw a link between the
food situation and bigger and more sympathetic audiences at peace meetings in late 1917, and military censors reported discontent among soldiers
about the food shortages their families were facing at home. A shortage of
potatoes in Glasgow in March 1917 led to a protest march by 2000 women
who cheered references to peace and the Russian Revolution. In late 1917
and early 1918, there was a series of work stoppages across the country in
protest over the food situation, and strikes were occasionally accompanied by the looting of food shops.[60]

Lord Rhondda, the new Food Minister, moved quickly to reorganize
the Department and impose greater government control and regulation,

something the Labour movement had been demanding for many months. Rhondda introduced a bread subsidy, reducing the price of a standard loaf from 1s. to 9d.; it was estimated that this saved 2s. a week in a working-class budget. Civilian rationing began with sugar on 1 January 1918, but was soon extended to meat, butter, and other foodstuffs. Individuals were limited to a weekly allowance of 8 ounces of sugar, 5 ounces of butter and margarine, 4 ounces of jam, and 2 ounces of tea. Bread remained unrationed and meat was rationed by price. Rationing embodied a leveling principle, limiting the food intake of the upper classes to minimize shortages among workers. *Punch* encapsulated the new spirit in a cartoon: a laborer and a nobleman were peering into a butcher's window. 'What's your choice, Guv'nor?' asks the worker. 'Mine's a couple of sausages.' The peer looks forlorn. 'I was just wondering how much shoulder of mutton I could get for fivepence.'[61] Enough food had always been available, but without control over supply and distribution, not all citizens had access to a fair share. Eventually, 85 percent of all food consumed in wartime Britain would be bought and sold through government agency, and 94 percent would be subject to price controls. A serious food crisis never materialized in Britain, unlike in Germany, where severe shortages and actual starvation undermined civilian and military morale in 1918 and contributed to the collapse of the German war effort.[62]

During the war there was a marked improvement in civilian mortality rates and an overall improvement in the working-class standard of living. The destitution that had seemed endemic in Edwardian times virtually disappeared. Poor Law relief declined significantly, as did the number of schoolchildren claiming subsidized school meals.[63] Life expectancy for men in England and Wales rose from 49 to 56 years between 1911 and 1921, and for women from 53 to 60 years. Although this was part of a longer trend, the increase during the war decade was substantially greater than during either the first or third decades of the century. Infant mortality in the first 30 years of the century also experienced its steepest drop during the war years, declining from 130 deaths per 1000 live births in 1911 to 89 per 1000 in 1919.[64] While there were important improvements in social welfare policy during the war, especially with regard to maternal and infant health, the impact of these measures lay mostly in the future. Wartime improvements in nutrition and longevity are primarily attributable to the increased earning power of the working class. Full employment, increased wages, plentiful overtime, jobs for women, separation allowances, and rent control created an exceptionally favorable economic climate for workers.[65]

Signs of a new affluence were everywhere visible. Improved wartime incomes allowed many in the working class to acquire status goods that had only been available to the artisan sector or the middle classes. Laborers became accustomed to reading newspapers and to having their photograph taken. They could buy more interesting food and better clothes. Clogs and shawls gave way to shoes and hats, though a censorious middle class often condemned workers for 'wasting' money on 'flashy' apparel. For many of the unskilled, expectations rose as a result of tasting 'the honey of affluence.'[66] Robert Roberts, the child of shopkeepers, recalled that 'the once deprived began to savour strange delights . . . One of our customers, wife of a former foundry labourer, both making good money now on munitions, airily inquired one Christmas time as to when we were going to stock "summat worth chewin." "Such as what?" asked my father, sour faced. "Tins o'lobster!" she suggested, "or them big jars o' pickled gherkins!" Furious, the old man damned her from the shop. "Before the war", he fumed, "that one was grateful for a bit o' bread and scrape!"'[67]

* * *

The home front was not unique in being shaped by wartime class dynamics. In many ways the Army itself recreated the British class system in miniature: aristocratic generals, middle-class officers, and a working-class rank and file. The Army structured itself around class, the military authorities trusting background rather than experience in forming the officer corps in the newly raised battalions. Until the last year of the war, when two-thirds of the officers were appointed from the ranks, a rigid class structure was in place for recruiting, training, and field service. At the outset of the war, over 40 percent of the military high command came from the aristocracy or gentry. The remainder of the officer corps was mostly middle class.[68] As Britain's tiny Army swelled to millions by 1915, there were insufficient officers to go around. The call was made to men of 'good education' to become officers. Their social and educational background was assumed to give them an air of authority that would compensate for their youth and lack of military experience. Before 1914, 150 schools and 20 universities had established Officer Training Corps. The public schoolboy therefore had such rudimentary military training as basic drill and marksmanship, but it was the public school ethos, with its ideals of manliness, duty, honor, sacrifice, and honesty that was believed to best prepare the nation's elite for leadership, military or otherwise.[69]

The Army tended to reinforce traditional social hierarchies, which has led some historians to downplay the egalitarian possibilities created by the war. Gerard DeGroot argues that 'it requires a precarious leap of reason to believe that barriers were broken down in the army, which was even more rigid and hierarchical than civilian life.'[70] 'For the soldier-worker', Eric Leed maintains, 'the war meant a new range of tasks that were dirty, hard, and compulsory.'[71] Long-standing prejudices of the British class system ensured that enlisted men were treated almost like children. Equality of sacrifice was no more apparent at the front than at home. Officers each had a soldier-servant who acted as a sort of military valet, attending to their uniforms and waiting at table. Officers' families regularly sent them hampers from Fortnum and Mason, containing all manner of delicacies – game, foie gras, fresh fruits, chocolates, and wine.[72] Robert Graves was shocked by his first visit to the Battalion Headquarters, which 'happened to be unusually comfortable, with an ornamental lamp, a clean cloth, and polished silver on the table. The Colonel, Adjutant, doctor, second-in-command, and signaling officer had just finished dinner: it was civilized cooking – fresh meat and vegetables. Pictures pasted on the papered walls; beds spring-mattressed, a gramophone, easy chairs . . .' Graves found it hard to reconcile this picture of officerly comforts with the vision 'of troops waist-deep in mud, and gnawing a biscuit while shells burst all around.'[73]

Much wartime propaganda, however, sought to depict the Army as a unifying force and promoter of social harmony. For example, in Ian Hay's patriotic novel *Carrying On* (1917), a middle-class soldier explains: 'When you have experienced a working-man's courage and cheerfulness and reliability in the day of battle, you can't turn around and call him a loafer and an agitator in time of peace – can you?'[74] Likewise, in his postwar novel, *Waiting for Daylight* (1929), H. M. Tomlinson celebrated the bravery of ordinary soldiers: 'And those Nobodies of Mons, the Marne, and the Aisne, what were they? The "hungry squad", the men shut outside the factory gates, the useless surplus of the labor market . . . Yet the Nobodies stood to it at Mons.'[75] Such sentiments were not merely propaganda, for the most unexpected people often proved themselves resilient under fire, challenging the accepted status hierarchies. Some memoirists and historians of the war have emphasized that the 'camaraderie of the trenches' could override the class-bound nature of the Army, promoting greater sympathy and understanding between the classes. The military historian John Keegan maintains that as a result of their close dealings with ordinary soldiers, 'officers were to conceive an affection for the disadvantaged which would eventually fuel that transformation of middle-class attitudes to the poor which has been the most important social trend in Twentieth-Century Britain.'[76] If so, such attitudes were not much apparent in the 1920s, when there were drastic cuts in government spending on social services.

Active service on the Western Front provided an opportunity for interaction between individuals who would have been unlikely to socialize in peacetime because of the class-bound nature of society. Trench warfare provided exceptionally favorable circumstances for the development of close inter-rank relationships. All shared the same discomforts and all needed to cooperate closely to ensure survival. A number of middle- and upper-class men later asserted that their attitudes toward the working class were altered by the war. Anthony Eden claimed that he had gained a 'sense of the irrelevance and unreality of class distinction' from his friendship with his platoon sergeant during the war.[77] A similar transformation is evident in the career of the novelist Christopher Reynolds Stone. In Stone's prewar novels, working-class characters were depicted as either cockney clowns or dangerous revolutionaries. But his experience as an officer softened his Tory attitudes and he developed real feelings of respect and admiration for his men. Stone's postwar novels are radically different; working-class characters are now central to the story and no longer a source of ridicule. They speak normal English rather than the artificial cockney of his earlier works. Stone helped found the Old Comrades Association and was active in fighting for pension rights for disadvantaged members.[78]

By the end of the war, the exclusive nature of the officer corps was breaking down. High attrition rates among officers enabled lower middle-class and even some working-class soldiers to rise through the ranks. Referred to as 'temporary gentlemen' to underscore their peculiar position and to emphasize that true gentlemanly status remained a birthright, they sometimes experienced snobbery.[79] Alfred Burrage lamented the appearance of officers from humble backgrounds at West End clubs: 'Judging by the manners and accents . . . they were nearly all "Smiffs", late of Little Bugginton Grammar School, who had been "clurks" in civil life.'[80] These new officers, however, performed admirably as leaders of men, ultimately earning the respect of their social superiors and casting doubt on the military caste system. In his autobiography, *Soldier from the Wars Returning* (1965), Charles Carrington affirmed: 'The "temporary gentlemen" who became temporary officers in Kitchener's Army proved the worth of their grammar-school educations by revealing their talent for responsible leadership even though their accents were not refined.'[81] There was much talk during the war of the inversion of class, 'of the clerk being the superior officer of his employer, of the squire taking orders from his gardener.'[82] While this characterization is grossly exaggerated, it nonetheless seems likely that when thousands of officers had risen from the ranks, and men of all classes shared the same trenches, traditional class attitudes would prove harder to maintain.

* * *

At the end of the war, the British social structure stood essentially as it did before 1914, but there were important modifications in its composition, attitudes, and modes of interaction. Some of the worst prewar poverty had been eliminated, while some large upper-class incomes were reduced. Between these two extremes, there was decreased social stratification within the principal classes, caused by a narrowing of middle-class salary differentials and working-class wage differentials. The upper classes lost some of their luster while the working classes gained influence and stature through their greater inclusion in the national community.

For many Britons the war called into question the fitness of the upper classes to rule. Blunders, mismanagement, and the extraordinary loss of life in wartime hardly inspired continuing confidence in the established ruling class. The aristocracy's own self-confidence and belief in its invulnerability was also seriously undermined by the experience of war. For a young aristocratic woman like Lady Diana Manners, the war meant 'nightmare years of tragic hysteria.' In her memoirs she recorded the dissolution of her world, as one after another of her friends and suitors was killed. It was in this context of utter disintegration that Lord Lansdowne shocked the nation with his letter to the *Daily Telegraph* (29 November 1917) calling for an end to the war and a negotiated peace with Germany. Lansdowne's younger son had been killed in Flanders in 1914. The continuing carnage and military stalemate had convinced him that the war could not be won, and that its senseless prolongation would 'spell the ruin of the civilized world.'[83]

In the aftermath of the war, a belief was created that an entire generation of Britain's elite had been wiped out. This view was given its most famous expression by C. F. G. Masterman in his book *England After War.* In his chapter 'The Passing of Feudalism', he extolled the sacrifices made by aristocratic officers and concluded that as a result of the war, 'the Feudal System vanished in blood and fire, and the landed classes were consumed.'[84] More recently, David Cannadine has demonstrated that the myth of a 'lost generation' of the elite cannot survive careful scrutiny, as the vast majority of nobles who fought in the war returned. Nonetheless, he argues, 'the British aristocracy was irrevocably weakened by the impact of the First World War. Not since the Wars of the Roses had so many young patricians died so suddenly and so violently.'[85] Aristocratic losses were proportionately greater than those of other social groups. Among peers and sons of peers who fought in the war, one in five was killed; for all members of the armed services, it was one in eight. The disproportionate casualties suffered by the upper class were a consequence of the social selection of the officer corps. Most officers came from the elite classes, and officer casualties were the highest in the war. In the first year of fighting, 14 percent of the officer corps was killed as against 6 percent of the rank and file.[86]

Wartime tax increases cut deeply into upper-class incomes, seriously eroding the elite's ability to maintain its traditional lifestyle. Income tax rates rose dramatically, and permanently, to a new level, from 6 percent in 1913 to 30 percent in 1918, and never fell below 20 percent again. The rich could not help but look back to the war as the beginning of their decline in prosperity. 'The old order is doomed', wrote the Duke of Marlborough in 1919 when death duties were raised to 40 percent.[87] The vicissitudes of war hastened the disappearance of the great landed estates that had been underway since the agricultural depression of the 1880s. In the years immediately following the war, more land changed hands than in any period of British history since the Norman Conquest. Six to eight million acres were sold between 1918 and 1921, much of it to sitting tenants. Owner occupiers thereby increased from 11 percent of farmers in 1914 to 36 percent in 1927, resulting in 'a new race of yeomen.'[88] As great landowners sold out altogether or trimmed down their estates, the traditional basis of the old-style county politics was also undermined.

The visible eclipse of the landed aristocracy hardly meant the disappearance of an upper class. The wealthiest among the agrarian elite continued their consolidation with the newer fortunes of finance and industry. Britain's changing social order was the subject of much discussion, as in Archibald Marshall's wartime novel, *Rank and Riches* (1915). The book chronicled the rise of Armitage Brown, a millionaire businessman, who acquires the country estate of a decayed aristocratic family. The war had provided tremendous opportunities for business growth and investment, mostly for the already wealthy. A postwar estimate prepared by the Inland Revenue calculated that 69 percent of the total increase of wealth went to the 340 000 persons with a net worth of £5000 or more. Disenchantment during the postwar years often found expression in laments for the disappearance of the old landed elite with its presumed values of honor and responsibility, replaced by a ruthless *nouveau riche* plutocracy – the 'hard-faced men who had done well out of the war.'[89] Iconic images of capitalist oppressors, as fat men in frock-coats and top hats sitting on money bags, long familiar to readers of socialist papers, gained wider circulation after the war, most surprisingly in middle-class publications. A great deal of postwar fiction also vilified capitalists. In particular, many crime and detective novels included 'profiteer' villains – corrupt businessmen who had shirked military service so as to enrich themselves at the nation's expense.[90]

As the upper class came to be redefined as a commercial and financial plutocracy, the middle class increasingly saw itself as a stratum between capital and labor – an image impossible in Marxist terms and one that would have been incomprehensible to the Victorians, who saw the middle class primarily as an industrial and commercial group. The composition of the middle class changed in the war years as the number of white-collar workers increased by over a million between 1911 and 1921, from 12 percent to 22 percent of the employed population. Furthermore, the middle class became more economically compressed during the war as income differentials between the wealthiest professionals and those at the lower end of the salary scale were narrowed. Now when people spoke of the middle class, the emphasis tended to be on suburban clerks, civil servants, shopkeepers, and low-level professionals like teachers – groups that more and more saw themselves as 'crushed' between big business and labor. This view is illustrated by a 1914 article in *Cassells' Journal*: 'Society today tends ever to divide itself into two main sections – those of Capital and Labour, with a smaller but important section, that of the hard-working Middle Classes between, which runs the risk of being ground to powder in the coming impact of the upper and nether millstones of the two big sections.'[91]

Many in the middle class experienced unaccustomed hardships during the war, which they came to see as primarily benefitting capitalist 'profiteers' and trade unionist workers. A number of charitable agencies sprang up in wartime to assist middle-class families in 'distress.' For the first time, according to the *Charity Organization Review*, many had had to cope with 'a smaller house, less food and clothing, fewer servants, and a cheaper education' for their children. Things seemed little better in the postwar world. In *England After War*, Masterman described the difficulties of maintaining a comfortable suburban lifestyle in an atmosphere of rising prices and taxes. He quoted from a *Daily News* symposium on how the middle class, the 'new poor,' were economizing: vegetable gardens, lodgers, remaking dresses, meatless dinners.[92] Eugenicists added to the chorus of woes by lamenting the continuing fall in the middle-class birthrate induced by postwar economic constriction.[93] This middle-class pessimism, however, should perhaps not be taken too seriously. Not only had the war created abundant growth opportunities for business, but it had led to a tremendous expansion of the civil service, and professional expertise was more highly valued than ever. And in the long run, the economic deflation of the 1920s and 1930s proved highly beneficial to the salaried middle class, whose incomes remained fixed as prices declined.

Of all the social classes, the working people of Britain would appear to have gained the most from the war, though of course they had had the most to gain. The two biggest contributors to pre-war poverty – low wages and unemployment – all but vanished during the war. Wages more than doubled between 1914 and 1918 and kept pace with rising prices. The worst prewar poverty disappeared, and unskilled workers experienced upward job mobility never before possible, resulting in an erosion of caste distinctions between the poorest workers and the elite labor aristocracy. After the war, Robert Roberts noticed this growing homogenization among Manchester's working class: 'Socially, the barriers of caste that had previously existed between the skilled worker and his family and the lower industrial grades were permanently lowered; the artisan felt less superiority, the laborer and semi-skilled man more self-assurance.'[94] All sectors of the working class had also been drawn more fully into the political life of the nation through military service and munitions work. Total war had demonstrated the nation's dependence on working people, or as G. D. H. Cole, the socialist intellectual, observed in 1919: 'Never before has the extent to which the whole community depends upon the working class been so fully realized, either by the other classes or by the workers themselves.'[95]

As the war progressed, contemporary commentators increasingly noted an erosion of deferential and servile behavior as well as greater working-class self-confidence. 'At home people remarked continually of the change among the undermass: regular wages and the absence of class pressure from above had wrought in many a peculiar quality which looked uncommonly like self-respect.'[96] The war reduced many workers' fatalistic acceptance of poverty while increasing their expectations, aspirations, and general sense of entitlement. W. H. Edwards, a union organizer in Shropshire, declared that workers 'went out to fight Prussian autocracy and now they must get rid of Prussianism that prevailed in their own country.'[97] In June 1917, a Socialist Convention was held in Leeds to celebrate the Russian Revolution and plan a network of soviets throughout Britain.[98] Although nothing came of this, it certainly alarmed the government, as did the upsurge in strikes during the final year of the war.

In 1917–18, to counteract war weariness and to rekindle national enthusiasm, the government began to foster expectations of social change among civilians, especially the working class. Lloyd George promised 'a land fit for heroes to live in', and, as an expression of the new democratic spirit, proposed an extension of voting rights. In January 1918, the Representation of the People Act was passed, granting the vote to an additional 12 900 000 men and, for the first time, 8 400 000 women over 30. The Act also enfranchised 19- and 20-year-olds on active military service. The electorate was thus vastly enlarged, increasing from 7.75

million voters in 1910 to 21.25 million in 1918, the largest single exten-sion of the franchise in British history.[99]

The wartime growth of trade unions and the Labour Party attests to the increasing political awareness of the working class. Trade union membership doubled from 4 million in 1914 to 8 million in 1920, while the Labour Party's vote had multiplied nearly sixfold, from 400 000 in 1910 to 2 300 000 in 1918, and it had replaced the Liberal Party as the official opposition to the Conservative Party.[100] Labour MPs gained val-uable governing experience by participating in the wartime coalition governments, and from late 1917 the Labour Party made a determined bid to function as a national party and a potential alternative govern-ment. In 1917, a new Party Constitution was drafted by Sidney Webb and Arthur Henderson, and later adopted by the Party Conference in February 1918. This document proclaimed an explicitly socialist vision of society: '. . . to secure for the producers by hand and by brain the full fruits of their industry and the most equitable distribution thereof that may be possible upon the basis of the common ownership of the means of production and the best obtainable system of popular administration and control of each industry and service.' A new program of policies was further outlined in the official booklet *Labour and the New Society*, includ-ing the public ownership of land and certain key industries, central eco-nomic planning, maintenance of full employment, and the provision of adequate social welfare benefits. These policies were to constitute the core of Labour's domestic agenda for the next 25 years.[101]

Labour broke with the Lloyd George Coalition at the announcing of a General Election for December 1918. Labour had only fielded 56 candidates in 1910; in 1918, it fielded 388. Especially significant was the decision by the Trades Union Congress to throw all its support, and its considerable financial resources, behind the Labour Party. There were still great difficulties in opposing the Coalition, which enjoyed the advantages of incumbency and the popular leadership of Lloyd George, 'the man who won the war.' Labour won only 57 seats, though it secured 24 percent of the popular vote.[102] The war had made workers less toler-ant of social inequality and created high expectations for social 'recon-struction.' The Labour Party embodied these expectations in its policies, and attracted even more supporters when the government failed to carry through on its promises of postwar social reform.[103]

* * *

Hopes were high for a better postwar world, and the King's speech to the new Parliament caught this spirit of optimism: 'The aspirations for a better social order which have been quickened in the hearts of my people by the experience of war must be encouraged by prompt and comprehensive action. Before the War, poverty, unemployment, inadequate housing, and many remediable ills were aggravated by division. But since the outbreak of the war every party and every class have worked and fought together for a great ideal . . . We must continue to manifest the same spirit.'[104] Important new legislation was enacted concerning unemployment, housing, and education, but a postwar economic depression and resurgent labor unrest during the 1920s soon soured the mood of social harmony.

The granting of unemployment payments to soldiers and war workers returning to civilian life severed the traditional insurance principle, whereby beneficiaries had to make contributions, and drew the government away from the support of paupers toward income maintenance of all workers. The Unemployment Insurance Act of 1920 provided near universal coverage. Although the Act only provided support for a limited number of weeks per year, and only to those who had paid into the fund for a stipulated time, it nonetheless represented an important step toward the principle that all citizens should be prevented from falling below a minimum level of existence. Workers themselves had come to view such support as a right of citizenship. 'When unemployment struck,' Robert Roberts noted, 'with a new authority, men no longer begged, as their elders had done, for the "right to work"; they insisted on the right to be maintained with a voice and vigour unheard of before, and maintenance of a sort the State grudgingly allowed.'[105]

The 1918, Fisher Education Act breached the class barriers in favor of a more egalitarian school system. It provided for universal compulsory education to the age of 14, abolished fees in elementary schools, and improved educational standards. The 1920 Report of the Departmental Committee on Scholarships further condemned 'an undesirable segregation of social classes' in the educational system, an attitude that would never have been articulated before the war. The greatest impetus for working-class mobility to non-manual occupations probably arose from the new education policy. In 1921, there were twice as many working-class children at secondary schools than there had been in 1913. Although economic recession and cuts in government spending curtailed this growth, it still continued at a slower rate, drawing workers' children into commercial and clerical employment. A class-based education nonetheless remained in place. Throughout the 1920s, almost 40 percent of middle-class boys went to secondary school and 8.5 percent to university, while figures for working-class boys were only 10 percent and 1.5 percent.[106]

Politicians promised 'homes for heroes' and the Addison Housing Act of 1919 set out to build 500 000 new houses within three years through state subsidies to local authorities. The history of the housing program is emblematic of many postwar social programs: ambitious plans and high expectations undermined by harsh economic realities. By 1921, Addison's program had built 200 000 houses, but the cost to the central government exceeded £130 million – far more than had been anticipated. A downswing in the economy gave rise to budget cuts which eliminated the program entirely. The abrupt abandonment of the housing program was an important factor in the general postwar disillusionment stemming from the government's failure to fulfill wartime promises.[107]

A brief postwar economic boom ended in 1921 with financial collapse, industrial depression, and rising unemployment. Unemployment, which had been only 3 percent in 1920, jumped to 13.5 percent in 1921, and over the next 20 years the number of jobless never dropped below a million.[108] Social programs and reconstruction fell victim to a new austerity as Lloyd George set up a committee under Eric Geddes to institute massive budget cuts. Broken promises and dashed hopes gave rise to bitter disenchantment, reflected in this stanza of the poem 'For Services Rendered':

> Where are those home-fires of welcome?
>   Have they all burnt away?
> Have Tommy and Jack, now they've come back,
>   In the unemployment ranks to stay?

The entire poem, printed on a card, was sold on street corners for 2d. by unemployed ex-servicemen.[109]

The war in part contributed to a heightening of class antagonisms during the 1920s. Ironically, the improvement of the working class's economic position and the decline of its traditional deference did not imply the attenuation of class conflict.[110] The working class emerged from the war with greater expectations and a greater sense of entitlement, while the middle class was more defensive, having experienced an erosion of its economic security. This situation proved to be a formula for disaster. Wartime cooperation gave way to expressions of mistrust and hostility. By 1922, Masterman noted: '"Our boys", who had fought so gallantly that nothing could be too good for them when they returned, had become "these men" who refused to give a fair day's work for a fair day's wage, and who were supposed to have an eye upon the imitation of Russian Revolutions.' The resurrection of Ramsay MacDonald's political career signaled a growing skepticism about the war's ideals. Voted out of office in 1918 for his pacifist views, MacDonald was back in Parliament in 1922 and the first Labour Prime Minister in 1924. His hostility to the war was no longer a political liability, and to many on the Left now appeared justifiable.[111]

In industrial relations, the uneasy truce between capital and labor dissolved, as employers sought to reassert their control and unions to build on their wartime gains. The resulting strikes and lockouts were far more aggressive and bitter than prewar industrial conflicts had been. The very words used by contemporaries to describe the unrest were infused with the language of the war, including references to 'retrenchment', 'campaigns', 'battles', and 'blockades.' The major postwar labor actions – the national railway strike of 1919, the miners' strike of 1920, the miners' lockout of 1921, and, most famously, the General Strike of 1926 – all resulted in defeats for the unions. Labour's wartime victories had led to overconfidence, while both lack of cooperation among the various unions and strong government determination, including the use of troops, undermined labor's resolve. The massive unemployment of the 1930s further weakened labor militancy and restored much industrial discipline.[112]

* * *

The working class's postwar defeats did not mean outright victory for capital, nor did they cancel out all of its wartime gains. The lessons of the war were not forgotten as the corporate model reasserted itself during the 1930s, bringing together business managers, union leaders, and politicians in an increasingly cooperative partnership to keep the system going and avoid crises.[113] Despite years of depression, there was never a return to the chronic poverty of the prewar era. In fact, the working-class standard of living continued to rise, a circumstance due in large measure to the government's commitment to social spending – another legacy of the war. The war did not destroy class feeling, despite a great outpouring of social solidarity at its height, but it did undermine the old hierarchies of Edwardian society. The old social order remained, albeit in a less rigid and less deferential form.

Chapter 3: Gender, Sex, and Sexuality

The First World War raised considerable discussion regarding the proper social roles for British women and men. In wartime, the course of action for men seemed clear and straightforward – enlist and fight. Women, however, had no clear path to follow and no role model. Debates over women's war work became battlegrounds for gender politics – setting limits on what women should do and defining how they should behave. While much wartime propaganda attempted to reinforce traditional gender ideology, the actual experience of war made enforcing such an agenda more difficult. The need for female labor on the home front opened a world of new possibilities for women. During the war women received a great deal of praise and positive attention for their work as nurses, munitions workers, and military auxiliaries, but were also the subjects of gossip, parody, and censure whenever their behavior seemed too unconventional.

The war also seemed to offer release from all manner of stuffy Victorian social customs and sexual prudery. The erosion of chaperonage, a freer style of courtship, and a franker public discussion of hitherto taboo subjects such as illegitimacy, venereal disease, and homosexuality all reflected a less inhibited sexual culture. While some progressives welcomed this new openness, more conservative elements in British society saw only a decadence that, if left unchecked, would sap the nation's fighting strength and undermine the Empire's moral fiber. Social purity campaigns were therefore mounted against prostitution, obscene literature, and 'unnatural' sexuality.

Historians remain divided over the extent to which the war brought about greater freedom for women, and greater sexual liberation for society as a whole. Until recently, the prevailing view emphasized the war's dismantling of Victorian gender roles and sexual mores. Arthur Marwick argued in *The Deluge* that women 'in their awareness that they were performing arduous and worthwhile tasks, were living through experiences once confined only to the most adventurous males . . . gained a new self-consciousness and a new sense of status.'[1] Most recent feminist scholarship, however, has cast doubt on this view, instead stressing the resilience of traditional gender ideology and the conservative backlash of the postwar years.[2]

* * *

The First World War found its most dramatic popular representations in images of sex and gender. The 'rape' of Belgium, the sensationalized accounts of female victims of German atrocities, and the bravery of soldiers all drew on traditions which equated combat with sexual virility and manly adventure.[3] The seeds of this imagery had been sown in the prewar years, as manliness and 'muscular Christianity' were increasingly emphasized in the late Victorian and Edwardian eras as vital to the imperial mission. Romantic and heroic images of warfare were especially promoted among youths by the adventure novels of Henty and Kipling, new periodicals like the *Boy's Own Paper*, and new organizations like the Boy Scouts and the Boys Brigade. By 1914, over 40 percent of British adolescents belonged to some kind of youth organization – many of them paramilitary in nature.[4]

When war broke out, many welcomed it as an opportunity to redeem the nation's manhood. H. G. Wells's fictional alter ego Mr Britling immediately broke off a romantic entanglement as there was no room in his heart 'for any love but the love of England. He loved England now as a nation of men.'[5] Wells was not alone in seeing the war as an antidote to the presumedly decadent state of Edwardian society, where men had become soft and effeminate, women hard and aggressive. The war, it was hoped, would regenerate manliness in men and femininity in women. The young writer J. B. Priestley saw the war as 'a challenge to what we felt was our untested manhood. Other men, who had not lived as easily as we had, had drilled and marched and borne arms – couldn't we?'[6] Oscar Wilde's elder son, killed on the Western Front in May 1915, had joined up 'to retrieve a name no longer honoured in the land.' He hoped, through his valor and bravery, to erase the blot of his father's homosexuality: 'first and foremost, I must be a *man*. There was to be no cry of decadent artist, of effeminate aesthete, of weak-kneed degenerate.'[7]

Soldiers were held up as the embodiment of true manhood, while men who held back from volunteering or who refused to fight were branded 'unmanly.'[8] Richard Aldington makes this point in *Death of a Hero*, where his protagonist George Winterbourne, returning to the front from leave in England, exclaims to himself upon seeing other soldiers: 'By God . . . you're men, not boudoir rabbits and lounge lizards . . . you're the first real men I've looked upon. I swear you're better than the women and the half-men, and by God! I swear I'll die with you rather than live in a world without you.'[9] This comparison between the manly soldier and effete civilian found comic expression in the popular wartime postcard entitled 'He, She and It', which depicted a robust young soldier out walking with an adoring young woman. They pass a monocled dandy who looks forlornly at the woman who ignores him. The designation 'It' implies that any man not in uniform isn't really a man.[10]

Much recruiting propaganda promised the approval of women and threatened the humiliation of appearing unmanly. The Mayoress of Keighley struck a powerful note at a 1914 recruiting rally, where she proclaimed:

> There are Yorkshire women as well as Yorkshire men, and I can assure the lads left behind that they will get nothing like the welcome, when the struggle is over, that will be given by the girls to those who have been to the war. When I see an able-bodied, well-built young man walking about the streets enjoying himself, I am ashamed of him.[11]

Baroness Orczy, author of popular romances like *The Scarlet Pimpernel*, founded the Women's Service League in September 1914 to assist the recruiting effort. The League placed ads in newspapers, containing a membership form which women were urged to sign and return. The prospective member pledged to persuade 'every man I know to offer his services to his country' and 'never to be seen in public with any man who . . . has refused to respond to his country's call.' Official government recruiting posters frequently appealed to women: 'Won't you help and send a man to join the Army today? Is your "best Boy" wearing Khaki? . . . Don't pity the girl who is alone – her young man is probably a soldier – fighting for her and her country, and for YOU . . . Think it over, then ask him to join the Army today . . . ' Most notoriously, a group of especially zealous women handed out white feathers, a symbol of cowardice, to any young men not in uniform.[12]

In much popular fiction, the war became an arena in which men could prove their manhood and win the love of women. For example, in Ruby Mildred Ayres's *Richard Chatterton, VC* (1915), the heroine Sonia jilts Richard because she believes him a slacker. He thereupon enlists and performs deeds of great heroism in battle, which win him the Victoria

Cross and Sonia's love. The hero of William Locke's *Rough Road* (1917) also finds his manly identity through battle. James Marmaduke Trevor has been overprotected since birth by his mother, who convinces him that he is 'delicate.' His lap-dog existence earns him the contemptuous nickname 'Doggie.' When the war begins, James accepts a commission, but his fear and incompetence lead to his dismissal. He experiences a shameful revelation of his effeminate nature and determines to remake himself. After enlisting as an ordinary soldier, he at last finds his courage. Sidney Dark's *Afraid* (1917) tells a similar tale of Jasper Sedley, a young man without courage. The very thought of physical suffering makes him weak and helpless, and he loses the woman he loves, since she cannot respect one so unmanly. Only the war provides the circumstances for Jasper to discover his latent courage, and to become a true man. The great number of such novels suggests that many saw British manhood in need of redemption, or conversely that they realized that masculinity was a fragile entity and that men's insecurities could easily be exploited for the war's benefit.

If the war gave men the opportunity to discover their manhood, it also enabled women to find their 'true' nature. For example, in Beatrice Harraden's novel *Where Your Treasure Is* (1918), the war transforms the hard business woman Tamar Scott into a compassionate and self-sacrificing being. Abandoning the competitive 'male' world of commerce, she finds a higher purpose aiding Belgian refugees. In both novels and the press, charity work and nursing were held up as the 'natural' feminine counterpart to masculine combat, and the gentle, nurturing woman was compared favorably to the Flapper and Suffragette. In Alice Askew's *Nurse!* (1916), for instance, the noble, self-sacrificing nurse, Elizabeth, serves as the ideal woman, contrasted with the vain and shallow Amy who lives only for pleasure. Likewise, in Maud Diver's *Unconquered: A Romance* (1917), the hero-soldier, Sir Mark Forsyth, ultimately chooses the kind, gentle Sheila over the radical suffragist Bel Alison.

The ideal British man and woman were most often embodied in the images of soldier and nurse – he representing the masculine virtues of bravery, strength, and courage, she the feminine ideals of compassion, nurturing, and virtue. Early in the war, the romantic soldier-poet Rupert Brooke, and Edith Cavell, the British nurse shot by the Germans for helping Allied soldiers escape in Belgium, filled the public's need for a hero and heroine who embodied the best of Britain's manhood and womanhood. There is some irony in a bisexual poet and an independent career woman filling these roles, but the nation memorialized them differently. Brooke's death in the Aegean from blood poisoning was recast as the sacrifice of a modern Achilles, while Cavell, a 50-year-old, unmarried principal of a nursing school, was consistently represented as a delicate 'girl.' The Bishop of Norwich, for instance, eulogized her as 'an innocent, unselfish, devout, and pretty girl.'[13] The need to recast the intrepid and courageous Cavell as a helpless girl says much about wartime Britain's gender politics. Pushing women back into the role of powerless victim in need of male protection was one response of men threatened by women's demands for greater freedom.

The image of women as victims of war was most ruthlessly exploited by stories of rape. Sexual outrage was a frequent symbol of German aggression, as in the 'rape of Belgium,' and specific allegations of German sexual depravity were a mainstay of propaganda. As one minister addressed a recruiting rally:

> To be shot dead is bad, but there is a worse fate for them. Our mothers and grandmothers would have gone crazy at the thought of their men tamely submitting to the imposition of a mixed race in England. Yet that would, we know, be the result of a German invasion. Half the children born next year in a town occupied by German troops would have a German soldier for a father ... I cannot speak plainer than I do.[14]

The Suffragette Christabel Pankhurst also insinuated allegations of rape in an early wartime speech: 'We know what the women of Belgium and France have had to suffer more than the newspapers have told, and more than the newspapers dare ever tell.'[15] Propaganda's emphasis on rape called on men to defend women, home, and family.

If wartime literature initially sought to portray women as compassionate nurses or as the victims of Hunnish 'beastliness,' this was a willful denial of the recent past. The immediate prewar decades had seen British women make unprecedented advances in education and employment, while their political demands were voiced more forcefully than ever before. Most famously, suffrage marches and Suffragette violence had been prominent in the news from 1910 to 1914. So heated was the conflict between feminists and the Liberal government that many wondered whether suffragists would support the war. Yet, as was the case with the labor movement, the war proved a unifying force for the nation. Millicent Garrett Fawcett, president of the National Union of Women's Suffrage Societies (NUWSS), suspended suffrage agitation for the duration of the war and pledged her organization's support for the war effort. 'Let us prove ourselves worthy of citizenship whether our claim be recognized or not', she patriotically instructed her followers.[16] Emmeline

Pankhurst, leader of the more radical Women's Social and Political Union (WSPU), also rallied to the flag, suspending Suffragette violence, lending her voice to recruiting rallies and eventually changing the name of her organization's newspaper, *The Suffragette*, to the more patriotic *Britannia*. The government responded in kind, releasing from prison all Suffragettes it had jailed for acts of civil disobedience.

Pankhurst's daughter, Christabel, articulated the Suffragette position on the war in a widely reprinted speech, given at the London Opera House in September 1914. She pointed out that 'the might-is-right principle upon which German power is now based is altogether contrary to the principle upon which women's claim to citizenship depends.' A standard argument against women's suffrage was that since women couldn't defend their country in the military, they were not entitled to all the rights of citizenship. Yet, as the war would soon make clear, women's support was needed for victory: 'The brains, the energy, the patriotism of women are being offered in the service of the Empire, and this is one of the chief signs and means of its regeneration.' The Pankhursts, like Fawcett, believed that women's war work would demonstrate to the government its dependence on all its citizens, women as well as men, and that the vote could no longer be denied. 'Sooner or later', Christabel concluded, 'this war will end in victory, and, when that day comes, women who are paying their share of the price will claim, will insist upon being brought into equal partnership as enfranchised citizens of this country.'[17]

While most suffrage organizations came out in support of the war, a number of prominent feminists like Olive Schreiner and Sylvia Pankhurst (to the horror of her mother and sister) refused to support the war and condemned those suffragists who, in their view, had become part of the machinery of war. However, even within the major suffrage societies, there were voices of dissent. When a proposal for a Women's Peace Conference at the Hague was put forward in December 1914, many suffragists thought they should attend. Millicent Fawcett strongly opposed attendance, and she got her way, but not before most of the office holders in the NUWSS and ten members of the executive committee had resigned. The Hague Conference went ahead, and it became the founding event of the Women's International League for Peace and Freedom, which continued to press the government for a list of its war aims and to advocate for a negotiated peace. Helena Swanwick chaired the British section; other prominent members included Catherine Marshall, Maude Royden, and Emmeline Pethick-Lawrence.[18]

Pacifist women frequently drew on notions of love and peacefulness rooted in maternity to oppose nationalist agendas. As one correspondent wrote in *Jus Suffragii*, the journal of the International Women's Suffrage

Alliance: 'What does nationality matter! All mothers feel for each other in sorrow; it binds them together in spite of all differences of nationality or rank or religion. The mother's heart is the same throughout the world.'[19] Such sentiments were decidedly in the minority during the war, and the women who espoused them faced fierce opposition as they were seen as undermining the armed forces. Nonetheless, the women's peace movement remained the most effective and broad-based voice of opposition during the war. As war weariness mounted, the Women's Peace Crusade gained tremendous support in certain parts of the nation. One of its rallies in Glasgow, for example, attracted over 10 000 people in July 1917.[20]

Not all suffragists abandoned their struggle for the vote to pursue war work or to campaign for peace. The Women's Freedom League in particular continued to hold suffrage rallies in London parks, but the mainstream press rarely covered them. The League pushed back against the state whenever it saw the war infringing on women's rights. It advocated more generous separation allowances for soldiers' wives and better compensation for women war workers. The Women's Freedom League also condemned the government's attempt to regulate prostitution as well as other wartime moves to restrict women's movements or activities.[21]

* * *

From the start, there was a great deal of soul-searching and hand-wringing about the appropriate manner in which women should support the war. They might encourage men to enlist through gentle persuasion: the hostility that greeted the white feather campaign suggested that haranguing in public was considered entirely too unladylike. It was also acceptable for women to gather parcels for war refugees, roll bandages for the Red Cross, and otherwise 'keep the home fires burning' by maintaining a comfortable home for the soldiers' return. After all, no one predicted a long war. Many upper-class women established charitable organizations to assist the families of soldiers or Belgian refugees. A widespread response by middle-class women was the knitting of scarves and socks for soldiers – an acceptable occupation, but one that hardly satisfied everyone's desire to be useful. Some women offered their assistance in odd, though poignant, ways. A personal column in *The Times* from 1915 stated 'Lady, *fiancé* killed, will gladly marry officer totally blinded or incapacitated by the War.'[22]

At first there was great reluctance to take women away from their homes. Women's magazines offered narrow perspectives on wartime roles. *Everywoman's Weekly* and *Woman's Own* published war recipes and military sewing patterns, but urged women not to be seduced by the glamor of war into 'inappropriate' war work. When a group of women doctors offered their services to the War Office in 1914, they were curtly instructed to 'go home and sit still!' No doubt many feared that unconventional war work might 'unsex' women and lead to a further breakdown of patriarchal authority. This seems to have been the concern of the soldier who wrote to his fiancée from overseas, warning her away from war work:

> Whatever you do, don't go in Munitions or anything in that line – just fill a Woman's position and remain a woman – don't develop into one of those 'things' that are doing men's work . . . I want to return and find the same loveable little woman that I left behind – not a coarse thing more of a man than a woman – I love you because of your womanly little ways and nature, so don't spoil yourself by carrying on with a man's work – it's not necessary.[23]

But what was considered 'necessary' changed dramatically as labor shortages and the demands of total war overwhelmed popular prejudices.

A number of women had longed for something more active than knitting and rolling bandages. Vera Brittain, for one, had chafed at the suburban complacency of her mother's friends who 'provincialized' the war by serving tea to Red Cross doctors and playing at first aid.[24] Suffrage leaders criticized the government for not involving women more, and when a shortage of shells was revealed in the spring of 1915, certain government ministers concurred. Munitions Minister Lloyd George encouraged Emmeline Pankhurst (with a £2000 grant) to organize a massive Suffragette demonstration and march on the theme 'Women's Right to Serve.' Held on 17 July 1915, the march attracted thousands of supporters on to the streets of London. Addressing the marchers, Lloyd George warned: 'Without women victory will tarry, and the victory which tarries means a victory whose footprints are footprints of blood.' Millions watched newsreels of the women's march in cinemas across the land. One caption approvingly commented: 'The British Lion is awake – So is the Lioness!'[25]

As more men entered the armed forces, women were needed to replace them. By the war's end, hundreds of thousands of women had entered the workforce, many of them in traditionally 'masculine' occupations such as engineering, munitions, transport, business, and eventually even the military. The war produced a leap in women's employment from 24 percent of the workforce in 1914 to 38 percent by 1918. One million women worked in munitions industries, 40 000 served as nurses, 20 000 joined the

Women's Land Army as agricultural workers, and 80 000 served in women's military auxiliary corps. Not only did the number of women in the workforce increase dramatically, but these women were much more visible in jobs on buses and trains, and in banks and post offices. Government propaganda also created a sense of novelty about women workers through its efforts to publicize their contributions in numerous photographic and newsreel images. For some of these women, especially the young and the middle class, work outside their homes was indeed a new experience. For most, especially the working class, paid work was not new, but the type of work was. Many left low-skill, low-wage jobs, especially in domestic service, for better paying skilled labor in factories and workshops.[26]

Nurses were the category of female labor recruited earliest in the war. The nature of warfare, with high explosives and machine guns, meant an unprecedented rate of injury and serious mutilation, and a serious shortage of trained nurses at the front. Professional nurses were supplemented by Voluntary Aid Detachment (VAD) nurses recruited from genteel upper- and middle-class backgrounds. Working-class women were deemed too immoral to mix with young soldiers. Furthermore, VADs received no salary; they paid their own way. The class dynamic caused serious tensions between the professional nurses and the VADs they supervised. Nurses viewed the VADs as amateurs who undercut their wages and had no long-term commitment to the profession, while VADs resented the authority exercised by women who were usually their social inferiors, and they often adopted a patronizing tone. Later in 1915, the government decided to pay VADs in hopes of boosting their numbers. They were given £20 per annum with increases of £2.10s. for each additional six months served. This was less than many servants were paid, but reflected the ideal that with 'ladies' patriotism was its own reward. By September 1916, 8000 VADs were serving in military hospitals; tens of thousands more joined up by the war's end.[27]

Nursing, unlike other forms of women's war work, met with almost universal approval. Photographic and artistic images of nurses and VADs were reassuringly feminine. They wore starched white uniforms almost like religious habits and were shown tenderly caring for wounded soldiers. They were frequently likened to 'angels' or 'madonnas.' For example, the sheet music for the popular song 'The Rose of No Man's Land' depicts a beautiful Red Cross nurse looking heavenward with a beatific expression on her face as a shaft of light shines down upon her.[28] The nobility and selflessness of nurses was also reflected in much wartime literature. A typical example can be found in Wilfred Meynell's novel *Who Goes There?* (1916), which extolls the experiences of Pauline Vandeleur, a saintly young Englishwoman nursing wounded soldiers in London.[29]

The reality of nursing was seldom so pretty. Few young women were prepared for the gruesome and squalid conditions at frontline hospitals. Caring for severely wounded young men – changing their bandages, bathing them, emptying their bedpans – caused sheltered young women to lose their reticence and sexual ignorance quickly. Some nurses engaged in work more adventurous and intrepid than anything the public imagined. More dashing and showy, for example, were the women of FANY (First Aid Nursing Yeomanry) who acted as ambulance drivers and mechanics near the front line. Many VADs, like Vera Brittain, experienced exhilaration after 'twenty years of sheltered gentility,' escaping the suburbs and their mothers' watchful eyes. She spoke for many young middle-class women who were nurses during the war: 'It is quite thrilling to be an unprotected female and feel that no one in your immediate surroundings is particularly concerned with what happens to you so long as you don't give them any bother.'[30] The experience of nursing proved more liberating than its 'madonna' image would suggest.

Clerical work for women, like nursing, aroused no social concerns, as it was clean, respectable, and low-wage. The feminization of clerical workers had begun before the war, but expanded significantly during the conflict because of the great profusion of paperwork in all walks of life. The greatest numerical increase of women workers during the war was in the areas of banking, finance, and commerce, which took on an extra 429 000 women, and unlike other areas, such as industry and transport, most of these women kept their jobs after the war. The feminization of banking was especially dramatic, with women growing from only 5 percent of total employees in 1914 to more than 40 percent by 1918. Women in Civil Service jobs also increased sharply, from 5,000 in 1914 to 107,000 by 1918. Activists like the Pankhursts and Millicent Fawcett were initially unenthusiastic about factory work for women, preferring women to replace men in clerical and secretarial posts – a clear reflection of suffrage organizations' middle-class membership and concerns.[31]

Serious wartime food shortages also led the government to recruit women as agricultural workers. At first there were few volunteers; the work lacked the romance of nursing or the high wages of munitions. In order to more effectively persuade women to return to the land, the Women's Land Army was created in July 1917. Land Army recruiting material appealed to women's patriotism and rhetorically linked food production to combat: 'Every woman who helps in agriculture during the war is as truly serving her country as the man who is fighting in the trenches, on the sea, or in the air.' Romantic literature like Berta Ruck's *The Land Girl's Love Story* (1918) also idealized pastoral life. Here, Joan leaves her job as a London typist and is regenerated in the countryside, finding love along the way. Although the Women's Land Army ultimately hired some 23 000 women, recruitment was a constant struggle. The work was backbreaking, badly paid, and geographically isolated. The writer Rose Macaulay, who worked on a farm during the war, joked about how unglamorous it was, shivering in cold fields and spreading 'wet manure.'[32] Most city girls did not long for a return to 'rural bliss.'[33]

Munitions factories had little trouble attracting women workers, once the initial opposition of male workers and trade unions was overcome. At first the industrial sector did not seek to fill labor shortages with women, but rather with the unemployed, retired, and young. However, the tremendous increase in weapons production soon exhausted these sources of workers. The government also wanted to send women into munitions production in order to release more men for the army. The trade unions fiercely opposed the introduction of women, fearing that management would use them as a permanent, cheap alternative to skilled union labor. Trade unions only agreed to the 'dilution' of skilled labor with women when the government promised to pay women the same as men, and to fire women once the war was over. Most skilled male workers resented women making good wages; they supported equal pay to protect the prestige of their profession, not to recognize women's worth. Furthermore, the Agreement of March 1915 between the government and 35 trade unions provided an escape clause that allowed employers to pay women considerably less than men, when work was subdivided so that individual women were only doing *part* of a skilled task.[34]

Although women in munitions work made only about half the wages of men, their pay was considerably higher than anything most working women had ever known. Before the war women factory workers earned on average 10–*14s.* a week. By the war's end, women in munitions earned on average 30–*35s.* a week, often supplemented by overtime and bonus pay. It was no wonder that women flocked to munitions factories, many of them leaving jobs in domestic service – which lost 400 000 workers during the war. By the time of the Armistice, 216,000 women worked at establishments run by the Ministry of Munitions. Women's union membership tripled during the war, from 437 000 in 1914 to 1 342 000 by 1920. Most women joined the National Federation of Women Workers (NFWW) since they were usually barred from such skilled unions as the Amalgamated Society of Engineers.[35]

Women munitions workers labored for long hours and often under dangerous conditions. One firm, Greenwood and Batley, was prosecuted for working women 82 hours a week. Yet as long as production quotas were met, the government usually turned a blind eye to long hours and excessive overtime. Working with chemicals and explosives also posed serious risks. TNT poisoning was quite common, its most prominent symptom being jaundice. The bright yellow faces of many munitions workers earned them the nickname 'canary girls.' The most serious cases proved fatal, with 109 women dying from TNT poisoning over the course of the war. Hundreds of women were killed in wartime factory explosions, which were usually covered up by the government so as not to damage wartime morale. Many munitions workers were very young and didn't fully appreciate the dangers they were facing at the time. Nor did the authorities go out of their way to apprise them of the risks.[36]

The importance of the munitions worker found expression in much wartime propaganda, which celebrated her as 'the girl behind the man behind the gun.' One factory recruiting poster proclaimed: 'On Her Their Lives Depend,' while another asked: 'Do you realise that every woman who works in these factories is helping to win the War and to save the lives of our soldiers?' Romantic fiction, aimed at a young female readership, idealized the experience of munitions workers. Novels like Bessie Marchant's *A Girl Munition Worker* (1916) or Brenda Girvin's *Munition Mary* (1918) were part romance, part adventure story, in which women captured German spies and fell in love with soldiers, all the while working hard to increase production. Official attitudes articulated in the press or by government-sponsored works like Hall Caine's *Our Girls: Their Work for the War* (1916) sentimentalized 'Tommy's Sisters' as young sweet things, temporarily putting aside their feminine reticence and shyness to make munitions.[37]

Behind the exaggerated, patriotic press accounts, there remained a hard reality of male prejudice against women's employment wherever it could be avoided, as well as alarm at the independence and good wages that munitions jobs gave young women. Some people were full of indignation at women spending their war wages on fine apparel, going to pubs and cinemas, and dining out in restaurants. This seemed to go against the wartime spirit of austerity and self-sacrifice, but also reflected middle-class resentment of working-class upward mobility.[38] Madeline Ida Bedford's poem 'Munition Wages' is a case in point. Written in 'cockney' dialect, the poem represented the experiences of a woman worker who earned 'five quid a week' in a munitions factory and shamelessly spent 'the whole racket on good times and clothes.'[39] Bedford's verse embodies middle-class snobbery and condescension toward an 'uppity' munitions worker, and reflects an increase in class tensions engendered by the new-found independence of traditionally subordinate groups like domestic servants.

The munitions factory was often portrayed in propaganda as a melting pot in which all social classes mixed. For example, an article from *The*

Times in May 1916 maintained that 'the titled woman has been thrown into contact with the girl at the lathe, just as Tommy has come into close and affectionate contact with his officers. They find themselves on a new footing. Battle is a wonderful leveller; so is labour.' The *Manchester Guardian* also reported the story of a titled lady who gave a party to celebrate her first month's work at a munitions plant. Guests included a duchess, the wife of a Cabinet Minister, and a working woman, introduced as 'Mabel, my mate in the shop.' The hostess carved and guests helped themselves to the vegetables. 'The simple life', said the hostess. 'Mabel and I only get fifteen bob a week . . .' Such stories were given great play in the press as evidence of class solidarity, but they were open to other interpretations. Sylvia Pankhurst commented darkly, 'What fun indeed for the titled few – and behind it the trenches. What ghoulish sport!'[40]

Only about 9 percent of female munitions workers were from the middle and upper class, and they were concentrated in skilled and supervisory jobs, mirroring the social hierarchy. Middle-class women were specifically recruited to act as supervisors in munitions factories on the assumption that their class background suited them to leadership. Variously called 'welfare supervisors' or 'lady superintendents', they were expected both to look after their charges' well-being and to control their behavior, meting out punishment for bad timekeeping or other infractions of factory discipline. Far from promoting class harmony, interactions of women from different social backgrounds in munitions factories tended to exacerbate class tensions.[41]

No realm of women's war work met with greater resistance or aroused more controversy than military service. Although not even the most ardent feminists suggested that women should go into combat, many believed that women could assist the armed services in active ways. Katherine Furse, who had organized Voluntary Aid Detachments early in the war to supply nurses, proposed a women's auxiliary for the Army, using the VAD as a model. The War Office fiercely resisted such a departure from custom. Since the state discouraged their participation, a number of middle- and upper-class women organized themselves into paramilitary units, beginning in 1914 with the Women's Emergency Corps and the Women's Volunteer Reserve. Their leadership was an unusual mix of liberal suffragists, the Hon. Evelina Haverfield and Emmeline Pethick-Lawrence, and conservative aristocrats, the Duchess of Sutherland and the Countess of Pembroke, united by their belief that the government was not doing enough to recruit women.[42]

These first uniformed women's paramilitary units were established to help defend the British Isles in the event of a German invasion, but as the war settled down on the Western Front, they assumed the role of auxiliaries. They initially required members to pay their own way, including the costs of uniforms and training, thereby restricting membership to the propertied classes. In July 1915, however, the Marchioness of Londonderry, who had important political connections, formed the Women's Legion to appeal to a broader section of the population than had the more elite groups. The Women's Legion was organized into Canteen, Ambulance, and Cookery Sections, and was recognised officially by the Army in February 1916. The group had tens of thousands of members by 1917, and its success convinced the authorities that an official military unit for women would be workable, thereby freeing more men for combat service.[43]

In March 1917, the Army finally created the Women's Army Auxiliary Corps (WAAC). Pains were taken to differentiate the women from regular soldiers. For example, there were to be no military ranks in the WAAC; instead of officers, there were controllers and administrators, and, instead of NCOs, forewomen. These responsible positions were mostly filled by the middle classes, while working-class women swelled the ranks. Most WAACs performed traditional women's chores, such as cleaning, cooking, and clerical work, but they did this in uniform, at the front, and under fire. In November 1917, the Navy created its own auxiliary, the Women's Reserve Naval Service (WRNS), and in April 1918, the Women's Royal Air Force (WRAF) began operating. Military service clearly appealed to some women's sense of adventure, but recruitment was still a problem, as the Army paid much less than did industry. Only when there were massive layoffs in munitions factories in early 1918 (because of enormous reserves and a sharp drop in demand after the Russian Revolution) did enlistment really take off. By the war's end, there were over 80 000 women serving in the military.[44]

While women in the military auxiliaries were more maids than amazons, at least one Englishwoman saw combat duty during the war. Flora Sandes, a Red Cross nurse in the Balkans, became an officer in the Serbian army. With short-cropped hair and wearing a man's uniform, she was hailed in the press as the 'Serbian Joan of Arc.' In 1916, she published *An English Woman-Sergeant in the Serbian Army* and toured Britain to raise funds for war relief. No doubt most viewed her as a novelty, though some saw her as a trailblazer. The creation in revolutionary Russia of the first female combat brigade, the Women's Death Battalion, also found admirers in Britain. Christabel Pankhurst regarded it 'as the greatest event in the world's history.'[45]

Although some celebrated the martial woman, and official propaganda praised WAACs as 'worthy to stand side by side with the men', many in Britain expressed disapproval at women seen as imitating men. Even Lady Londonderry, who had organized the Women's Legion, found some of her volunteers entirely too aggressive: 'We had to contend with a section of "She-Men" who wished to be armed to the teeth and who would have looked quite absurd had they had their way.'[46] A more general hostility to women in uniform frequently surfaced in letters to the press, as in the following angry missive to the *Morning Post* from a man who had seen women marching near his home:

> I do not know the corps to which these ladies belong, but if they cannot become nurses or ward maids in hospital, let them put on sunbonnets and print frocks and go and make hay or pick fruit or make jam, or do the thousand and one things that women can do to help. But for heaven's sake, don't let them ride and march about the country making themselves and, what is more important, the King's uniform, ridiculous.[47]

Women in military-style units not only raised suspicions about their femininity, but their morality was also constantly being called into question. For instance, a racy cartoon in the *Sporting Times* asked: 'Would you rather have a slap in the eye or a WAAC on the knee?' Persistent rumors of promiscuity among the WAACs became so virulent that in February 1918, the Minister of Labour appointed a Commission of Inquiry – which entirely exonerated the force. There was, nonetheless, a strong postwar backlash against women military auxiliaries. Proposals to extend women's military service into peacetime were firmly rejected. As the *Times* noted with approval, 'the public has grown tired of uniformed women.'[48]

Ambivalent attitudes toward women's war work may account for the provisions of the 1918 Representation of the People Act, which enfranchised all British men, but only women over 30 who were ratepayers or the wives of ratepayers. At the time suffragists saw women's contributions to the war as key to getting the vote, and historians have typically endorsed this view, but the provisions of the 1918 Act excluded young and working-class women who constituted the majority of war workers. Some politicians may have felt that young women had experienced too much freedom during the war and needed to be reined in. Others probably hoped that the enfranchisement of older, more affluent women would counterbalance the millions of working-class men added to the voter rolls in 1918.[49]

Balancing the demands of total war proved especially difficult for women. On the one hand, the war required them to be strong, energetic and self-reliant. They should display grit and 'the British bulldog spirit.'

On the other hand, women were cautioned not to become 'unsexed' by their war service, but to retain their soft, tender, mothering ways. Maintaining this balancing act was no easy feat.

* * *

While women struggled to find their place in the war and many of them experienced exciting new opportunities, millions of men in the Army quickly discovered that this war was a far cry from the chivalric fantasies of their youth. The horrifying nature of trench warfare, with its unprecedented number of mutilations and deaths, created a nightmare existence for the British soldier. The war seemed to have turned the world upside down, liberating women and constricting men. That so many women appeared positively to enjoy the war, inevitably led to male resentment and an escalation of misogynist rhetoric.

In an influential article in the journal *Signs*, Sandra Gilbert argued that the First World War liberated women, but emasculated men by depriving them of autonomy and 'confining them as closely as any Victorian woman had been confined.' Soldiers' immobility and passivity, and their inability to act out their prescribed aggressive role, gave rise to a new disorder, termed 'shell-shock', which mirrored the symptoms of hysteria, a condition exclusively attributed to women before the war.[50] Emotionally disturbed men provided a shocking contrast to the heroic masculine ideal embodied in the fiction of Kipling, Henty, and H. Rider Haggard that had done so much to shape the public's fantasies of war. The First World War can thus be seen as a 'crisis of masculinity.'[51]

Recent work by Ana Carden-Coyne and Julie Anderson has detailed how severely wounded and disabled soldiers were often feminized in wartime discourse as weak and dependent beings. Therapy and rehabilitation aimed not only at improving physical mobility, but at re-masculinizing the soldier by restoring his sense of sexual confidence and psychological toughness. Wounded men were discouraged from giving way to 'feminine' displays of emotion and praised for stoicism and 'manly' endurance of pain. Sports frequently played a role in soldiers' rehabilitation, as it fostered both physical strength and masculine competitiveness.[52] A popular physical culture movement in the postwar world also sought to rebuild veterans as muscular strongmen, drawing heavily on Classical ideals of strength and beauty.[53]

The traditional gender order was restored by re-masculinizing men, but also by attacking women's new-found freedoms. Sandra Gilbert and Susan Gubar in Volume 2 of *No Man's Land* (1989), and Susan Kingsley Kent in *Making Peace* (1993) emphasized the estrangement felt by men at the front toward women left at home in relative safety. That many women were apparently deriving great pleasure from prosecuting the war only led to more alienation and bitterness on the part of men. Kent argues that war had become 'sex war,' and that soldiers saw women as emasculating them and benefitting from their absence.[54] Such attitudes are found in soldier's memoirs, journals, and poetry. Perhaps most famously, Siegfried Sassoon's 'Glory of Women' condemns British women for upholding the fiction of war's nobility:

> You worship decorations; you believe
> That chivalry redeems the war's disgrace.[55]

For Sassoon, the war has become a kind of ritual sacrifice to femininity.

Some even came to see the war as the fault of women. Lord Sydenham, for example, blamed the outbreak of war on Suffragette violence, arguing in Parliament in 1917 that 'it helped the Germans to believe that a country in which educated women perpetrated outrages on churches and public property was not in a position to wage war.' Others pointed to the active role some women played in recruitment, imagining in retrospect that women had heartlessly driven men off to the slaughter. In Wifred Owen's poem 'Disabled', a badly crippled soldier bitterly realizes that he had enlisted 'to please the giddy jilts.'[56] The 'white feather campaign', in particular, was resurrected and flogged in postwar memoirs and writings. What had been a minor patriotic outburst in the early months of the war, came to be remembered as 'an emblematic act of feminine betrayal.'[57]

Literature of the postwar years was also marked by antifeminism and misogyny. D. H. Lawrence expressed considerable anger and resentment at women's new-found power. In his short story, 'Tickets, Please' (1919), women conductors take over a Midland tram line. The one remaining male conductor, significantly named John Thomas, futilely tries to assert his authority until the women attack him in crazed fury. 'Who wants him?' one cries; 'Nobody!' the others respond. In Richard Aldington's story, 'The Case of Lieutenant Hall' (1930), the protagonist savagely rejects a proposed visit to a frontline brothel: 'I don't want your bloody whores! I don't want ever to touch a bloody woman. Didn't they urge us into that hell, and do their best to keep us there? Look at Stanton, with his genitals mangled, becoming a bloody parson – poor devil. Women? Pah!'[58] Emasculation was a frequent theme in postwar literature, represented by figures like Clifford Chatterley, suffering from genital wounds.

Some men felt threatened by the perception that the war had liberated women at their expense. This viewpoint, however, was far from universal and probably emphasizes the middle class at the expense of other social groups. The views of famous writers like Sassoon or Lawrence were hardly representative of most British men. Nor did all women experience the war as a liberating event. Gilbert and Gubar's feminist reading of women's participation in the war as a 'festival of sexual liberation' needs to be modified. After all, women were not a homogeneous category.[59] Texts that focus on the working class, like Sylvia Pankhurst's *The Home Front*, show that for many poor women the war was far from liberating, but burdened them with new problems, like the loss of a breadwinner, inadequate separation allowances, rising prices, and shortages of basic necessities. Other female voices from the time challenged the division between a suffering masculine battle front and a privileged feminine home front. In her novella, *Love's Last Leave* (1925), Violet Hunt argued:

> But women, who had no vote, fought too, for they worked too and endured the beastliness of living in what were practically beleaguered cities. Food queues and tramping for lack of transit wore them out by day, while nights, punctuated by Zeppelins, put the finishing touch on the instability of their nerve centres and horrified their children so that they threatened to grow up idiots.[60]

Hostility to women and other civilians who blithely endorsed the war was not an exclusively masculine or soldierly response, but was echoed by many women at the time. Nurses like Vera Brittain reacted angrily to women in England who 'played at war' and boasted of the sons they sent off to battle. In her postwar novel, *Not So Quiet* (1930), Helen Zenna Smith fantasizes about taking her mother, who was active in recruiting to the front, and showing her the bodies of battle-scarred soldiers as they were placed in an ambulance: 'See the man they are fitting into the bottom slot. He is coughing badly. No, not pneumonia. Not tuberculosis. Nothing so picturesque . . . He is coughing up clots of pinky-green filth. Only his lungs . . .'[61] Soldiers were not alone in feeling alienated from some aspects of civilian society.

* * *

Just as the war overturned certain assumptions about gender roles, it seemed to offer release from all sorts of sexual restraints. This could be observed in the new fashions – shortened hemlines and freer use of cosmetics, as well as in heightened challenges to Victorian mores. The British Society for the Study of Sex Psychology was founded in 1914 and, during the war, published numerous tracts proclaiming the benefits of sexual liberation, including Stella Browne's *Sexual Variety and Variability among Women* (1915) and Havelock Ellis's *Erotic Rights of Women* (1918). Given the apocalyptic atmosphere of the war, adherence to the old codes seemed pointless to many. Vera Brittain maintained that 'for the younger generation life had grown short, and death was always imminent; the postponement of love to a legal occasion might mean its frustration for ever.'[62] A character in Helen Smith's *Not So Quiet* echoed this sentiment, responding sarcastically to some people's concern with the morality of women war workers: 'Personally, if I were choosing women to drive heavy ambulances, their moral characters wouldn't worry me. It would be "Are you a first-class driver?" not "Are you a first-class virgin?"'[63]

Not all Britons welcomed such ideas. Conservatives especially feared that moral laxity would undermine the war effort, and many felt they were observing a rising tide of promiscuity and vice. The Women's League of Honour saw war conditions as a special threat to chastity, and they called for 'prayer, purity, and temperance' to shore up national preparedness. Social purity therefore remained a formidable concern throughout the war. The state had the power to terminate women's separation allowances for intemperance or immorality – 'irregularity of conduct' – and, despite objections to this action as an invasion of privacy, did so in a number of cases. In 1915, D. H. Lawrence's novel, *The Rainbow*, was denounced in the press as a 'monotonous wilderness of phallicism', and the National Purity League mounted a successful prosecution for obscenity. The novel was banned and existing copies publicly burned. In 1916 an act was passed to restrict the opening hours of nightclubs, which were attacked as dens of iniquity where soldiers were preyed on by 'harpies of the underworld.'[64] Patriotism thus became the justification for enforcing conventional morality in all walks of life.

The earliest moral panic of the war concerned the phenomenon of 'khaki fever' – the name given to the reportedly immodest behavior by young women in towns near army camps. Press accounts, which reflected fears of women's sexual independence, denounced girls for running after soldiers, apparently unable to resist the attractiveness of uniforms. The Chief Constable of Huntingdon told the Home Office that 'real' prostitutes posed less danger to the army than flighty girls who pursued soldiers 'in a most indecent manner.' Nonetheless, in 1916 the Defence of the Realm Act (DORA) was amended to make it an offense for any woman convicted of prostitution or vagrancy to remain in the vicinity of military camps. The wives of England's bishops also published an appeal to women and girls: 'Don't let your excitement make you silly and lead you to wander aimlessly about. Remember that war is a very solemn thing.' Working-class women were more vulnerable to charges of sexual impropriety than middle- and upper-class women, whose 'respectability' shielded them from much harassment, in spite of their own unconventional behavior during the war.[65]

Adeline, Duchess of Bedford, and other upper-class women, convinced of the immorality of many working-class women, secured the Home Secretary's consent to form women's patrols to police the behavior of women in the neighborhood of military camps. Most famously, Margaret Damer Dawson, a member of the National Vigilance Association, organized the Women's Police Volunteers to protect women from prostitution and prevent the mixing of soldiers and young women near training camps. Women's patrols were eventually recognized by local authorities, and used to enforce curfews in garrison towns and inspect the homes of suspected prostitutes. Some women volunteers from suffragist backgrounds, like Nina Boyle, objected to the surveillance and harassing of working women, but their concerns were little heard. By 1916, the success of the voluntary groups had led the Metropolitan Police to employ for the first time 30 professional policewomen. Women police continued to uphold the gender division of labor, as they acted as guardians of other, mostly working-class women, in addition to going after prostitutes.[66]

The exigencies of war led some to advocate traditional family values, while others re-evaluated the very institutions of marriage and the family. Early in the war it was discovered that a large number of working-class soldiers were not married to the women they lived with. Nonetheless, the Executive Committee of the National Relief Fund decided that 'where there was evidence that a real home had been maintained allowances should be made to unmarried mothers and their children.'[67] The usual stigmas attached to irregular unions and illegitimacy seemed to be breaking down. Such was even more apparent in the 'War Babies' panic of 1915, when a supposed upsurge in illegitimate births led to widespread concern. (There was a slight rise in the percentage of illegitimate births during the war, though a fall in the actual number of such births.) According to Sylvia Pankhurst: 'Alarmist morality-mongers conceived most monstrous visions of girls and women, freed from the control of fathers and husbands who had hitherto compelled them to industry, chastity and sobriety, now neglecting their homes, plunging into excesses, and burdening the country with swarms of illegitimate infants.'[68] This view was tempered by the countervailing belief that during wartime all children were a national asset. The Conservative MP Ronald McNeill argued that 'the mothers of our soldiers' children are to be treated with no scorn or dishonour, and that the infants themselves should receive a loyal and unashamed welcome.'[69]

The casualties of war brought to a head fears of depopulation and degeneration that supposedly required radical new ways of thinking. The sexologist Havelock Ellis argued: 'Never before has it been so urgent to enlarge and requicken our sexual morality and social customs in such a way that women may be enabled to allow free play to their best impulses and ideals in the purification and fortification of the race of the future.' Ellis mentioned a 1917 poll taken from *Physical Culture* magazine in the United States, where 'a notable proportion' of readers favored polygamy and the legal and social acceptance of unwed mothers. In a wartime play, ominously titled *The Race*, Marie Stopes also praised the decision of a young woman to have a child by her soldier lover as a eugenic act. In response to her mother's assertion 'that for an unmarried woman to have a child is wrong,' the heroine questions: 'Is it not *more* wrong that not only Ernest, but all the fine, clean, strong young men like him who go out to be killed, should have no sons to carry on the race; but that the cowardly and unhealthy ones who remain behind can have all the wives and children?' Such provocative views remained decidedly in the minority. The Bishop of Oxford probably spoke for most Britons when he warned that 'there seems a danger of people going as far as to make a glory out of shame.'[70]

A great deal of public anxiety and voyeuristic attention was devoted to the sexuality of British women during the war. Much less publicity was given to the sex lives of soldiers, although the Army must have initiated many young men in the ways of the flesh. In his 1965 memoir, *Soldier from the Wars Returning*, Charles Carrington discussed the sex life of the British soldier based on his own experience as a young, middle-class officer. Having had a very sheltered upbringing before the war, nothing had prepared him for army life in France, where few taboos existed. Towns near the lines, like Le Havre, were wide open, with well-developed red-light districts and well advertised brothels on two scales of payment – first-class for officers, second-class for other ranks. As Carrington recalled:

> There were fastidious soldiers and strait-laced soldiers; there were faithful as well as unfaithful husbands; there were middle-aged men who regulated their conduct; but the popular line the Army followed, at every grade, was the pursuit of sex, on the rare days when opportunity offered. A compensation was found for sex-starvation in the recourse to bawdy jokes and rhymes, of which there was a never-failing supply.[71]

A perusal of troop magazines and other artifacts of popular culture from the war years reveals a great deal of sexual innuendo and fantasy on the part of soldiers, though most of it seems rather tame by today's standards. There was much flirting with French women, for example, but little else. As a poem from a troop newspaper lamented:

> Oh! madamerselle, chery madamerselle,
> You come for a nice promenay?
> Yes, it's always the same with your 'apres la guerre,'
> And your 'me no compris' what I say.[72]

The innocence of much sexual banter is reflected in postcards, as in one which depicts a soldier with his arms around two women, captioned 'Our Army is extremely well armed.' Another shows a soldier caressing his girlfriend accompanied by the silly pun: 'I'm still a *raw* recruit, that's why I'm so *tender*.' Most romantic imagery, however, was of the sentimental hearts and flowers variety, often portraying soldiers embracing their sweethearts, above some tender verse:

> I long to be with you, dear heart,
> But countless miles us sever,
> So send this token just to prove
> A love that lasts forever.[73]

Given the sexual reticence of Edwardian society, and the sexual isolation of most soldiers, it took very little to awaken desire. The most popular pictures among soldiers were the 'Kirchner beauties,' ethereal women in translucent garments drawn by Raphael Kirchner for the *Daily Sketch*. Pin-ups in the dugout were frowned upon by military authorities, which made them even more desirable to love-starved troops. Soldiers also devoured the society magazine *The Tatler* for its fashion reports and underwear advertisements depicting women in camisoles and night-gowns. Female impersonators in troop shows also generated a great deal of sexual excitement among soldiers. Performers rarely presented comic drag acts, but tended to emphasize feminine glamor and allure. Impersonators significantly took great care over their wardrobes, having lingerie sent to them, or going on special trips to Paris to select their finery themselves.[74]

The prevalence of venereal disease in the Army is another indicator of how sexually active troops were, as well as how little the military provided by way of disease prevention or education. By 1918, some 60 000 British and dominion soldiers were receiving treatment for venereal disease, or 32 out of every 1000 soldiers in the Army. Britain was almost alone among the combatants in having no general instruction or preventative treatment for venereal disease during most of the war. Initially, young recruits were given a printed message from War Minister Lord Kitchener in their pay books: 'In this new experience you may find temptations both in wine and women. You must entirely resist both temptations, and while treating all women with perfect courtesy, you should avoid any intimacy. Do Your Duty Bravely.'[75] Kitchener's appeal to self-restraint, though widely mocked at the time and since, was perfectly in keeping with the military thinking which continued to uphold Victorian ideals of character and morality. Major H. Waite's *Soldiers' Guide to Health in War and Peace* (1915) typically advised that desire could be conquered by 'avoiding impure conversation, thought, and temptation' and 'by regular employment of muscular and mental exercises.' Soldiers also suspected that medical officers sought to dull their libidos by spiking their tea with bromide, believed to inhibit desire.[76]

The ineffectiveness of moral restraint was underscored by the military's statistics on venereal infection as well as by the 1916 Royal Commission on Venereal Diseases, which found that 8–12 percent of the adult male population was infected. VD came to be seen as a pressing public health problem, greater government funds were made available for diagnosis and treatment, and greater openness was now possible in discussing the problem. The British Army and public, however, remained deeply divided over the issue, many still favoring sexual continence, others medically regulated prostitution, and still others new technologies of prevention. There was much public criticism of the French system of licensed military brothels and, when it was discovered in March 1918 that the British Army was operating its own brothels in Le Havre and Cayeux-Sur-Mer, the outcry in Britain, especially from the churches, was intense. Lord Salisbury warned the government that: 'Everything depends now upon keeping the people keen about the war, but if the notion which has already taken root is allowed to spread that instead of being a sacred cause the war is a vehicle of vice and demoralization, there will arise an uneasiness amongst the soundest part of the people . . . that the war is under a curse.' The Cabinet therefore declared licensed brothels off-limits for British troops, though this proved difficult to enforce. Conservative social attitudes also hindered medical alternatives, and it was only in 1918 that the Army Medical Service widely distributed prophylactic tubes of permanganate of potash against venereal infection.[77]

In wartime discussions of controversial sexual topics like VD, soldiers, as the nation's heroes, were above reproach. Women, therefore, tended to receive the harshest criticism as potential seducers and despoilers of brave young men. In February 1917, Arthur Conan Doyle wrote to *The Times*, condemning the 'vile women' who 'prey upon and poison our soldiers.'

Later that year, another correspondent referred to women as 'sexual free-lances' who 'stalked through the land, vampires upon the nation's health, distributing and perpetuating among our young manhood diseases which institute a national calamity.' The most paranoid minds even imagined a German conspiracy employing a system of syphilitic prostitute spies.[78] The ubiquitous image of the female spy, both in wartime fiction and in the notorious case of Mata Hari, brought together fears about the enemy alien, the wayward woman, and sexual decadence. In a popular wartime book on espionage, Hamil Grant encapsulated prevalent misogynist fantasies. 'Woman,' he argued, 'when intent on turpitude, is capable of sounding lower depths than the vilest of the male species.'[79]

Prostitution became a political issue at the highest levels of wartime policy making when the Canadian and New Zealand Prime Ministers protested against the aggressive prostitutes of London who were pur-portedly seducing innocent boys from the colonies. In March 1918, DORA was amended to make it a criminal act for any woman with VD to solicit or have intercourse with any member of the military. Women suspected of violating this law could be detained for medical inspection and imprisoned for up to six months. The law was seen as an attempt to reimpose the Victorian Contagious Diseases Acts, which had unfairly persecuted women and imposed no penalties on men, and it was vigor-ously denounced by women's suffrage societies and other feminist and religious organizations. Nevertheless, by October 1918 there had been 201 prosecutions and 102 convictions under the new law, and the regula-tions remained in force until after the war.[80]

The war brought greater openness in the discussion of sexual mat-ters, but it also aroused fears that the nation could be undermined from within by immorality and decadence. In her book, *The Hidden Scourge* (1916), Dr Mary Scharlieb sounded an alarm that the British Empire was at a crisis point and that venereal disease posed 'a national danger as great and more insidious than defeat on sea, on land and in commerce.' The New Zealand Prime Minister, Massey, similarly warned the mother country: 'Whenever an Empire has fallen, the downfall has always been preceded by an orgy of immorality, and I am afraid . . . we are getting perilously near that state of things in Great Britain.'[81] Sexual promiscu-ity and perversity became, in the minds of many, almost as great a dan-ger to Britain as the German Army.

* * *

No aspect of human sexuality aroused greater anxiety during the war than homosexuality, which struck at the heart of traditional assumptions regarding gender roles and the family. The war heightened both public awareness of homosexuality and greater self-awareness among British homosexuals. Large numbers of gay men and lesbians, especially those from small towns and isolated regions, were brought together either in the military or through migration to cities to do war work. In certain large cities such as London, distinctive gay and lesbian subcultures were becoming more visible both during and after the war. Wartime discussions of homosexuality were also becoming franker and more open, but not everyone urged greater tolerance and understanding.

The all-male environment of the military helped foster intimate friendships between men and furthered the expression of male emotion. There was greater potential for experimentation in intimacy between men in the army than in civilian life. Fortitude and tenderness could coexist in ways strikingly at odds with the wartime ideal of aggressive masculinity.[82] Close, affectionate relations developed between men at the front. Among officers these relationships often mirrored the romantic friendships of their public school days. To what extent these relationships were homosexual is difficult to say, and many of the men involved were probably not entirely clear about their own feelings. Homosexuality was not widely discussed or understood, but a general negative attitude toward homosexuality, together with its illegality, worked to suppress its discussion, if not its practice. Richard Aldington's autobiographical novel, *Death of a Hero* (1929), stated emphatically that 'there was nothing sodomitical in these friendships.' Eric Hiscock, however, whose war memoirs were published in the 1970s, observed greater latitude and presented both homosexuality and passionate, demonstrative friendships between men as quite common in the military.[83]

While the war made it possible for gay men to find each other, it also exposed them more to the public gaze. The presence of large military camps near many towns, and mass troop movements through major cities and ports created unprecedented opportunities for all manner of sexual encounters. Moral crusades to protect the nation's youth and shore up imperial resolve drew attention to nightclubs where unchaperoned mannish women and effeminate men congregated and 'flaunted' themselves. Social purity organizations reported that naval towns such as Plymouth, Southampton and Portsmouth were venues for homosexual soliciting in the streets. An especially shocking wartime discovery was that some London cinemas were the site of gay sex and male prostitution. An investigator reported to the Home Office that in one cinema men tipped the usher a shilling to be allowed to have sex with each other in the balcony. At another cinema he observed male patrons paying boys to fondle them.[84]

Authorities realized that the all-male atmosphere of the trenches might lead to homosexual behavior among soldiers, but were not prepared to tolerate it. Between 1914 and 1919, 22 officers and 270 soldiers were court-martialed for homosexual acts in the British Army. According to Jeffrey Weeks, the armed services 'believed themselves to have special problems of order and discipline: sexual contact between men, and especially across ranks, threatened to tear asunder the carefully maintained hierarchy.' Homosexual acts in the military carried much heavier punishment than among civilians. The shame and humiliation attendant on the mere accusation of homosexuality could produce extreme reactions. For example, there was a wartime case of a West Indian soldier who murdered a fellow conscript who had reported him for an 'unnatural offense,' before the alleged crime could even be investigated. The Army was quite ruthless about enforcing its own code of morality, even in other nations, like Egypt, where homosexuality and male prostitution were tolerated under native law. In order to 'protect' British and dominion soldiers from the homosexual subcultures of Cairo and Alexandria, large parts of those cities' red-light districts were placed under military rule, thus circumventing Egyptian law.[85]

A number of recent literary studies of the war have focused on the disillusionment soldiers experienced in the trenches and the compensations many found in male comradeship and love. Paul Fussell and others have noted that a surprising amount of war poetry concerned the love of soldier for soldier.[86] In 'Ten Years After', W. G. Thomas wrote:

I found in Hell
That love of man
For men – a love more true
Than women tell
Since love began.

Herbert Read's 'My Company' is even more explicit about the object of desire:

A man of mine
    lies on the wire...
And he will rot
And first his lips
The worms will eat.
It is not thus I would have him kissed,
But with the warm passionate lips
Of his comrade here.[87]

When Fussell first published his work in 1975, drawing attention to the homoerotic nature of some soldiers' writings, the initial critical reaction included much embarrassment and denial.[88]

A surprising number of positive depictions of homosexuality emerged from the war. T. E. Lawrence, for instance, romanticized homosexual relations among his Arab comrades in his postwar memoir, *Seven Pillars of Wisdom* (1926). Most famously, Rose Allatini's *Despised and Rejected* (1917) had as its hero Dennis Blackwood, a homosexual and pacifist. Allatini must have been influenced by the ideas of Victorian sexologist Edward Carpenter in her belief that the homosexual had 'the soul of a woman in the body of a man.' She saw homosexuality and pacifism as intimately related in their defiance of established notions of manhood. Most provocatively, she argued that homosexuals were 'the advance-guard of a more enlightened civilization . . . From them a new humanity is being evolved.' She also linked the persecution of homosexuals to that of Christ: 'They're despised and rejected of their fellow men today. What they suffer in a world not yet ready to admit their right to existence, their right to love, no normal person can realise.'[89] Not surprisingly, Allatini's novel was suppressed under DORA as a threat to the war effort.

Conservative literature equated homosexuality and all other things thought to be perverse with Germany. In a wartime article, 'Efficiency and Vice', Arnold White accused Germany of attempting 'to abolish civilisation as we know it, to substitute Sodom or Gomorrah for the New Jerusalem, and to infect clean nations with Hunnish erotomania.' In John Buchan's novel *Greenmantle* (1916), the villain is a sadistic German officer who is also homosexual, which the protagonist discovers when he enters the German's private quarters: 'At first you would have said it was a woman's drawing room. But it wasn't. I soon saw the difference. There had never been a woman's hand in that place. It was the room of a man who had a fashion for frippery, who had a perverted taste for soft delicate things . . . I began to see the queer other side of my host, that evil side which gossip had spoken of as not unknown in the German army.'[90]

In January 1918, the right-wing MP and journalist Noel Pemberton Billing published an article in his newspaper, the *Imperialist*, alleging a pro-German conspiracy involving British homosexuals. The article reported the existence of a secret German dossier which contained the names of 47 000 English men and women who practiced vices 'all decent men thought had perished in Sodom and Lesbia.' The names purportedly included Cabinet ministers and Privy Counsellors, who were being blackmailed by Germany to reveal war secrets. In February, under the headline 'The Cult of the Clitoris', the *Imperialist* condemned a private production of Oscar Wilde's *Salome* being given in London and starring the Canadian dancer Maud Allan. The paper claimed that the audience would consist of many of 'the 47 000.' Maud Allan sued Billing for libel, but the trial, held in June, became a media circus in which Billing was able to gain a wider audience for his absurd allegations. Defense witnesses like Wilde's former lover Alfred Douglas claimed that Wilde was 'the greatest force for evil that has appeared in Europe during the past 350 years.' Billing was acquitted amid popular rejoicing.[91]

Although public awareness of male homosexuality had already been raised by late Victorian scandals such as the Cleveland Street Affair or the trials of Oscar Wilde, lesbianism remained almost invisible until the war. *Despised and Rejected* included lesbian characters as did Violet Tweedale's *The Heart of a Woman* (1917) and D. H. Lawrence's *The Rainbow* (1915). Most significantly, Christabel Marshal, under the masculine pseudonym Christopher St John, wrote *Hungerheart* (1915), a first-person narrative of Joanna 'John' Montolivet which follows her through a series of rapturous affairs with other women.[92]

Public understanding of same-sex desire, especially between women, emerged slowly, as a much-reported case from 1916 demonstrates. That year a 32-year-old laborer from London was called up for military service, but revealed to be a woman by the medical exam. The press was unclear how to explain this behavior. Was it merely the act of an 'adventurous girl?' Her ability to 'pass' as a man seemed to cast doubt on such an explanation. As a soldier who saw her said, 'She was the most perfect male impersonator I have ever seen. Not one of the women who wear men's attire on the stage – and I have seen all the best of them – could approach her. We were absolutely deceived, and I can tell you that when the truth came out there was something like consternation in the barracks.' More ominous still was the fact that this 'man-woman,' usually referred to as Albert, had been living and working as a man for four years, and lived with another woman as 'husband and wife.' Yet most press accounts refrained from accusations of impropriety. Most writers did not have the vocabulary or conceptual framework to label Albert a lesbian. Instead they characterized her 'masquerade' as a desperate device to escape an abusive husband and to find better-paying work. The romantic novelist Berta Ruck later commented on the case in the *Illustrated Sunday Herald*, where she concluded that it was natural that a woman would want to 'do her bit' during wartime 'by killing a few brutes of Germans with her own hands!' Somewhat incredibly, however, Ruck also included her own homespun version of sexological discourse: 'Every now and then a woman is born who feels she's only a woman by mistake. She has the character, the strength, the capabilities of a man. Her male individuality is clothed in a feminine body; but it seems an oversight, just as if pickles had been packed into a labeled jam-jar.' Thus scientific theories of sexual inversion began to make their way into popular media.[93]

The war proved to be essential to the emergence of a lesbian identity, both through a greater openness in discussing the topic, and by bringing together large numbers of like-minded women in war work and the military. A number of British lesbians played a prominent role in activist wartime organizations that pushed the boundaries of traditional feminine behavior. Mary Allen and Margaret Damer Dawson established the Women Police Volunteers, Barbara Lowther set up an all-women ambulance unit that operated in France, and Evelina Haverfield founded the Women's Volunteer Reserves, to recruit women drivers to replace men who had joined the army.[94]

In her ground-breaking lesbian novel, *The Well of Loneliness* (1928), Radclyffe Hall argued that the war had in fact given 'a right to life' to lesbians like her heroine Stephen Gordon, who wished to escape the conventions of femininity and marriage. For Hall the war enabled lesbians to display heroic qualities and to recognize their own natures: 'A battalion was formed in those terrible years that would never again be completely disbanded.' Gordon meets her lover Mary Llewelyn serving with her in the 'Breakspeare' ambulance unit in France, and after the war they achieve a 'new and ardent fulfillment.' After they discover their sexual identities in the war, Hall's heroines experience the postwar rejection of lesbian women. 'England had called them and they had come; for once, unabashed, they had faced the daylight. And now because they were not prepared to slink back and hide in their holes and corners, the very public whom they had served – was the first to turn round and spit upon them.'[95]

Many feared that the war had awakened in women a dangerous desire for masculine occupations and behavior. In the postwar period, psychologists' theories of 'sexual inversion' fed into the backlash against women's new roles. Female soldiers, for example, were now recast as deviants in psychological writings and popular discourse. When Violet Douglas-Pennant, commandant of the WRAF, was fired in 1918, there were widespread rumors that it was because she had engaged in immoral acts with young women in the force. In 1931 the press revealed that her dismissal had indeed been on account of certain generals' belief that she was a 'deviant.' In the 1934 collection, *The Sexual History of the War*, a number of medical experts now identified a woman's desire to enter the military as a sign of transvestism, homosexuality, or even sadism. The heightened visibility of lesbianism during and after the war led Parliament in 1921 to attempt to amend the criminal code to include 'acts of gross indecency by females' which the 1885 Act criminalizing male homosexual relations had ignored.

The proposal was rejected in the House of Lords as likely to give lesbianism undesirable publicity. It was thought best not to discuss it at all.[96] The postwar 'return to normalcy' might best explain the most celebrated sex book to emerge from the war – Marie Stopes's *Married Love* (1918). A best-selling sex manual that advocated frequent and mutually satisfying sexual relations between husbands and wives, Stopes's book has usually been presented as a surprising departure from Victorian prudery that signaled a new climate of sexual liberation. Stopes herself claimed that she published *Married Love* because 'I felt psychologically the time was ripe to give the public what appeared to me a sounder, more wholesome, and more complete knowledge of the intimate sex requirements of *normal* and healthy people than was anywhere available.'[97] Stopes's emphasis on the term 'normal' is instructive, as she presents sexual pleasure as an ideal that will save and transfigure marriage and the family. Well-known for her advocacy of birth control, Stopes nonetheless saw the begetting of children as inseparable from normal relations. 'Every lover desires a child,' she insisted. 'Those who imagine the contrary, and maintain that love is purely selfish, know only the lesser types of love.'[98] Stopes's work posed far less of a challenge to prewar gender ideology than many feared.

* * *

Both contemporaries of the war and historians have probably focused a disproportionate share of attention on the novelties and oddities of wartime sexual experience, especially with regard to women. Many people at the time feared the unravelling of conventional morality and gender roles, though such fears proved mainly unfounded. Most British women never worked outside the home during the war, nor were they expected to. Domesticity and motherhood remained a constant bulwark against radical innovation. Most wartime women's literature emphasized being supportive sweethearts and wives as the most important role for women, taking precedence over the new opportunities for national service. For instance, E. M. Delafield's *The War-Workers* (1918) satirized the overzealous attitude and self-importance of some lady volunteers through the persona of Miss Charmian Vivian, manager of the Midland Supply Depot. She is contrasted unfavorably with Grace Jones, the ideal woman who remembers her responsibilities to home and family. Annie Swan's best-selling *Letters to a War Bride* (1915) celebrated the joys of housekeeping, and venerated domestic duties as women's principal responsibility during the war. Rather than representing a disruption of domestic life, the war gave many women an opportunity to rediscover its importance.

Women's weekly magazines like *Woman's World* and *Mother and Home* concentrated on effective domestic economy during the war, including ideas for remaking dresses and recipes for stretching limited food supplies. The patriotic housewife could do her bit by making 'war cake' – a crude dark loaf which kept well and cost little. It used no eggs or milk, little sugar, and bacon grease rather than butter – the taste hidden by additions of cinnamon and cloves. Recipes like this, or the ubiquitous lentil loaf, were circulated to promote patriotic restraint and to involve women more intimately in the war effort. *Win the War Cookery Book* elevated domestic economy to the level of combat: 'The British fighting line shifts and extends and now *you* are in it. The struggle is not only on land and sea; it is in *your* larder, *your* kitchen, and *your* dining room. Every meal *you* serve is now literally a battle.'[99] Such appeals seemed to ignore class differences since middle-class women had the leisure to experiment with new recipes. For many working-class women, the extra burdens of rationing, queuing, and creative cookery often came on top of war work outside the home.

The war also emphasized motherhood as women's primary patriotic role, and as such continually undercut their attempts to break out of the doll's house. The journalist Alex Thompson warned that by promoting women's war work, the nation was neglecting 'another trade at which they shine unrivaled – and that is the useful trade of motherhood.' J. Arthur Thomson, professor of natural history at the University of Aberdeen, agreed, arguing that 'If there is patriotism in dying for our country, there is conceivable patriotism in marrying for her and in bearing children for her.'[100] This view, far from being upheld only by conservative ideologues, was maintained with equal vigor by the nation's leading feminists and suffragists. Millicent Fawcett told mothers who stayed at home that 'the care of infant life, saving the children, and protecting their welfare was as true a service to the country as that which men were rendering by going into the armies.' Christabel Pankhurst also reminded a wartime audience 'that if the men fight, the women are the mothers. Without the mothers you have no nation to defend.'[101] By raising motherhood to an act of citizenship equivalent to military service, feminists like Fawcett and Pankhurst hoped to advance women's political rights. Ironically, they also reinforced the Victorian ideology of 'separate spheres' for men and women.

Much wartime art and literature extolled motherhood as a sacred calling, encouraging women to emulate the Virgin Mary. For instance, the much-reproduced Red Cross poster, 'The Greatest Mother in the World,' depicts an oversized woman cradling in her arms the miniature body of a wounded soldier in a kind of 'bizarre intersection of the madonna and child and the Pieta.'[102] Lilith Hope's novel, *Behold and See!* (1917), tells the story of Sister Rose, a Belgian nun raped by a German soldier. Discovering that she is pregnant, she decides to keep the child despite the prejudice and disapproval she encounters. She is presented as a saint who realizes that motherhood is the holiest calling of all. Annie Vivanti Chartres' novel *Vae Victis* (1917) also extols the decision of a Belgian woman, Cherie, to bear the child of a German soldier who had raped her. She refuses her family's pressure to have an abortion. 'She heard no other voice but that child-voice asking from her the gift of life, telling her that in the land of the unborn there are no Germans and no Belgians, no victors and no vanquished . . .'[103] Such pro-life and maternalist sentiments constituted a powerful countervailing force to wartime innovations in women's roles, and were to emerge with even greater strength in the postwar world.

* * *

Wartime disruptions in the realms of sex and gender were followed by a conservative backlash in the 1920s and 1930s. In 1917 the feminist Stella Browne even predicted that the war would be succeeded by 'a specialised education for girls concentrating on the sentimental and the domestic, and a fevered propaganda in favour of what some would call the normal family.' During the war, the news media, government propaganda, and even commercial advertisements had celebrated women's non-traditional war work, though almost as soon as the war was over, these popular representations reverted to images of women in the home, as wives and mothers. For example, 'Glitto', a grease remover, which had been promoted during the war as the munition worker's friend, later proclaimed in its ads that it made the kitchen glitter. Likewise, an 'Oatine' face-cream ad from February 1919 showed pretty women applying the product at home, accompanied by the caption: 'Back to Home and Duty.' 'Now the war is won', the text explained, 'many women and girls are leaving work, their war job finished. They are naturally desirous of regaining their good complexions and soft white hands freely sacrificed to the National need.'[104]

Toward the end of the war, government propaganda began preparing women for a return to domesticity. One pamphlet declared: 'A call comes again to the women of Britain, a call happily not to make shells or fill them so a ruthless enemy can be destroyed but a call to help renew the homes of England, to sew and to mend, to cook and to clean and to rear babies in health and happiness, who shall in their turn grow into men and women worthy of the Empire.' The government might represent this 'call' as a welcome choice, though in fact the Restoration of Pre-War Practices Bill forcibly deprived many women of their jobs, especially those in high-paying, skilled industries. While some women quietly accepted this turn of events, others clearly did not. In June 1918, thousands of women marched to Westminster to demand to keep their factory jobs. The surprise and hostility with which women were met when they again moved into new jobs during the Second World War also suggests that the First World War had not significantly altered social attitudes toward working women.[105]

There was also a desire to domesticate the returning soldier, as many feared that the war had awakened savage 'animal' instincts in men that would not easily be quelled. 'Khaki riots' in the summer of 1919 only confirmed such fears. Most seriously, Victory Day (19 July 1919) celebrations turned violent in several towns with soldiers attacking civilians. In Luton, ex-servicemen set the town hall on fire and fought a pitched all-night battle with policemen. Yet there was a return to domesticity for men as well as women after the war, and a greater emphasis on companionate relationships. Men's social lives revolved more around their homes and families, and less around their male friends than before the war.[106]

The marriage rate increased markedly during the 1920s. Nonetheless, a myth still persists that a generation of women was condemned to single status as a result of so many male fatalities. As Jay Winter has demonstrated, there was actually a greater sexual imbalance in the decade before the war due to male emigration, which halted in the 1920s. Some women who lost sweethearts in the war may have chosen to stay single, but this was not for lack of available men.[107]

Although it has long been a cliché that the war swept away the last vestiges of Victorian prudery, the sexual liberation of the 1920s was extremely superficial. During that decade, considerable press coverage of the antics of upper-class youth, theater people, and 'the flapper' focused attention on bohemian hedonism and sexual license, though this was largely a myth generated by the media. The reality for most Britons was far more prosaic and conservative. A mounting list of obscenity prosecutions in the years after the war, most notably the 1928 trial involving *The Well of Loneliness*, hardly pointed to a permissive society. Both *Ulysses* and *Lady Chatterley's Lover* had to be published abroad. Film censorship was also strengthened, with a long list of subjects that were strictly taboo, such as prostitution, rape, or drunkenness among women.[108] While the Church of England modified its position on birth control in 1930 and divorce laws were slightly liberalized in 1937, there was no mass exodus from marriage and family as some alarmists had feared. The domestic ideal was actively promoted by the vast expansion of women's magazines, which added 60 new titles between 1920 and 1945, including *Woman's Illustrated*, and *Housewife*. These publications were full of advice on home-making and childrearing, with special emphasis on the importance of a woman pleasing her husband.[109]

A number of historians have emphasized the decline in organized feminism after the war. Susan Kingsley Kent, for one, argues that wartime tensions between the sexes and the link between war and sex war had become so strong that postwar feminists 'made peace.' Many women in the mainstream suffrage movement accepted theories of sexual difference that advanced the 'separate spheres' ideology, and the deaths of hundreds of thousands of men further underscored the importance of maternity. Feminists' demands now tended to be less about the rights of women, and more about the needs of women as mothers.[110] There was little place in the postwar world for the intrepid WAAC or doughty munitionette, and some of these women felt lost and betrayed. Radclyffe Hall gave voice to such women's feelings in her story 'Miss Ogilvy Finds Herself, ' where her protagonist, the commander of an ambulance unit, is now plunged back into dull provincial life with her two unmarried sisters. 'Had she ever stood tranquilly under fire, without turning a hair, while she issued her orders? Had she ever been treated with marked respect? She herself was beginning to doubt it.'[111]

* * *

Postwar society and culture were dominated by conservatism, but this should not blind us to new freedoms which emerged from the war, or to the survival of alternative views on gender and sex. In 1918 millions of women over 30 were enfranchised. In 1928 the vote was extended to women in their twenties, the so-called "Flapper Franchise." Parliament also passed the Sex Disqualification Removal Act, which opened the Civil Service and professions to women at the war's end. In 1920 Oxford University finally allowed women to take degrees. Feminism was less vis-ible in the 1920s, but it had by no means disappeared. British feminists remained active in the postwar peace movement, education reform, and Labour politics.[112]

Despite the renewed emphasis on motherhood, women were exercising greater control over their fertility than ever before. Women who married in the decade before the war had borne on average 3.5 children. Women who married in the 1920s averaged 2.4. Wartime publications such as the Women's Cooperative Guild's *Maternity* (1917) or Marie Stopes's *Married Love* (1918) helped raise public consciousness of the awful consequences of frequent childbirth for women, and helped break down traditional

opposition to birth control. Increased use of condoms by soldiers as a pre-
ventive against VD also spread contraceptive knowledge. Among working-
class women, the expansion of wartime employment greatly increased
the knowledge of birth control. Diana Gittins, who conducted an oral
history of women from the period, found that they mostly learned about
contraception from their workmates in factories, shops, and offices.[113]

Most recent scholarship on women in the war emphasizes the temporary nature of their wartime gains, which were negated by a later
resurgence of the domestic ideal and an antifeminist backlash. This
approach, however, tends to obscure the deeper meaning of the war
for many women. The war also revealed new possibilities and raised
women's consciousness of their oppression. Many working-class women
were politicized during the war through union membership, through
their anger at demobilization and their often fractious interaction with
middle-class factory officials.[114] A number of contemporary observers
also noted that women's personalities were often transformed by the war,
and that they gained in self-confidence and independence. For example,
the *New Statesman* reported on the new women workers in 1917:

> They appear more alert, more critical of the conditions under which
> they work, more ready to make a stand against injustice than their
> pre-war selves or their prototypes. They have a keener appetite for
> experience and pleasure and a tendency quite new to their class to
> protest against wrongs even before they become "intolerable."[115]

These lessons were not forgotten after the war, even among those women
who lost their factory jobs and returned to domestic service. Former war
workers interviewed by Deborah Thom reported that they now felt a
greater capacity to resist exploitation than before the war. As one woman
explained, she had learned from the war that 'I could just move on if
I didn't like the place.' Millicent Fawcett believed that the war found
women 'serfs and left them free.'[116]

Attitudes like self-confidence and independence are difficult to assess,
and certainly cannot be measured like wage levels and rates of employment. Still, they should not be lightly dismissed. Factory magazines
published by women munitions workers and commemorative histories
written by women in military auxiliaries expressed tremendous pride in
the work of women and a sense of themselves as a heroic vanguard. Some
historians might stress the transience of wartime gains, but the women
themselves felt they had done important, pioneering work and helped
open the doors to their emancipation.

Chapter 4: Nation, Race, and Empire

Ideas and behaviors with regard to nationalism and race greatly influenced the course of the war, and were themselves transformed by it. An international conflict that pitted nation against nation and involved far-flung empires necessarily heightened its participants' awareness of their own national and racial identities – which were inevitably formed in opposition to a nationally or racially 'inferior' enemy. In Britain, which had experienced considerable social conflict during the decade preceding the war, the concept of 'nation' proved a particularly effective rallying cry and unifying force – overriding, for example, the more conflict-based class and gender identities of trade unionists and Suffragettes. In the words of one recruiting agent, 'there were no rich and no poor now, no Protestants and Catholics, no Conservatives and Liberals; we were all Britishers!'[1] Nationalism attempted to focus conflict outward – against a German foe invariably constructed as a degenerate, barbaric 'throwback': the 'Hun' of popular propaganda. As successful as such ideas were in garnering support for the war effort, they created problems of their own since 'the nation,' as defined, clearly could not accommodate the diverse citizenry of Britain itself, let alone its vast, diverse Empire. An 'Anglo-Saxon' nationalism might embrace Canadians and Australians, but what of Jews or the Irish? Indians and Africans could be British citizens, but could they ever be 'British'? Did they even want to be? The British Empire itself proved an especially rich and problematic site in which to play out ideas of 'nation' and 'race.' Ironically, at the very moment when Irish nationalism threatened to shatter the bonds of imperial union, the war saw subject peoples throughout the Empire rush forth to defend the very instrument of their subjugation. The war represented a highpoint in imperial expansion and imperial cooperation, but it was also clearly a turning point. For while the common struggle may have strengthened imperial bonds among some peoples of the dominions and colonies, it also caused them to develop a heightened sense of their own self-worth and to claim with greater vigor new rights and privileges inconsistent with British supremacy.

Until recently most histories of the First World War focused almost exclusively on the war in Europe. Since the 1980s important new scholarship has highlighted military campaigns in the Middle East and Africa as well as the crucial contribution of imperial resources to the British war machine. Little of this work, however, has informed histories of the home front or of domestic war culture, giving the impression that the Empire was disconnected from the metropole and had little impact on either British society or the popular imagination.

While historians have been slow to recognize that the Great War was in fact a worldwide/imperial conflict, contemporaries had no doubts about it. Indeed, early Allied victories over German forces in Africa and the Far East were widely reported on, as optimistic counterparts to the stalemate on the Western Front. Official pronouncements about the war spoke of 'the Empire' as frequently as they did of 'England' or 'Britain,' and a great deal of wartime propaganda and popular culture also featured imperial themes. Most significantly for the home front, imperial troops enabled Britain to delay the conscription of its own population until 1916.

* * *

In the great national struggle with Germany, British propagandists sought to depict their foe as the antithesis of enlightenment and civilization. Germany and its people were held to embody the worst possible characteristics of a nation: militarism, intolerance, despotism, and slavish obedience to authority, while Britain and the British represented the diametric opposite: peacefulness, broad-mindedness, democracy, and individualism. According to the Reverend Studdert-Kennedy, a popular army chaplain: 'The individual German is the most easily governable, easily biddable, do-as-I'm toldable, get and get underable person in the world. The individual Briton is the most independent who-the-devil-are-ye-talking-toish, I won't-be-made-a-doormat-of-for-nobodyish person in the world.'[2] In this analysis the British saw themselves as the last bulwark of civilization against barbarism. They were the modern Roman Empire which had spread peace, learning, and good government throughout the world, whereas the Germans were the 'Huns': untutored savages intent on destroying the Pax Britannica and plunging Europe into another Dark Age. Although this view required a tortuous rereading of history and the denial of much of Germany's scientific, literary, and artistic accomplishments, there was no shortage of persons espousing it, from erudite scholars to hack novelists. Early in the war, the Oxford don A. H. Sayce wrote to *The Times*, explaining that Germans had made no significant contributions to European culture or science. He maintained that most so-called German thinkers had borrowed or stolen their ideas from other countries and that the only original characteristic of German culture was militarism. According to Sayce, 'They are still what they were fifteen centuries ago, the barbarians who raided our ancestors and destroyed the civilization of the Roman Empire.'[3]

This view of Germans permeated British culture, finding expression in the popular press, novels, cinema, and even juvenile literature. For example, in a wartime story serialized in the *Girl Guides Gazette*, Teutonic character defects are manifest in the German girl Estelle, who is found to be working against England. The young English heroine recognizes the foreigner's shortcomings from the beginning: 'Estelle does not strike me as up to the mark. She was in some fuss with Dot last term, and she didn't own up, but let Dot take all the punishment; that wasn't conduct "befitting an officer and a gentleman," was it? Well, she happens to be neither – not even a guide yet, and, after all, what can you expect from a German?'[4] In Herbert Strong's adventure story for boys, *With Haig on the Somme* (1917), the German agent gives himself away with his repulsive, hoggish table manners – a confirmation of his bestial nature. Another patriotic novel of the war, Charles Agnew MacLean's *Here's to the Day!* (1915), chronicled the obsessive, violent character of the German militarist, Count von Hollman. As one character describes him, 'the only trouble with him was that you had to kill him to cure him of what was the matter with him.'[5] This view of German barbarism was cemented early in the war through a barrage of atrocity stories circulated in the British press, involving almost unspeakable acts of sadism supposedly committed by German soldiers against Belgian civilians and prisoners-of-war. 'A Hun is a Hun' the adage went, and there was little expectation of reformation, since national defects were thought by many to be congenital rather than the product of social organization or historical development.

For contemporaries, the Great War represented not merely a national, but a 'racial' struggle. After all, since the nineteenth century, the concepts of 'nation' and 'race' had bled into each other. Victorian anthropologists and ethnographers had formulated racial hierarchies which placed Europeans on a higher plane of evolutionary development than Asians or Africans, but within Europe itself there was further jockeying for position at the top of the racial scale. The English, Germans, Irish,

French, Russians, and so forth, were all understood to be separate races unto themselves, who possessed innate mental qualities – temperament, character, and genius – that were carried in the blood and revealed in the lineaments of the face.[6] National characteristics (like German militarism or British love of fair play) were therefore presumed to be as racially fixed as skin color – the inevitable products of evolutionary development.[7] In one explicitly racist formulation, the Germans were referred to as the 'Zulus of Europe.' The British commander Lord Kitchener compared German behavior in Belgium to that of 'dervishes in Sudan.' J. H. Morgan argued that they demonstrated atavistic characteristics which suggested that they were not truly European, 'but a throw-back to some Tartar stock.'[8]

Britain's military and imperial competition with Germany was bound up with post-Darwinian anxieties of racial degeneration and 'the survival of the fittest.' Ever since the late nineteenth century, many Britons had been preoccupied with fears of national and racial decline, seeing their country's flagging industrial sector, falling birthrate, urban poverty, and lackluster performance in the Boer War as unmistakable manifestations of racial decay.[9] In popular discourse the British referred to the Germans as Huns, a negative designation to be sure, but one that also expressed fears that their rivals were a more vital, warrior race, capable of overwhelming the British Empire. In the years just before the war, for example, H. M. Hyndman advocated school drilling because he believed that the German working class was in better physical shape than the British. 'It is sad to witness,' he wrote, 'the decay of any great nation; it is saddest to witness the deterioration of our own.'[10]

Who would inherit the earth? Nothing less seemed at stake in the war than the future development of humanity. Leonard Darwin, president of the Eugenic Society and son of the great Victorian evolutionist, made clear that German victory would result in a worldwide decrease of such 'inborn characteristics' of the British race as the 'idea of liberty.' Little would now stand in the way of the Germanization of the species. Speaking to a wartime audience, Darwin asked: 'Do we wish to see a world-wide increase in the qualities which have made Germany such a terribly dangerous foe, namely her love of power over other nations, her preoccupation in warlike matters in times of peace, and her determination to win at all costs, moral or material?'[11] Eugenics, the pseudo-science of heredity and selective breeding, had gained tremendous influence among British intellectuals in the generation before the war.[12] As such it lent a spurious scientific authority to racial and class hierarchies and reinforced Social Darwinist notions of an inevitable struggle between the races.

Given this extreme rhetoric of nationalism, it is not surprising that British society became saturated with Germanophobia. All things German were now tainted and suspect. German language classes were canceled, and German music banned from concert halls, considerably limiting an orchestra's repertoire. A paranoid atmosphere developed whereby the Kaiser's agents were thought to be everywhere, and anyone with a foreign accent came under suspicion. 'Spy fever' became rife and eventually developed into a theory of a 'Hidden Hand' of German influence which controlled Britain and hindered the war effort. A popular novel by Mrs Belloc Lowndes, *Good Old Anna* (1915), centers on naturalized Germans living in an English cathedral town. Most are loyal, but in their midst is a secret agent of Germany who manages to snare a simple servant, 'good old Anna,' into his evil schemes. The novel warns of the dangers of enemy aliens, and helped create a climate conducive to internment.[13] German ancestry (however distant) and 'German-sounding' names were enough to arouse suspicion. Lord Battenberg diplomatically became Lord Mountbatten and even the royal family thought it best to alter their dynastic name from Saxe-Coburg-Gotha to Windsor.[14]

The most extreme domestic expression of nationalist feelings was a series of anti-German riots directed against German shops and businesses across Great Britain. The German community in Britain was one of the country's largest ethnic minorities, numbering some 60 000 at the outbreak of the war. Many were engaged in retail trade, with German butchers and bakers especially common. German-owned shops were obvious targets for xenophobic mobs, who looted and destroyed them in August and October 1914, May 1915, June 1916, and July 1917. The worst rioting took place in 1915, following the sinking of the passenger ship *Lusitania* by a German submarine. Almost every part of the country was affected, and authorities had considerable difficulty restoring order.[15] The government never seriously considered German residents a disloyal element, but decided to imprison many of them for their own 'protection.' Over the course of the war, some 30 000 resident alien German men were placed in prison camps on the Isle of Man. Alien internment was a tremendous waste of energy and resources, as many aliens had been employed in munitions or other war work. Canada and Australia followed Britain's lead, interning large numbers of German immigrants in their own nations.[16]

The growth of intolerance and decline of liberalism in Britain can no doubt be accounted for by the perceived decline in domestic security engendered by the war. All Britons, however, were not of one mind in these matters. Liberal newspapers like the *Westminster Gazette* and the *Manchester Guardian* decried attacks on aliens, Conservative Unionist papers like the *Evening News* and *Daily Mail* were more sympathetic to the rioters, and populist, jingoist papers like *John Bull* positively incited violence. Indeed, on 15 May 1915, *John Bull*'s publisher, Horatio Bottomley, called for the extermination of all Germans in Britain: 'I call for a vendetta – a vendetta against every German in Britain – whether "naturalized" or not . . . You cannot naturalize an unnatural abortion, a hellish freak. But you *can* exterminate him.'[17]

In rallying to cries of 'nation' and 'race', the line between anti-German sentiment and hatred of all foreigners was easily erased. Mobs that began by destroying German shops often ended up looting businesses owned by Italians and Russians (British allies), or attacking blacks and Chinese (British citizens), many of whom lived in port cities working as seamen and dockers. Anti-Semitism, especially, flourished amid wartime xenophobia, and was directed most strongly against the tens of thousands of Russian Jews who lived in London as resident aliens.[18] Lacking citizenship, they were not eligible for the draft, and most were reluctant to volunteer for a war in which Britain was allied with Tsarist Russia, their old oppressor. Alien Jews became the target of increasingly scathing press comment and public hostility once they were the only group of young, able-bodied men left in British cities.[19] The *East London Observer*, particularly known for its anti-Semitic rhetoric, editorialized in 1915 that 'Jew Boys . . . who hang about street corners and public houses, the cheap foreign restaurants and similar places, ought to be made to do something for the country they honour with their presence.'[20] Unfortunately, such language was not limited to the gutter press, but was commonly employed by MPs and other public officials, many of whom accused Jews of 'profiteering' and 'job snatching.' The common use of the term 'German Jew' further encouraged popular confusion between enemy aliens and other foreigners.[21] In May 1917, the British government introduced a bill forcing resident aliens to enlist in the armed services or be expelled from the country. The *East London Observer* called repeatedly for Jews who continued to resist service to be placed in concentration camps. In September 1917, in the worst civil violence since the 1915 *Lusitania* riots, between 2000 and 3000 Jews and gentiles fought a pitched battle in the streets of Bethnal Green, East London.[22]

Extreme nationalism and wartime paranoia created an unfriendly climate for all foreigners, including friendly aliens. For example, people even turned against the Belgian refugees who had been the objects of so much compassion at the beginning of the war. It was absurdly alleged that tens of thousands of Belgian and French refugees were working as prostitutes in London. In 1916, the Metropolitan Police investigated and harassed cafes set up by Belgians in central London, believing them to be sites of 'immorality' and 'meeting places for alien enemies and spies.' No enemy aliens were found, but the authorities still put the premises under strict control and surveillance.[23]

British citizens of foreign descent or colonial origin, such as the Anglo-Jewish community, were especially troubled by questions of identity and acceptance. Gladys Stern's novel, *Children of No Man's Land* (1919), dramatized the plight of the Jewish community, with its conflicting loyalties and a sense of not belonging anywhere. Some British Jews favored the creation of a special Jewish battalion as a means of visibly demonstrating their loyalty to the nation, whereas others condemned the idea of a separate fighting force as a 'ghetto unit' that would further isolate them from their fellow Britons.[24] British Jews also sought to condemn anti-Semitic attacks against their Russian co-religionists in East London, while still appearing loyal to Britain's cause. That their loyalty should ever have been in doubt testifies to the growing inflexibility of nationalist discourse both before and during the war. If membership in the British 'nation' was defined narrowly to include only those of 'Anglo-Saxon' descent as some kind of distinct 'biological' race, then many groups could never hope to belong, regardless of their political allegiance, degree of cultural assimilation, or even military service. One cruel irony of the war, as David Cesarani states, was that many people 'died for an England and an idea of Englishness that remained stubbornly impermeable to the particular needs and aspirations of the varied peoples which comprised the country's true population.'[25]

* * *

Issues of race and national identity are magnified many times over when we consider the British Empire as a whole. In 1914 the British Empire covered nearly a quarter of the Earth's surface and embraced hundreds of millions of people, embodying an immense racial, religious, ethnic, and linguistic diversity. Britain's ability to marshal, however imperfectly, the vast human and material resources of its Empire gave the nation tremendous advantages. Yet efforts to extract conscripts and raw materials from the dominions and colonies exacerbated tensions within the Empire and further alienated already disaffected elements in the population. Unequal, even racist, treatment of imperial soldiers who fought and died for a British victory increased colonized people's resentment of the Empire. Likewise, Britain's authoritarian rule over its colonies proved difficult to reconcile with the claim that it was defending democracy and the rights of small nations like Belgium. The Empire called upon subject peoples to defend the institutions of their subjugation.

That so many of them were willing to do so highlights the complexities of imperial relationships.

Fighting in overseas colonies and by colonial soldiers is largely what made the Great War a 'world war.' The first 'British' shot of the war was actually fired by West African soldiers invading German Togoland, and fighting between British and German soldiers in East Africa continued after the Armistice. The public's unbounded confidence in War Minister Lord Kitchener derived from his heroic past in imperial campaigns. The Army's essentially imperial character was even reflected in a great deal of Indian military slang. For instance, the soldiers' term for Britain, 'Blighty,' came from the Urdu word for home, and khaki from the Hindi word for dust.[26]

The resources of Empire especially helped Britain redress the imbalance of a struggle with such a larger and more populous nation as Germany. The United Kingdom, with a prewar population of some 45 million, was able to mobilize around 6 million soldiers over the course of the war. Germany, with a population of almost 68 million and a tradition of universal military service, fielded a total of 13 million troops. Dominion and colonial soldiers were therefore vital to the British military. Nearly one million Indian soldiers served overseas. So many Indian recruits were raised in the Punjab alone that it became another home front for the British war effort. The massive Indian forces were joined by almost 500 000 Canadians, 300 000 Australians, 100 000 New Zealanders, and 80 000 white South Africans. Of the 101 British and imperial divisions stationed on various fronts, 71 were from Britain, 30 from the dominions and India.[27] In addition, hundreds of thousands of Indians, Africans, Chinese, and West Indians served in military labor units outside their nations.[28] The arrival of many of these colonized peoples in Britain greatly expanded the nation's racial diversity.[29] The war service and contributions made by colonized peoples gave them a new sense of entitlement to the rights of British citizenship, despite the fact that throughout the war, the British sought to maintain colonial racial practices and power relations.

The war put great pressure on the Empire and its peoples, but it also created tremendous opportunities. As H. G. Wells's fictional hero Mr Britling said when war broke out, 'Now everything becomes fluid. We can redraw the map of the world.'[30] A number of the most die-hard imperialists drawn into the wartime government hoped to do just that. Lord Curzon joined the Cabinet in 1915, Lord Milner in 1916, and Jan Smuts in 1917.[31] With men like this in charge and with the German and Ottoman (Turkish) Empires available to the victors, there would be no holding back.[32] Dominion and imperial troops quickly set to work. In 1914, New Zealand forces captured German Samoa, Australians seized

German New Guinea and Nauru, South Africans captured German South West Africa, and colonial soldiers invaded German Togoland and Cameroons in West Africa. Large-scale fighting lasted several years in German East Africa as well as in the Ottoman Empire, where it was largely the work of Indian and dominion soldiers.[33]

The British Empire grew over the course of the war. In 1914 Egypt was made a British protectorate. In 1916 the British conquered the sultanate of Darfur in Sudan and 'liberated' Qatar from Turkish rule, only to place it under British 'protection.' At the war's end, Britain and the dominions were given control over many of Germany's African and Pacific colonies, in addition to large parts of the Ottoman Empire such as Palestine and Iraq.[34]

A great deal of British propaganda emphasized the imperial aspects of the war, downplaying the grab for land and instead presenting an idealized, multiracial brotherhood working together for peace and democracy. The poet Julian Grenfell wrote: 'don't you think it has been a wonderful, and almost incredible, rally to the Empire; with Redmond and the Hindus and Will Crooks and the Boers and the South Fiji Islanders all aching to come and throw stones at the Germans.'[35] First and foremost, the war was presented as a struggle of 'righteous, moral Empire pitted against upstart, undeserved Empire.'[36] Early in the war, London buses were covered in posters containing extracts from Pericles' 'Funeral Oration' from the *Peloponnesian War*.[37] To a nation schooled in the classics, the message was clear: Britain stood for the Athenian Empire and its rich cultural legacy of learning, art, and democracy, while Germany was the despotic, militarist Sparta. Relieving the Germans of their colonies was a simple act of charity. As a writer for *The Christian World* maintained, unlike the benevolent British, 'the German attitude of overlord is in fact destructive of the native races. Ought such a nation to be permitted to have dominion over subject people?'[38]

Germany, however, delighted in pointing out that the defender of Belgium was the oppressor of Ireland and India. Indeed, the whole history of British imperial expansion could be seen as the conquest of the weak by the strong. While Edwardian Britain was a far more open and democratic society than Wilhelmine Germany, Britain's dependent colonies seldom benefitted from its democratic traditions. German propaganda in neutral countries focused on the autocratic nature of the British Empire, as well as the charge of betraying the white race through the use of Indian soldiers against white Europeans. British reliance on its colonial peoples was constantly ridiculed by the Germans. For example, an anti-British postcard depicted 'England's only available Army' as a rag-tag assortment of cartoonish, spear-carrying Africans.[39]

British apologists for imperialism responded that their Empire was unlike any other, but rather 'a colossal experiment in international government with a minimum of compulsions and a maximum of freedom.'[40] In a pamphlet explaining the war to young people, J. Holland Rose argued that 'the motto of the British Empire is "Live and let live." It is not a close preserve kept for ourselves; it is a free and hospitable community where all peoples share alike on equal terms.'[41] The most extreme propaganda saw the Empire as a manifestation of divine providence. In *God's Dealings with the British Empire* (1916), John Hancock maintained 'We are God's chosen people, His inheritance, the salt of the earth, His loved ones, His glory, the people He delights in, His sons and His daughters.'[42]

Nationalist propaganda characterized the war as a joint imperial venture, uniting mother country, white dominions, India, and the dependent territories in a crusade for freedom.[43] In a religious pamphlet, *Brothers All: The War and the Race Question*, the imperial war effort symbolized Christian unity: 'we find brown men and yellow men and black men joined with ourselves in one colossal struggle, pouring out their treasure, pouring out their blood, for the common cause . . . ' The author Edwyn Bevan argued that while the old Empire was hierarchical, albeit benevolently paternalistic, the war would bring about a more egalitarian 'new relation built on the consciousness of great dangers faced and great things done together, feelings of mutual friendship and respect and trust.'[44] Newspapers, propaganda films, and adventure stories frequently celebrated the contributions of colonized peoples, though often in a patronizing manner typical of the time. For example, in March 1917, the *Newcastle Daily Journal* rhapsodized over: 'splendid-looking Zulus . . . sturdy Basuto . . . and deep-chested Pondos – willing volunteers every one of them, who have exchanged their sunny luxuriance for the bitter cheerlessness of this particularly severe winter in order to do their bit towards winning the war.'[45] Visual depictions of the imperial 'family of nations' appeared frequently on war posters and commercial advertisements, though the images typically privileged the British people by placing them front and center, flanked by people from the white dominions, with Indians and Africans in the background.[46]

The war conveniently provided innumerable opportunities for promoting the importance of Empire at the very time when Irish and Indian nationalists seemed poised to dissolve imperial bonds. With the great novelist of Empire John Buchan as director of the new Information Ministry, imperial issues were given high priority. The creation of the British Empire Union in 1915 'to inculcate a greater interest in and knowledge of the Empire' also helped shore up the nation's imperial consciousness by promoting the teaching of imperial history in schools and encouraging the wider celebration of Empire Day. Emphasis on imperial themes enabled the media to paint a more optimistic picture of the war, highlighting, for example, naval superiority, a series of quick and easy victories in Africa, and diverting images of 'colorful' peoples and 'exotic' locales. In his pioneering 1927 study of British propaganda, Harold Lasswell revealed that 'in order to illustrate the unity of the Empire, a number of profusely illustrated volumes were put out, showing the history of British beneficence and the degree of Empire co-operation at the front.' *India and the War* (1915) glorified the British Raj and included numerous color pictures of Indian regiments in native uniforms. Literary anthologies such as *The Anzac Book, Canada in Khaki,* and *Indian Ink* were also published to promote imperial unity and highlight the contributions of colonial troops.[47]

Popular adventure novelists frequently linked the war to imperial themes. For example, in Talbot Mundy's *King of the Khyber Rifles* (1916), the hero, Athelstan King, defuses a holy war German agents are attempting to foment in India against British rule. He is aided in his endeavors by a mysterious Indian woman, Yasmini. The novel is an orientalist fantasy in which Indian unrest is seen as the result of outside agitation, though most Indians are depicted as loyal to the Empire. The greatest romanticizer of Empire, Rudyard Kipling, wrote *The Eyes of Asia* (1917), an epistolary novel, purportedly representing the correspondence of Indian soldiers in Europe with relatives and friends at home. Throughout the book, the soldiers express their loyalty to the King and Empire, their awe of European society, and their gratitude for the kindness they have experienced from the Army and civilians.

Government-sponsored propaganda films also made effective use of imperial themes. *The Empire's Shield,* for instance, celebrated the British navy, while *Sons of the Empire* touted imperial brotherhood through the rich pageantry of colonial troops on parade.[48] Dominion loyalty was also emphasized in films like *Canadians on the Western Front* (1918) or *New Zealand Troops in France* (1917). Films about the colonized peoples of Asia and Africa likewise stressed their devotion to the mother country, but also underscored the difference between these people and the British. A scene from *A Chinese Labor Contingent* (1917) depicts a group of incredulous Asian workers being shown how to open a can of food. In the film *A South African Native Labor Contingent* (1917), men are shown working under white supervision. On their lunch break, they demonstrate native dances. A white officer throws a coin in the air and laughs as the men scramble for it.[49]

A great deal of wartime propaganda gave prominence to fighting in the Middle East. In many ways the region was the ideal 'theater of war', providing as it did exotic locations, 'picturesque' colonial troops, and dramatic emphasis on the importance of the Indian Empire.[50] Unlike the horrors of trench warfare on the Western Front, the war in the Middle East could be depicted as a war of movement, a 'romantic' war with affinities to the Crusades. In a series of swift attacks in 1916–17, General Allenby and his Arab allies captured Jerusalem and overran Palestine and Syria. Out of these campaigns, the British officer T. E. Lawrence emerged as the heroic 'Lawrence of Arabia' – a nearly mythic embodiment of the imperial spirit. Almost wholly a media creation, Lawrence was catapulted to stardom by a series of laudatory newspaper reports penned by the American journalist Lowell Thomas. Lawrence's Arabian 'adventure' satisfied the public's desire for a heroic British identity in a conflict where the mass death of the trenches seemed to render individual heroism impossible. The image of Lawrence as the deliverer of the Arab peoples from their Turkish bondage further idealized the British imperial mission, creating a fantasy of national liberation at the very time when the British were expanding their hold over the region.[51]

* * *

The propaganda of Empire notwithstanding, the First World War posed serious challenges to British imperial unity. Would Britain's various dominions and dependencies support its war effort, or would they take advantage of the turmoil for their own ends? Would colonial cooperation come at too high a price? Ultimately, the bonds of Empire held, but the strains of so long and bloody a struggle seriously altered imperial relationships and identities.

Initially, the most spontaneous and enthusiastic support for Britain came from the so-called 'white dominions': Canada, Australia, New Zealand, and South Africa.[52] These nations, though autonomous and self-governing, were linked to the mother country through shared traditions of law, government, culture, and history. Many dominion citizens traced their descent from British settlers, or had been born in Britain themselves. Indeed, almost 50 percent of military volunteers from Canada, Australia, New Zealand and South Africa had been born in Britain. Although dominion governments frequently pursued domestic political agendas markedly at odds with British politics (Australia had a Labor government and New Zealand had given women the vote), they generally accepted British management of their foreign policies. Yet dominion entry into the war was not merely a question of political allegiance, but also of economic common sense given the close financial and trade links within the Empire and the virtually total dependence of the dominion economies on British credit.[53]

Dominion contributions to the war in terms of men and material were impressive. Canada mobilized more than half a million men, Australia over 300 000. New Zealand with a population of only one million, fielded more than 100 000 soldiers – almost half its eligible male population. The New Zealand contingent included over 2000 Maori soldiers out of a male Maori population that numbered no more than 30 000. Altogether, the dominions added another million men to Britain's overseas fighting forces. Dominion soldiers served in all theaters of war. Anzac (Australia and New Zealand Army Corps) forces played a vital role in the Middle East, most famously at Gallipoli, while South African soldiers proved essential in capturing Germany's African colonies. Dominion troops were widely praised as effective combat forces. In addition to their roles as soldiers and sailors, dominion citizens also served as laborers, merchant seamen, medics, and nurses. Most significant in this regard were the 70 000 black South Africans who served in labor battalions in Africa and Europe. By the war's end they constituted 25 percent of the military workforce on the Western Front. Imports from the Empire more than doubled during the war years, and many of these came from the dominions. Australia shipped huge supplies of meat to Britain during the war. Canada produced vast quantities of wheat for the Allied war effort, as well as significant amounts of shells and explosives. During the last two years of the war, one third of the British Army's munitions were made in Canada.[54]

Not all dominion citizens, however, identified with the Empire, and attempts to enlist soldiers especially alienated such disaffected populations as Afrikaners, French-Canadians, and Irish-Australians. Most threatening to imperial unity was the situation in South Africa, where a bitter resistance to British rule had been waged by Afrikaners (white South Africans of Dutch descent) only 12 years earlier in the Boer War. Many Afrikaners continued to resent British rule and sympathized with Germany, although South African Prime Minister Louis Botha and Defense Minister Jan Smuts, both former Boer commanders, worked assiduously for British victory. Late in 1914, 12 000 Afrikaner rebels led by a number of former Boer War generals attempted to overthrow the Botha government on account of their opposition to the war and to South Africa's invasion of German South-West Africa. The rebellion proved unsuccessful, but certainly soured the spirit of imperial cooperation.[55] French-Canadians likewise expressed little enthusiasm for the war, and volunteered at extremely low rates. In 1917, only 30 000 of some 400 000 Canadians serving overseas were French-Canadian, although they comprised a third of Canada's population. French-Canadians fiercely opposed Canada's 1917 Conscription Act. Anti-draft riots broke out in Quebec at Easter 1918, during which five protesters were killed and the provincial legislature debated secession.[56] Australians twice defeated proposed compulsory military service in public referenda owing in large part to the opposition of Irish-Australians who made up nearly a quarter of the country's population.[57]

Even among dominion citizens most loyal to Britain, resentment grew over what they perceived as British arrogance and indifference. Dominion society tended to be more egalitarian and less class-bound than Britain, and soldiers, especially, bristled at the haughty and condescending manner of the British officer class. Other dominion personnel also resented British airs of superiority, as in the case of a Canadian nurse who told an officious British sister that she had not voluntarily traveled 3000 miles 'to be spoken to like that by anybody.' The British, for their part, tended to criticize dominion soldiers as rowdy and undisciplined. Stories abounded concerning their unwillingness or inability to show proper deference and respect. One oft-quoted anecdote concerned an Australian private who, passing an overweight British general bathing on the beach, not only failed to salute, but remarked 'My bloody oath mate, you 'ave been among the biscuits!'[58]

More serious still was the belief that incompetent British commanders were sacrificing dominion troops needlessly. Among Australian soldiers, who experienced one of the war's highest casualty rates (82 percent), this feeling mounted after the disastrous Gallipoli campaign.[59] Dominion leaders also came to the conclusion that London was all too willing to take risks at their expense and to fail to engage in adequate consultations. They felt that their contributions to the war entitled them to a greater role in imperial policy making. British Prime Minister Lloyd George agreed and in 1917 convened the Imperial War Cabinet, a meeting of dominion prime ministers that aimed at closer cooperation. At the same time, Jan Smuts of South Africa joined the Prime Minister's inner War Cabinet.[60] Of course, Lloyd George's decision to involve the dominions more in leadership underscored the British plight after the especially great losses in the Somme campaign of 1916. As he explained to the colonial secretary: 'We want more from them [the dominions]. We can hardly ask them to make another great recruiting effort unless it is accompanied by an invitation to come over to discuss the situation with us.'[61] Britain's problems, it seems, were the dominions' opportunity.

The experiences of war for the dominions ultimately stimulated local nationalisms more than a common imperialism.[62] Dominion governments increasingly demanded greater autonomy, and in 1918, Canada, Australia, New Zealand, and South Africa were allowed to represent

themselves at the treaty negotiations at Versailles with separate delegations. The other allies resented the packing of the peace conference
by the British Empire, but these delegations hardly spoke with one
voice. Serious disagreements emerged among British and dominion
delegates over the division of the spoils of war, especially with regard
to the annexation of former German colonies.[63] Dominion histories
of the war, as well as postwar commemorations, downplayed the imperial theme and instead emphasized national pride and the unique
contributions (and suffering) of their own people. For Canadians, the
battle at Vimy Ridge was as essential for constructing a national consciousness as Gallipoli had been for Australians and New Zealanders.
Annual Anzac Day celebrations on 25 April became national holidays
in Australia and New Zealand, where even the smallest towns erected
war memorials.

* * *

Unlike the dominions, Britain's dependencies (India, the African colonies,
the West Indies) had little choice but to support the war. The dependencies were governed from London via a British-controlled civil service and
military, and their societies were dominated by a small, white elite of merchants, landowners, and missionaries. Colonized peoples had little control over their political destiny, though their antipathy to British rule was
well known to the white elite and was increasingly expressed through
nationalist organizations like the Indian National Congress. The British
government was aware of potential colonial opposition to the war, but
could not refrain from squeezing the colonies for all they were worth
in terms of money, material, and manpower. The colonial government
of India raised £100 million for the war effort (more than a full year's
revenue) and was ultimately to send more than one million Indian soldiers to fight overseas. The cost of supporting these troops (£20–30 million annually) would normally have been borne by Britain, but was now
paid for by the Indian taxpayers, who of course were unrepresented in
government and were not consulted about their generous 'gift.' Colonial
raw materials, such as metals, rubber, jute, and petroleum, were sucked
up by the war effort at phenomenal rates. They were often obtained by
colonial administrators at fixed prices well below market rates.[64] In most
African colonies, the war increased taxation and decreased expenditure
on public works and social welfare, which had never been high to begin
with.[65] Hundreds of thousands of Africans served as carriers and general
laborers for the imperial military forces that fought in German colonies
across the continent. Wartime propagandists like Harry Johnston argued

that Africans willingly aided the British war effort because British rule had 'won their sympathy and even their gratitude,' though in truth the goodwill of colonized peoples took Britain by surprise.[66]

At the outset of war, the British were very unsure of Indian and African loyalty. In March 1915 Britain devised a repressive Defense of India Act that empowered special courts to arrest and detain without trial any people suspected of undermining the war effort. With the removal of the regular Indian Army, Britain sent Territorial Army units to India to act as an imperial police force for the duration of the war. At one point British forces were reduced to 15 000, but there was little unrest. A notable exception was among Indian soldiers stationed in Singapore, who mutinied in 1915. For a time the whole colony was threatened, and when order was restored, 47 mutineers were sentenced to death. The Theosophist and Indian nationalist Annie Besant was later interned by the Viceroy of India in 1917, when she called for a Home Rule campaign advocating violence.[67] Likewise in Africa, although whites feared that blacks would rise up if the able-bodied men went off to war, this fear mostly did not materialize. In fact, the elite and middle-class spokespersons of the colonized peoples hurried forth to offer their support.

In India nationalist leaders like Dadobhai Naoroji and Surendranath Banerjea made loyal speeches on the Empire's behalf. Mohandas Gandhi organized ambulance units for the Army and helped the authorities recruit Indian soldiers. Other prominent Indians like Mancherjee Bhownaggree, a former MP, and Bhupendranath Basu, a past member of India's Legislative Council, wrote pro-war tracts. Basu's *Why India Is Heart and Soul with Great Britain* (1914) argued that 'India is not a conquered country, nor are her people a subject population.' Instead, Britain had rescued India from anarchy and civil war in the eighteenth century and brought the blessings of civilization – law and order, education, and modern technology. The war enabled Indians to demonstrate their loyalty to the Empire, and, Basu hoped, secure greater self-rule.[68] The leadership of the Indian National Congress and the Muslim League also hoped that Indian cooperation would be rewarded with more autonomy, and both organizations invoked the democratic rhetoric of the war to their own ends.[69]

In South Africa the SANNC (South African Native National Congress), a middle-class organization working for the betterment of black South Africans, came out in favor of the war, since they too believed that by proclaiming their allegiance to the British Crown, they would pressure the authorities into granting meaningful political reforms.[70] Like the Indian National Congress, the SANNC was quick to equate the democratic pretensions of British war propaganda with their own plight.[71]

West Indian blacks also sought to participate in the war as they saw this as a real opportunity to demonstrate their equality with whites and challenge the objectionable idea of 'the white man's burden.'[72] Although British and colonial governments were gratified by pledges of loyalty from colonized peoples, they realized that any support accepted would come with expectations of reform. They therefore sought to limit and contain colonial participation.

The most problematic and hotly contested issue regarding colonial people's role in the war was military service. The official policy of the War Office was against black enlistment in the British Army, though many black persons living in Britain tried to enlist. In June 1918, at a time of severe manpower shortages, the War Office offered to lift the color bar, but the Army Council still excluded blacks from British regiments. Imperial recruiting practice was much influenced by Victorian race theory, which posited the existence of 'martial races' and 'cowardly races.' In India, for example, the Army recruited almost exclusively among certain Muslim peoples and Sikhs in the north who were believed 'naturally' warlike. Likewise, in Africa, some peoples like the Hausa were considered martial races, and recruited for local militias, while others like the Mende were only deemed suitable for porterage and other manual labor.[73]

The white colonial elite also opposed blacks joining the Army, fearing that it would give them aspirations above their station and lead to the erosion of racial boundaries. In the West Indies governors were officially instructed by the Colonial Office to discourage black enlistment, and only intervention by the King embarrassed the authorities into allowing the creation of a segregated West Indies Regiment. Nonetheless, Bonar Law, the Secretary of State for Colonies, was determined to keep black soldiers away from the Western Front because he believed their serving in Europe would create difficulties for white supremacy once the war was over.[74] Offers of military service by black South Africans were rejected absolutely by the Union government, which was simply afraid to arm blacks, and also believed that using black soldiers would undermine white prestige. Yet by 1916, large-scale British offensives created an urgent need for manpower, and the decision was made to recruit black laborers, who were organized into the South African Native Labor Contingent (SANLC), a uniformed, but non-combative military unit. By the war's end the SANLC was comprised of more than 70 000 men engaged in digging fortifications, and loading and hauling supplies for British troops in France. Even the performance by blacks of their traditional manual labor created anxiety among white South Africans, at whose insistence blacks were isolated and housed in closed compounds to prevent them from acquiring ideas harmful to white rule and from mixing with white women. Tens of thousands of Chinese 'coolies' also labored on the Western Front, where they too endured brutal treatment and segregation.[75]

There was never any question that Indian soldiers would participate in the war given the enormous size of the Indian Army and the long tradition of military service by 'native races' on the Asian subcontinent. The nature of Indian service, however, was subject to much debate. For example, should Indians continue to serve merely as soldiers of the line, or might not some be promoted to the officer class? Should Indians fight against Europeans? Some members of both the British and colonial Indian governments opposed sending Indian troops to Europe, for fear that experience in fighting white men might undermine the colonial racial hierarchy. Acute manpower shortages in the early stages of the war soon vitiated this objection, and Indian troops were rushed to the Western Front, where, by 1915, some 138 000 were serving.[76] From the start, Indians in France experienced horrible culture shock, not only in leaving their homeland for an alien clime, but in adjusting to the horrors of trench warfare and fighting a war few understood or believed to concern India. In addition, Indian soldiers had to contend with segregation and racist attitudes on the part of their British officers and the Army high command.[77]

Morale suffered, and some Indian soldiers writing home expressed their disenchantment and urged friends and relatives not to enlist.[78] Censors of the Indian mail uncovered much that was distressing. Many letters home simply expressed stunned bewilderment: 'Do not think that this is war. It is not war. It is the ending of the world. This is just such a war as was related in the *Mahabharata* about our forefathers.' Other writers were more forthright in blaming the British and voicing their sense of betrayal: 'We have crossed the seven seas and left our homes and our dear ones and our parents, and for the honour of such an unjust and false-promising King. We have sacrificed our lives . . . No doubt before them we are regarded as inarticulate animals, but who can say that to oppress and dishonour us is good?'[79]

Historians are divided about the combat experience of Indian troops on the Western Front. Some have emphasized that morale problems, a cold climate and sickness undermined the Indian Army's effectiveness. More recent work by George Morton Jack argues that trench warfare was no more disorienting for Indians than for Europeans and that Indian soldiers fought ably and bravely. Jack maintains that Indians were withdrawn from France in 1915 to counter Turkish threats to Egypt, not because of poor performance.[80]

No one doubts the vital role of the Indian Army in the Middle East. Here, they were closer to home and fighting a war that could better be justified as protecting India. Indian troops repulsed a Turkish attack on the Suez Canal in 1915 and they maintained British control over Persian Gulf oil. By the war's end more than a million Indians had fought campaigns in Mesopotamia, Palestine, and Syria.[81] In the end, the victories they won and the hardships they endured heightened Indians' sense of their own soldierly qualities, diminished the stigma of racial inferiority, and increased their sense of entitlement as citizens of the Empire.

West Indian soldiers' attempts to serve the Empire were similarly frustrated by racial prejudice. In the face of official discouragement, 16 000 black soldiers from the Caribbean volunteered for overseas service, more than 10 000 of them from Jamaica. Not allowed to fight on the Western Front for fear that the color line would be eroded and that Germany would mock Britain for needing the help of 'savages' to win the war, West Indians were assigned their traditional role as servants. They carried water and ammunition, under heavy fire, to frontline troops. Like Indian soldiers, the West Indies Regiment was later given combat duty against the Turks, where they performed impressively. They continued, nonetheless, to receive unequal treatment, resulting in one of the most famous mutinies of the war, at a demobilization camp in Taranto, Italy. Here, in December 1918, the black soldiers were denied a pay increase given to whites and were expected to clean the segregated latrines of the white soldiers. The West Indians rioted against their second-class status and were harshly punished. Several soldiers were given prison terms of 8–14 years, and one was executed by firing squad.[82]

No imperial subjects labored under harsher conditions than the black soldiers and carriers pressed into service for the campaigns against Germany's African colonies.[83] Several thousand black soldiers, mostly from Nigeria, fought for Britain in Cameroons and East Africa, though their contribution is little remembered. The British downplayed their victories, gave them few medals, and built them no memorials. To add insult to injury, the Colonial Office decided it would be 'impolitic' to allow black troops to march in victory parades in London.[84] Less celebrated still are the hundreds of thousands of carriers whose efforts had much to do with Allied victory in Africa. The basic work of carriers was porterage, but in military campaigns they also acted as general laborers – cutting roads, unloading ships, and driving lorries. Britain's wartime need for African labor was almost insatiable: over 50 000 carriers were drawn from West Africa, nearly a quarter of a million carriers were recruited in British East Africa, and even the small colony of Nyasaland (Malawi) provided 200 000 men for a job the Africans called *thangata* – work without benefit. Officially, all the men serving were volunteers, but in reality many were either sent by chiefs or forcibly taken in quotas. 'Carrier recruitment' was a contemporary euphemism for forced labor, and carriers often worked under conditions little better than slavery. They were overworked and underfed, their pay often in arrears, and unlike soldiers, had no prospect of a pension or disability allowance. In 1915 in Nyasaland, John Chilembwe, an African Baptist minister, led an unsuccessful uprising against the despotic recruiting methods of the British military. He also sought to protest the huge numbers of Africans killed in the war. Carrier deaths alone in East Africa probably exceeded 100 000, mainly from disease and starvation brought about by official incompetence and neglect. This death rate was scandalous, but no scandal ensued, because as one Colonial Office note baldly stated, 'who cares about native carriers?'[85] Needless to say, such racist attitudes were not confined to the British Empire, but, at the time, were widespread throughout Europe and North America.

One of the war's great hypocrisies was the contrast between the rhetoric of imperial brotherhood on the one hand, and the attempt by the British and dominion governments to maintain colonial racial practices on the other. This was apparent in their resistance to black people fighting against white, their preference for colonized people performing menial, low-status jobs, and their attempts to keep colonial-style segregation in place even in the more egalitarian societies of Western Europe or under combat conditions. The South African government made certain that African labor companies remained segregated from white units and civilians on the Western Front, for fear that black veterans of the war would 'demand the vote' or aspire to be 'the equal of your wives and children.'[86] South African labor companies were housed in closed compounds. The only other wartime laborers so treated were German prisoners-of-war. Similarly, wounded Indian soldiers convalescing in England found their access to nearby towns greatly restricted. Indian hospitals, surrounded by barbed-wire fences, seemed more like prisons. An Indian surgeon at the Kitchener Hospital, J. H. Godbole, was so upset by these restrictions on the 'liberty of the individual' that he attempted to shoot the British officer in charge as a protest.[87]

Anxieties about race-mixing meant that the authorities were especially vigilant about keeping Africans and Asians away from white women. A white South African officer, on learning that French women had served tea to black dock workers at Rouen, told the men concerned: 'When you people get back to South Africa again, don't start thinking you are whites just because this place has spoilt you. You are black and you will stay black.'[88] Similar attitudes meant that there was great resistance to having English women nurse Indian soldiers. English nurses were finally allowed, but only in a supervisory capacity – no touching would take place. Official reports worried that too much casual contact with white women might cause Indian men to conceive wrong ideas about the 'honour' of English women, and that this 'would be most detrimental to the prestige and spirit of European rule in India.' Censors of the military mails also carefully deleted any sexual references by Indian soldiers to white women.[89] Few things threatened the notion of white supremacy as much as the possibility of miscegenation.

* * *

Despite the racist treatment meted out to colonial soldiers and the heavy burdens the war placed on the dependent territories, colonial subjects for the most part remained loyal to Britain. The greatest wartime blow to Empire came much closer to home, in Britain's oldest colonial possession – Ireland. Here, on Easter Monday 1916, a small group of radical nationalists launched a rebellion against British rule that within a few years would result in Irish independence. Although Ireland had been ruled by the English for centuries, politically it had only been part of the United Kingdom since 1801. Yet in many ways it remained an occupied nation, dominated by a Protestant Anglo-Irish elite of landowners and professionals.[90] Many Britons viewed Irish Catholic peasants through the same racist, colonial lens with which they saw Indians or Africans. In spite of their skin color, Irish were hardly thought of as 'white.' Victorian racial theory, still very influential, depicted the Celtic peoples as a primitive, atavistic race.[91] Irish Catholics had been denied many basic civil rights until the nineteenth century, and for their part had demonstrated their opposition to British rule through a long series of rebellions and revolutionary movements. More recently, Irish nationalism had focused on the constitutional Home Rule movement which sought to secure greater autonomy for Ireland within the British Empire, especially through the creation of a separate parliament for domestic affairs. In the years just prior to the war, Home Rule had been approved by the British Parliament and was set to commence in 1914. Protestants in northern Ireland, however, were horrified at the prospect of their nation being politically dominated by Irish Catholics, and they threatened armed opposition to Home Rule. A civil war between Irish Catholic Nationalists and Protestant Unionists seemed all but certain in 1914, until war with Germany intervened.[92]

Irish Nationalist leaders agreed to postponing Home Rule until the war had ended and they pledged their support to the British war effort in hopes of further indebting Britain to them. Historians have argued that despite the war's initial unifying effect, it soon highlighted the 'racial'

divide between Catholics and Protestants. The Irish Protestants of
Ulster, most of whom were descendants of seventeenth-century Scottish
settlers, saw themselves as 'British' and volunteered to defend Britain
and the Empire in large numbers. Many Irish Catholics, however, felt
themselves to be victims of imperialism and were reluctant to fight for
Britain. Only 65 000 Catholics enlisted out of 140 000 Irish volunteers,
although Catholics outnumbered Protestants three to one.[93]

Recent work by Catriona Pennell has suggested that an Irish
Protestant/Catholic divide over the war was not so great as suggested
by the above recruitment figures. Irish enlistment rates mimicked
Britain's urban/rural divide whereby city dwellers joined the army
in large numbers, while farm workers did not. Urban enlistment in
Ireland actually compared favorably to that of England. In Belfast
Catholics joined the forces almost as readily as Protestants. But since
Ireland, especially Catholic Ireland, was mostly rural and agricultural,
recruitment followed the typical British pattern of farm laborers holding back. Nationalist and Unionist leaders attempted to link their
communities' war service to their political aspirations, further compli-
cating the overall picture. Thus, as Pennell demonstrates, Irish entry
into the war was 'a much more cautious, calculated, negotiated, and
gradual process.'[94]

The most radical nationalists, like the Sinn Fein party, certainly
opposed British recruitment in Ireland. One of their arguments (revers-
ing the usual eugenic discourse) was that the British were a soft, effete
race who could not win the war without help from the more potent
Irish.[95] Sinn Fein hoped to take advantage of the war, which saw the with-
drawal of most British troops from Ireland, by launching the 1916 Easter
Rising.[96] Involving only a few hundred armed rebels in Dublin, the revolt
was crushed by the British military and condemned by Irish Nationalist
leaders who feared it might endanger Home Rule. Yet the extraordinarily harsh British repression of the Easter rebellion alienated many Irish
Catholics, who otherwise had little sympathy for the rebels' demand for
an independent Irish republic. The imposition of martial law, the execution without trial of rebel leaders, and the wholesale internment of anyone suspected of republican leanings, led most Irish Catholics to reject
Home Rule and opt instead for Sinn Fein and independence.[97]

British repression of the Irish also proved an embarrassment inter-
nationally, given Britain's claim to be protecting small nations from
German aggression. The Irish found sympathetic audiences in the
United States and the dominions, where so many of their countrymen
had settled. In Australia, 23 percent of the population was of Irish-
Catholic descent, and that nation's Senate petitioned the King in March

1917 to immediately grant Home Rule.[98] Meanwhile, the newly formed Irish Republican Army maintained a guerrilla war against British rule that lasted until 1921. The struggle could have gone on indefinitely, but a war-weary British public had no will to hold on to Ireland if to do so required a prolonged campaign and a massive occupation force. Representatives of Sinn Fein and the British government met in London and negotiated a treaty whereby most of Ireland was granted dominion status as the Irish Free State. Six Protestant-dominated counties in the north remained part of the United Kingdom.

* * *

The loss of Ireland was a harbinger of things to come, but the most sanguine imperialists could still congratulate themselves on the war's outcome. Britain won the war and victory was widely interpreted as the joint achievement of the Empire. The years between the First and the Second World War probably marked the highpoint of imperial propaganda and the cultural mythology of Empire. In 1919, imperial boundaries were swelled by the addition of former German and Turkish possessions. In Africa, Togoland, Cameroons, and Tanganyika could now be colored red, as could the Middle Eastern territories of Palestine, Transjordan, Iraq, and the Persian Gulf States.[99] These new acquisitions were technically 'mandates', meaning that they were entrusted to Britain by the newly constituted League of Nations, to be administered in the interests of their inhabitants with a view to eventual independence. But in point of fact, they were treated as colonies.[100] The British Empire was larger than ever before.

In spite of the Empire's expansion, there remained considerable room for pessimism. After all, Britain had only barely won the war, even with the assistance of its Empire. The contributions of the dominions and colonies strengthened their national pride and self-reliance and gave them greater claims to autonomy. Victory had also depended on the material and financial contributions of Britain's allies. Reliance on American money destroyed Britain's status as a creditor nation; it now owed the United States some £850 million, much of it borrowed from New York banks.[101] Indebtedness weakened Britain's imperial resolve and limited its means to respond effectively around the world. War weariness further created a climate of disengagement whereby not only Ireland, but also Egypt was granted independence in 1922. The war had fanned the flames of Empire, but could the British control the fire?

Britain held on to most of its colonies and even gained a few new ones, but the war weakened the bonds of dependence among imperial subjects.

The particular savagery of the First World War and its unprecedented carnage seriously undermined the notion of European cultural superiority.[102] Official bungling and mismanagement of the war effort further undermined belief in British efficiency and invulnerability on the part of colonized peoples, and the prestige and authority of Empire suffered an irreparable blow. The presumption of European racial superiority was also dented by the specter of colonial soldiers fighting and killing white men. As one Indian soldier remarked on his experience in 1915: 'What are the Germans in the face of Indian troops? They do nothing but run away in front of us.'[103] Colonial soldiers and laborers developed a heightened sense of their contributions to the war, despite official British attempts to limit their engagement. Black South Africans, for instance, were assigned the most menial tasks on the Western Front, but still saw their work as the equivalent of military service. As one laborer put it, 'when we heave a heavy load, we know that we kill a Hun.'[104]

Many Africans and Asians serving in Europe were surprised by the friendly behavior they experienced from French civilians and ordinary British soldiers. This did not fail to leave an imprint. What impressed them the most was that working-class whites displayed little color prejudice and treated them as equals.[105] Exposure to European class hierarchies was an eye-opening experience for colonized peoples. Seeing poor white people contradicted the basis of colonial society, where whites never labored and where 'whiteness' automatically conferred privileged status. Fraternization with white people occurred in ways not possible in the colonies. This helped break down the color bar, psychologically as well as physically, and suggested possibilities for a new political order. An Indian soldier stationed in Britain wrote to relatives that 'the Englishmen at home are also very good people. It is only the ruling class that thinks so much of itself and stands in the way of Indian reform.'[106]

Not surprisingly, imperial subjects who worked and fought for British victory were unlikely to simply resume their old 'subject' status once the war was over. Surely their contributions and sacrifices entitled them to the 'rights of freeborn Britons.' Many were not slow to assert such rights, like the former colonial soldiers who were unable to find work in Britain after the war because of their color. They formed a delegation and petitioned the government in June 1919. 'We ask for British justice', they wrote, 'to be treated as true and loyal sons of Great Britain.'[107] Where sacrifice for Empire was met with a racist response, or where expectations were raised only to be dashed, there was bound to be bitterness.

By the end of the war, there were some 20 000 black people in Britain, many of whom had served in the merchant marine, labor battalions, or the military. With the onset of postwar unemployment, there was growing hostility to black workers, and in the summer of 1919, there were race riots across Britain – in Barry, Cardiff, Glasgow, Liverpool, London, Newport, and South Shields. White mobs attacked blacks at labor recruiting centers and lay siege to their boarding houses. In Liverpool, 120 black workers were dismissed from factories because whites refused to work with them. In Cardiff, some 2000 people attacked shops and houses associated with black workers. The mobs contained many demobilized soldiers, including a number of Australians and white South Africans.[108]

There was little sympathy for the blacks among the authorities or in the press, who felt they should return to their homelands or that they had brought the violence on themselves by associating with white women. According to the *Liverpool Courier*: 'One of the chief reasons of popular anger behind the present disturbances lies in the fact that the average negro is nearer the animal than is the average white man, and that there are women in Liverpool who have no self-respect.'[109] In 1925, the Home Office issued the Colored Alien Seamen's Order, which allowed all 'colored' seamen to be treated as 'aliens' and expelled from the country unless they could establish their birth in a British colony, which few of them had the documents to prove.[110]

In Jamaica, Trinidad, and British Honduras, there was also a wave of postwar riots in which returning soldiers and sailors heavily participated, attacking whites and shouting slogans such as 'this is our country.' For some West Indian soldiers, their wartime experiences sparked an abiding desire for social justice. Clennell Wickham, for example, became editor of the *Barbados Journal* after returning from the war, and his paper supported early campaigns for civil rights in the Caribbean.[111] Many African servicemen were likewise radicalized. According to Edward Roux, the pioneering historian of black resistance in South Africa, 'After 1918, there were thousands of black men in the country who were not willing any longer to endure the anti-Native laws, men who were prepared to stir up their fellow Africans to revolt against the system.'[112]

American President Woodrow Wilson emphasized national self-determination at the Versailles Peace Conference, which clearly did not benefit Britain's colonies, though the idea certainly resonated with many colonized peoples.[113] Indian nationalists probably saw the greatest gains from the war. British rule seemed especially insecure once the Indian Army had left to fight in Europe and the Middle East, and the government hoped to strengthen Indian loyalty through a series of promised reforms. In August 1917, the Secretary of State for India, Edwin Montagu, proposed responsible government for India at the provincial level and in 1918 produced a plan for postwar constitutional reform. When British

Prime Minister Lloyd George met with dominion leaders in 1917, he included for the first time two Indian representatives, the Maharaja of Bikaner and Sir S. P. Sinha. India was also allowed separate representation at the Versailles Peace Conference.[114] The economic burdens of the war had greatly augmented membership in the Indian National Congress as well as compounding its grievances, and the postwar climate was such that any concessions made by the British would only whet India's appetite for more. The Montagu Reforms were tempered by the Rowlatt Act of March 1919 which attempted to make permanent the wartime system of special courts and restrictions on Indian civil liberties. Mounting demonstrations against British rule in 1919 precipitated an armed attack by soldiers on Indians protesters in the Punjabi city of Amritsar where 400 people were killed on April 13. The Amritsar massacre became the occasion of Gandhi's first mass campaign of civil disobedience against the colonial government of India, and as such marked the beginning of the modern Indian independence movement.[115]

* * *

The British Empire was seriously weakened by its participation in the First World War. Although imperialists saw the war as a wonderful opportunity, it actually brought about greater nationalism among colonial subjects and undermined the old ideals of imperialism. The possibility of constructing a common bond of imperial citizenship without regard to color, ethnicity, or religious traditions appeared less likely given the resurgent nationalism in Britain and the attendant hardening of racial boundaries. The war saw Britain become more racially diverse, but not more racially tolerant or inclusive. It seemed that as British imperial hegemony began to weaken, Britons at home and abroad took increasing refuge in the privileges of 'whiteness.' For instance, Japan's desire for a declaration of racial equality in the League of Nations' Covenant was scuttled by Australian Prime Minister Hughes, who threatened to mobilize public opinion throughout the 'Anglo-Saxon' world against it.[116] Of course, colonized peoples hardly needed to take part in the war to experience racism, but their wartime service proved crucial in convincing many of them that no amount of devotion to their British governors would grant them the racial status apparently necessary for full citizenship in the Empire. Perhaps the war's greatest tragedy was its tendency to promote an exclusive concept of 'Britishness', narrowly defined along ethnic and racial lines, rather than an inclusive 'Britishness' based on a common citizenship of shared rights and responsibilities.

Chapter 5: Propaganda and Censorship

The First World War was a 'total war' that required the direct or indirect participation of millions of combatants and civilians. The continuity of public morale and support could not be taken for granted, as the war dragged on for years with no end in sight. Propaganda became a crucial means of rallying support for the nation and maintaining commitment to the war effort. The combination of mass literacy and new techniques of communication like the poster and motion picture gave propaganda an importance it had never had before, and which it has retained ever since. In the words of the British press magnate Lord Beaverbrook, who later directed official propaganda: 'Since strength for the purposes of war was total strength of each belligerent nation, public opinion was as significant as fleets and armies.'[1]

Not all wartime propaganda originated from official government sources. In Britain the state played a smaller role in directing public information and orchestrating cultural production than in the other belligerent nations. Britain possessed a strong and diverse civil society with a deep-rooted Protestant voluntary tradition that rallied in support of the war.[2] Most propaganda was a product of this civil society: commercial advertising, newspapers, sermons, musical productions, novels, films, and postcards. Although propaganda usually originated from patriotic writers, artists, and voluntary organizations, the government increasingly involved itself in such operations – professionalizing output and bringing more of it under official state supervision.

In its attempt to maintain a high level of support for the war, the government and its allies in the press, churches, and schools conducted an intense propaganda campaign in which they bombarded the eyes and ears of British citizens with posters, parades, pamphlets, films, martial music, and military spectacles. In an important postwar study of official

British propaganda, Harold Lasswell argued: 'No government could hope to win without a united nation behind it, and no government could have a united nation behind it unless it controlled the minds of its people.'[3] This notion of propaganda as 'mind control' has been the subject of intense criticism since the war. Writers, historians, and political progressives have condemned the wartime government and its allies in civil society, emphasizing the ways in which they manipulated information – highlighting upbeat stories, exaggerating military successes, suppressing military failures, and silencing voices of dissent. The negative connotations attributed to the term 'propaganda' today owe much to the experience of the First World War.

* * *

During the Great War, the British government, for the first time in its history, mounted a campaign of official propaganda in a determined attempt to win support for its war-related policies at home and abroad. In August 1914, C. F. G. Masterman, a journalist and Liberal politician, was asked by the Cabinet to find some way to counter anti-British pamphlets being circulated abroad by the Germans. Masterman responded with a well-thought-out system of opinion manipulation, intended initially to promote the British cause among neutral countries and the dominions. He established a War Propaganda Bureau, headquartered at Wellington House, and usually referred to by its location. Masterman recruited distinguished writers and intellectuals, including Arnold Bennett, Arthur Conan Doyle, Lewis Namier, and John Galsworthy, to offer advice and to write pamphlets and articles in support of the war. Wellington House also coordinated propaganda from a multitude of unofficial organizations such as the Cobden Club, the Victoria League, the British Empire Union, and, most important, the Central Committee for National Patriotic Organizations (CCNPO).[4]

Initially, Wellington House and the CCNPO invited prominent individuals to write or lecture about the war, with a view to justifying Britain's position in it. This intellectual approach was somewhat old-fashioned, being directed at the educated classes rather than the masses.[5] The principal tool utilized was the pamphlet. In 1914, 45 different titles were produced, rising steadily to 132 in 1915, 202 in 1916, and 469 in 1917. Hundreds of thousands of copies were distributed, though Wellington House was careful to disguise their official nature. The pamphlets appeared to be written by private individuals and printed by private publishing houses. They were distributed through private channels like book dealers, voluntary organizations, and steamship companies.

So secret were the dealings of Wellington House that even Parliament was largely unaware of its existence and activities.[6]

Much of Britain's official propaganda was initially directed less at its own citizens, whose commitment was taken for granted, than to neutral nations, especially the United States. Wellington House, in fact, was under the authority of the Foreign Office. Sir Gilbert Parker, a popular Canadian novelist and MP for Gravesend, was in charge of American propaganda. Parker compiled a list of several thousand influential Americans – politicians, academics, journalists, and businessmen – for the use of Wellington House. Typically, these people would be sent pamphlets, along with a personal cover letter from Parker, who was apparently writing to them as a concerned citizen. The writers G. M. Trevelyan and John Masefield went on lecture tours of the United States in 1915, sponsored by Wellington House. Masterman also recruited the popular novelist Mrs Humphry Ward to visit the front and write up her experiences for the American reading public. The result, *England's Effort: Letters to An American Friend* (1916), was an epistolary novel which praised the splendid work being done by all the fine young people she met at army camps and in munitions factories.[7]

While the Foreign Office worked through Wellington House, the War Office created its own separate propaganda bureau, MI7, which arranged press visits to the front, prepared special articles concerning military news, and intercepted and analyzed German cable and wireless communications. The German propaganda network was also infiltrated by postal censorship, which intercepted pro-German literature destined for neutral nations, replaced it with pro-British material and sent it on its way. The haphazard growth of different official and private propaganda organizations within Britain resulted in a certain amount of overlap and duplication of effort, and even rivalry. Here, as elsewhere in society, the government gradually extended its control and coordination efforts.[8]

The earliest literature produced by Wellington House was intended to justify Britain's entry into the war and to brand Germany as the aggressor. Cynics abroad and socialists at home might characterize the war as a conflict about Empires, trade, and markets, but when Germany invaded Belgium, propagandists emphasized Britain's honorable mission of protecting a defenseless and trusted friend. Prime Minister Asquith claimed on 6 August 1914: 'We are fighting to vindicate the principle that small nationalities are not to be crushed in defiance of international good faith, by the arbitrary will of a strong and overmastering power.'[9] Praise for 'gallant little Belgium' became a stock of British propaganda. A cartoon in *Punch* from 12 August 1914 personified Belgium as a plucky peasant boy who staunchly bars access to his farm to a club-wielding thug, representing Germany.

The defense of Belgian neutrality could also be seen as a defense of Britain. In an early propaganda piece, the headmaster of Eton argued that Britain's worldwide interests and eventually her national survival, depended on keeping Belgium's ports out of enemy hands. This was a reasonable position, but hardly one to inspire the masses. More convincing narratives were constructed, in particular the story that Bethmann-Hollweg, the German Chancellor, had berated the British Ambassador, Sir Edward Goschen, for expressing concern for Belgian neutrality that had been guaranteed by a treaty signed in 1839. Surely Britain would not go to war 'just for a word – "neutrality," a word which in war time is so often disregarded – just for a scrap of paper . . .'[10] This story had profound influence on British sensibilities, symbolizing the dialectic of German dastardliness and British rectitude. The scene was worthy of melodrama, and one could easily picture the Chancellor twirling his moustaches and shaking his fist while Goschen stood his ground, stalwart and unblinking. Indeed, clergymen wrote Sunday School plays about 'A Scrap of Paper' and the expression became one of the infamous phrases of the war. A popular recruiting poster reproduced the very 1839 treaty under assault – a treaty signed by both Britain and Prussia – with the caption: 'A Scrap of Paper – Prussia's Perfidy – Britain's Bond.'[11]

British academics also invoked the past in justifying their nation's entry into the war. In September 1914, the Oxford History Faculty published *Why We Are At War: Great Britain's Case*, in which they self-servingly recounted a century of German aggression and duplicity. The most famous academic defense of the British cause was Gilbert Murray's *Foreign Policy of Sir Edward Grey* (1915), which argued that British diplomacy had played no role in the build-up to war, but was motivated by a desire to avoid war. These works were part of a long series of 'Oxford pamphlets', which employed some of the most distinguished thinkers in Britain to justify 'both historically and morally England's position in the struggle.' They often set forth the intellectual origins of the war, and emphasized the warped, sterile, and militaristic nature of German culture.[12]

Much British propaganda focused on the idea that an autocratic, anti-liberal Germany was bent on trampling the freedoms and independence of the democratic nations of Western Europe. This line of thought was given early and eloquent expression by H. G. Wells in his influential book, *The War That Will End War* (1914). A left-wing intellectual and socialist, Wells argued that Prussian militarism must be defeated to make the world safe for democracy. Wells was an early supporter of a League of Nations and maintained that a British victory could abolish war altogether. This theme was taken up by other writers, such as Arnold Bennett, a popular novelist and advisor to Wellington House. In *Liberty: A Statement of the British Case* (1914), Bennett claimed that the British also fought for the freedom of Germans, who were ill-served by 'the monstrous chicane of the military caste' which wanted not only to dominate Europe, but to crush democracy at home. Bennett concluded: 'We have a silly, sentimental, illogical objection to being enslaved. We reckon liberty – the right of every individual to call his soul his own – as the most glorious end. It is for liberty we are fighting.'[13]

Critics abroad responded that British imperial history was one long litany of conquering small, defenseless nations, and that the defender of Belgium was the oppressor of Ireland. That Russia, a far more despotic regime than Germany, was Britain's ally also required some hasty revisions of history. Numerous pamphlets defended the British Empire as a free association of nations held together by mutual bonds of affection and trust. Propaganda glossed over Tsarist tyranny and attributed the shortcomings of Russian society to a pro-German aristocracy. 'Holy Russia' became a dominant theme, as in the 1915 *Punch* cartoon which depicted the Tsar as a modern crusader. 'Who follows me for Holy Russia's sake?' he asks inspired troops, as a priest leads them in prayer.[14]

In the long run, a war to defend Belgian neutrality or to promote democracy proved less effective as a propaganda theme than an emotional plea to rescue Belgian women and children from German barbarism. During the last weeks of 1914, the *Daily Chronicle* published an illustrated booklet entitled *In the Trail of the German Army* which included numerous photographs of the destruction wrought in Belgian towns. The German military, surprised and enraged by unexpectedly stiff resistance by the Belgian Army, and erroneously believing in the existence of guerilla bands of snipers, turned its fury on the Belgian civilian population. Recent research by John Horne and Alan Kramer has carefully documented a pattern of terror on the part of German forces: widespread burning of homes and entire villages, the use of civilians as human shields, and the mass execution of hostages in retaliation for supposed guerilla resistance. More than 5000 Belgian civilians, including many women and children, were killed by the German Army in a series of atrocities that clearly violated the 1907 Hague Convention on 'The Laws and Customs of War.'[15] Such serious violations of the rules of warfare were soon eclipsed by even more sensational (and imaginary) stories of atrocities against civilians, especially the raping and mutilation of women and children.

Rumors spread by refugees were printed in newspapers and gained widespread belief. German soldiers were accused of raping nuns, and cutting off women's breasts and children's hands. Among the most famous of the false atrocity stories was the report that the Germans 'crucified' a captured Canadian officer near Ypres.[16] This new atrocity propaganda was hysterical and apocalyptic in tone, as in Barry Pain's poem 'In the Trail of the Hun':

> Villages burned down to dust;
> Torture, murder, bestial lust,
> Filth too foul for printers' ink,
> Crimes from which the apes would shrink.[17]

The stories of rape and sadism were concocted by neither the British government nor the press, but began as 'urban myths' among Belgian refugees. British newspapers printed the stories with little attempt at verification, though in fairness to the press, its access to the war zone was highly restricted.[18]

In the face of official German denials, the British government in December 1914 appointed a committee to investigate the widespread reports of atrocities in Belgium. The committee was chaired by Lord Bryce, a former ambassador to the United States and a respected scholar. The other six members included distinguished historians, lawyers, and journalists. The material under investigation consisted of 1200 depositions recounting acts of German barbarism made by Belgian refugees now living in England, or by British and Belgian troops stationed in France. The committee did not select the cases it would investigate, nor did it interview any of the persons making allegations. In fact, the committee carefully avoided verifying the evidence, but took the approach that although 'individual cases' might have been doubtful, they probably represented a 'general truth.' The committee did not dwell on the stories of rape and mutilation, but nonetheless lent credence to them on the flimsiest of evidence.[19]

The Bryce Report was released in May 1915, by a lucky coincidence, a week after the *Lusitania* sinking. The Report concluded that Germans had committed atrocities in Belgium as part of a deliberate strategy of terror. Masterman had the Bryce Report translated into 30 languages and sent thousands of copies abroad. Although it was 600 pages long, the report was sold for 1*d*., the price of a newspaper.[20] The Report's findings were given wider circulation in popular works such as William Le Queux's *German Atrocities* (1915) and Theodore Cook's *Crimes of Germany* (1915). In 1915, Phyllis Campbell also published *Back of the*

Front: Experiences of a Nurse, a sensational ghost-written 'memoir' meant to substantiate the Bryce Report. Campbell recounts her horror at meeting a Belgian refugee whose clothing was 'saturated with blood from her cut-off breasts.' She then comes across a kitten which had been tied to a tree and tortured by German soldiers: 'Of all the devilish cruelties I had seen, none so brought home to me the utter depravity of the German soul . . . It seemed to me that all the wickedness, all the fear and filthiness unimaginable that exists can be summed up in one word: GERMAN.'[21]

The image of the beastly Hun dominated the most inflammatory, mass-market propaganda. Cartoons, posters, and films presented sensational, boiled-down versions of the Bryce Report. Most frequently, German soldiers were depicted as rapists and sadists. Edmund Sullivan, for instance, drew numerous 'hate cartoons' which were widely published and later collected in *The Kaiser's Garland* (1915). One of them, 'The Gentle German', depicts a bestial soldier impaling a winged cupid on his bayonet. The most famous cartoonist of the war was Louis Raemaekers, a Dutch illustrator who moved to London in 1915 and produced a vast number of sinister images, emphasizing the brutality and cruelty of the Germans. Typical images include 'Kultur has passed here', which shows a dead woman and child lying amid rubble, and 'I crush whatever resists me', in which a figure representing German militarism chops down a crucifix with an axe.[22]

The alleged sado-sexual crimes against women and girls were given the most publicity in propaganda. Posters and cartoons depicted German soldiers brutalizing women. Artists now represented Belgium as a woman, stripped to the waist, bound and violated, replacing the earlier image of the nation as a brave boy defying Goliath. Recruitment speakers shocked and titillated crowds by informing them that in the event of a German victory, thousands of British girls would be taken to stud farms in Germany. Wartime films took special delight in portraying sexual assault. In *The Unpardonable Sin* (1918), the popular actress Blanche Sweet is menaced by German soldiers who attempt to rape her. In the climax of *Hearts of the World* (1917), the hero levels a pistol at his sweetheart's head as German soldiers are battering down the door to the Belgian house in which they have taken refuge. The implication is that he is saving her from certain rape and that death is a preferable fate.[23]

A number of events in 1915 turned out to be a godsend to British propagandists. In April Germans used poison gas against allied troops, on 7 May the passenger ship *Lusitania* was sunk by a German submarine, in October Turks began massacres against Armenian Christians, and the Germans shot Nurse Edith Cavell for helping Allied soldiers escape from Belgium. None of these events were invented, but they were presented so as to maximize their propagandistic effect and to make the case for

systematic German barbarism, especially against the weak and defenseless. For example, 1201 passengers drowned when the Germans torpe-
doed the *Lusitania*. Many of them were women and children whose bodies
later washed ashore on Irish beaches, where they were photographed
to devastating effect. A widely circulated recruitment poster depicted a
woman sinking beneath the sea, her child clutched in her arms. A single-
word caption exhorted viewers: 'Enlist.' Although the ship was widely
suspected of carrying contraband, including thousands of explosive artillery shells, it was presented as another example of German 'beastliness.'
In a further propaganda coup, Captain Reginald Hall, head of Naval
Intelligence, had 300 000 'copies' struck of a medal said to have been
ghoulishly issued by the German government to celebrate the sinking.[24]

The execution of Edith Cavell in Brussels on 12 October 1915 was
also widely exploited for propagandistic purposes. A Red Cross nurse
in German-occupied Belgium, she was shot for helping Allied soldiers
cross enemy lines. Dozens of books were written and films produced,
commemorating her sad fate, and Cavell's portrait hung in schoolrooms
throughout the country. A new recruiting poster depicted Cavell accompanied by the bold-faced text: 'Murdered by the Huns! Enlist and Help
Stop Such Atrocities.' Soon a Spanish exporter was sending 'Cavell
oranges' to England, wrapped in tissue decorated with etchings of her
final hour. Her wax figure remained the most popular wartime exhibit
in Madame Tussaud's Museum in London.[25] Whether politically or commercially motivated, homages to Cavell presented her as a madonna of
sorrows whose death was the ultimate self-sacrifice. Such representations reinforced notions of female purity and called upon men to defend
hearth and home, lest their wives and daughters suffer Cavell's fate.[26]

* * *

In the first years of the war, the aim of most domestic propaganda was
to encourage enlistment in the armed services. Since Britain had no
tradition of conscription or mass military service, recruitment propaganda was essential. A 30-member Parliamentary Recruiting Committee
(PRC), consisting primarily of party whips and party organizers, operated under the supervision of the War Office. The PRC's main mode of
appeal was the mass rally. During the first big recruiting drive in 1914,
800 meetings were organized across the nation and four million leaflets distributed. Rallies took the form of patriotic pageants. They began
with military bands leading a procession of local dignitaries through the
town, and culminated in an open-air meeting where recruiters made
fiery speeches exhorting young men to answer their country's call. The

mayor and local ministers usually spoke, but the PRC also brought in MPs and generals, literary celebrities, and music hall entertainers.[27] Speakers utilized a vast range of rhetorical strategies in appealing for recruits. H. Rider Haggard, the author of popular adventure novels like *King Solomon's Mines*, employed emotional patriotic rhetoric and invoked the glories of Britain's past: 'By the spirits of your fathers, by the women who bore you and the children whom you love, by those who have already shed their sacred blood for you, by the glories of your ancient story, in the name of the God who made you free, and of the splendid flag that from age to age has floated above your homes, I charge each one of you to play his part today.' The familiar list of German atrocities was often rehearsed, and men were called on to defend their homes and families. Recruiters even suggested that those who failed to enlist were less than men, as did Arthur Conan Doyle in his pamphlet *To Arms!*: 'All our future lives will be determined by how we bear ourselves in these few months to come. Shame, shame on the man who fails his country in this its hour of need!' Among the most popular recruiting speakers was the MP and journalist Horatio Bottomley, who specialized in a potent mixture of jingoism and populism. Bottomley typically demanded the dismantling of the German Empire, the confiscation of its navy, and the hanging of the Kaiser. With its rival demolished, Britain would then, Bottomley insisted, redirect its own military spending to social welfare policies for the working classes.[28]

A continual call for recruits was maintained by posters displayed on every conceivable surface. In January 1915, one Londoner observed: 'Posters appealing to recruits are to be seen on every hoarding, in most shop windows, in omnibuses, tramcars, and commercial vans. The great base of Nelson's Pillar is covered with them.'[29] The poster had emerged in the late nineteenth century as an important advertising medium, and had even achieved a measure of artistic respectability through the efforts of painters like Toulouse-Lautrec and Alphonse Mucha. Its low cost and immediate visual impact made it an ideal means of mass propaganda. Shortly before the war broke out, the government for the first time employed professional advertisers to assist in recruiting. Hedley Le Bas and Eric Field of the Caxton Advertising Agency began working for the War Office in 1913. They later organized a committee of advertising agents to advise the PRC and to assist in the poster campaign for recruits.[30]

In spite of the hired advertising experts, the earliest PRC posters lacked dramatic impact. They contained no visual images, but were merely simple block-print texts such as 'Your King and Country Need You.' Other posters lacked mass appeal, instead directing their message to the nation's elite: 'Have you a Butler, Groom, Chauffeur, Gardener, or Gamekeeper serving *you* who at this moment should be serving your King and Country?' At the time many criticized the low artistic quality of the posters, which were mainly designed by the printing firms employed by the PRC. Acting on its own, the London Underground began commissioning posters of greater artistic merit in early 1915, employing talented illustrators such as Frank Brangwyn and Savile Lumley. PRC posters soon began to incorporate illustrations and made more emotional appeals. The PRC's first great success, and the most famous image from the war, was its Kitchener poster, based on a design by Alfred Leete. The stern-faced commander gazes outward, his finger pointed directly at the viewer. His expression commands obedience as does the simple text: 'Join Your Country's Army!' The image of Kitchener recalled Britain's past imperial victories and seemed to embody the nation's resolve.[31]

The poster campaign grew in sophistication and psychological complexity. Appeals were made not merely to duty, but to young men's desire for adventure and comradeship. One popular poster, designed by the painter Lucy Kemp-Welch, depicted a soldier on horseback charging across a battlefield. It was simply captioned 'Forward!' John Hassall's recruiting poster for the Public Schools Brigade shows a young soldier waving his hat at the viewer. He has just captured a German trench and calls out: 'Hurry Up! Boys – Fill the Ranks.' Another poster invoked chivalric associations, showing St George, England's patron saint, slaying the dragon. Some recruiting posters even adopted a jaunty style, as in the picture of three jolly comrades playing cards in the trenches. 'Will you make it a fourth?' they ask the viewer.[32]

Appeals to manhood or guilt were also common in recruiting posters. One poster simply states: 'Your friends need you. Be a man.' Perhaps the most famous example of this approach was designed by Savile Lumley. In a postwar scene, a young girl asks her father 'Daddy, what did *you* do in the Great War?' The man looks out at the viewer with an expression of intense shame. In other posters, women urge their men to enlist. 'Women of Britain say GO!' was the message of one poster. In another, an Irish woman grasps a rifle and points in the direction of a burning Belgian town. 'Will you go or must I?' she asks a hesitant man. Most posters did not portray women in such aggressive stances. More commonly women were shown as vulnerable and imperiled, needing male protection. 'Remember Belgium' encaptioned a poster of a woman and child fleeing from a burning village. Another poster showed a bombed house in Scarborough, which had been shelled by German battleships. An orphaned child stood alone in the rubble. The bold-face title asked: 'Men of Britain! Will You Stand For This?'[33]

Plate 5.1   Alfred Leete, 'Kitchener Wants You' (Imperial War Museum, London)

Plate 5.2 Savile Lumley, 'Daddy, what did YOU do in the Great War?' (Imperial War Museum, London)

All the techniques of mass advertising, developed in the prewar generation to sell consumer goods, were now enlisted in the drive for recruits: posters, postcards, banners, rallies, and even film. In 1915, the PRC commissioned the London Film Company to produce a recruiting film, *You!*, which was a call for Britons to support the war. The film opens with a scene of General Dallaway writing to his son Hugh, asking him 'What are YOU doing for your country?' Hugh tosses the letter away and it is blown out of a window and across London, where it is found by several different people in succession. Its accusatory message shames all of them into action. A young cockney slacker enlists, a rich woman decides to do war work, a financier hoarding gold buys war bonds, and finally, the letter returns to Hugh Dallaway, who is now inspired to enlist. The film premiered in January 1916, by which time its message was less urgent, because the first conscription bill had passed. By this time, the PRC had distributed 54 million copies of some 200 different posters and organized 12 000 recruiting meetings. In the final weeks before the Military Service Act went into effect on 2 March, public hoardings were covered with one last message from the PRC: 'Will You March Too, Or Wait Until March 2?'[34]

The end of the recruiting campaign did not diminish propaganda appeals directed at the British public. There were calls for nursing volunteers, for women workers in munitions factories, and for the land army. Citizens were exhorted to restrict food consumption and avoid waste. Above all, posters and advertisements constantly urged Britons to buy war bonds or to contribute to a vast array of war-related charities. The same sentimental and guilt-inspiring advertising techniques that had promoted recruitment now pleaded the case for war orphans, disabled soldiers, and Belgian refugees. Many of the posters commissioned by British charities achieved high artistic standards, like the work of well-known illustrators Louis Raemaekers and J. B. Beadle.[35]

Appeals for money reflected the unprecedented costs of the war, which nearly bankrupted the British state. Taxes were increased and overseas loans secured, but even this was not enough. Public borrowing through domestic war loans raised desperately needed funds, and Britain was blanketed with appeals to buy war bonds. Three major campaigns to promote War Savings Certificates were launched by the government in November 1914, June 1915, and January 1917. These drives utilized all the tools of mass propaganda employed elsewhere, including posters, rallies, and film. One poster depicted a German soldier being crushed by a gigantic British coin. Another proclaimed: 'Every Hun dreads/ Every Hundred/ Put into National War Savings Bonds.' Popular music hall artists like Harry Lauder and George Robey were active in fund-raising drives. Appeals were made to theater audiences, and musical reviews often included songs encouraging donations:

> By silver bullets will the war be won
>   That is the stuff to give the Hun.
> So pay – pay – don't delay
>   Come along, make a splash
> Shell out, fork out, if not walk out
>   What we want is cash.

Plate 5.3   Louis Raemaekers, 'Ain't I a lovable fellow?' *Raemaekers' Cartoon History of the War*, vol. 1 (New York: The Century, 1918), 29. (From the author's collection)

Fund-raising rallies could be highly imaginative events, as was the 'Feed the Guns' campaign in October 1918. For this drive, Trafalgar Square was transformed into a replica of a shell-destroyed French village and battlefield. The statue of General Gordon was covered by a ruined church tower and the fountain became part of a destroyed farm house. Visitors walked along artificial trenches and put money inside howitzers placed about the square.[36]

The National War Savings Committee was among the first agencies to utilize motion pictures for war propaganda. It produced numerous short films encouraging both thrift and war bond purchase, including *The Small Capitalist*, *Her Savings Saved*, and *Stand By the Men Who Stand By You*. In 1916, the Committee commissioned the Gaumont Film Company to make *For the Empire* as part of that year's war loan drive. An emotional and allegorical film, it opens with an image of a despairing mother, symbolizing Belgium, kneeling by her dead children, followed by shots of damaged buildings in Ypres and Rheims. A title then asks 'Why are we safe?', followed in turn by images of the British Navy. The audience is then informed that 'One Dreadnought costs £2 000 000, but we must win the war. Never mind the cost.' People are then shown buying war bonds at the post office, and the film concludes with a scene of the British Lion (a real lion was used) tearing apart the Prussian battle standard.[37]

* * *

Propaganda was not only concerned with projecting a positive image of the war effort and rousing popular support. It also sought to censor bad news that might adversely affect civilian morale, and to restrict information that could be of use to the enemy. On the first day of Britain's entry into the war, the cable ship *Teleconia* cut the German transatlantic cables, thereby giving Britain a tremendous communications advantage. The Defence of the Realm Act was initially designed with the control of information in mind – to prevent the obtaining or relaying of information 'of such a nature as is calculated to be or might be directly or indirectly useful to the enemy', and to protect the vital centers of communications, such as railways, docks, and harbors. As the war progressed, DORA was expanded to grant the government regulatory powers over almost every aspect of British society, but control over communications remained fundamental. DORA was designed primarily to prevent valuable information from reaching the enemy rather than to control public opinion at home, though the latter was one of its consequences.[38]

On 5 August 1914, a Press Bureau was set up under the militant Tory, F. E. Smith. The Bureau, staffed largely by military officers, examined all press cables, issued news releases, and gave instructions to newspaper editors on the attitude they should take to questions of the day – what should be emphasized, what downplayed. Doubtful material was required to be submitted for censorship. Quickly dubbed the 'Suppress Bureau' by reporters, the agency banned all correspondents from the front and was so zealous about preventing valuable news from reaching the enemy, that it delayed publication of battle reports and provided scanty details. *Punch* joked that American papers published stories about the British Army days before the Press Bureau released the information in Britain. Official secrecy resulted in much confusion and bewilderment about the war. Lack of access to the front led to the proliferation of rumors, atrocity stories, and outright fabrication. Starved for news, the *Daily Mail* published a detailed account of an entirely fictitious naval battle.[39]

Newspapers were vocal in their criticism of the Press Bureau, attacking it frequently in editorials and cartoons. A cartoon from *London Opinion* in October 1914 depicts a blindfolded Britannia who is thinking: 'My boys are doing well, I am certain, but alas, I am allowed to know so little!'[40] Press relations only improved in May 1915 when reporters were finally allowed to visit the front and some journalists were added to the censorship staff, diluting the military secrecy. The new co-directors of the Press Bureau, E. T. Cook and Frank Swettenham, were more trusting of journalists and realized the benefits of having the press as an ally. After all, most newspapers were overwhelmingly patriotic and were happy to practice voluntary censorship, suppressing negative material and publishing upbeat stories. Editors generally accepted the Press Bureau's 'D-notices' advising papers of matters not to be discussed, such as air raids, food riots, or labor disputes.[41]

Most newspapers practiced self-censorship, but DORA enabled the government to suppress papers that printed anything they considered untruthful or harmful to the war effort – not always the same thing. Specifically, Regulation 27 of DORA allowed the government to prevent the spread of 'false reports' likely to cause 'disaffection.' This could be interpreted liberally, and was the most common pretext for silencing the press. Most famously, the *Globe* was forced to suspend publication for two weeks in November 1915 when it claimed that Kitchener was being forced to resign. Such actions against the mainstream press remained rare as the government courted its goodwill and could usually rely on its discretion. Pacifist and Labour papers bore the brunt of official suppression. The Glasgow socialist weekly *Forward* was suppressed in 1915 when it published an account of Lloyd George's hostile reception by the city's workforce. When it was discovered in 1916 that Germany was using material from the pacifist *Labour Leader* for propaganda purposes, the government banned the exportation of all pacifist papers. Yet, for the most part, the government refrained from suppressing even the radical papers, fearing this would 'have the effect of advertising the speeches and publications which are now, for the most part, left in obscurity.'[42]

Newspapers were the most important source of information at the time, and a ready-made vehicle for propaganda. Inexpensive, mass-circulation papers had only been around since the 1890s, though they had already pioneered a lively and sensational style well-suited to wartime stories. Newspaper sales soared during the war, reflecting the public's avid desire for information from the battle front. Over six million newspapers were sold each day – during times of great crisis, even more. At the start of the Somme offensive, for instance, the *Sunday Pictorial* alone sold nearly 2.5 million copies. For many in the working class, the war years represented their introduction to a daily paper.[43]

The press had a feeling for the public mood and a better understanding than did Wellington House of how to win people over to a particular point of view. Journalists were recruited as official propagandists from the beginning. In September 1914, G. H. Mair of the *Daily Chronicle* became director of the Neutral Press Committee. By the end of the war, the press barons Lords Beaverbrook and Northcliffe were directing the entire propaganda network.[44] The line between government-sponsored news and independent journalism was often hard to see. For example, the British government secured a controlling interest in Reuters News Agency in 1916. This fact was kept secret at the time, so the public imagined that the news service was independent and impartial, when it was actually a mouthpiece for official propaganda.[45]

The British press was comprised of more than one hundred newspapers including 16 London dailies, many of which were affiliated with either the Conservative or the Liberal Party. A handful of influential press lords, Sir George Riddell and Lords Northcliffe and Beaverbrook, controlled much of the circulation.[46] The British press has not fared well with historians of the war. At its worst, it has been accused of associating war with glamor and adventure, masking the slaughter on the Western Front, protecting incompetent commanders, and exaggerating German atrocities.[47] There is some truth to these charges, but the picture is rather more complex.

While most papers tended to focus on small, heroic actions rather than the larger, gloomier picture, in other respects the attitudes of the press were far from monolithic. Some papers were highly patriotic and supported an authoritarian approach to the war. Horatio Bottomley's *John Bull* was the most hate-filled paper imaginable, vilifying 'Germhuns' and later exhorting 'Hang the Kaiser', but it was hardly representative. Other papers favored more flexible and democratic methods of waging war. The *Daily Mirror*, for example, was tolerant of conscientious objectors, while *John Bull* wanted them all shot. Conservative and Liberal papers disagreed violently over the treatment of naturalized aliens or the employment of women war workers. Some papers like the *News of the World* presented an antiseptic view of the front, others like the *Daily Mirror* showed much of the mud and squalor of the trenches in its photos. The provincial press maintained closer, more personal links to individual fighting men, and therefore often contained more realistic and vivid accounts of battles and the conditions of trench warfare.[48]

The press did not create a patriotic public, but rather nurtured existing patriotism and concealed unpleasant facts that might undermine morale. Catastrophic British and French losses during the early months of the war were concealed. Instead, the public read of 'German Army Demoralized – Troops Starving' and 'Despairing Officers and Men Commit Suicide.'[49] The men who ran the newspapers, from the publishers and editors to the reporters, saw their mission not only as providing information, but also as bolstering the war effort. They never questioned the legitimacy of the war, though they sometimes drew attention to the problems of waging it. They might criticize certain politicians for their lack of zeal or organization, but they never dared criticize a general. (One of the few journalists to attack the military was the Australian Keith Murdoch, who drew attention to the British commander's disastrous strategy at Gallipoli.) Casualty lists were published, but no attempt was made to weigh losses against ground gained or damage inflicted on the enemy. Tens of thousands of British soldiers died in the opening days of the Somme offensive. No ground was gained, yet the headline in the *Times* read: 'The Day Goes Well.'[50]

Wartime press accounts committed few outright lies, though there were many significant omissions. Perhaps what made news most difficult to assess was the euphemistic language, formulaic expressions, and boiler-plate constructions it generally employed. British soldiers never retreated; they offered 'splendid resistance' and 'brilliant counter-attacks.' The Army was always 'heroically fighting against tremendous odds', 'wiping out enemy masses', and 'firmly holding our withdrawn lines.'[51] The *Daily Mail* referred to 'going over the top' at the Battle of the Somme as a 'gay, impetuous and irresistible leap from the trenches.'[52] This fanciful and overblown rhetoric not only made it almost impossible to know what was actually happening, but also elevated the most ordinary and squalid engagements to the realm of myth and chivalry. A generation of Britons had been schooled in this 'essentially feudal language' through the adventure stories of Henty Rider Haggard, the poetry of Lord Tennyson and Robert Bridges, and the pseudo-medieval romances of William Morris. In these heroic fantasies, soldiers were 'warriors', horses were 'steeds', and warfare was 'strife.' You didn't defeat the enemy, you 'vanquished the foe', and you didn't die, you 'perished.'[53] It was only natural that writers and journalists would resort to this 'high diction' when narrating what they imagined to be their own crusade or national epic. Yet in seeking to elevate, they merely succeeded in obfuscating.

Romanticized depictions of the war, however, were not entirely the work of naïve journalists and government propagandists, as recent scholarship has demonstrated. Even soldiers were not immune to representing the war in euphemistic and elevated terms. As Robert Wohl argues, most officers had been 'trained in a literary tradition that translated quotidian and unpleasant reality into elevated sentiment and diction.' In their letters and diaries they often referred to death as 'crossing the bar, a kiss, or an embrace.' Nor was this merely window dressing. The Christian ideal of self-sacrifice gave the war a deeper meaning for soldier and civilian alike, and they spontaneously employed an idealized vocabulary, without prompting from above. Catriona Pennell studied several hundred firsthand accounts of the war by Britons from all geographic regions and social classes. She found that ordinary people employed the same language about the war as found in official publications. 'They used "big words" like honour, justice, defense, righteousness, and therefore the high diction of 1914 was speaking to a mood, not dictating it.'[54]

* * *

A great deal of the inflated rhetoric employed by propagandists was religious in origin, and the Church of England played an important role in wartime propaganda. The Church helped transform a campaign to safeguard national interests into a veritable holy war. Many churchmen were active in recruiting drives, preached patriotic sermons, and wrote pamphlets equating Britain's 'cause' with God's. Notions of Christian brotherhood quickly evaporated as the Church proclaimed a virtual crusade against German infidels. A leading theologian labeled Germany a nation of 'demoniacs' whose Kaiser was the 'Antichrist.' The most aggressively rhetorical of church leaders, Arthur Winnington-Ingram,

Bishop of London, made the crusade imagery explicit in a June 1915 appeal to the Church: 'I think the Church can best help the nation first of all by making it realize that it is engaged in a Holy War, and not be afraid of saying so. Christ died on Good Friday for Freedom, Honour and Chivalry, and our boys are dying for the same things . . . Mobilise the Nation for a Holy War!'[55]

Ministers frequently compared Germany to biblical aggressor nations like Babylon or Assyria, in which case Britain was linked to God's chosen people, the Israelites. The language of churchmen often rivaled that of the biblical prophets, as in the Reverend C. R. Ball's assertion that Germany was 'perverted of moral sense, possessed of national dementia, sunk in the depths of moral infamy, shrinking from nothing in its mad lust and worship of the will to power.' An army chaplain told his congregation on the Western Front, 'the god that the German leaders worship is the idol of the earth – a cruel and crude monster who lives on human blood.' In 1916, a clergyman from Wimbledon warned that in the event of a German invasion, they planned (in the manner of Herod) to kill every male child. Students of prophecy, especially evangelical laymen, were quick to identify Germany with the scarlet, seven-headed, ten-horned Beast from Revelations 17:3 and the Kaiser with the mighty king in Daniel 11:3. To some writers he was no other than the Antichrist, easily proven by the fact that he was 666 months old when the war began.[56]

The war seemed to be part of a divine plan. The Anglican philosopher C. C. J. Webb argued that God had used war throughout history as a key instrument in molding mankind. Hymns with martial imagery, 'Onward Christian Soldiers', 'Fight the Good Fight', and 'Soldiers of Christ', were sung more frequently, supplemented by new battle hymns freshly composed:

> Not ours, O Lord, to wake the sword,
>   Or cannon's deadly rattle;
> But while we laboured long for peace
>   Our foes prepared for battle.
> Be with us, then, and keep us safe
>   From all who sore assail us,
> For justice, truth, and freedom's sake,
>   Let not thine arm now fail us.[57]

Some army chaplains became notorious for their fiery rhetoric and calls to battle. The Reverend G. A. Studdert-Kennedy not only preached powerful sermons before battle, but was also accompanied to the trenches by a veritable vaudeville show: a champion boxer, wrestlers, and an officer who had bayoneted 18 Germans. His companions demonstrated their martial prowess as an 'opening act' for his sermons.[58]

Religious images from the war attempted to evoke a pious atmosphere and underscore the Christian mission of Britain's cause. Typical was the print 'The White Comrade', depicting an ethereal Jesus hovering compassionately above a wounded soldier and accompanied by the verse: 'Lo, I am with you always.' Much religious writing during the war equated soldiers' deaths with Christ's sacrifice. This gave the war a religious cast and sought to console those whose friends and relatives had been killed. The Christ symbolism was spelled out explicitly in a short story by Florence Barclay, 'In Hoc Signo Vince' (1915). At the request of a nurse, a soldier improvises a Red Cross flag out of a sheet and bloody bandages. The blood-stained cross reminds all of the crucifixion and, by extension, comforts them that war's sacrifices will also lead to resurrection. Many believed that since soldiers were fighting a holy war, they would naturally go to heaven if they were killed. Some in the Church even connived at this unorthodox theology. The Bishop of London, for one, wrote a prayer book for soldiers that included the following Good Friday meditation: 'Christ died for others today; then if I am called to die for others I shall be only following Him; He will look on me as His comrade-in-arms and will be with me in the hour of death and afterwards.'[59]

In the church militant there seemed to be no place for the gospel of brotherly love. The Society for the Propagation of Christian Knowledge published a series of 'Wartime Tracts for Workers', which included Reverend P. Burns' *On Forgiving Our Enemies*. Burns assured his readers that Christians don't have to forgive the enemy, and in fact it would be wrong to do so when the enemy commits 'foul injury to the weak and helpless.' The Methodist minister Joseph Dawson similarly advised his flock in a sermon entitled 'How Would Christ Treat Germany?': 'What is the good of a Christianity that sickens into sentimentalism, that slobbers over the transgressor, and is afraid to have him punished?' A sermon by the Bishop of London, strangely titled 'A Word of Cheer', exhorted Britons 'to kill Germans; to kill them not for the sake of killing, but to save the world, to kill the good as well as the bad, to kill the young as well as the old . . .' Archdeacon Wilberforce also proclaimed: 'To kill Germans is a divine service in the fullest acceptation of the term.'[60]

Not all churchmen embraced the holy war propaganda, though voices of outright dissent were rare. The Bishop of Chelmsford was almost alone in stressing that the Christian God was the Father not only of the people of Britain but also of 'the men with whom we are at war . . . It is for

them equally with ourselves, that Christ bled and died upon the Cross.'
Clergymen may have been reluctant to espouse the brotherhood of man,
as this generally provoked bitter criticism. In 1917 when some bishops
reminded Britons of their duty to love their enemies, the tabloid press
mocked 'the flabby-babby babble of the Boche-defending Bishops.'[61]

* * *

Between official censorship and patriotic support for the war on the part
of newspapers, universities, and churches, there was little space for dissenting voices to be heard. Most socialist and pacifist papers had few
resources, small circulation, and faced constant harassment – not all of
it official. For example, many newsagents and public libraries refused
to carry them. One of the few high-profile venues for dissent was the
Cambridge Magazine, an unofficial student publication, which achieved
a circulation of 25 000 during the war. It was not a pacifist paper, but
was cosmopolitan in outlook and open to viewpoints besides the official patriotic line. Among its contributors were Bertrand Russell and
Siegfried Sassoon, and it routinely published excerpts from German and
Austrian papers. The Liberal *Nation* stood alone among mass-circulation
journals in its more moderate and nuanced positions on the war. It, too,
published Sassoon's anti-war poetry, and was frequently banned from
export by the government.

Overall, there was little tolerance for critics of the war, and they
were dealt with in a wide variety of ways, from public harassment to
imprisonment. When George Bernard Shaw ridiculed the patriotic
rhetoric of the war in his 1914 essay, *Common Sense About the War*, he
became the focus of vitriolic attacks in the press, and found his plays
removed from library shelves. When Siegfried Sassoon issued a protest
against the continuation of the war in July 1917, newspapers refused
to print it and his friends gave exaggerated evidence about his mental
state. The Army preferred to pack Sassoon off to a mental hospital in
Scotland, rather than to create more publicity for pacifism or punish
a highly decorated war hero. When the philosopher Bertrand Russell
wrote a pamphlet in 1916 criticizing the government for imprisoning
conscientious objectors, he was fined, and when he refused to pay,
his library was confiscated and sold. Trinity College, Cambridge,
deprived him of his lectureship, and the government refused to let
him accept a teaching offer from Harvard University. His movements
were restricted and he was forbidden to give public lectures. Finally,
Russell was imprisoned for six months in 1918 for publishing an article
urging a negotiated peace.[62]

In its suppression of dissent the government received much help from a supportive population. Patriotic crowds frequently broke up anti-war demonstrations. The right-wing British National Workers League was especially energetic in launching violent attacks on peace meetings. Thousands of Britons also denounced radicals and suspected spies to the police or the Home Office. In such cases popular patriotism drove rather than followed government initiative.[63]

The government was keen to avoid the appearance of heavy-handedness or to make martyrs out of those who opposed the war. It mostly sought to deny dissenters a mass audience for their views. While avoiding public prosecution, the state busied itself behind the scenes, keeping close tabs on dissenters. There was considerable police surveillance of people who spoke out against the war. Postal censorship also allowed the government to intercept anti-war publications, preventing them from reaching neutral nations like the United States. By 1918 the War Office had accumulated 38 000 dossiers on persons suspected of pacifism or anti-militarism.[64]

A wide battery of official and unofficial sanctions and punitive measures worked to isolate, marginalize, and silence dissenting voices, but could not eliminate them altogether. The Independent Labour Party, the Women's International League, and the Society of Friends continued their opposition to the war despite public disapproval. The National Council for Civil Liberties was formed to protest government restrictions on freedom of expression, and the Union for Democratic Control (UDC) to oppose the authoritarian manner in which the war was waged. The UDC was a small, but vocal group of liberal and socialist intellectuals like J. A. Hobson, E. D. Morel, Arthur Ponsonby, and Norman Angell, who spoke out in favor of greater parliamentary control over foreign policy and an end to secret diplomacy. The UDC opposed conscription and argued that the war should be ended by negotiation and compromise. The government maintained close watch over the organization's activities and forbade the export of its literature.[65]

Britain, alone among the belligerents, made provision for conscientious objection to military service, but the men who took advantage of this allowance were widely abused. The Conscription Act appeased Liberal opinion by allowing appeals before some 1800 local tribunals. The vast majority of appeals against military service (90 percent) were for family or economic reasons and many of them were granted. Those appeals have mostly disappeared from histories of the war, which have overwhelmingly concentrated on the statistically small number of men who resisted the draft for reasons of conscience. Many of them were Christian pacifists, others international socialists. When conscription went into effect early in 1916, some 16 500 men registered as conscientious objectors, and the term 'conchie' became an expression of opprobrium.[66] Conscientious objectors had to make their case to a local tribunal of clergymen, prominent citizens, and retired army officers. As James McDermott has shown, the tribunals were not as hostile to conscientious objectors as has generally been assumed. 'If a man was courteous and indicated a willingness to "do his bit" in any other way than to fight, most tribunals usually responded favorably.' Those who refused any alternative service, such as caring for the wounded, or 'expressed their convictions with defiant self-assurance,' were dealt with more harshly. Those in the Quaker tradition generally accepted alternative service, but some 1350 'absolutists' refused to perform any work that might assist the war effort. They were subjected to scorn and abuse out of all proportion to their numbers. In an attempt at intimidation, the military sent some conscientious objectors to France, where, once in the war zone, they could be shot for refusing to follow orders. They were later imprisoned, and 73 died as a result of harsh treatment. After the war, they were disenfranchised for five years and many found it impossible to secure employment, given their record.[67]

* * *

During the early years of the war, few Britons had much sympathy for the war's critics. Yet by 1917, the initial enthusiasm of the population was showing signs of waning in the wake of horrifying casualties, continued military stalemate, rising prices, and food shortages. The overthrow of the Tsar in February 1917 and the socialist takeover of Russia in October further rejuvenated the peace movement, and lent confidence to more radical and oppositional voices in Britain. Peace marches in the summer of 1917 attracted thousands of people. Industrial unrest rose dramatically in 1917, and some trade unions began to split into patriotic and pacifist wings. U.S. President Woodrow Wilson's message on war aims (Fourteen Points) in December 1917 energized the Labour Party to approve its own war policy, which called for a negotiated peace without annexations and, like Wilson, the creation of a supranational authority, or League of Nations. The British government feared losing the initiative and responded with a heightened propaganda campaign aimed at the domestic audience. In the final years of the war, the government came to see propaganda as more and more important in steeling national resolve and boosting civilian morale.

The whole propaganda structure was overhauled in February 1917 with the creation of a new Department of Information under John

Buchan to supersede Masterman's Propaganda Bureau at Wellington House. Masterman's propaganda, directed principally to leaders and opinion makers, had been increasingly criticized as old-fashioned and elitist. On coming to power in December 1916, Lloyd George asked his friend Robert Donald, editor of the *Daily Chronicle*, to review the government's propaganda network. Donald's report, which led to the creation of the new Department of Information, found Masterman's approach too literary and rational. Donald urged a more vigorous and strident propaganda aimed at the masses and, when necessary, outright fabrication.[68]

John Buchan's accession as Director of Information marked a departure from Masterman's more gentlemanly approach. A journalist and colonial civil servant, Buchan had risen to prominence as a protégé of Milner's in South Africa. He was also the author of popular adventure novels like *Prester John* and *The Thirty-Nine Steps* which invoked conservative, pro-imperial themes. As an indication of its new popular orientation, Buchan's Department of Information included a Cinema Division and News Division. The Cinema Division sought to exploit more vigorously the nation's over 3000 movie houses, and the News Division was guided by a committee of newspaper magnates, including Lords Northcliffe and Beaverbrook, who already had considerable experience in appealing to the masses. The Department's most infamous creation – and a sign of the new mood – was its pamphlet *A Corpse Conversion Factory* (1917), which accused the Germans of boiling down dead bodies, including those of Allied soldiers, to make soap. It was sheer invention.[69]

In May 1917, the Department of Information created the National War Aims Committee (NWAC) to counteract pacifism and defeatism and to reinvigorate the nation's commitment to the war. The Committee sought 'to keep before our nation both the causes which have led to the world war and the vital importance to human life and liberty of continuing the struggle until the evil forces which originated this conflict are destroyed for ever.' NWAC drew much of its personnel from the former Parliamentary Recruiting Committee, and like that earlier body appealed directly to the people by means of patriotic rallies. Brass bands would play, politicians and celebrities would speak, and an airplane might drop leaflets on the crowd. Frequently, the presence of a tank or large gun would add drama to the proceedings. NWAC also operated five cinema vans which toured the country showing films on the sides of buildings. Between August and October 1917, NWAC organized over 3000 public meetings. An additional 10 000 meetings took place in 1918.[70]

The key to NWAC's approach was to abandon the vague generalities of earlier nationalist propaganda and instead to focus on specific and concrete ways in which the war effort would benefit the British people. NWAC urged its speakers 'to dwell on the democratic development and improvement of the lot of the working classes which state control and other war changes have already secured; to suggest the prospect of further improvement and greater freedom when the war is over.' Lloyd George began promising 'homes fit for heroes' and other utopian schemes of postwar reconstruction. For the first time, British statesmen made specific and progressive statements about the purpose of the war along the lines of American President Woodrow Wilson's 14 Points. In January 1918 Lloyd George finally declared Britain's war aims, including the restoration of Belgian independence, national self-determination for peoples living under Austrian and Turkish rule, and the creation of an international organization to 'diminish the probability of war.'[71]

The late war propaganda effort combined the carrot and the stick approaches, for while NWAC promised democracy and prosperity, the censorship provisions of DORA were enforced with renewed vigor. From 1917 the Home Office under George Cave increased its suppression of dissent. In September and October of 1917, 24 raids were carried out against socialist and pacifist organizations and a massive quantity of literature was seized. Police often damaged presses and other printing equipment during raids, to the great hindrance of future production. The success of the Bolshevik Revolution in Russia increased the mood of apprehension and caused the government to clamp down even more on dissent. DORA was amended so that all writings about the making of peace had now to be submitted for censorship before publication. MI5, the intelligence service responsible for national security, expanded from ten employees in 1914 to 850 in 1918. By 1918 more than 4000 censors were examining the nation's letters.[72]

In February 1918, the Department of Information was upgraded to the status of Ministry under the control of the press baron Lord Beaverbrook, owner of the *Daily Express* and the *Globe*. That same month, Lord Northcliffe, proprietor of *The Times* and the *Daily Mail*, was enlisted to head the new Department of Enemy Propaganda, which aimed at psychologically undermining German and Austrian resolve. Lloyd George had long had close relations with the press, so there was little surprise that he wanted to bring in professional newspapermen to shake things up. The appointments of Beaverbrook and Northcliffe, however, created an outcry in Parliament. A number of MPs, led by Austen Chamberlain, argued that by placing newspaper proprietors in charge of official propaganda, the government was undermining the freedom of the press.[73]

Lloyd George's new regime certainly altered the approach to official propaganda. By the end of the war, the Ministry of Information was producing fewer books and pamphlets and more leaflets, posters, and films. There was, in particular, a greater emphasis on visual materials. By 1917, the government was distributing over 4000 war photographs weekly. It also began producing six different illustrated magazines modeled on the popular *Illustrated London News*. The most famous of them, the *War Pictorial*, was selling 750 000 copies a month by November 1917. Its official origin was unknown to its readers – government propaganda was being successfully passed off as a slick, commercial publication. NWAC also had great success with its 'German Crimes Calendar', which depicted a different enemy atrocity for each month of the year, including the burning of Louvain, the execution of Edith Cavell, and Zeppelin raids on London. Other more popular media now being employed for propaganda included lantern slides, postcards, and cigarette cards.[74]

There had been no official photographers at the front until 1916, and after that only 16 photographers covered all the theaters of war. While they produced thousands of images, they revealed little about the nature of modern warfare. Battles per se were difficult to photograph and the enemy was rarely seen. Pictures of soldiers sitting in trenches lacked drama and heroism, so they were kept to a minimum. Most photos were posed shots of soldiers at rest or play, usually smiling cheerfully for the camera. Other favorite subjects were ruined towns and scenes of civilian distress which highlighted German brutality. Certain subjects were forbidden by the censor, especially badly wounded or dead British soldiers. Yet photographers, like journalists, were guided as much by the publishing standards of the day as by censorship. They were concerned with creating positive images of the war. Patriotism and bourgeois standards of decency did not always permit full disclosure.[75]

The most important means of visual propaganda was the motion picture, a form of mass entertainment only about ten years old when the war began, but one that was ripe for exploitation. In 1914 seven million Britons were attending the cinema weekly, though the audiences were largely working class. By 1917, 21 million tickets were sold each week to members of all social classes. The war was crucial in turning a working-class entertainment into a universal pastime. Newsreels and propaganda films drew audiences from all classes, eager for any glimpse of the front or news about the war. According to film historian Kevin Brownlow, 'by the time the conflict was over, the film had become a social force. It had grown out of the stage of mild diversion and into an era when life without it was unthinkable.'[76]

At first there was some resistance to film propaganda among Britain's leaders, many of whom were contemptuous of the cinema as a vulgar,

working-class entertainment and skeptical of its ability to seriously contribute to the war effort. The Canadian government even banned all
war films in 1915 in the belief that actual scenes of the war might discourage enlistment.[77] News that German war films were reaching wide
audiences in neutral countries caused officials to reconsider. The first
government propaganda film, *Britain Prepared*, was a compilation created from footage supplied by the War Office. It premiered in December
1915 and featured scenes at army training camps and on board a battleship. The success of this venture led the government to organize an
official Committee for War Films, consisting of representatives from the
British film industry. The government would ultimately produce more
than 200 films in support of the war effort.[78]

The Committee would be permitted to send cameramen to France
to film troops, and in 1916 reached an agreement with the government
to produce a documentary film based on the Somme offensive. Most
of the film was shot on the front lines of battle, although one scene of
soldiers going over the top was later staged, as suitable footage could not
be taken at the time. *The Battle of the Somme* (1916) electrified audiences
and convinced the government of the value of film as propaganda. It was
not without controversy, however, as it contained images full of suffering
and agony, including several shots of actual corpses. The government
was careful to avoid such grim reality in later war films. *The Battle of Arras*
(1917), for instance, concentrated on scenes of happy, smiling soldiers.[79]

A heightened emphasis on film propaganda began with the newly
organized Department of Information in 1917 and continued to the end
of the war. Film propaganda was expanded to include a number of films
about the British war effort at home. A newsreel series was launched in
May, consisting of short subjects to be screened before feature films. The
newsreels usually conveyed positive images of life on the home front and
praised the civilian workforce. Typical examples included *A Day in the Life
of a Munition Worker* (1917), *The Life of a WAAC* (1918), and *Woolwich Arsenal
and Its Workers* (1918). Films often appealed directly to their audiences,
urging them to buy war bonds or conserve food. For instance, *Fighting
U-Boats in a London Back Garden* (1918) showed one family's small garden
which, it was claimed, provided them with a daily supply of vegetables. The
housewife is seen proudly holding up a turnip as a title proclaims: 'This is
why the U-boats don't worry ME.' Private film studios had long been making fiction films based on the war, but now the government began experi-
menting with this genre. In 1917, the Ministry of Food produced *Everybody's
Business*, a dramatic film about food conservation featuring popular actors
like Gerald du Maurier. Its success convinced the government of the need
to make entertaining fictional films about the war.[80]

A newly formed War Office Cinematographic Committee commissioned the renowned American film director D. W. Griffith to make a propaganda film based on the war. The British government provided no funding, but gave Griffith free use of its soldiers, training camps, and weapons in staging scenes. Griffith quickly found himself out of his depth in dramatizing a war of stalemate. His visit to the front proved disillusioning and he concluded 'real war made poor drama... Everyone is hidden away in ditches. The dash and thrill of wars of other days is no longer there.' He later confessed: 'The life of a soldier in modern war is the life of an underpaid, overworked ditch digger compelled to live in discomfort and danger. All the glamour has gone . . .' Unable to stage a heroic and realistic picture, Griffith fell back on the model of *The Birth of a Nation*, his 1915 epic of the American Civil War. Publicity for the film claimed that it was photographed on the battlefields of France, though most of it was actually shot in Los Angeles. Mock battle scenes were staged featuring cavalry charges, running infantry, long columns of charging men, and cannons bombarding the enemy.[81]

The resulting film, *Hearts of the World* (1917), proved immensely popular both in Britain and in the United States. Griffith ultimately downplayed the battle scenes in favor of a domestic drama involving a family's struggle to survive under the German occupation of Belgium. The melodramatic plotline involved the heroine, played by film star Lillian Gish, being menaced by brutal Germans and saved by her soldier sweetheart. Griffith was inspired by J.M. Barrie's one-act war play, *The Old Lady Shows Her Medals*, which he had seen in London. He decided that this was the proper way to dramatize war, not on the battlefield, but with poignant scenes of home life.[82]

Other fiction films followed. In 1918, the government released *Mrs John Bull Prepared*, which underscored the importance of women's war work through a cast of dramatic characters, including the male chauvinist Mr Smith. When this stern patriarch discovers his daughter reading a book entitled *Woman's Place in the War*, he flings it to the ground, declaring 'Woman's place is AT HOME. She is not fit for anything else.' This twentieth-century Scrooge is then visited by the 'Spirit of British Womanhood', who reveals to him images of women's war work and forces him to acknowledge his error. The most ambitious propaganda film, unfinished at the time of the armistice, was known by its working title, the *British National Film*. Scripted by the popular writer Hall Caine, it was to depict a German invasion of Britain, the occupation of Chester, and resistance by the local women. The film sought to make explicit the notion that Britons were fighting for their homes. The scenes of invasion would be intercut with footage contrasting German barbarism (the sinking of the *Lusitania*) with British virtue (Edith Cavell). To drive home this contrast, the film had the same man who ordered the sinking also preside over Cavell's execution (even though he had fallen in love with her!). In the last months of the war, the Ministry of Information planned to build its own studio to produce even more dramatic features.[83]

* * *

The extent to which wartime propaganda actually influenced people's attitudes and behavior has been the subject of continuing debate. Charles Higham, an advertising agent active in the recruiting drive, invested propaganda with tremendous psychological power: 'Most men and women thought they were acting on their own initiative . . . yet probably not half those self-sacrificing decisions would have been made without the continual galvanization of heart and thought and energy. Government publicity, throughout the war, was like the beating of drums; except that they were silent drums, and the beating was not on parchment but on consciences.' Propaganda may well have reinforced feelings of patriotism and steeled flagging resolve, but it would be misleading to suggest that Britain was a suggestible nation easily manipulated by master hypnotists. People did not believe everything they read, nor did they believe everything they heard. There were clear limits to how much the public could be manipulated. For the most part it could be led only where it wanted to go. When the *Daily Mail* blamed the public's darling, Lord Kitchener, for the shell shortage in 1915, people would have none of it. Although Kitchener was indeed to blame, advertisers canceled their contracts with the paper and circulation plummeted. Calls to patriotism were not always enough either. When Lloyd George tried to win over striking Glasgow workers in 1915 with patriotic platitudes, they shouted him down.[84]

Propaganda posters have been cited as classic examples of psychological manipulation, but did they work? The evidence is mixed. Louise Saunders, for example, was inspired to join the WAACs when she saw a poster modeled on the famous Kitchener image, with a woman in uniform declaring 'Your Country Needs YOU.' 'That settled it for me', she recalled. 'I thought that is what I'll do – I'll go and help win the war.' Saunders, however, was probably already susceptible to this call. Those who were critical of the war or who objected to women in the military would not have responded so favorably. Not everyone found such images inspiring. H. G. Wells dismissed the entire poster campaign as 'ridiculous placards and street corner insults.' Bob Smillie, the Scottish miners' leader, openly mocked the poster in which a girl asks her father

'Daddy, what did you do in the Great War?' He said his reply would be: 'I
tried to stop the bloody thing, my child.' Nor was defacement of propaganda posters unknown. In Glasgow, for instance, a Kitchener image was
scrawled over with the verse:

Your King and Country Need You
Ye hardy sons of toil
But will your King and Country need you
When they're sharing out the spoil?

In Ireland the propaganda campaign was heavily countered by Sinn
Fein, which vandalized recruitment posters and produced parodies of
British propaganda.[85]

Nicholas Hiley has shown that the largest surge of enlistment was actually *before* the PRC campaign got off the ground. During the period when
the most psychologically manipulative posters dominated, enlistment
levels were declining. The brash approach was favored by advertising
men, not by civil servants or the military. Recruitment officers felt that
the most effective posters were not those that tried to shame potential
recruits, but those that projected 'a delightful geniality.' Kitchener himself disliked the bullying style of so many posters, and Liberal politicians
condemned the commercial approach as 'contrary to the whole spirit
of voluntary enlistment.'[86] Ian Beckett points out that the scale of the
government's recruitment drive was not as impressive as historians have
imagined. Although the PRC printed around 6 million posters and 14
million leaflets at a total cost of £24 000, this was less than the choco-
late manufacturer Rowntree's had spent on advertising a single brand of
cocoa in 1912.[87]

Soldiers often dismissed wartime propaganda as nonsense and political cant. They disbelieved many atrocity stories and ridiculed the sentimental 'Tommy' created by the popular press. R. H. Tawney, when a
wounded sergeant, wrote an angry letter to the *Nation* on the topic: 'This
Tommy is a creature at once ridiculous and disgusting. He is represented
as invariably "cheerful" and reveling in the "excitement" of war, of finding "sport" in killing other men, or hunting Germans out of dugouts as
a terrier hunts rats . . . Of your soldier's internal life, the sensation of
taking part in a game played by monkeys and organized by lunatics, you
realize, I think, nothing.' Troop journals also dissented bitterly from the
upbeat, patriotic tone of the British press:

You write about the 'fray,'
From some place far away,

You're giving us what Tommy calls the 'dirts.'
With your 'majesty of war,'
And our 'eagerness for more' –
Remember that this rubbish sort of hurts.

Another troop paper parodied a war correspondent's report, concluding 'inset is a typical photo of one of our troops who has been in the
great advance and is longing to get at them again.' The inset was
blank.[88]

The home front press and many civilians continued to endorse bellicose propaganda and anti-German sentiments long after most soldiers
had lost faith in 'a war to end war.' An especially notorious example was
the letter of a 'Little Mother' published in the Conservative *Morning Post*,
written in angry response to a letter by a 'common soldier' calling for
peace:

> We women, who demand to be heard, will tolerate no such cry as
> 'Peace! Peace!' where there is no peace . . . There is only one tem-
> perature for the women of the British race and that is white heat . . .
> We women pass on the human ammunition of 'only sons' to fill up
> the gaps, so that when the 'common soldier' looks back before going
> 'over the top' he may see the women of the British race on his heels,
> reliable, dependent, uncomplaining.

The letter was reprinted in pamphlet form and sold 75 000 copies in
a week. Robert Graves encountered it while on leave and believed it an
example of 'the war madness that ran about everywhere, looking for a
pseudo-military outlet.' Such propaganda perplexed and even angered
some soldiers, like Graves, who held no such enthusiasm for the war,
nor such hatred for the Germans.[89] This much-remarked-upon division
between soldiers' and civilians' attitudes toward the war is often attributed to the combined effect of censorship and propaganda. According
to this line of reasoning, the upsetting realities of the war – horrid frontline conditions, the gruesome nature of combat, military blunders – were
assiduously suppressed by the government and its allies in the press, thus
allowing people at home to retain their comfortable illusions. There is
some truth in this argument, but soldiers' alienation from civil society has
been exaggerated, and the ignorance of the home front to battlefront
realities has been overdrawn.

Many civilians were skeptical of rosy press reports about the war and
were better informed about the awful conditions of trench warfare than
has generally been acknowledged. Soldiers were continually returning

home on leave, and British towns were full of injured and convalescing soldiers, some of them seriously wounded. Many were reluctant to discuss their experiences, though others did so freely and in graphic detail. Official government reports in 1917 referred to industrial workers as possessing a 'much more vivid realization of the actual horrors of war due to the large numbers [of soldiers] who have returned here with the experience of it fresh upon them.' Optimistic press accounts also began to lose their credibility when the same editions contained daily casualty lists occupying several pages in small print.[90]

British soldiers on the Western Front also sent home millions of letters a week. Their correspondence was censored and they sometimes sanitized their experiences so as not to worry their families, but their letters were often frank and graphic. Lieutenant Ernest Smith wrote to his mother about the water continually flooding his trench: 'It would not matter so much if it were ordinary water, but unfortunately it has passed a good many corpses on the way and stinks most horribly!' After the Battle of the Somme, John Masefield wrote to his wife: 'There was a cat eating a man's brain, and such a wreck of war as I never did see, and the wounded coming by, dripping blood on the track, and one walked on blood or rotten flesh, and I saw bags of men being carried to the grave. They were shoveling parts of men into blankets.' This correspondence did not always remain private, as hometown papers often published graphic stories based on soldiers' letters. For example, in October 1914 the *Evesham Journal* included a report from a local recruit: 'Sometimes the slaughter is terrific. It is often impossible to bury the dead and the stench from the decomposing bodies is very bad indeed... Sometimes explosions lift men eight or nine feet into the air and then they simply go to pieces.'[91]

A number of wartime novels and memoirs written by combatants and other eyewitnesses also contradicted the rosy pictures offered by the propagandists. Hugh Walpole's *The Dark Forest* (1916) presented a harsh, unromantic view of the war based on his service in an ambulance unit in Russia. The thinly fictionalized experiences of a Red Cross doctor, *Red Cross and Iron Cross* (1916), offered graphic descriptions of fighting and the most gruesome details imaginable of trench warfare. Mrs St Clair Stobart, who worked as a nurse in Serbia, also sought to deglamorize the conflict in her memoirs, *The Flaming Sword in Serbia* (1916), by emphasizing the suffering of the common soldier. At one point, she encounters a corpse on the battlefield: 'flies, flies, flies, and no one to beat them off. Only flies knew where he was. His mother was, perhaps, at this moment, picturing him as a hero, and he was – food for flies. That night, in old parlance, would have been called glorious. But is there glory on this blood-stained earth?'[92] Henri Barbusse's wildly popular *Le Feu* (1916)

became available in English in 1917 as *Under Fire*. Perhaps more effectively than any book written during the war, it depicted harrowing scenes
of death and dismemberment.

Although much information about the 'real' nature of modern warfare was available, not everyone was able to process it. It was certainly
difficult for civilians to understand things so utterly outside their own
experience and so alien to the myths they had cherished since child-
hood. As one young person from the time explained:

> War to my generation implied campaigns on the Indian frontier, in
> Egypt or South Africa. My ideas of European war were derived from
> panoramas of the Franco-Prussian conflict to be seen in continen-
> tal cities. It was the war of tradition. Cavalry charged the foe. When
> death came, it was a heroic death brought about by heroes on the
> other side.[93]

For some, this idealized image was so ingrained that no amount of graphic
reportage could dislodge it. Others clung to the old, heroic version of war
because it transfigured and hallowed the deaths of their loved ones. The
alternative version – random, unceremonious, mechanized death – was
too ghastly to contemplate. Propaganda thus constricted people's com-
prehension and imagination as much as it limited their information.

* * *

Propaganda cast a pall over the postwar world. The virulence of anti-
German atrocity stories certainly contributed to the punitive nature
of the peace settlement at Versailles that led in part to another world
war. During the 1920s, much official propaganda was exposed as false
and denounced as a betrayal of the nation. C. E. Montague's memoir,
Disenchantment (1922), detailed the distortions of the wartime press
in a chapter entitled 'Can't Believe A Word.' The invention of the
corpse-conversion story was exposed in the Commons in 1925. Arthur
Ponsonby's *Falsehood in Wartime* (1928) exposed other dishonesties,
especially with regard to atrocity propaganda. This further undermined
people's trust in government and led to an unfortunate disinclination
to believe stories about Nazi treatment of Jews during the next war,
while the actual atrocities committed by the German Army in 1914 are
now largely forgotten.

Feelings of being lied to and manipulated became more general,
especially by the late 1920s, when a spate of postwar memoirs and novels unleashed the pent-up resentments and disillusions of a decade.

Books such as Robert Graves's *Goodbye to All That* (1929) and Richard Aldington's *Death of A Hero* (1929) highlighted the contrasts between the propagandists' image of the war and the experiences of ordinary soldiers. Aldington embodied the cynicism of his generation when he concluded that responding to 'Your King and Country Need You' meant 'getting killed to further the material aims of people who manipulate those gross symbols.'[94]

Chapter 6: Art and Literature

The First World War provided a spur to cultural production on a scale unprecedented in British history. Composers, painters, dramatists, poets, and novelists all produced works inspired by the war, some of which continue to shape contemporary understanding of the conflict. The war evoked complex and powerful emotions among British writers and artists, many of whom called for a new purity in culture and a move against the 'degeneracy' of modern art. Most establishment figures promoted the war in a straightforward, patriotic manner, portraying the conflict as a just and heroic national crusade. As the war dragged on, however, doubts grew and new artistic voices, especially among poets and painters who had experienced combat firsthand, began presenting the war in a harsh and unflattering manner. This new anti-heroic stance represented a radical change in cultural sensibility.

Many of the men and women who sought to de-mythologize the Great War were part of a younger generation of artists and writers, like Robert Graves and Paul Nash, whose work still influences modern perceptions of the war. The postwar growth of artistic modernism has also led a number of cultural historians to draw connections between the war and a new, avant-garde aesthetic. These scholars have especially characterized the war as an artistic watershed which displaced an older generation of staid, establishment writers and artists and helped usher in new 'modern' forms of artistic expression.[1] Other scholars have instead emphasized continuity with the prewar art scene and the stubborn survival of heroic representations of the war.[2]

* * *

Many British writers and artists greeted the outbreak of war with enthusiasm. They hoped it would bring liberation from crass materialism, petty
political bickering, and cultural decay. For example, the young poet
Rupert Brooke rhapsodized:

> Now, God be thanked Who has matched us with His hour,
> And caught our youth, and wakened us from sleeping,
> With hand made sure, clear eye, and sharpened power,
> To turn, as swimmers into cleanness leaping . . .[3]

The distinguished critic and editor Edmund Gosse also welcomed the
war as a purifier. Shortly after hostilities began, he celebrated the war's
artistic possibilities in an essay, 'War and Literature', published in the
Edinburgh Review: 'War is the great scavenger of thought. It is the sover-
eign disinfectant, and its red stream of blood is the Condy's Fluid that
cleans out the stagnant pools and clotted channels of the intellect.'[4] For
Gosse, Brooke, and many others, there was an apocalyptic and transcen-
dental dimension to impending war.

The war inflamed British cultural insularity and led to attacks on
German art and literature. Even icons of European Romanticism like
Goethe and Beethoven were subjected to patriotic scorn. Nietzsche, in
particular, was often singled out as an invidious influence on German
culture. His works were subjected to the most facile, reductive readings
in order to make him into a Machiavellian apostle of might over right.
One London bookshop placed a sign next to Nietzsche's works urging
its customers to 'read the Devil in order to fight him better.' When the
German military shelled the cathedral at Rheims and burned the library
of the University of Louvain, these acts were presented as further proof
of 'Hunnish' insensitivity to learning and the arts:

> Religion, books, carved stone, and storied pane
>   Pleaded as vainly as the men you shot,
>   Wherefore our indignation burns red-hot
> Above the fiery ashes of Louvain.[5]

German 'Kultur' meant Nietzsche and the discordant music of Richard
Strauss. British culture, by contrast, was represented by the wisdom of
Shakespeare, and the pastoral beauty of Keats and Wordsworth. Public lectures were widely organized in 1916 to mark the 300th anniversary of the
death of Shakespeare. These commemorations were often stridently patriotic in tone, invoking the Bard as evidence of British cultural supremacy.

Another cultural aspect of propaganda consisted of sending the 'classics' of British literature and science to libraries in neutral countries. Presumably, an acquaintance with Dickens or Newton would help convince foreigners of the superiority of British civilization. Others also sought to inspire British soldiers with their nation's literary heritage. *The Times*, for instance, produced a series of patriotic broadsheets for the trenches excerpted from the works of Shakespeare, Wordsworth, Macaulay, and Kipling.[6]

The war at first encouraged artistic conservatism, the patriotic extolling of the classics, and the attacking of modernism, which came to be associated with alien, foreign influences. *The Times* reviewed a 1915 exhibit by the London Group of Futurists under the title 'Junkerism in Art.' Wartime exhibits of Continental poster art (mostly Austrian) were also condemned as 'squat, ugly, lowering and decadent.' A letter to the *Poetry Review* in October 1914 characteristically welcomed the war as an antidote to the avant-garde: 'The war will save us from the whirlpool and will bring us back to the realities of life and drive the mists away from the hills of vision. With German culture . . . will die the arrant nonsense that has passed for "high-browed" culture over here, the growing disrespect for all things sacred to simple folk, the disdain of religion and morality by those inoculated with the Nietzsche virus.' Xenophobia worked to create a conservative climate of opinion hostile to artistic innovation.[7]

Many modernists, however, also welcomed the war, hoping that it would sweep away not themselves, but a moribund, establishment culture. The abstract painter and writer Percy Wyndham Lewis condemned British art as being obsessed with nostalgia and tradition and unwilling to engage in radical transformation. He heralded the war as a cataclysmic event that would blast away cultural philistinism. Lewis had founded the artistic movement of Vorticism, which included the poet Ezra Pound and the painter Edward Wadsworth. Much influenced by the Italian Futurists, the Vorticists favored geometric abstract painting and bold free verse. The first issue of their journal *Blast* (20 June 1914) declared war on Edwardian art. One week later, Archduke Franz Ferdinand was shot at Sarajevo and the Great War began. For the cultural avant-garde as well as for artistic conservatives, the war over culture intertwined with the war of the trenches.[8]

The most famous and popular contemporary authors put their services at the disposal of the state. The propaganda chief, C. F. G. Masterman, gathered together most of Britain's leading writers for a meeting at Wellington House on 2 September 1914. Among the 24 men present were James Barrie, Arnold Bennett, G. K. Chesterton, Arthur Conan Doyle, John Galsworthy, Thomas Hardy, Gilbert Murray, H. G. Wells, and Israel Zangwill. After the meeting, Gilbert Murray drafted a statement on behalf of the group, calling upon Britain and 'all the English-speaking race' to defend the 'ideals of Western Europe against the rule of "Blood and Iron" . . .' The document was eventually signed by 52 writers and appeared in both *The Times* and the *New York Times* on 18 September 1914. Many of these writers, who now included Rudyard Kipling, Rider Haggard, May Sinclair, and Mrs Humphry Ward, were to support the war through propaganda work, both official and unofficial.[9]

Anthony Hope Hawkins, author of the swashbuckling *Prisoner of Zenda*, was appointed by Masterman as literary advisor to the War Propaganda Bureau. Almost immediately, Wells wrote the idealistic *The War that Will End War* and Chesterton, the sensational *Barbarism of Berlin*. The popular novelist Hall Caine gathered dozens of literary contributors to compile *King Albert's Book*, which was sold to benefit Belgian charities. Masterman sent Mrs Humphry Ward on a tour of the United States and persuaded her to write *England's Effort*. The War Office commissioned Arthur Conan Doyle to write an official history of the war, which appeared between 1916 and 1919. By the end of the war, the novelists John Buchan, Arnold Bennett, John Galsworthy, and H. G. Wells were all employed by the Ministry of Information.[10]

There were few voices of dissent among Britain's literary establishment. George Bernard Shaw and Thomas Hardy were almost alone in their inability to work up much enthusiasm for the war. Shaw, especially, remained aloof, publishing *Common Sense About the War* in November 1914. The pamphlet began by asserting provocatively that 'No doubt the heroic remedy for this tragic misunderstanding is that both armies should shoot their officers and go home and gather in their harvests in the villages and make a revolution in the towns.' Shaw went on to insist that Britain shared equally in the war guilt and that the Kaiser's arrogance was more than matched by that of the British ruling class, quoting Lord Roberts on 'the will to conquer which has never failed us.'[11] Hardy, too, after penning a few patriotic poems, quickly became disenchanted with the war and his poetry grew increasingly more gloomy and pessimistic. By the time of the Armistice, he wondered what it had all even been about:

> Calm fell. From Heaven distilled a clemency;
> There was peace on earth, and silence in the sky;
> Some could, some could not, shake off misery:
> The Sinister Spirit sneered: 'It had to be!'
> And again the Spirit of Pity whispered, 'Why?'[12]

Among younger writers, Francis Meynell was so disgusted by literary jingoism, especially Edmund Gosse's 'War and Literature', that he responded with 'War's a Crime' published 19 December 1914 in the

radical *Herald*: 'The lands are rotted with blood and the seas are swallowing
their dead, and the clean, sweet rivers are full of mangled corpses – amen,
amen, it is all a tonic for Mr Gosse . . .'[13] D. H. Lawrence also opposed
the war and his novel *The Rainbow* (1915) was banned as a danger to wartime morality. Married to a German, the 'red baron's' cousin Frieda von
Richthofen, Lawrence was even accused by his neighbors of being a spy
in 1917. Several of his later novels reflect bitterly on the war, especially
Kangaroo (1923), which recounted Lawrence's wartime experiences in a
chapter entitled 'The Nightmare.'[14]

* * *

Most of Britain's artistic community supported the war unreservedly
and was eager to offer its help. The nation's concert halls and theaters
responded enthusiastically to the outbreak of war. Patriotic concerts
of English, French, and Russian music were hurriedly arranged and
Britain's leading composers began producing war-related music. Sir
Edward Elgar composed *Carillon*, which set a Belgian war poem by Emile
Cammaerts to music. It became the unofficial anthem of the war, only
rivaled by Elgar's earlier hymn 'Land of Hope and Glory.' Elgar later
created works incorporating patriotic verse by Laurence Binyon and
Rudyard Kipling. Sir Charles Stanford and the poet Sir Henry Newbolt
collaborated on *Song of the Sea* and Sir Hubert Parry set William Blake's
'Jerusalem' to music as a hymn of national determination:

> I will not cease from Mental Fight,
> Nor shall my Sword sleep in my hand,
> Till we have built Jerusalem
> In England's green and pleasant Land.

Patriotic concerts were extremely popular, though not to everyone's
taste. Virginia Woolf complained of a 1915 performance that 'the patriotic sentiment was so revolting that I was nearly sick.'[15]

Anti-German feeling quickly found musical expression. The Music in
Wartime Committee was created to protect the interests of British musicians, and soon orchestras, hotels, and restaurants fired all their German
and Austrian musicians. Debates took place over the morality of performing German music. An article in the *Fortnightly Review* declared musical war:
'The hour has come to put aside and to veil with crepe the scores of the men
who have crystallized in so unmistakable a manner the spirit of the modern
Huns . . . The future belongs to the young hero who will have the courage
to exclude from his library all the works of Handel, Mendelssohn, Wagner,

Brahms, and Richard Strauss . . .' Thomas Beecham organized patriotic concerts that excluded all German music. Henry Wood's Promenade Concerts replaced their long-standing Wagner night with a Russian night. German operas, if performed at all, were sung in English.[16]

Theater managers also scurried to find something 'military' to stage. There were revivals of *Henry V* and Thomas Hardy's *The Dynasts*, which recounted Nelson's victories. Any topically appropriate lines would typically be played up so as to bring down the house, like these in Shakespeare's *King John*:

This England never did and never shall
Lie at the proud feet of a conqueror . . .

An avalanche of new war plays descended on London and provincial theaters. No fewer than 24 such plays were licensed in September and October 1914, including *England Expects, Call to Arms, God Save the Empire, Your Country Needs You*, and *Soldiers' Honour*. Most of these plays were meant to encourage recruiting, and often included interludes of military music and recitations of patriotic poems. Recruiting officers would be present in the lobby. The custom began (which continued into the 1960s) of playing the national anthem at the close of all plays and concerts.[17]

Spy plays remained the most common war-related dramas, capitalizing on anti-German sentiment. Between 1914 and 1916, 50 such plays were performed. They were mostly in the melodramatic tradition, featuring unbelievably virtuous soldier heroes and unbelievably evil German villains who were inevitably foiled in their attempts to bomb munitions factories, poison reservoirs, or steal state secrets. Belgian atrocities were frequently restaged, for, as in most melodramas, the villains revealed their depravity through the brutal treatment of women and children. Many of these dramas also featured the Kaiser, who was vilified as the embodiment of German evil. As 'William the Wicked' or 'Attila II,' he plotted the downfall of civilization, all the while prancing about the stage like a martinet and cackling with sadistic delight.[18]

There would always be an audience for patriotic pageants and spy thrillers, but most wartime plays were light-hearted, diversionary entertainments. As Shaw later explained, audiences thirsted for 'silly jokes, dances, and brainlessly sensuous exhibitions of pretty girls. The author of some of the most grimly serious plays of our time told me that after enduring the trenches for months without a glimpse of the female of his species, it gave him an entirely innocent but delightful pleasure merely to see a flapper.' The most popular show of the war was undoubtedly *Chu Chin Chow*, which ran for more than 2000 performances. It was an extravagant musical fantasy set in the Orient, featuring harem girls and comic songs.[19]

There was frequent criticism of musical reviews and comic plays by social purity crusaders, who found them an affront to wartime morality. Most famously, General Sir Horace Smith-Dorrien and his wife spoke out against what they saw as the salacious nature of much theatrical material. In 1916, the general appealed to theaters and music halls to 'place patriotism before their own interests' by 'eliminating anything that might be suggestive of vice.' Lady Smith-Dorrien suggested the ideal plays were 'pieces with pretty music, charming scenes and nothing at all to stir unworthy passions.' Others found the essential frivolity of theater at odds with wartime austerity. Neville Chamberlain, then the Director-General of National Service, argued that 'in war time amusements should be taken in moderation. And I am not sure that the sight of long queues of pleasure-seekers during the day in war time is calculated to conduce to the seriousness of spirit, that appreciation of a necessity for putting all our efforts into the struggle, which is what we want so much to impress upon the great mass of the people today.' In this spirit, an Amusement Tax was enacted in April 1916, which imposed surcharges on all theater tickets, from a half-penny for the cheapest seats to a shilling for the most expensive ones.[20]

Theaters experienced a host of practical problems, from the loss of personnel due to military conscription to the danger of air raids. Zeppelin attacks on London kept people at home, especially on dark nights when the raiders could operate with virtual impunity. Audiences shrank as the moon waned, and some theaters began advertising 'moony nights' as safe from attacks. At the Alhambra Theatre, where the popular *The Bing Boys Are Here* was playing, the management advertised: 'Come and see the Bing Boys: it is a full moon tonight so you need not fear the "Bang Boys."' Another theater advertised that its reinforced concrete roof offered 'a veritable Gibraltar of safety.' In spite of air raids and rising ticket prices, the theater flourished as it provided a much-needed distraction from wartime anxieties.[21]

Unlike novels or poetry, there was little room for dissent in the theater, as it had to appeal to the broadest possible audience and was the most heavily censored of the art forms. No play could be performed before securing a license from the Lord Chamberlain's Office, which vetted wartime dramas with special vigor. The censor forced plays to remove scenes depicting dying British soldiers or Zeppelin raids as hurtful to home front morale. Anything critical of the armed forces was also likely to be excised. In one play, the censor went so far as to object to an Indian spying for Germany as an insult to the colonials fighting for Britain. In another play, a scene with a drunken sailor had to be removed. The most subversive wartime play was probably Shaw's mildly sardonic *Augustus Does His Bit*, performed in London in 1917. The play was a comic take on a vain, incompetent aristocrat who insists on meddling in wartime affairs. At one point the Germans capture the protagonist, but immediately set him free when they realize how stupid he is. They certainly would not want to deprive Britain of such leadership! By 1917, some audiences had become receptive to this viewpoint, and the play proved especially popular with soldiers.[22]

Shaw's more serious and sustained indictment of the war and the British establishment was *Heartbreak House*, written during the war but not published or performed until 1919. The play takes place at a country house party and features an assortment of feckless representatives of Britain's elite. The characters allow civilization to fall because they lack the strength to sustain it. The collective wisdom and expertise of the nation only leads to war, and the play ends with a Zeppelin dropping bombs. Shaw realized that wartime audiences were not ready for his message: 'When men are heroically dying for their country, it is not the time to show their lovers and wives and fathers and mothers how they are being sacrificed to the blunders of boobies, the cupidity of capitalists, the ambition of conquerors, the electioneering of demagogues . . .' In other words, grim realism and satire were 'not compatible with the defense of the realm.'[23]

Another playwright dubious of the war was Allan Monkhouse, now largely forgotten, but at the time as successful and critically admired as Shaw. Monkhouse's war plays center on the ambivalence and honest doubts that thoughtful young men had about joining the fight. His one-act play *Shamed Life* (1916), for instance, depicts enlistment as necessary and inevitable, but ridicules 'talk about romance and honour and sacrifice.' *The Conquering Hero*, written during the war but not performed until 1923, was one of the earliest literary works to question the values of the war. It is a sympathetic account of a young writer who is reluctant to enlist and the abuse he endures from his own family and neighbors. Monkhouse studiously refused to glamorize the war and portrayed the most vocal patriots as strident bigots and bullies.[24]

* * *

The world of visual arts, like its theatrical and musical counterparts, also responded to the drums of war. Museums and art galleries vastly increased in attendance, and exhibits often took on a martial theme. Painters sought to demonstrate their patriotism by creating inspiring and heroic images of war. Loyalty might also include expressions of artistic xenophobia and intolerance. For example, one London gallery owner announced that 'no enemy aliens, conscientious objectors, or sympathizers with the enemy were permitted to exhibit in his galleries.' The Royal Society of British Artists expelled all members of 'foreign origin,' including many who were naturalized British citizens. In the arts as elsewhere 'Britishness' was defined in narrow, racial terms, rather than as adherence to the state and loyalty to king and empire.[25]

Patriotism, however, did not altogether shield art from charges that, in wartime, it was a costly and unnecessary luxury. For a short period in 1916, a number of public museums and art galleries were closed, both as an economic measure and a symbolic gesture about the seriousness of the war effort. An entertainment tax was later levied against art galleries as well as cinemas, circuses and music halls. The Royal Academy, indignant at being classed with such vulgar pastimes, protested that it was not an 'entertainment.' In 1918 paintings, drawings and sculptures became subject to luxury duty, as they were deemed 'wasteful and extravagant.' For some, there was no place in the war for leisure, recreation, or art. Shaw later condemned such 'war delirium' in which 'all pretense about fine art and culture and the like must be flung off as an intolerable affectation; and the picture galleries and museums and schools at once occupied by war workers.' Saner minds, for the most part, prevailed, especially as the visual arts were seen as an important element of national propaganda.[26]

The most popular and widely circulated war art depicted soldiers engaged in heroic acts of bravery – irresistible infantry attacks and cavalry charges. Grandiose battle scenes were painted by home-based artists like John Charlton, Christopher Clark, and R. Caton Woodville, based purely on their imaginations and earlier traditions of war art. An especially large number of anachronistic and unrealistic cavalry charges were painted, such as Allen Stewart's *The Charge of the Scots Greys at St Quentin* (1915) and Lucy Kemp-Welch's *Forward the Guns!* (1917). Lady Elizabeth Butler, an academic artist who had specialized in painting battle scenes since the 1870s, also brought her talents to bear on this war. She, too, favored outmoded cavalry charges, and her canvases more accurately reflected the warfare of Napoleonic Europe. These paintings evoked the thrills of war, but did not depict the stark reality of blood and dismemberment. Their influence was widely felt, as they were disseminated via illustrated magazines and postcards.[27]

Most painters, as well as magazine and newspaper illustrators, got nowhere near the front, but rather produced images based on 'information received' or on their own flights of fancy. Visual depictions in the press of the 1916 Somme offensive conveyed a false impression of order and success, depicting troops advancing rapidly, unimpeded by either barbed wire or enemy fire. These illustrations were based on artists' false assumptions that British bombardments had destroyed German resistance. As late as April 1918, *The War Illustrated* depicted a heroic cavalry charge on its cover, long after such actions had been rendered useless by modern weaponry. Most artists no doubt believed in the veracity of their images. Others recognized that a certain amount of idealization was necessary. Lady Butler, for example, cautioned that 'the painter should be careful to keep himself at a distance, lest the ignoble and vile details under his eyes should blind him irretrievably to the noble things that rise beyond.'[28] Such 'vile details' as bloody, dismembered corpses would hardly boost civilian morale.

The idealized version preferred by most artists is best exemplified in *The Great Sacrifice*, a painting by James Clark that first appeared in *The Graphic* at Christmas 1914. A dead soldier lies peacefully at the foot of a crucifix. He looks as if asleep and no blood mars his handsome appearance. Clark's work became the most popular painting of the war. The original was purchased by Queen Mary. It was reproduced extensively and hung in homes, schools and church halls across the nation. It inspired numerous sermons and its religious imagery provided consolation to the families of dead soldiers. After the war the painting was copied in memorial windows and monuments around Britain and the Empire.[29]

Victorian-style genre paintings which told a story visually, often a sentimental or inspirational one, also remained popular among British artists and the viewing public. Fred Roe's *The Foster Parent* depicts the interior of a French farmhouse, where a kilted soldier watches over a sleeping infant. F. Matania's *The Last Message* shows a dying soldier whispering into the ear of his comrade, who strains to hear every fading word. One of the best known genre painters – and a favorite of the army high command because of his romanticized style – was Richard Caton Woodville. A number of his paintings depicted blinded soldiers, such as *When Night Sets In* or *Memories*, in which a blind, convalescing soldier sits in a garden, while images of his past activities float above him – horse riding, cricket, tennis. He will never be able to do these things again. Woodville's sentimental images circulated widely on postcards, sold to benefit soldiers' benevolent funds.[30]

Not all artists found it easy to keep up this ebullient mood. The academician Charles Sims, for example, was deeply depressed by the death of his son at the Front in 1915. He had begun a painting before the war, *Clio and the Children*, which he now radically reworked. The original canvas had been an idyllic scene of the muse of history reading to a group of children in a sylvan landscape. Sims now repainted Clio in a mournful attitude, her head bowed and her parchment stained with blood, suggesting that history had been defiled by the war. By 1916, other artists

Plate 6.1   James Clark, *The Great Sacrifice* (Imperial War Museum, London)

were reflecting this darker mood in their work as the horrifying casualties of the Somme obliterated any hope of an easy or early victory. For instance, Mark Gertler's *Merry-Go-Round* depicts a group of soldiers and civilians spinning maniacally about on a carousel. The painting implied that the war was an infernal dynamo whirling out of control.[31]

Most paintings of the war were initially produced on an artist's own initiative, or as commissions for magazines or private charities. The government's preference for literary propaganda meant that it was slow to approach artists. Wellington House only began recruiting painters in 1916. The first official war artists were Muirhead Bone, sent to the front to sketch military scenes, and Francis Dodd, commissioned to paint portraits of Britain's leading military and naval figures. They were both conservative choices. Bone produced numerous drawings of soldiers playing football or at rest, and of the movement of men and equipment to and from the front lines. The effect was to give the war a calm quality, and Shaw dismissed Bone's work as 'too good to be true.'[32]

With the creation of the Department of Information in 1917, there was greater emphasis on visual propaganda, and a younger generation of war artists, many of whom had seen military service, were actively recruited. Paul Nash, C. R. W. Nevinson, and Eric Kennington were the most famous of the soldier-painters. They had all trained as artists before the war, but their careers were interrupted by frontline service as soldiers or medics. By 1917, they had each been sent home wounded, where they worked up sketches and paintings based on their experiences in the war zone. Exhibitions of their work attracted critical attention and they were recruited as war artists. Their work contrasted dramatically with the prevailing, idealized vision of the war, embracing instead the squalor of the trenches and the blighted landscapes of Flanders.

The paintings of Nevinson, Kennington, and Nash combined a savage anger at the war's destructiveness with compassion for its soldier victims. Nevinson's gritty and stark canvases made soldiers' sufferings palpable, as well as conveying the mechanized nature of modern warfare. In *La Mitrailleuse*, for instance, he shows three soldiers grimly manning a massive machine gun. A dead comrade lies nearby and barbed wire frames the horizon. Nevinson believed that 'war was now dominated by machines and that men were mere cogs in the mechanism.' Nevinson's *The Doctor* shows all the pain and suffering of wounded soldiers. Unlike earlier, sanitized paintings of military hospitals, where cheerful soldiers rest calmly, Nevinson's patients display open, bloody wounds and writhe in pain. Nevinson insisted that the war should be depicted 'without pageantry, without glory, and without the over-coloured heroic' of academic art. Kennington also sought to deglamorize army life. His painting of

The Kensingtons at Laventie depicts bedraggled and exhausted soldiers in the midst of a ruined village.[33]

The harsh quality of the young artists' work did not always meet with official approval. The Army Censor, Colonel Lee, objected to much of Nevinson's output. He suppressed *A Group of Soldiers* on the grounds that the tired, hard-faced men who the artist painted were 'not worthy of the British Army.' Nevinson responded angrily: 'I will not paint "castrated Lancelots" though I know this is how Tommies are usually represented in illustrated papers, etc. – high sounding eunuchs looking mild-eyed, unable to melt butter on their tongues and mentally and physically incapable of killing a German. I refuse to insult the British Army with such sentimental bilge.' Nevinson was later forbidden to exhibit *Paths of Glory*, since it depicted the taboo subject of dead British soldiers. Nevinson defiantly included the painting in a show, covering it with a paper banner marked 'CENSORED.' Kennington's work was sometimes too graphic for the censor as well. When his sketch of soldiers delousing was suppressed, he replied: 'I see you have cut the lice . . . It is *staggering*. Tommy endures the persistent torture and his mother and sister must not think of the "disgusting little things."'[34]

Paul Nash's experience at the front also transformed him into an angry opponent of the war's futility. In a letter to his wife, he reflected on the horrors of the war and on his own mission as an artist:

> Evil and the incarnate fiend alone can be master of this war, and no glimmer of God's hand is seen anywhere. Sunset and sunrise are blasphemous, they are mockeries to man, only the black rain out of the bruised and swollen clouds all through the bitter black of the night is fit atmosphere in such a land. The rain drives on, the stinking mud becomes evilly yellow, the shell holes fill up with green-white water, the roads and tracks are covered in inches of slime, the black dying trees ooze and sweat and the shells never cease . . . It is unspeakable, godless, hopeless. I am no longer an artist interested and curious, I am a messenger who will bring back word from the men who are fighting to those who want the war to go on for ever. Feeble, inarticulate, will be my message, but it will have a bitter truth, and may it burn their lousy souls.[35]

Nash's letter could well serve as a description of several of his paintings. *Void*, *The Menin Road*, and the ironically titled *We are Making a New World* all depict blighted landscapes of shell holes, blasted tree trunks, barbed-wire entanglements, and stagnant pools of filthy water. Nash saw little hope for a humanity who could so savagely destroy the natural world.

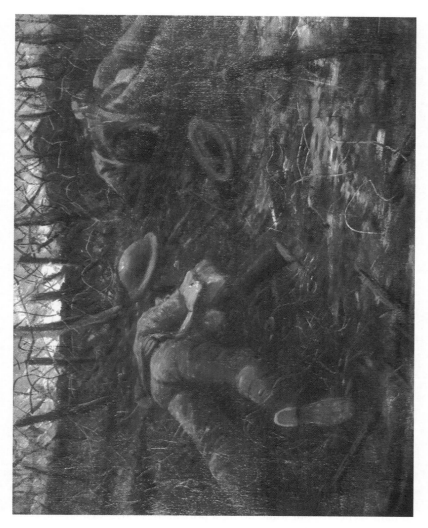

Plate 6.2   C. R. W. Nevinson, *Paths of Glory* (Imperial War Museum, London)

In 1918, the new Minister of Information, Lord Beaverbrook, set up the British War Memorials Committee to promote a more aggressive accumulation of artwork based on the war. The Committee compiled lists of subjects they wanted painted and found artists to do the work. They greatly expanded the circle of war artists, most notably including John Singer

Plate 6.3   Paul Nash, *The Menin Road* (Imperial War Museum, London)

Sargent, a painter of international renown. Sargent was eager to participate, but found it extremely difficult to capture modern warfare artisti-
cally: 'How can there be anything flagrant enough for a picture when
Mars and Venus are miles apart whether in camps or front trenches. And
the farther forward one goes the more scattered and meagre everything
is. The nearer to danger the fewer and the more hidden the men – the
more dramatic the situation the more it becomes an empty landscape.'
Sargent was later moved by a scene of hundreds of victims of a mustard
gas attack suffering from temporary blindness. The resulting panoramic
painting, *Gassed*, depicts medical orderlies leading long lines of blinded
soldiers off the battlefield. It proved one of the most famous and popular
of all war paintings.[36]

Another established artist, the Irish society painter William Orpen, was
transformed by his experience as a War Artist. He was initially tapped
to paint generals, but while doing a portrait of Douglas Haig, the commander told him: 'Why are you wasting your time painting me? Go and
paint the men.' Thereafter Orpen wandered about behind the lines, drawing soldiers and the battle scared landscape. His work highlighted 'the
human frailty and vulnerability' of the men and often included images of
dead and wounded soldiers. Art critics and the press disliked Orpen's war
art, which they found harsh and irreverent, but soldiers loved it.[37]

Orpen and Sargent were among the few Royal Academy types included
in the expanded War Artists scheme. Most were outsiders to the art establishment and a number of them were bold choices indeed. Joining the

expressionist Nash and cubist-influenced Nevinson were the Vorticist Wyndham Lewis, the Fauvist John Duncan Ferguson, and other 'moderns' like Stanley Spencer and Bernard Adeney. At least one art critic applauded the choice of modern and abstract painters, arguing that 'the explosive style of the Futurists is eminently suited to the character of modern warfare.'[38] The Ministry of Information's artistic advisors were receptive to innovation and agreed that the war lent itself to the abstractions of modern art. Only the unreal colors of Nash's landscapes could convey the bizarre nature of frontline destruction. The geometric distortions of cubism and futurism likewise lent themselves to an industrialized warfare that seemed to transform men into machines. In a number of paintings by Nevinson and Wyndham Lewis, soldiers appear to be more robotic than human. According to Samuel Hynes, 'a modernist method that before the war had seemed violent and distorting was seen to be realistic on the Western Front. Modernism had not changed, but reality had.'[39]

Connections between camouflage and abstract art seemed obvious as well. In 1917, the Naval Commander Norman Wilkinson devised the 'dazzle' camouflage technique of painting ships with vibrant geometric patterns in sharply contrasting colors, making it difficult to determine their size and direction when seen through a periscope. They resembled nothing so much as large cubist paintings. Appropriately enough, most of Britain's 'dazzled' ships were supervised by the Vorticist painter Edward Wadsworth, who conceived especially wild and explosive zig-zag patterns for them.[40]

Not everyone appreciated or understood the efforts of the modernist war painters. The military censor, for one, hardly knew what to make of Nash's bold, abstract works: 'I cannot help thinking that Nash is having a huge joke with the British public, and lovers of "art" in particular.' Exhibits in 1918 of official war art also drew attacks from the popular press, mostly directed at the cubist-inspired works of Wyndham Lewis, William Roberts, and David Bomberg. In some accounts, their avant-garde canvases were equated with subversion. One paper referred to 'Bolshevism in Art', and another thought the paintings should be labeled 'Made in Germany.' To many Britons the anti-heroic images were unacceptable. Questions were even asked in Parliament about 'freak' pictures in public galleries and the government expenditure on them.[41]

* * *

The First World War is probably remembered through its poetry more than any other medium. Amateur patriotic verse filled the newspapers and magazines of the day. Thousands of volumes of poetry were published over the course of the war and were avidly read by millions. For the first time in history, numerous soldier-poets wrote about their own experiences of battle. The history of this war poetry in particular became emblematic of the nation's evolving attitude toward the war, early enthusiasm giving way to disenchantment and disillusion. As a popular saying of the time explained, 'I went to war with Rupert Brooke and came home with Siegfried Sassoon.'[42]

At the outbreak of war, newspapers across the country were deluged with amateur verse on patriotic themes. *The Times* alone estimated that it received as many as 100 such poems a day in the Autumn of 1914. Well-known writers also offered up their poems in the hopes of inspiring the nation. Kipling's 'For All We Have and Are' especially captured the mood of urgency and commitment:

> For all we have and are,
> For all our children's fate,
> Stand up and meet the war.
> The Hun is at the gate!
> . . .
> There is but one task for all –
> For each one life to give.
> Who stands if Freedom fall?
> Who dies if England live?[43]

Poetry remained a staple of wartime literature, allowing people to express their deepest emotions in an especially decorous manner. The presumed sanctity of the war apparently called for an unusual and 'elevated' mode of discourse.

The great mass of war poetry was patriotic doggerel and most of it has long since been forgotten. A typical collection of such verse, *Songs and Sonnets for England in War Time* (1914), included poems such as 'To "Little" Belgium' by Coulson Kernahan:

> That 'little' but loyal race whom, near and far,
>   A world acclaims for glorious, deathless deed,
>   Rather than fail GREAT Belgium in her need,
> Rather than this, in God's own name, be war![44]

The war's most popular poet was probably John Oxenham, whose writings brimmed with optimism and a belief in the war's religious mission:

> As sure as God's in His Heaven,
> As sure as He stands for Right,

As sure as the Hun this wrong hath done,
So surely we win this fight![45]

Britain's poet laureate, Robert Bridges, also dutifully churned out tur-
gid patriotic verse, such as his ode to 'Lord Kitchener': 'Unflinching
hero, watchful to foresee/ And face thy country's peril wheresoe'er,/
Directing war and peace with equal care . . .'[46] Much war poetry followed
the conventions of Georgian poetry in which rural subjects and pastoral
imagery predominated. In the popular anthology, *Poems of To-Day* (1915),
nearly a third of the poems are celebrations of England and the English
landscape for which the nation fought.[47]

The war's first literary celebrity was the soldier-poet Rupert Brooke.
His sonnet cycle, *1914*, crystallized the early idealism of the war, celebrat-
ing the sacrifice of young men who 'poured out the red/ Sweet wine
of youth.' Brooke's poetry was given wide circulation when the dean of
St Paul's Cathedral in London quoted 'The Soldier' while preaching on
Easter 1915:

If I should die, think only this of me:
    That there's some corner of a foreign field
That is forever England. There shall be
    In that rich earth a richer dust concealed . . .[48]

The poem was reprinted in *The Times*, and shortly thereafter Brooke died
in the Aegean, where he had been sent to fight the Turks. His early death
granted him the status of a national martyr, and he remained a focal
point of Britain's ideals and aspirations. Winston Churchill eulogized
him as 'all that one could wish England's noblest sons to be in days when
no sacrifice but the most precious is acceptable, and the most precious
is that which is most freely proffered.' Brooke's *1914 and Other Poems* was
published in June 1915, and over the next decade this and his *Collected
Poems* sold 300 000 copies.[49]

Brooke was but the first and most famous of countless war poets.
Julian Grenfell also died early in the war and also idealized the conflict
in poems such as 'Into Battle':

The fighting man shall from the sun
    Take warmth, and life from the glowing earth;
Speed with the light-foot winds to run,
    And with the trees to newer birth;
And find, when fighting shall be done
    Great rest, and fullness after dearth.[50]

Other less-talented poets were inspired to follow the example of Brooke and Grenfell. One troop journal even joked that 'an insidious disease is affecting the Division, and the result is a hurricane of poetry. Subalterns have been seen with a notebook in one hand, and bombs in the other absently walking near the wire in deep communion with the muse.' Richard Aldington later condemned the 'vogue for "war poets," which resulted in the parents of the slain being asked to put up fifty pounds for the publication (which probably cost fifteen) of poor little verses which should never have passed the home circle.'[51]

Among the first soldier-poets who refused to idealize the war was Charles Hamilton Sorley. He was sickened by the outpouring of patriotic literature, and criticized Brooke as 'far too obsessed with his own sacrifice . . . whereas it is merely the conduct demanded of him (and others) by the turn of circumstances . . .' Sorley saw the war as tragedy and refused to adopt conventional patriotic rhetoric. In his sonnet 'To Germany', he expressed pity for the enemy as fellow sufferers:

> You are blind like us. Your hurt no man designed,
> And no man claimed the conquest of your land.
> But gropers both through fields of thought confined
> We stumble and we do not understand.[52]

By 1916, in the face of the continuing slaughter on the Western Front, most soldiers found Brooke's idealism difficult to sustain. Their poems increasingly presented the war in a harsh and unglamorous light, as in Arthur Graeme West's 'The Night Patrol':

> Only the dead were always present – present
> As a vile sickly smell of rottenness;
> The rustling stubble and the early grass,
> The slimy pools – the dead men stank through all . . .

West even wrote a savage poetic rejoinder, 'God! How I Hate You, You Young Cheerful Men!', to those soldier-poets who persisted in exulting in war in the manner of Brooke or Grenfell.[53]

Among a growing number of anti-war poets were Siegfried Sassoon, Robert Graves, Isaac Rosenberg, Gilbert Frankau, and Wilfred Owen. According to Frankau, they sought to strip 'The glamour from this outrage we call war,/ Shewing it naked, hideous, stupid, vile –/ One vast abomination.'[54] They wrote graphically of the conditions at the front – the cold, the mud, the rats and lice, and they wrote of the tragedy and waste of so many young men dying for an uncertain cause. In 'Dead Man's Dump', Isaac Rosenberg describes an apocalyptic scene of battlefield carnage:

> The wheels lurched over sprawled dead
> But pained them not, though their bones crunched,
> Their shut mouths made no moan.
> They lie there huddled, friend and foeman,
> Man born of man, and born of woman,
> And shells go crying over them
> From night till night and now.[55]

The awful suffering of ordinary soldiers seemed especially obscene when set against the hollow clichés of patriotic propaganda.

At the time, Siegfried Sassoon was the most widely read of the anti-war poets; his work appeared in the *Nation*, the *Cambridge Magazine*, and two wartime collections, *The Old Huntsman* (1917) and *Counter-Attack* (1918). Sassoon wanted to use his poetry to impress upon civilians the awful realities of war. For example, in 'They' he sardonically contrasted the brutal consequences of war with its facile patriotic rhetoric. In the poem, a bishop addresses a group of soldiers, assuring them that 'they will not be the same' for having fought in a holy war. The soldiers reply that they are indeed changed: 'For George lost both his legs; and Bill's stone blind;/ Poor Jim's shot through the lungs and like to die;/ And Bert's gone syphilitic . . .'[56] In July 1917, Sassoon published a protest against the war in Sylvia Pankhurst's paper, *The Workers' Dreadnought*: 'I have seen and endured the sufferings of the troops, and I can no longer be a party to prolong these sufferings for ends which I believe to be evil and unjust . . . I believe that I may help to destroy the callous complacence with which the majority of those at home regard the continuance of agonies which they do not share, and which they have not sufficient imagination to realize.'[57] Rather than court-martialing him, the military authorities decided that Sassoon was suffering from 'shell-shock', and they sent him to a mental hospital in Scotland. While there, he met another soldier-poet, Wilfred Owen, and encouraged him in his own assault on the war's hypocrisy.

While the anti-war poets developed new modes of expression based on their experience of trench warfare, most civilians continued to uphold traditional attitudes and to write patriotic verse. Christian sacrificial symbolism remained popular on the homefront, as in Lucy

Whitmell's 'Christ in Flanders' or Muriel Stuart's 'Forgotten Dead,
I Salute You':

> There was his body broken for you,
> There was his blood divinely shed...[58]

Poems like this tended to anger soldiers, who believed the religious language merely served to mask the awful reality of the trenches. Especially
galling were hectoring appeals by civilians who knew nothing of the horrors of the war and who were in no danger of being sent themselves. Jessie
Pope's 'The Call' is typical:

> Who's for the trench –
>   Are you, my laddie?
> Who'll follow French –
>   Will you, my laddie?
> Who's fretting to begin,
> Who's going out to win?
> And who wants to save his skin –
> Do you, my laddie?[59]

Many of the poems of Sassoon and Owen expressed their anger at civilians, especially the jingoists and the 'old men' of the Church and government who sent the young men to their deaths. Sassoon mocked the
'smug-faced crowds' who 'cheer when soldier lads march by.'[60] Owen's
'Dulce et Decorum Est,' originally and sarcastically dedicated 'to Jessie
Pope', invites patriotic civilians to imagine a dying soldier being trans-
ported from the battlefield:

> If you could hear, at every jolt, the blood
> Come gurgling from the froth-corrupted lungs,
> Obscene as cancer, bitter as the cud
> Of vile, incurable sores on innocent tongues, –
> My friend, you would not tell with such high zest
> To children ardent for some desperate glory,
> The old Lie: Dulce et decorum est
> Pro patria mori.[61]

The anti-war poets hoped to shock the home front out of its complacency
by smashing patriotic clichés and exposing the war in all its raw savagery.
   The chasm between soldier and civilian poets had grown wide, but
was not unbridgeable. Some poets like Thomas Hardy and Edith Sitwell

articulated feelings of grief and pity about the war, eschewing heroic language altogether. Others like Helen Hamilton condemned warmongers as ghouls 'Who gloat with dulled old eyes,/ Over those lists,/ Those dreadful lists/ Of young men dead.'[62] Mary Borden also wrote graphically about war's physical brutality, as in her 'Unidentified,' where an exploding shell renders a soldier's face 'a mass of matter, horrid slime/ and little splinters.'[63] Borden's work has more in common with that of Wilfred Owen than with Jessie Pope's work, and vitiates any absolute division between the poetry of civilians and soldiers.

The poetry of disillusionment remains the best-remembered body of work written during the war, though it was hardly representative of the whole. G. S. Streets' 1918 survey of wartime poetry remarked how upbeat it all was, with the exception of Sassoon, whom he dismisses as 'not of English blood.'[64] John Oxenham and Jessie Pope were widely read; Isaac Rosenberg and Wilfred Owen barely at all. The anti-war poets were little published during the war, or even immediately afterwards. Rupert Brooke continued to outsell them all. Only in the late 1920s, when there was a critical re-examination of the war, did the soldier-poets of protest find an appreciative audience. The anti-war movement of the 1960s added to their popularity and Paul Fussell's *The Great War and Modern Memory* (1975) enshrined the notion, now much challenged, that the soldier-poets embodied the most authentic vision of the war.

* * *

Apart from formulaic stories of adventure and romance, most mainstream wartime fiction concerned the lives of ordinary Britons and their efforts to understand the war and to find an appropriate place for themselves in it. A vast number of sentimental 'home front novels' celebrated quiet domestic virtues or depicted the war as revitalizing a selfish, decadent society by replacing materialism with spiritual values. Such novels often portrayed the war as a 'social revolution', transforming all levels of British society which were united in serving King and Country.

One of the most popular novels of the war was Wilfred Meynell's *Aunt Sarah and the War: A Tale of Transformations* (1914), which followed the lives of Aunt Sarah, her nephew at the front, and her niece in training for the Red Cross. At first Aunt Sarah views the war as an inconvenience in her comfortable life, and she complains about shortages of food and servants who enlist. Eventually, however, she is swept up in the patriotic fervor, converting her house into a hospital and devoting her time to nursing the wounded. Howard Keble's *The Smiths in War Time* (1917) was another idealized novel of home front life, intended to cultivate support for the war. Mr and Mrs Smith, a middle-class couple in their seventies, make a determined effort to economize; they rent out their villa and take a small cottage for the duration, release their maid for war work, and observe meatless days. As in much of this genre, there is little reference to the front; a grandson is reported missing in action, but is later found safe.

Many home front novels were written by women, as they usually detailed the war's impact on domestic life and those left behind. Annie Jameson's *War-Time in Our Street* (1917) focused on a group of neighborhood women, offering a series of upbeat, cheerful tales full of resilience and hope. Jameson's later *The Silent Legion* (1918) celebrated the 'heroes of the home front,' especially the women who sacrificed their health and happiness for the welfare of others. During the war, the Simpson family lose their business and their only son. Mrs Simpson's health fails, and her daughter, Barbara, gives up nursing wounded soldiers to care for her mother. Mrs Simpson, however, refuses her daughter's help, realizing that her own life is less important than the nation's cause. Women's nurturing qualities were a staple of wartime novels, in none more so than in Margaret Sherwood's *The Worn Doorstep* (1917). The book was written as a series of letters from the heroine to her dead soldier sweetheart detailing her benevolence to stray animals, Belgian refugees, and war orphans.

Much wartime literature was concerned with scenes of rural England, even though only 20 percent of the population still lived in the countryside. For many Britons, village life seemed to embody the more wholesome, communal values that were especially prized in wartime. Agnes Castle's *Little House in Wartime* (1915) presented an idealized, sentimental picture of family life in a Surrey village. Sheila Kaye-Smith's *Little England* (1918) was set among a Sussex farming community and depicted the inhabitants' deep love of the land, which inspires them to great sacrifices: 'They had died for a little corner of ground which was England to them, and the sprinkling of poor, common folk who lived in it. Before their dying eyes had risen not the vision of England's glory, but just these fields, with the ponds and the woods and the red roofs.'[65]

Most home front fiction shied away from stories of the atrocities and horrors of war, preferring to present tales of quiet fortitude and perseverance. Not so Rudyard Kipling's 'Mary Postgate', an especially violent and xenophobic story. The title character, a stereotypical mild-mannered spinster, finds that the war 'did not stay decently outside England and in the newspapers, but intruded on the lives of people whom she knew.' A bomb drops on her village and kills a young girl. Later, Mary finds a badly wounded German pilot in her back garden.

Rather than assisting him, she grimly stands by, ignoring his pleas for help, and watches him die. When his death rattle begins: 'She leaned forward and listened, smiling. There could be no mistake. She closed her eyes and drank it in.'[66] The pain and anguish of women on the home front was also the subject of Mrs Humphry Ward's *Missing* (1917), which centers on a young bride's collapse when she learns her husband is missing in action.

Most of the novels and short stories written during the war have been forgotten by critics and readers alike. They entertained contemporaries, but offered few profound insights about the war, preferring to depict it in predictable and patriotic ways. Notable exceptions include the wartime fiction of H. G. Wells and May Sinclair, and a small body of anti-war novels. Wells's initial enthusiasm for 'a war to end war' had become more difficult to sustain by 1916, when he wrote *Mr Britling Sees It Through*, one of the most popular and critically acclaimed novels of the war. The book detailed the effects of the war on a middle-class family, especially its head, a thinly disguised version of Wells himself. Their comfortable existence is shattered. Mr Britling's aunt is killed in a Zeppelin raid and his eldest son dies in the trenches. Britain's initial unpreparedness is also dramatized, as are the ineptitudes of politicians and the military. Wells maintains faith in Britain's cause, but moves beyond narrow patriotism and anti-German prejudice. Mr Britling points out that German atrocities in Belgium had their counterpart in British colonial warfare. And yet, despite doubts and criticisms, the novel maintains a stubborn hope for a better world. Mr Britling pieces together a higher purpose for the war, and hence 'sees it through' in a future vision of international cooperation and permanent peace.

May Sinclair, a suffragist and well-regarded novelist, served briefly in an ambulance unit in 1914. Like Wells, she struggled to reconcile the cataclysmic nature of the war with her political progressivism and a desire for a better world. In an early wartime story, 'Red Tape', she celebrates the war's potential for breaking down class barriers and rescuing people from narrow, self-centered lives. A middle-aged man and woman who work at a charitable organization are swept up in the excitement of war: 'It made them do things, vehement and orgiastic things, that they had never done before. It drove them forth together at six o'clock into England's Bohemia. It compelled them to dine together feverishly, in a low restaurant in Soho. It flung them out under the lamplight on to the surge of the crowd in Trafalgar square.' Yet the 50-year-old Sinclair also expresses how useless the old felt. Her protagonists, Mr Starkey and Miss Delacheroy, eagerly take first-aid classes and offer their services to the War Office, only to be informed that 'they won't look at you if you're over forty.'[67] Sinclair's later novel, *The Tree of Heaven* (1917), traces the war's shattering impact on the progressive Harrison family, whose members at first resist being swept up in the vortex of mass patriotism. Eventually, they all embrace the war as a means of constructing a selfless community, although it costs several of them their lives. Sinclair, like Wells, endorses the war in her fiction, but utterly rejects the jingoism of much wartime writing and engages in candid criticism of British society and its wartime leaders.[68]

A few war novels rejected the legitimacy of the conflict altogether or else maintained a very wide critical distance from it. Anti-war fiction never achieved the popularity of the patriotic novels, though by 1916, as casualties mounted and war weariness set in, it could no longer be dismissed as the work of cranks or traitors. In 1916, the Quaker Theodora Wilson wrote *The Last Weapon* as a Christian pacifist allegory about a battle between Love and Fear. After much struggle, Christ's love is held out as a more powerful weapon than all the deadly arsenals of the belligerent nations. Mary Hamilton's *Dead Yesterday* (1916) and Rose Macaulay's *Non-Combatants and Others* (1916) both featured sympathetic and charismatic heroines who were peace activists. Macaulay ridiculed the notion that war was glamorous or thrilling, and Hamilton emphasized the socialist argument that money spent on war and armaments prevented meaningful social reform.

Criticism of the war was sometimes masked as fantasy, as in Arthur Machen's novel *The Terror* (1917). In rural Wales, munitions workers, miners, and farmers begin to die in mysterious, violent ways. German treachery is suspected until it is discovered that the 'terror' is due to animals rising against their human overlords. The war has reduced people to the level of beasts and the spirit of this brutality has cast a spell on the animals. In a similar vein, John Snaith's fantasy *The Coming* (1917) critiques the war through the device of 'Christ' living in wartime Britain. John Smith, a village carpenter, incites suspicion and mistrust among his neighbors since he won't join the army and doesn't attend church. The pompous vicar is so appalled that Smith hears inner voices that he has him committed to an asylum. Snaith clearly saw wartime standards of patriotism as fundamentally un-Christian.

Anti-war fiction was never common, though its very existence is testimony to the determination of certain writers and publishers. It also suggests a somewhat greater climate of artistic freedom in Britain than is often acknowledged by historians of the war. Censorship of novels certainly existed, but was never as great as that of newspapers or plays, since the government realized that the readership of 'serious' books was rather limited. A few select prosecutions, such as that of Allatini's

Despised and Rejected, put publishers on their guard and discouraged them from releasing anything too controversial. Access to anti-war fiction was further hindered by the refusal of many bookstores and libraries to have it on their shelves.

* * *

A number of war-related artistic and literary developments seemed to signal a cultural shift, in particular a greater receptivity to modernism – a self-consciously radical sensibility that rejected the certainties of reason and science. Seen through the lens of modernism, truth was not absolute, but ever-changing and open to a multitude of interpretations. In painting, this gave rise to abstraction and multi-perspectivism, whereby there no longer existed a single point around which a canvas was organized. In literature, this meant that stories could be narrated by multiple voices, with none given privilege or omniscience. In music, the rules of scale and harmony were abandoned in favor of discordant energy and passion. Artistic modernism experienced its first flowering in the decade before the war, though primarily on the Continent, where Picasso, Stravinsky, and Kafka had made their mark. The British artistic establishment was aware of these innovations, but regarded them with contempt and derision, believing them to be unmistakable signs of decadence and degeneration.

The war, however, produced a major rift between literary generations. After the war, the 'old men' (and women) of the literary establishment, Bennett, Barrie, Galsworthy, Mrs Humphry Ward, were seen as fatally compromised by their support for the war, as well as hopelessly old-fashioned in outlook. The 'civilization' for which men had died, was a sham – 'an old bitch gone in the teeth,' in the provocative words of Ezra Pound.[69] A younger generation of writers – Virginia Woolf, T. S. Eliot, D. H. Lawrence, Wyndham Lewis – saw the war through a darker lens. That they also promoted bold, new literary styles suggests that the war had acted as a catalyst of the modernist movement.

British modernism certainly took off during the war. Official sponsorship of abstract and cubist painters such as Paul Nash, Christopher Nevinson, and Stanley Spencer gave modern art wider exposure. James Joyce began *Ulysses* in 1914, and modernist literary journals began to spring up – *Wheels* in 1916, *Arts and Letters* in 1917, and *New Paths* in 1918. They published writers like T. S. Eliot, Edith Sitwell, and Aldous Huxley, who were to dominate the postwar literary scene. Milestones of literary modernism started to appear. In 1916, the author known as H. D. published *Sea Garden*, a collection of poetry full of allusions to the war.

In 1917, Eliot published *Prufrock and Other Observations*, and Ezra Pound *Homage to Sextus Propertius*, in which the corruption of the British Empire is compared to that of ancient Rome. After the war, the soldier-poet Herbert Read published *Naked Warriors* (1919), which employed avant-garde literary techniques such as free verse, disjointed images, and non-linear narratives to advance a chaotic vision of the war. Eliot's *The Waste Land* (1922) revolutionized modern poetry while invoking dark memories of the war through its images of rats, dead men, blasted landscapes, and ruins.[70] Virginia Woolf's novels of the 1920s – *Jacob's Room* (1922), *Mrs Dalloway* (1925), *To the Lighthouse* (1927) – form a kind of modernist war trilogy. As works of literary modernism, Woolf's novels are more concerned with displaying the fragmented contents of people's consciousnesses than with recounting a story. Yet the war continually intrudes into the narrative in oblique and impressionistic ways. Woolf especially explores the false values that produced the conflict, and illustrates the devastation the war wrought in individual lives. In *Mrs Dalloway*, a young victim of shell-shock commits suicide rather than submit to the cruel treatment of the medical establishment. Perhaps the most remarkable modernist meditation on the war is David Jones's *In Parenthesis*, written between 1928 and 1937. Jones, an ex-soldier, ignores traditional literary conventions by constructing a fractured pastiche of poetry and prose, memoir and myth. The work follows a Welsh private, John Ball, through the Flanders' trenches, superimposing on his story snatches of ancient Welsh legends.

The extent to which the war represents a modernist watershed remains controversial. Some scholars have argued that the war heralded a modern age in the arts, characterized by cynicism, relativism, and despair. Paul Fussell, the best-known exponent of this view, depicted the war as a cultural watershed in his influential study *The Great War and Modern Memory* (1975). Fussell argued that writers created a new paradigm – an ironic mode of expression – that displaced earlier romanticized and elevated ways of representing warfare. The disillusioning experience of war undermined traditional sources of cultural identity and stimulated a literary and artistic revolution. Modernists like Eliot, Woolf, and Lawrence all presented 'recent history as discontinuous and fragmented, civilization as ruined, the past as lost.'[71] But other scholars, such as Jay Winter, have pointed out the stubborn survival in Britain of artistic and literary conservatism.[72] Winter argues that the modernist thesis rests too heavily on a small group of avant-garde figures who, at the time, were neither widely known nor representative of their artistic peers. Much popular art and literature continued along traditional paths laid out long before the war.

Of course, the rise of new cultural forms does not preclude the persistence of older ones. Some intellectuals and middle-class Britons, especially among the younger generation, embraced new artistic and literary styles, while others, especially among 'the masses', remained blissfully ignorant of these new developments, or else met them with derision or blank incomprehension. Avant-garde art and literature made little impression on popular culture.

Chapter 7: Popular Culture

As the previous chapter has demonstrated, a great deal of attention, scholarly and otherwise, has been devoted to studying artists' and intellectuals' reactions to the war, especially to those of persons who challenged heroic representations of the conflict. This emphasis represents a long-standing elite bias on the part of historians and literary critics which has only recently been challenged by studies of popular culture. This is not to deny the importance and influence of such figures as Robert Graves, Wilfred Owen, H. G. Wells, Paul Nash, and Virginia Woolf, but to point out that they do not comprise the whole picture, and, in many ways, they are far from representative of it. Their poems, novels, and paintings were known to a small minority of Britons, and, in some cases, their work only achieved recognition years after the war. Most people viewed the conflict through the lens of popular culture: music hall reviews, films, postcards, cartoons, adventure stories, and sporting contests. The profound and pervasive influence of the war was also felt in commercial culture and advertising. All manner of consumer goods promoted the war while at the same time using it to sell their merchandise. The popularity of war toys and war literature for children suggests an especially high degree of socialization amounting to a veritable 'militarization of culture.'

Popular culture tended to be even more uncritical, jingoistic, and patriotic in its attitudes toward the war than was elite culture, and it kept alive heroic representations of the war long after they had lost favor elsewhere. Among the popular arts, there were no protests against the war, and no sympathy for pacifism. The notable exception to this rule was among soldiers, who developed a distinct and rich culture of their own. The popular culture of soldiers differed markedly from that of civilians in its more skeptical and fatalistic attitudes toward the war. Soldiers created their own satirical trench magazines and composed their own songs that often mocked or subverted the patriotic culture of the home front.

* * *

Critically acclaimed novelists like Arnold Bennett, H. G. Wells, and May Sinclair were by no means the most widely read authors in wartime Britain. Among civilians and soldiers alike, the most frequently requested books in shops and libraries were adventure tales and detective stories. Sensational paperback 'penny novelettes' printed on cheap paper were the mainstay of the mass-market book trade. The adventure genre was particularly well suited to adopting the war as a literary theme. A reviewer in *The Times Literary Supplement* pointed out in 1916 that 'war has become as much the stock-in-trade of the novelist as are treasure islands, pirate schooners, or the Great North road.'[1] Mrs Humphry Ward understood the wartime appeal of sensational fiction, even as she was unable to fill the need herself: 'Novels have a special function nowadays – when one sees the great demand for them as *délassement* and refreshment. I wish with all my heart that I could write a detective – or mystery – novel! That is what the wounded and the tired love.'[2] The Library Fund, which collected thousands of books for military camps, hospitals, and ships, found that the men's favorite authors were Nat Gould, Jack London, Rudyard Kipling, William LeQueux, Ian Hay, and Robert Louis Stevenson, all of whom were associated with adventure and suspense writing.[3] Thousands of rousing, yet formulaic, war books were churned out to meet popular demand. A typical example was S. Nevile Foster's *Plain Tales from the War*, a collection of inspiring 'true life' stories illustrative 'of hardships bravely endured, of wounds honourably won, of danger met with a smile, of death received as a friend, which must quicken the pulse of every Briton.' The cover illustration shows a young officer mounting a barricade and rallying his troops to follow him into battle.[4]

The most popular novelist of the war was undoubtedly Nat Gould, now all but forgotten. He specialized in thrilling adventure stories, often centered on the world of sport and racing. He simply grafted the war on to his usual plotlines, as in *The Rider in Khaki* (1917), the story of Alan Chesney, who survives a dangerous battle, returning home just in time to win a prominent horse race. Another popular adventure novelist, Escott Lynn, wrote several action-packed war novels such as *In Khaki for the King* (1915), *Knights of the Air* (1918), and *Tommy of the Tanks* (1919). Cyril McNeile, a professional soldier in the Royal Engineers, enjoyed great success with adventure stories he published under the pseudonym 'Sapper', including *Men, Women and Guns* (1916), *No Man's Land* (1917), and *The Human Touch* (1918). After the war McNeile scored again with his 'Bull-Dog Drummond' novels, 'the adventures of a demobilized officer who found peace dull.'

A number of war novels sought to dramatize Kitchener's New Army for the home front reading public. Of these books, Ian Hay's *The First Hundred Thousand* (1915) proved phenomenally successful and remained one of the war's biggest sellers. Hay, in reality Captain John Hay Beith of the 10th Argyll and Sutherland Highlanders, supposedly based the novel on his own wartime experience. If so, one would be hard-pressed to find a work more at odds with the later, less heroic accounts of Robert Graves or Siegfried Sassoon. *The First Hundred Thousand* is a deeply conservative, patriotic book, which celebrates the reactionary politics of certain Scottish and Ulster Protestant soldiers, such as Major Wagstaffe, who praises the war for destroying 'all the small nuisances of peace-time' like Suffragettes, Bernard Shaw, and Liberal politics.[5] Hay's 'true life' stories, like those of his many imitators – A. Neil Lyons, *Kitchener Chaps* (1916), Boyd Cable, *Between the Lines* (1917) – were mixtures of patriotism and light-hearted optimism which sought to reassure the folks at home by not painting too gloomy a picture of the front.

In adventure novels, the war frequently becomes an arena in which men can prove their manhood and win the love of women. For example, John Joy Bell's *Cupid in Oilskins* (1916) tells the story of a naval gunner who must sink a German submarine in order to be worthy of his sweetheart. St John Ervine's *Changing Winds* (1917) follows the adventures of four Irishmen, three of whom enlist in the British Army and die at the front. The fourth, Henry Quinn, is prevented by fear from volunteering, earning him the contempt of his fiancée Mary. Later, he is caught in the middle of the Easter Rising, where he discovers untapped reserves of courage. Having found his manhood, he then enlists in the Army and is reconciled with Mary. Adventure novelists not only used the war to make men out of cowards and weaklings, but also showed how wastrels could redeem themselves by dedication to a noble cause. In Clemence Dane's *First the Blade* (1918), the war transforms Justin Cloud, a frivolous upper-class snob whose only prior concern had been collecting birds' eggs. Justin goes off to the front and at last finds real meaning in his life.

Spy novels were among the most widely read of the war's popular fiction. The masters of this genre were E. Phillips Oppenheim and William Trufnell LeQueux, both of whose output was prodigious. Typical examples of their work include Oppenheim's *The Double Traitor* (1915), in which a young British diplomat discovers a list of German spies in England, and LeQueux's *The German Spy* (1914), in which the hero, Rupert Manton, infiltrates and exposes a spy ring, resulting in the arrests of hundreds of

German agents. LeQueux's obsession with spies was not confined to his best-selling novels. He helped fan the flames of wartime spy hysteria with his non-fiction book *German Spies in England* (1915), which argued that hundreds of German agents were 'daily, nay hourly, plotting our downfall.'[6] Arthur Conan Doyle even brought his fictional detective Sherlock Holmes out of retirement in 1917 in order to frustrate German spies in 'His Last Bow.' Spy novels often alleged German infiltration of the highest levels of British society, lending credence to the 'hidden hand' belief held by some that British military defeats were the work of traitors. In Dorota Flatau's *Yellow English* (1918), wealthy Germans who had married into the British peerage are revealed to be spies.

Spy novels expressed popular race hatred and national paranoia, both of which helped nurture a real spy mania and xenophobia that were one of the war's more unpleasant by-products. F. E. Eddis's spy novel, *That Goldsheim* (1918), emphasized the need to restrict foreign immigration and ensure a Britain for Britons. The story concerns a successful German businessman who marries an Englishwoman and becomes a naturalized British citizen, but who proves to be a traitor and a spy. No amount of social assimilation can rid Goldsheim of the taint of his German blood. Eddis even suggests that German immigration had been part of a scheme organized by the German Imperial government to infiltrate British society and commerce. The author was a former secretary to the Royal Commission on Alien Immigration and the novel was published under the auspices of the conservative British Empire Union. Not surprisingly, Scotland Yard received an average of 300 spy accusations a day during the war, almost all of them unfounded. Many persons of British nationality were reported as spies simply because they 'looked odd', because they were heard 'whispering', or they had 'voices like Germans.' An urban legend circulated widely about a German governess who didn't show up to lunch one afternoon. A search of her room revealed a trunk with a false bottom, filled with explosives. Such rumors flourished in the vacuum created by heavy censorship of hard news about the war.[7]

The spy novel, like the adventure genre in general, enabled men to prove their courage and resourcefulness. A common plot involved the hero stumbling upon enemy plans or a spy ring, but being unable to convince skeptical officials. The hero is then menaced and hunted by ruthless assassins, and must prove his mettle by eluding them and securing the proof necessary to defeat them. John Buchan's *The Thirty-Nine Steps* (1915) and John Alexander Ferguson's *Stealthy Terror* (1917) are notable examples of this genre. While these novels celebrated manly courage, they often included a strong misogynist element, as enemy agents were frequently seductive women in the manner of real-life spy Mata Hari. In

John Buchan's *Greenmantle* (1915), for example, the master spy Hilda von Einem plots to foment a holy war of Islamic peoples against the British Empire. Likewise, in one of the stories written by 'Sapper', the wife of a high-ranking British officer is revealed to be a German agent. The hero observes 'how devilish dangerous a really pretty and fascinating woman can be – especially when she's bent on finding things out and is clever enough to put two and two together.'[8]

Adventure stories tended to assert traditional gender roles, and the readership of action and spy novels was overwhelmingly male. Nonetheless, as more women were drawn into war work, and even the military, they began to write adventure narratives, no longer the exclusive province of male authors. A number of women who had seen front-line service in the medical corps or military recounted their stories in print as intrepid and thrilling adventures. Sister Martin-Nicholson's *My Experiences on Three Fronts* (1916) and Flora Sandes's *An English Woman Sergeant in the Serbian Army* (1916) are but two notable examples of a burgeoning genre. Some adventure novels also began featuring women as main characters. In Brenda Girvin's *Munition Mary* (1918), the heroine uncovers a spy ring at a defense plant. The title character of Martha Trent's *Alice Blythe: Somewhere in England* (1918) drives an ambulance in France, flies a plane, and captures a German spy.

Whatever their gender politics, wartime adventure stories were unswervingly patriotic. Britain's cause was divinely sanctioned and Germany was the embodiment of evil. Popular adventure and spy novels testify to the persistence in wartime culture of Victorian ideology with its melodramatic themes contrasting 'cads' and 'heroes', cowardice and courage, dissipation and moral regeneration.[9] These heroic attitudes and the popular fiction which embodied them was later mocked by anti-war writers, but maintained a persistent popularity. Despite the revelations of the war's horrors by Aldington, Sassoon, Graves, and others, *The First Hundred Thousand* was still in print in the 1980s. Ernest Raymond's 1922 novel, *Tell England*, which described the hero's death in Arthurian language – 'Doe had done a perfect thing at the last, and so grasped the grail' – was still in print 60 years later and had long been a popular gift to schoolboys.[10]

Romance novels represented the war's other popular literary genre. Like adventure stories, they had been a staple of prewar publishing, and also found it easy to adapt their literary conventions and formulaic plotlines to wartime service. For example, in a number of the wartime novels of Ruby Ayres, such as *The Long Lane to Happiness* (1915) and *Invalided Out* (1918), the war merely provides background color for typical romantic stories of courtship and inheritance. The most popular romance writer of the period, Berta Ruck, churned out numerous love stories involving girls and soldiers, including *The Lad with Wings* (1915), *The Bridge of Kisses* (1917), and *The Land-Girl's Love Story* (1918). In one of her most popular wartime novels, *The Girls at His Billet* (1916), three sisters living on the east coast of England find their humdrum lives transformed when an army training camp is created nearby. A young officer is housed temporarily with their family and a number of romantic complications ensue. By the end of the story, all the sisters are engaged to dashing officers. Novels like this provided an opportunity for escapism and an antidote to the austerities of the war.[11]

If adventure books appealed primarily to men, encouraging enlistment and endorsing 'manly' values like courage and endurance, then the romance genre was their feminine counterpart, promoting compassion, domesticity, and self-sacrifice. Romance novels were conservative in their gender politics, reinforcing the accepted norms of feminine behavior. When the heroine of Dorothy Black's *Her Lonely Soldier* (1916) volunteers as a Red Cross nurse, she discovers her lost love, wounded and suffering from amnesia. Under her care, he is cured and they live together happily ever after. In Hugh de Selincourt's *A Soldier of Life* (1916), James Wood returns home wounded and emotionally scarred from the front. Yet, he is ultimately redeemed and able to live a normal life through the love of a compassionate woman, Corinna. The war was sanitized and sentimentalized within the conventions of the romance novel. Soldiers were often wounded, but seldom died. Even in death, however, love and honor cast a redemptive glow over the war's losses. One of the best-selling books of the war, *Love of an Unknown Soldier* (1918), purported to be a series of letters written by a British officer to an American Red Cross nurse and found in a trench after his death. The work's chivalric formula imagines the soldier as a gallant knight of old and the nurse as his lady fair. The war's popular romance and adventure novels were dismissed by contemporary critics as sensational trash or formulaic potboilers, and they have been largely forgotten today. Yet they were far more widely read than were Shaw or Wells or the later antiwar writers, and were thus important in helping millions of Britons to construct a meaningful image of the war or to reconcile themselves with the war's problems.[12]

* * *

Music halls and cinemas were the working-class alternative to concert halls and theaters, and they played a vital role in sustaining the war effort. Popular musical entertainers aided in recruiting and war bond drives, and performed for troops at training camps in Britain or at the front lines. Harry Lauder, an extremely popular music hall comic and singer, lost his own son in the war and was especially active in entertaining troops. Musical comedy artists like Nellie Taylor and Phyllis Dare specialized in 'naughty' recruiting songs, in which – dressed in uniform – they encouraged young men to 'be manly' and enlist. Their reward would include the devotion of the nation's women. In a popular music hall routine, a female singer boasts how on each day of the week she goes out with a different member of the armed services. She then concludes by addressing the men in the audience: 'on Saturday, I'm willing, if you'll only take a shilling, to make a man of any one of you.'[13]

Music halls had a long tradition of employing patriotic rhetoric, which easily lent itself to support of the war. As M. W. Pope has argued, 'it was at the halls you learnt your patriotism, were told you had a navy, a British navy, which kept your foes at bay, that a Little British Army went a damned long way, that the soldiers of the Queen (or later the King) always won, and that you couldn't beat the boys of the bulldog breed who made Old England's name. And you believed it all.'[14] Routines were essentially crude political cartoons set to music. Fat German soldiers, with sausages hanging from their pockets, and a bumbling, cowardly Kaiser and Crown Prince, 'Little Willy', were popular objects of ridicule. Light-hearted and boastful songs, such as 'To Hell with the Kaiser' or 'Gilbert the Filbert, the Colonel of the Nuts', extolled the invincibility of British soldiers.[15] The flippancy of the music hall approach to the war came to be resented by some soldiers. For example, after a visit to the Liverpool Hippodrome in 1917, Sassoon wrote 'Blighters,' in which he imagined a tank lurching menacingly down the theater aisles: 'And there'd be no more jokes in Music-halls/ To mock the riddled corpses round Bapaume.'[16]

Music publishers churned out vast numbers of patriotic songs that were performed in music halls and sold as sheet music for the parlor piano. The songs ran the gamut of themes from jingoist ('The Bulldog's Bark', 'Stick to Your Guns', 'We'll Fight Till We Win or Die') to comic ('Sister Susie's Sewing Shirts for Soldiers', 'When An Irishman Goes Fighting') to sentimental ('Brave Women Who Wait', 'Khaki Boy', 'Where Are the Lads of the Village Tonight?'). Melancholy, romantic ballads like 'Annie Laurie' and 'Roamin' in the Gloamin' were great favorites of the wartime public – soldiers and civilians alike. Songs of nostalgia and homesickness were particularly popular, such as 'Home, Sweet Home', 'Tipperary,' and 'Keep the Home Fires Burning,' with lyrics by Lena Guilbert Ford:

Keep the home fires burning,
While your hearts are yearning
Though your lads are far away

They dream of home.
There's a silver lining
Through the dark cloud shining
Turn the dark cloud inside out,
Till the boys come home.[17]

American music also gained in popularity during the war, especially rag-time and jazz and the dance styles they inspired, such as the Charleston. This caused a great deal of alarm, as such music was associated with African-Americans and thus assumed to be degenerate.[18]

The war also transformed the British gramophone industry. The outbreak of hostilities initially devastated the industry as more than half its players and records were made in Germany. The business soon rebounded, however, with domestic production and consumption of records increasing dramatically during the war. Improved working-class pay allowed more people to purchase record players. The shrinking of many public forms of leisure, such as sporting events and pubgoing, also meant that entertainment became more home-centered. This trend ben-efitted sales of both sheet music and records. After an outburst of patri-otic songs in 1914–15, there was little ongoing demand for war-themed recordings. The most popular records with both soldiers and civilians were romantic ballads like 'Roses of Picardy' and 'If You Were the Only Girl in the World.'[19]

Like music halls, cinemas also attracted a vast working-class audi-ence, and they also sought to promote the war. By 1917, the more than 4000 British cinemas sold a total of some 20 million tickets weekly, a threefold increase over 1914. As drink prices rose and public drinking hours were restricted, the cinema provided an inexpensive alternative to a night at the pub. It also served as a popular courtship rendezvous for young working-class men and women, sitting together in the dark. The military also maintained its own cinemas for frontline troops. By 1917, the 11 divisions of the 4th Army alone had 25 cinemas attracting 40 000 soldiers a week.[20]

Over the course of the war, the government increasingly made use of film as propaganda, though most wartime films were still commercially produced. Commercial film companies easily adapted their usual fare of melodramas and sentimental romances to the war, as in the tear-jerker *Christmas without Daddy* (1914). A whole series of films was devoted to the capture of German spies, including *The Kaiser's Spies* (1914) and *A Munition Girl's Romance* (1916). Like popular novels, many wartime films also gave men the opportunity to prove their bravery and win the love of a good woman. *Saving the Colours* (1914), *They Called Him*

Coward (1915), and *The Happy Warrior* (1918) were all tales of battlefield redemption cast in the familiar melodramatic mode. These films usually featured cruel and lecherous German villains who menaced helpless civilians. In *The Heart of Humanity* (1917) a brutal German soldier tosses a baby out of a second-story window because its crying annoyed him. British soldiers inevitably came to the rescue, summoned by intrepid heroines, brave children, or clever animals. The war remained a popular subject of films, but was by no means the universal one. The continuing popularity of adventures and dramas that had nothing to do with the war testifies to the public's need for escapist entertainment. Among the most popular films of the war years were *The Avenging Hand* (1915), the tale of an Egyptian mummy that comes to life and kills the violators of her tomb, and *Sally Bishop* (1917), a film version of a popular romantic novel.[21]

The economic constraints of wartime drastically curtailed domestic film production, resulting in an even wider showing of American films. These included Cecil B. DeMille's *The Little American* (1917), which recreated the sinking of the *Lusitania*. By placing beloved film star Mary Pickford on board, DeMille made the tragedy all the more palpable. The most popular American films were those starring Charlie Chaplin, a comic actor who had begun his career in British music halls. In *Shoulder Arms* (1918), Chaplin's resilient character of the 'Little Tramp' is drafted into the Army, endures the rigors of boot camp, bumbles his way across the Western Front, and, in the end, manages to capture the Kaiser. Chaplin's brand of irreverent humor especially appealed to soldiers. One wartime observer noted of frontline audiences that 'love plots didn't seem to interest them much, but a comedy – I mean regular slapstick stuff – started them shouting with glee.' Altogether nine-tenths of the films shown in wartime Britain were American. Just as with the introduction of American popular music, this phenomenon marked the beginning of an 'Americanization' of culture which became even more pronounced after the war.[22]

* * *

Sports were an important aspect of mass culture in Britain and played an active role in the war that has been little studied. For example, of the 1.2 million men who had volunteered for the Army by the end of 1914, nearly half a million had come forward through football organizations. One recruiting poster proclaimed: 'Hundreds of football enthusiasts are joining the Army daily. Don't be left behind . . . Join and be in at THE FINAL and give them a KICK OFF THE EARTH.' A rugby poster also urged young men to 'Play the Game!', touting Lord Kitchener as 'the team's' full back, General French and Admiral Jellicoe as three-quarter backs, and Sir Douglas Haig as a half back.[23] Football was wildly popular with the troops. A Scottish soldier recalled that 'most of our men were playing football within half an hour of finishing a heavy march after a fortnight in the trenches.' Sport was part of a common culture shared by almost all soldiers, and it provided them with some autonomy away from the discipline of the front.[24]

Despite sports organizations' support for the war, newspapers were filled with angry complaints against professional football teams which continued to play games as the nation fought overseas. *Punch*, in January 1915, dubbed football results 'The Shirkers' War News.' Sir George Young wrote to his son, serving in the navy, that 'the scandal of professional football, with the huge "gates" of loafing lads as spectators, is beginning to raise an outcry. How slow we English are!' This conflict was, in part, one of social class, in which the upper-class amateur tradition of sport opposed working-class professional athletics. Working-class crowds at football matches were denounced as slackers, criticism which was not leveled at wealthy spectators at horse races. Eventually, both football matches and horse races were suspended until the end of the war. Boxing, however, was enthusiastically promoted as it seemed the ideal pastime for a bellicose society. According to *The Times*: 'Here are something of the ingredients of war – blood and sweat and struggle, the cunning manoeuvring for blows and the taking of them cheerfully . . . here is the courage of the battle in miniature.'[25]

Sports metaphors permeated wartime oratory and propaganda rhetoric – 'play the game', 'play with a straight bat', 'fair play and foul.' Britain was held up as a sporting nation that, unlike Germany, didn't 'hit below the belt.' The presumed linkage between team effort and effective fighting was also emphasized. Robert Baden-Powell, for example, held that soldiers are like 'players in a football team: each has to be perfect and efficient, each has to adhere patiently to the rules and to play in his place and play the game – not for his own advancement or glorification, but simply and solely that at all costs his side may win.' A young officer wrote in his diary that 'a man who is used to sport, takes things – even in the great chance of life and death – as part of the game.' Most famously, in the Somme offensive Captain Nevill of the East Surrey Regiment led his men across the battlefield kicking a football. At the time the incident was interpreted as an example of British pluck and daring, but later it was regarded as tragic proof that Britons had viewed the war as just another game. Yet, the episode also dramatizes how sport was an important common bond between men of different classes and backgrounds.[26]

The war made itself felt in other leisure activities besides sport. Working-class pub culture, like professional football, was also seen as an impediment to the efficient waging of war. War provided a wonderful opportunity for temperance organizations and social purity campaigners to advance their respective agendas. Kitchener appealed to the public not to 'treat' soldiers to free drinks and a law against 'treating' was passed later. Factory managers blamed low munitions production on drunken workers, and Lloyd George rallied his Nonconformist supporters with the cry that 'Drink is doing us more damage in the war than all the German submarines put together.' On 15 April 1915, the King 'took the pledge' to refrain from drinking until the end of the war, but his example inspired few not already so inclined. Scarce supplies and punitive taxation, however, greatly reduced alcoholic consumption, as did the government's restriction of licensing hours. National sobriety increased dramatically, and prosecutions for drunkenness were five times higher in prewar London than by the war's end.[27]

Holidays at seaside resorts were at first another casualty of wartime austerity. There was widespread criticism of merry-making at resort towns in the early part of the war, though town fathers tried to justify the usual entertainments as morale boosting. Fear of attack also diminished the customary crowds at some east coast towns, but other resorts were quick to solicit this business. For example, the Buxton Information Office advertised that 'the German Navy cannot navigate the Buxton waters. Situated in the centre of England, Buxton is the *safest* and most restful place in the country.' Most holiday centers later made up business by housing Belgian refugees and British troops. As the war dragged on, the initial hostility to home front pleasure dissipated. Resorts like Blackpool did especially well, testifying to the expanding wartime incomes among the working class.[28]

* * *

The work of the official war artists is well known, though many of their paintings and drawings were not widely circulated at the time. Nonetheless, there was a rich wartime visual culture exemplified by popular media such as posters, magazine illustrations, cigarette cards, advertisements, and postcards. Like most commercial culture, popular images of the war tended to promote an upbeat, unwavering patriotism.

An important, though often neglected, visual repository of the war is the postcard. It was a vital means of communication between soldiers at the front and people at home. During the war, postcards were delivered at the rate of over a million a day. They were cheap at a penny a piece, and overseas postage was only another 1*d.* for civilians and 1/2*d.*

for soldiers. Postcards required a minimum of effort to send while indicating a maximum of thoughtfulness. No depth of sentiment was necessary, or even possible, in the small space available for messages, though the sender could convey a variety of feelings via his selection of the subject matter or images on the card. A number of postcard companies, such as Bamforth's, quickly adapted their cards to wartime themes. Sentimental images of children and home remained popular, invoking fond feelings for absent loved ones. Hundreds of postcards illustrated popular songs, such as one which depicted a pensive young woman accompanied by a verse from the ballad 'Somewhere in France with You':

> Somewhere in France,
>   Yonder across the sea,
> While I am here fondly dreaming of you,
>   There you are dreaming of me.

As the war became more ferocious and as casualties mounted, the subject matter became more serious, though no less sentimental, including many images of wounded or blinded soldiers.[29] Soldiers seemed to favor racy images of women and comic depictions of Army life. A popular postcard series among the troops was F. Mackain's 'Sketches of Tommy's Life.' This cartoon series comically depicted bullying officers, endless marching and drill, as well as the muddy disorder and discomfort of life in the trenches. These cards allowed soldiers to convey something of their lives to family and friends more clearly than many could explain themselves, though the comic tone undercut too sober reflection by civilians. Soldiers especially loved postcards that made fun of the bureaucracy and red tape which surrounded them. One postcard depicted a soldier frantically informing an officer that the enemy was advancing, as shells exploded nearby. The officer, who has just hung up the phone, calmly replies that 'HQ has just rung through to say that in the future all members of His Majesty's forces are to shave daily.'[30]

Other understudied visual artifacts of the war include the numerous advertisements on posters and in newspapers and magazines, which linked their products with national pride. Lifebuoy Soap, for instance, billed itself as the 'Royal Disinfectant' in an ad that depicted nurses looking after wounded soldiers in a military hospital. Advertisers also sought to promote a patriotic attitude toward the war and to perpetuate an idealized view of the front. The poster promoting Mitchell's Golden Dawn Cigarettes showed a group of happy smiling soldiers in a trench amidst lush green fields and blue sunny skies. The officer scans the horizon for the enemy, and, finding there's 'time for one more', passes his cigarette case around.[31]

Advertisers were quick to copy military rhetoric and images to sell their goods. Another Lifebuoy ad proclaimed that their soap 'will carry you to victory over the Germs and Microbes of Disease.' The kitchen cleaner 'Vim' represented its product as an artillery gun that could smash dirt, and Gibbs toothpaste was endorsed by a flying ace who claimed it was 'fragrant as the lofty air.' The pervasiveness of military language and imagery even affected the fashion industry, as exemplified in *Vogue*'s promise to watch the 'battlefields' of style. 'Do the lines of fashion shift and change – *Vogue* knows. Do the couturiers launch a stirring advance – *Vogue* knows. *Vogue* is a courier, and comes from Paris to drop bombs of fashion on expectant readers.' Much of this advertising might now appear to be in questionable taste. Especially shocking to our modern eyes are a series of ads the *Barnsley Chronicle* ran in July 1916, coincident with the Somme offensive, promising 'slaughter at the sales.'[32]

Businesses like Selfridges proclaimed their loyalty by establishing several 'war windows' at their store, which contained maps and war photographs, but which also advertised products for sale such as khaki clothing, first aid cases, and waterproof sleeping bags. Consumers were continually urged to send goods to frontline soldiers. An advertisement for Pears' Soap depicted two soldiers washing in a river and declaring, 'Oh for a cake of Pears now!' The Decca Company invited people to send portable gramophones to soldiers overseas; 'hundreds' of officers had supposedly provided testimonials that this was 'a valuable asset to the morale of the troops.' Other advertisements played on civilians' anxieties and guilt. Manufacturers of the 'Dayfield Body Shield' exhorted potential customers to 'Save His Life!' by purchasing their bayonet, lance, and shrapnel-proof vest.[33]

The wartime need for austerity and frugality put advertisers in an ambiguous position. They needed to promote consumption without appearing to advocate unpatriotic selfishness or excessive civilian comfort. Burberry's rebutted the government's savings campaign by arguing that consumption was patriotic:

> Is It Economy? to stop legitimate British Industries. To buy a dress of British materials, British made – wherein is Britain poorer? Money passes from one to another, and is distributed amongst needy workers – workers must live . . . True patriots will continue to drive motorcars and clothe themselves decently while they can afford it.[34]

A 1915 ad for Murray's Mellow Mixture likewise admonished consumers: 'Don't stop smoking because tax on tobacco has increased. It is your duty to the State to keep on Smoking. The Chancellor increased the duty on tobacco to give smokers an opportunity of contributing towards the successful issue of the war.'[35] Even the consumption of luxury goods could be justified during wartime. Wine reduced 'stress and anxiety', and enjoying a new piano was 'better for the folks at home than thinking about Zeppelins.' Cosmetics ads told women it was their 'duty' to beautify themselves for the fighting men. Ven-Yusa face cream exhorted women workers to 'remember, that while it is patriotic for girls to help their country with war-work, it is also patriotic for them to preserve the natural beauty of their skins and complexions. . .'[36]

In business and advertising, as in so many areas of British life, the war aroused nationalist sentiments. A number of firms proclaimed (proudly or anxiously) the 'Britishness' of their products and personnel. The chemists Boots' took out ads declaring 'The Truth About Eau de Cologne.' This product, customers were assured, did not come from the eponymous German city, but was of British manufacture. The laxative Kruschen Salts, despite its name, had been 'Entirely British for 160 Years.' The Royal Worcester Corset Company informed the public that 'the principals and every employee . . . are British-born, and the concern is run entirely upon British capital.' Companies ruthlessly exposed any supposed German connections of their rivals. Liptons accused J. Lyons and Company, rival tea merchants, of harboring German directors. Lyons responded with ads proclaiming they were an 'All British Company With All British Directors.' De La Rue Pens warned that Watermans were controlled by an Austrian firm. 'Every Waterman pen sold, therefore, in this country means profit to the King's enemies.'[37]

The commercialization of the war not only contributed to a generalized patriotism, but also tended to normalize and trivialize the conflict by allowing it to penetrate the minutiae of everyday things. War-themed advertisements, as well as objects like tank paperweights, battleship pincushions, and toy soldiers, made the war commonplace and familiar instead of frightening and horrible.[38] A vast range of war-themed commodities flooded the British market, from children's toys to jewelry to decorative accessories for the home. A patriotic cigarette case, for example, was engraved with the image of British soldiers storming a German artillery position, accompanied by a quotation from Kipling: 'Who stands if freedom fall? Who dies if England live?' British potteries produced hundreds of different china figurines which celebrated military heroes and fighting machines, including images of Kitchener and Edith Cavell, submarines and airplanes. People could eat off commemorative dishes decorated with the allied flags and pour tea from pots shaped like tanks.

The most ordinary artifacts of material culture promoted patriotic feeling and made military images a comfortable feature of daily life.[39]

* * *

Popular culture attempted to mobilize the nation as broadly as possible, and this included its youngest members who were socialized to be good Britons in a variety of ways – through education, youth organizations, games, and literature. War made combatants even of schoolchildren, who collected cooking fats for manufacturing explosives and scrap metal for use in munitions factories. They bought war bonds with their pocket money and cultivated garden allotments to increase the nation's food supply. The training of students became increasingly infused with a military ethos, and the War Office's influence in schools grew with the establishment of new programs of calisthenics and military-style drills. The health of working-class children, as potential future soldiers, also received greater attention, but their education was seriously neglected. Although children were supposed to remain in school until the age of 14, the need for wartime labor meant that this restriction was often ignored. The Education Minister, H. A. L. Fisher, later admitted that 600 000 children had been put 'prematurely' to work during the first three years of the war. Some 200 schools were requisitioned to house soldiers, further disrupting education.[40]

A distinctive British youth culture had existed since the late nineteenth century, organized around groups like the Boy Scouts and Girl Guides, and through a vast range of juvenile publications, all of which sought to promote 'wholesome' values and allegiance to the Empire. This culture proved to be an ideal forum for mobilizing young people in support of the war. Hundreds of thousands of current and former members of the Boy Scouts and Church Lads' Brigade joined the military. Boy Scouts worked directly with the Army as messengers and supply depot assistants. Scouts also patrolled coastal areas, on the lookout for submarines and Zeppelins, and a special war service badge was created for them. Military-style training among youth organizations and in schools was seen as a preparation for service in the armed forces. Many boys grew up with the war and fully expected to serve in it themselves. Claud Cockburn, who had been a public school student during the war, recalled that 'most of the sixth form was wiped out, year after year.' Each year 'they were called up and 80 percent of them would be killed. I know when I was in the sixth form, I think only about 10 percent or so of the previous year were still alive, and we thought that was life.'[41]

The First World War led to 'a wave of patriotic marketing' directed at youth. Illustrated souvenir cards were published for boys to collect, featuring regiments, war heroes, and the latest weaponry. Girls' papers like *Sunday Stories* and *Girls' Realm* gave away 'silks' of patriotic subjects with instructions for embroidering them into cushion covers. Girls were encouraged to scatter items of patriotic propaganda throughout the home. Girls dressed up in nurse costumes and bandaged sick dolls while their brothers wore soldier uniforms and marched with toy guns. Gamages, the London toy shop, advertised facsimile officer uniforms for boys aged 6 to 12. Numerous companies marketed war-themed toys like tanks, ships, artillery pieces, and the ever-popular toy soldiers. Children's board games like 'Scout Signaller' and 'Trencho' helped inculcate a heroic image of the war. In the game 'From the Ranks to Field Marshal', players advanced around the board by securing promotion and honors for heroic acts in battle.[42]

Not even infants were free from the attentions of propagandists. Captain Sir William Wiseman advised mothers 'not to reprove, but to encourage' children who fought in the nursery as this habit of play had rendered the British superior in hand-to-hand combat. Nursery rhymes were rewritten to reflect patriotic concerns:

Baa Baa, black sheep,
Have you any wool?
Yes sir, yes sir, three bags full,
One coloured khaki,
One of varied hue,
And one to make a Union Jack in red, white and blue.

Children's ABC books were also devised with wartime themes:

B is for Belgium	C's for our Colonies
Brave Little State	Loyal And True
So valiant for Honour	Bringing help to their mother
So reckless of fate.	From over the blue.

Some of this propaganda was surprisingly violent considering that it was aimed at very young children. 'The House that Jack Built' was destroyed by a Zeppelin, but this was only the beginning: 'This is the Hun who dropped the bomb that fell on the house that Jack built./ This is the gun that killed the Hun who dropped the bomb that fell on the house that Jack built.'[43]

Masterman and later John Buchan at the Department of Information subsidized propaganda directed at children, including James Yoxall's *Why Britain Went to War: To the Boys and Girls of the British Empire* (1914).

Yoxall, an MP and a member of the National Union of Teachers, told schoolchildren that 'we fight to free the whole world from war and the danger of war.' He then framed the conflict in terms of a schoolyard brawl: 'The Kaiser has been the bully in the European playground, and every boy well knows that there is no peace for others until a bully is tackled and knocked out.'[44] Another official work aimed at children, Henry Newbolt's *Tales of the Great War* (1916), claimed that Germans took pleasure in mutilating women and children through their air attacks on Britain. Newbolt contrasted the 'barbarity' of German pilots with the 'daring and chivalrous' conduct of British airmen. Schools disseminated patriotic tracts and staged propaganda pageants. In a typical play for children, *The Scouts* (1915), a Boy Scout, Albert Jones, and his friend Clara capture a German spy, Miss Corner (alias Frau Korner), who was posing as an artist at a seaside boarding house. As Korner is led away, she cries: 'What a humiliation to be tricked by those two children! What will the Kaiser think?'[45]

The war saw a huge outpouring of patriotic stories for juveniles still very much in the Victorian tradition. Generations of young men before the war had been nurtured on the patriotic adventure stories of G. A. Henty and popular periodicals like *The Boy's Own Paper* and *Young England*. During the war these publications continued to repeat the old themes, presenting the conflict as high, heroic adventure. Young men were pictured on the covers of the boys' magazines, standing before waving Union Jacks, or leading cavalry charges against the enemy. The magazines were filled with pictures of battleships and airplanes, and stories about Boy Scouts and young men's military training. They often featured the accounts of real-life 'boy heroes' like 16-year-old John Cornwell, a sight-setter for a gun on board HMS *Chester*, who was killed in the Battle of Jutland. Although Cornwell was badly injured and the rest of his gun crew killed, he stayed at his post until the battle was over, when he died. Cornwell's bravery was held up as an example for other boys to follow and his life narrated in terms of an adventure story. Sir Edward Carson summarized the 'message' Cornwell sent to the Empire's youth: 'Obey your orders, cling to your post, don't grumble, stick it out.'[46]

Numerous adventure novels for boys also presented the war as a 'great game.' In Albert Lee's *At His Country's Call* (1916), the Boy Scout Maurice Millard is sent to France to do first-aid work. There he is caught up in a series of adventures: he delivers a message in German-held territory and is captured by the enemy, but escapes by stealing a plane and proceeds to drop its bombs on German military facilities. Especially popular with juvenile readers were the many wartime novel series featuring the adventures of 'The Khaki Boys', 'The Boy Volunteers', 'The Navy Boys', or 'The Aeroplane Scouts.' One popular series by Robert Drake, 'The Boy Allies', chronicled the adventures of Jack Templeton, an English boy, and Frank Chadwick, his American chum. In *The Boy Allies with the Flying Squadron* (1915), Jack and Frank are decorated by King George V after a daring escape from Germany, and in *The Boy Allies at Jutland* (1917), they sneak into Bremen and hijack a German ship.

Books and magazines directed at British girls, like the *Girl's Own Paper* or *Girl Guides' Gazette*, eschewed heroics and advised their readers to endure the war's sorrows silently or to support the nation from within the home by knitting socks and canning food. But as women began participating more actively in the war, this development was reflected in juvenile literature. Adventure series for girls such as 'The Red Cross Girls' or 'The Khaki Girls' started appearing. Activist heroines were featured in May Wynne's *An English Girl in Serbia* (1916) and May Baldwin's *Irene to the Rescue* (1916). In Baldwin's novel, the intrepid and gutsy Irene Mathers cleared the name of a French family unjustly accused of spying for Germany. Many girls no doubt found this sort of book a welcome relief from the usual anemic romances, but a new image for girls proved controversial. One reviewer criticized Irene's bold demeanor, finding her an unfit model for young women. Children's books in which girl protagonists were equal to boys in embracing adventure and danger remained exceptional. More often the girls exhibited an ambivalent attitude toward their wartime roles, as in Alice Massie's *Freda's Great Adventure* (1917), where Freda uncovers German spies, but in the end, returns home with no other wish than to 'be a comfort' to her family.[47]

* * *

British soldiers had a distinctive culture of their own, which differed in some respects from the popular culture of civilians, but also shared common elements. Paul Fussell has argued that soldiers believed in a 'severe and uncompromising' division between themselves and civilians on the home front, but in fact the two groups were never entirely alienated. Popular culture provided strong links between battlefront and home front, as soldiers and civilians sang the same songs, watched the same films, and played the same games. Millions of letters were exchanged each week between soldiers and their families, and parcels from home often contained magazines, books, and gramophone records.[48]

Although millions of soldiers participated in a common mass culture of sport, music halls, cinema, and pulp fiction, they also came to eschew the more stridently patriotic elements of these activities and art forms.

Because of their firsthand experience of the horror and futility of modern warfare, soldiers developed a more critical, ironic, and fatalistic attitude toward the war than did civilians. An elite literature of disillusionment is well known from the work of soldier-poets and memoirists, but could be found even more broadly among the theatricals, songs, cartoons, and magazines produced by soldiers themselves, and widely circulated among the military forces at the time. The Army saw the benefit to morale of keeping soldiers occupied and entertained between bouts of frontline service, and it devoted much effort to providing recreation. Officers organized seaside excursions to Dunkirk or Boulogne, horse races, football and cricket matches, concert parties, and films. Soldiers actively participated in entertaining each other.[49]

Most army divisions sponsored theatrical troupes, which staged programs reminiscent of music-hall fare. Soldiers wrote and performed the usual comic songs and skits about mothers-in-law or fat ladies bathing at the seaside, as well as the sentimental ballads which were the other side of standard music hall entertainment. Much of the material mocked the misfortunes of war, reflecting the working-class attitudes of the halls: 'fatalism, political skepticism, the evasion of tragedy and anger, and a stance of comic stoicism.'[50] Troop theatricals favored satirical songs about Army life composed by the men:

> Hullo! hullo! what's their dirty game,
> Working us at ninety in the shade?
> It wasn't the tale they told when we enlisted,
> Now it's all parade, parade.

Making light of unbearable conditions made them seem more tolerable, as in 'My Little Wet Home in the Trench', a parody of the popular ballad 'Little Grey Home in the West':

> I've a little wet home in a trench,
> Where the rainstorms continually drench,
> There's a dead cow close by,
> With her hoofs toward the sky,
> And she gives off a beautiful stench.[51]

A common target of soldiers' humor was those in authority, especially officers:

> We've got a sergeant-major,
> Who's never seen a gun;

He's mentioned in dispatches
For drinking private's rum,
And when he sees old Jerry
You should see the bugger run
Miles and miles and miles behind the lines!

Sylvia Pankhurst related a play put on by convalescing soldiers at an army hospital in France. 'The Deserter' was a satire on Army life that was especially savage in its portrayal of pompous, overbearing officers. The soldiers laughed uproariously at the lampoons, but by the play's end, when a private is shot for desertion, the audience grew depressed and moody. 'The play was too real for them', Pankhurst concluded.[52]

One major element of music-hall fare absent from troop theatricals was xenophobia. Few of the frontline troops shared the virulent anti-German feelings of civilians; rather, they tended to have sympathy for the plight of their counterparts in the German trenches. As the troop journal, *The Outpost*, noted in 1917, Hun was 'a popular word with the pulpit and parts of the press', Bosche was 'a word much affected by the officers', but among the men it was the almost affectionate 'Old Fritz.' Soldiers often parodied the patriotic songs of the home front. For example, the popular recruiting song 'We don't want to lose you/ But we think you ought to go/ For your King and your Country/ Both need you so' was later sardonically answered by soldiers:

For we don't want your loving,
And we think you're awfully slow
To see that we don't want you
So please won't you go.
We don't like your sing-songs,
And we loath your refrain,
So don't you dare sing it
Near us again.[53]

Songs preferred by soldiers were satires on the military, celebrations of drink and sex, and burlesques of popular songs, even hymns. 'Lead, Kindly Light', for example, became 'We've Had No Beer Today.' Another popular song was a parody of 'What A Friend We Have in Jesus':

When this bloomin' war is over,
   Oh, how happy I will be;
When I get my civvy clothes on,
   No more soldiering for me.

No more pack-drill, heavy laden,
    No more asking for a pass;
We will tell the Sergeant-Major
    He's a silly blinkin' ass.

Soldiers made up irreverent lyrics to accompany the dreaded morning reveille call:

Get out – o'bed,
Get out – o'bed,
You lazy bug-gers.

They also composed humorous, and often obscene, marching songs:

Mademoiselle from Armentieres, parlez-vous?
Mademoiselle from Armentieres, parlez-vous?
Mademoiselle from Armentieres –
She ain't been f —d in forty years!
Hinky dinky parlez-vous.

The irreverence and bawdiness of soldiers' songs provided much-needed relief and humor to weary troops.[54]

Among soldiers, humor, even dark humor, could provide an emotional release from things too awful to contemplate seriously. For instance, troops sought to belittle or downplay the horrors of trench warfare by giving silly or familiar names to the instruments of mass death and destruction. Soldiers referred to nighttime shelling as 'free firework displays.' Exploding shells were 'crumps' and 'whizz-bangs,' and trench mortar bombs 'toffee apples.' The Germans' heavy artillery gun was called 'Big Bertha' and a mine thrower known affectionately as 'Minnie.' One frontline paper included a mock love poem, dedicated 'To Minnie':

No place is sacred, I declare,
Your manners most immodest are,
You force your blatant presence where
Maidens should be particular.

Soldiers' slang also humorously gave vent to their contempt for officious behavior. For example, official memoranda from headquarters were sardonically dubbed 'bum fodder.'[55]

For British soldiers, the French and Flemish languages also provided numerous possibilities for parody and comic misunderstandings. The 'unpronounceable' towns of Belgium and France were given cockney rechristenings; Ypres as 'Wipers', Godevaersvelde as 'Gertie wears velvet', and Fonquevillers as 'Funky Villas.' In army slang, food was 'mongey' and drink 'plonky' – from the French *manger* and *vin blanc*. There were frequent comic attempts at French speaking, usually for the purpose of 'fraternization.' A popular pamphlet among some British soldiers was the phrase book *Five Minutes' Conversation with Young Ladies* which contained such useful phrases as 'Voulez-vous accepter l'aperitif ?' or 'Permettez-moi de vous baiser la main.'[56]

The best-known object of humor among soldiers was 'Old Bill' – a cartoon character created by Bruce Bairnsfather satirizing Army life and mocking the heroic image of war. Bairnsfather, a junior officer in the First Royal Warwickshires, began a series of satirical sketches of soldiers' life in 1914 which appeared weekly in *Bystander* and proved wildly popular with the troops. The cartoons usually involved 'Old Bill' and 'Young Bert.' Bert was a naïve, wide-eyed volunteer, while Bill was more attuned to the ways of the world – and of Army life. He remains cynical about patriotic rhetoric, but nonetheless does his duty. He is especially adept at making the most of bad situations – testimony to the working-class capacity for endurance in the face of adversity. A typical cartoon shows Old Bill writing to his wife: 'Dearest, At present we are staying at a farm . . .' He sits in front of a shelled farmhouse surrounded by the carcasses of dead cows. The anti-heroic view of the war is especially highlighted by Bairnsfather's cartoon 'That Sword', which depicts a soldier charging into battle with his sword held aloft, and is captioned 'How he thought he was going to use it.' This image is contrasted with another of the same soldier toasting a piece of bread on the sword, captioned 'How he did use it.' Soldiers especially appreciated this deflation of home front propaganda.[57]

Perhaps the best illustration of a distinct soldiers' culture can be found in the hundreds of different trench papers and magazines produced during the war. Written and edited by the members of a particular infantry battalion or artillery battery, the papers were only a few pages in length and usually appeared on a monthly basis. Some were printed by the troops themselves on abandoned French presses or on Army equipment, others sent to agents in Paris or London for reproduction. The best known of the trench journals was *The Wipers Times*; others included *The Dud*, *The Dump*, *The Growler*, *The Shell Hole Advance*, and the *Dead Horse Corner Gazette*. These papers served to bind battalions closer together by giving soldiers a forum in which to vent their grievances, usually by means of humor or satire. Frequent themes included the ignorance of civilians and politicians, the incompetence of the War Office, and the

bad food and miserable conditions of trench life. Soldiers' papers presented a jaded and irreverent view of the war, completely at odds with the
heroic presentation of the home front press.[58]

Trench journals parodied civilian papers, with mock letters to the editor, advice columns, fashion news, poetry and prose, and 'in-jokes' which
only those initiated into the bizarre existence of the frontline soldier
could appreciate. *The Mudlark*, for example, contained a column 'Things
I have never seen at the front', which included staff officers taking exer-
cise before breakfast and army commanders eating bully beef and biscuits. The papers frequently included mock-romantic odes to rats and
lice as well as burlesques of wartime advertisements: 'Are you going over
the top? If so be sure to first inspect our new line of velveteen corduroy
plush breeches. Be in the fashion and look like a soldier.'[59]

Trench papers delighted in mocking the grandiloquent reportage of
war correspondents or civilian strategists like Horatio Bottomley and
Hilaire Belloc. In May 1916, the *New Church Times* published a spoof on
'How to Win the War' by 'Belary Helloc':

> The line held on all fronts is 1,500 miles (circa). This is 2,640,000
> yards. Now we must get that number of our troops and allot one yard
> per man. Give each man a bomb, and at a given signal let them all go
> over and each to account for his own particular opponent. This would
> account for 2,000,000 of the enemy (that is giving the generous allow-
> ance of 640,000 failures) ... I think I may safely say that, after the
> tenth or eleventh attack, the enemy would be ready to consider the
> advisability of making terms rather than continue the war.

Under cover of ridiculing ignorant civilians like Belloc, the piece implic-
itly criticizes the General Staff's approach to offensive warfare, and this
months before the Somme offensive. Another trench journal similarly
defined 'strategist' as 'a person who doesn't care how many lives he risks
as long as he doesn't risk his own.'[60]

Troop journals combined the mockery and irreverence found in soldiers' songs and the cartoons of Bruce Bairnsfather with the more sober
depictions of war associated with soldier-poets like Sassoon and Owen.
For example, one paper printed an 'Amateur's Alphabet' which traces
the disillusionment of a raw recruit:

> U is the uniform he donned at first with glee,
> But the pride and glamour's faded now, 'fed up,' 'sheer fed' is he.
> V is the volley of abuse he'd like to pour
> On decrepit politicians who caused this blanky war.

The last issue of *The Wipers Times* was even more explicit in summarizing the lessons of the war: 'Anyway though some may be sorry it's over, there is little doubt that the line men are *not*, as most of us have been cured of any little illusions we may have had about the pomp and glory of war, and know it for the vilest disaster that can befall mankind.'[61]

The disillusionment manifested in troop culture was neither pacifist nor defeatist in its outlook. Soldiers may have rejected the jingoist rhetoric of the home front, but they had no intention of giving up. The determination of the frontline soldier permeated popular ballads and the writings of trench papers. For example, a poem from *The Listening Post*, exhorted:

We must keep the line from breaking,
Though the trees and rocks are quaking,
And the earth with gunfire shaking –
'Play the game.'

'Playing the game' stood for a whole attitude: equanimity in the face of hardship, extreme endurance, and unwillingness to let the side down. Troops fought because their comrades expected it of them and because they still believed in the essential justness of the British cause. The soldier's poem 'To My Chum' captures this spirit of comradeship and determination:

Well, old lad, here's peace to you,
And for me, well, there's my job to do,
For you and the others who lie at rest,
Assured may be that we'll do our best . . .

Soldiers' writings acknowledge the brutal realities of the battlefield while at the same time affirming the sanctity of sacrifice. Soldiers fight on so that their friends will not have died in vain. The fatalism and endurance of ordinary soldiers may best be exemplified in their song:

We're here because we're here
Because we're here
Because we're here.[62]

* * *

The overwhelming diversity of British cultural production during the war years makes it difficult to generalize about the arts and habits of leisure in wartime. The books and papers people read, the music they heard, and the images they saw depended on numerous variables: their social class, sex, age, level of education, political inclination, and status as soldier or civilian. Middle- and upper-class Britons were far more likely than workers to read *The Times* or the *Nation*, the novels of H. G. Wells or John Galsworthy, and to attend concerts or visit art galleries and museums. Working-class Britons were more likely than their elite counterparts to read the *Daily Mail* or *John Bull*, the novels of Nat Gould or Berta Ruck, and to attend music halls and football matches. Of course, some forms of popular culture cut across class barriers, like the works of Kipling, popular songs, and, increasingly, the cinema. Over the course of the war, popular culture became more homogenized and national, less characterized by local and regional variations. It also became more dominated by mass entertainment, like cinema and hit songs, and more Americanized.[63]

Most wartime culture, whether elite or popular, promoted consensus, patriotism, and devotion to the nation's cause. The dominant artistic and literary view of the war as heroic and purposeful was only challenged by some few members of the avant-garde and by a steadily increasing number of soldiers. At the time of the war, these alternative voices remained largely unheard by the British public. In the years that followed, however, these minority voices emerged and reshaped the nation's understanding of the conflict, and they continue to influence modern attitudes toward the First World War and war in general. The popular novels, poetry, films, and music that entertained the majority of Britons during the war years have been largely forgotten.

Chapter 8: Remembering and Memorializing the War

The First World War was more aggressively memorialized and commemorated than any war before or since. The honoring of the war dead reached near cult-like proportions, and the experience of the war was both mythologized and demonized. Millions of Britons lost close friends and relatives in the war, and their attempts to cope with this loss had profound effects on the national consciousness and the way in which the war was historicized. The 'memory' of the war, in particular, has emerged in recent years as an important historiographical issue, reflected in a new scholarly interest in war memorials, the cultural implications of collective memory, and the making of history.[1]

War memorials and commemorations show how the bereaved came to terms with the war. Simple street shrines grew up spontaneously during the war. Afterwards, they took on a permanent form. The Great War produced more monuments in Britain than any previous event in history. Every village, town, and city had its memorial, as did many businesses and schools. During and immediately following the war, the need for solace in remembering the war dead predominated, and most monuments celebrated the heroism and sacrifice of soldiers. During the 1920s, Remembrance Day ceremonies also evoked profound respect and emotion through the communal laying of wreaths, the observation of a two-minute silence, and the singing of religious and patriotic songs. The wearing of Flanders' poppies, made of paper and sold by ex-soldiers, also expressed widespread national mourning and solidarity. By the late 1920s and 1930s, however, a more pessimistic and cynical view of the war had emerged and competed with earlier patriotic interpretations. A spate of memoirs and war novels, especially by veterans, contributed to a mood of disillusionment. Commemorations of the war dead increasingly were bound up with pacifist denunciations of war itself, as well as criticism of a social and political order which some people now held responsible for so many 'meaningless' deaths.

Since the 1960s the pessimistic and cynical view of the war has come to dominate public understandings of the conflict. Some of this grew out of an anti-war movement related to the Cold War and revulsion at the U.S. escalation of the war in Vietnam. The widely held belief that the First World War was a tragedy has found expression in popular films and television programs, best-selling novels, and a school curriculum that privileges the voices of anti-war poets like Wilfred Owen. Earlier views of the war as a necessary conflict and a hard-won victory faded from view. In recent years some scholars have attempted to complexify our historical understanding of the Great War, but their efforts thus far have made little impact on the prevailing view that still emphasizes a naïve populace manipulated by deceptive propaganda and heedlessly slaughtered at the whim of incompetent generals.

* * *

Memorialization of the war and the war dead began long before the war had ended. In December 1915, the Civic Arts Association was founded to advise on the design of war memorials, and from 1916 onwards there were regular conferences and publications on the subject. In London's East End, makeshift street shrines sprang up carrying the names of local soldiers who were serving overseas or who had died, along with flowers, flags, and pictures of the Royal Family. More private family commemorations of the death of loved ones also took place. For the rich this might entail a stained-glass window or stone tablet in the local church. For the poor, this might mean a mantel 'shrine' of a framed photograph of the dead soldier surrounded by black ribbons and flags. Nick Mansfield describes one such family memorial in his grandmother's front room: 'On one side was a faded sepia postcard of a smooth faced teenager, her son Walter, self-conscious in ill-fitting khaki, contained in a coloured embossed mount of generals, allied flags, battleships and aeroplanes; on the other, a crude oil painting of a sunlit and flowered war cemetery, hawked door to door by a penniless woman artist in the early 1920s who filled in name, rank, and number to order.'[2]

In 1916, as the Somme offensive raged and casualties soared, a government committee was established to develop a memorial artifact to be sent to the next of kin of slain soldiers. The committee decided on a commemorative medallion and a contest was held for its design. The winning entry depicted Britannia holding a victory wreath in one hand and a trident in the other, accompanied by a lion. The name of the deceased was engraved along with the motto: 'He Died For Freedom And Honour.' Over a million of these medals were eventually minted and came to be popularly known as the 'dead man's penny.' Accompanying the medal was an elaborate printed scroll, which commended the soldier in elevated terms: 'He whom this scroll commemorates was numbered among those who, at the call of King and Country, left all that was dear to them, endured hardness, faced danger, and finally passed out of the sight of men by the path of duty and self-sacrifice, giving up their own lives that others might live in freedom.'[3]

Soldiers' graves rarely appeared in photographs in 1914–15, probably as part of a general effort to downplay the number of casualties and deaths. By 1916, as deaths mounted, images of military cemeteries became more frequent, reassuring families that their departed relatives were properly buried and their graves well cared for. One widely circulated photograph showed an Army chaplain tending British graves in Flanders. Another postcard depicted a neat grave surrounded by verdant countryside at which angelic young French women are leaving flowers, accompanied by the sentimental caption: 'The little French girls keep green the memory of the brave Englishmen dead on the field of honour.'[4] The reality undoubtedly bore little resemblance to these images of propaganda.

Wartime necessity altered long-standing burial customs and mourning rituals. Soldiers were buried in the absence of family and friends, or even their comrades, in hastily dug graves near the sites of battle. Thousands of bodies were never recovered or properly identified. This represented a striking reversal of the ideal civilian death where a person died between clean sheets in the family home, surrounded by relatives and friends. Elaborate funerals and Victorian-style ritualized mourning disappeared during the war, and even mourning dress was rejected because of the need to maintain a more optimistic appearance. Otherwise, the nation would have been clothed in a boundless sea of black. The absence of deathbed farewells and proper funerals deprived families of any real sense of closure, which in turn led to a number of novel and unorthodox mourning practices. For example, ritual prayers for the dead, which had been very uncommon in the Church of England, became widespread over the course of the war. Some evangelicals were horrified by what they saw as a return to medieval Catholicism, but most people welcomed the practice as it comforted them and helped them acknowledge the reality of their loved one's death.[5]

Spiritualism also assumed a major significance for many seeking to come to terms with their bereavement or looking for one final conversation with a lost son or husband. Both during and after the war, seances experienced a tremendous resurgence of popularity. At one point, there were over 100 mediums practicing in the Kensington area alone. A best-seller of 1916 was Sir Oliver Lodge's *Raymond*, a memoir of his son killed in the war. The book, which went through numerous editions into the 1920s, contained a number of alleged spirit communications from his dead son received via a medium. Lodge's scientific reputation lent authority to spiritualism in the eyes of many people, as did the endorsement of the celebrated author Sir Arthur Conan Doyle. Doyle had also lost a son in the war and became an enthusiastic apologist for spiritualism. He wrote about the phenomenon in *New Revelation* (1918) and spent the last years of his life assiduously promoting his beliefs.[6]

* * *

Early in the war the decision was made not to return bodies to Britain for burial. The Graves Registration Commission was set up to record and care for the graves of the fallen. It was later replaced by the Imperial War Graves Commission which was to establish cemeteries in France and Belgium. For the first time in history, scattered bodies were to be disinterred, gathered together, reburied, and individually marked. After the war, land in France and Belgium was deeded in perpetuity to Great Britain for the creation of more than 1800 cemeteries which were laid out according to a systematic pattern. In the center of every cemetery was a 'Cross of Sacrifice' and a 'Stone of Remembrance' inscribed with the biblical verse 'Their name liveth for evermore.' Identical gravestones were arranged in neat, uniform rows with the dead soldier's name, rank, regiment, and date of death inscribed. By 1938, when the Imperial War Graves Commission completed its work, 557 520 soldiers had been buried in identified graves and another 180 861 unidentified bodies had been given individual, though anonymous, burials.[7] The uniformity of headstones for all ranks – although much resisted by the upper classes – and the great care taken to create individual graves, was widely hailed at the time as a democratic gesture and a tribute to the common soldier.[8]

The principal architects chosen for the War Graves Commission were Edwin Lutyens, Herbert Baker, and Reginald Blomfield, all well-established figures in their field. Lutyens, who later designed the Whitehall Cenotaph, favored a non-denominational and secular memorial stone as the centerpiece of every cemetery. He designed the 'Stone of Remembrance' based on classical precedents. The Church, however, insisted on the addition of a cross, which was designed by Blomfield. This so-called 'Cross of Sacrifice' was carved from stone and had a bronze sword superimposed on it. Rudyard Kipling, whose own son had died at Loos and was never found, also served as a War Graves Commissioner until his death in 1936. Kipling suggested most of the inscriptions used in the cemeteries: 'Their Name Liveth for Evermore' on the Stone of Remembrance, 'A Soldier of the Great War/ Known unto God' on head-stones of unidentified bodies, and 'Their Glory Shall Not Be Blotted Out' for graves which had been obliterated by bombardments.[9]

In addition to creating hundreds of war cemeteries, the government also decided to erect national battlefield memorials to commemorate significant events of the war. This work was overseen by the Battle Exploits Memorial Committee, whose most famous monuments were built to commemorate the Battles of Ypres and the Somme. Churchill had wanted the ruined town of Ypres to stand as a permanent memorial, though, unsurprisingly, the local residents preferred to rebuild. Instead, Reginald Blomfield designed a massive arch leading to a memorial hall, on whose walls were carved more than 54 000 names of soldiers who died near Ypres and whose bodies were never recovered. Edwin Lutyens's Somme Memorial at Thiepval honored the missing war dead from that battle. Lutyens designed a series of interlocking arches inscribed with the names of more than 73 000 British soldiers. These memorials were not traditional 'triumphal' arches, but existed essentially as rosters of the names of ordinary soldiers. They resisted a traditional or symbolic representation of the war and contributed to the 'democratization of memory.'[10]

Most Britons regarded the cemeteries and battlefields of northern France as almost holy sites, which they longed to visit. In 1922, George V visited the war cemeteries of France and Belgium. His trip, significantly known as the 'King's pilgrimage', embodied a profound expression of national grief. Many tours by ordinary Britons followed. The St Barnabas Society, named for the patron saint of consolation, was founded by an Anglican minister in 1920 to organize subsidized pilgrimages to Flanders for those too poor to pay for the trip. The YMCA, British Legion, and Red Cross also organized low-cost (£6 in 1920) trips to war cemeteries. Commercial tour companies, like Thomas Cook, offered a range of pack-age deals, and numerous guidebooks were also published. Books such as the *Michelin Guide to the Battlefields* (1919), *How to See the Battlefields* (1919), and *Seven Days in Belgium* (1925) were full of practical advice for those unaccustomed to travel abroad, explaining what to pack, how to navigate customs, and what to tip in foreign hotels. Battlefield tourism tended to perpetuate the most heroic images of the war. Elevated rhetoric was typically employed by tour guides and books: 'Here nearly 8000 of the flower of British manhood lie sleeping', or 'There is not a single acre from here on to Ypres that is not made sacred by the blood of men.' By 1931, visits to war graves by widows and parents ran to some 140 000 a year, increasing to 160 000 by 1939.[11]

Not everyone could visit cemeteries in France, and the need for memorials at home inspired numerous town and village monuments, as well as national sites of mourning in London: the Tomb of the Unknown Warrior in Westminster Abbey and the Cenotaph near Whitehall. The Cenotaph (a Greek word meaning 'empty tomb') was designed by Edwin Lutyens for the Victory Day celebrations held on 19 July 1919 to mark the signing of the Versailles Peace Treaty. The need for a focal point of observance arose, and Lutyens proposed a cenotaph, hastily constructed of wood and plaster, as a temporary solution. His simple classically inspired design consisted of a tomb chest set on top of a tall stepped pylon. The monument is devoid of traditional symbols and stands as a minimalist, almost abstract object. Lutyens hoped to transcend the narrow parochialism of religious or patriotic imagery and to achieve a more 'elemental' response to mourning. The cenotaph was so much admired that public opinion demanded it be replaced by a permanent version in stone, which was unveiled on 11 November 1920, the second anniversary of the Armistice. At that time, a seven-mile long line of mourners laid wreaths at its base. A number of cities built cenotaphs modeled on the one in London, including Manchester, Glasgow, Belfast, Newport, and Hull. Ceramic replicas were widely sold and displayed in households across the nation.[12]

The second anniversary of the Armistice also saw the creation of the Tomb of the Unknown Warrior. This national memorial was the idea of an Army chaplain, David Railton, who proposed a public funeral and burial for the body of an unidentified soldier to represent all the missing war dead. The method of selecting the soldier was highly ritualized: one body was exhumed from each of six cemeteries – Ypres, Cambrai, Arras, the Somme, the Aisne, and the Marne – and taken to Ypres, where a blindfolded officer picked one of the bodies. The body was then taken back to Britain in a coffin made from an oak tree from the grounds of Hampton Court Palace. After resting overnight at a temporary chapel in Victoria Station, the body was taken to Westminster Abbey on 11 November 1920, where it was interred beneath the floor with great ceremony. In the week following Armistice Day, nearly a million people visited the tomb. Britons, many of whose own relatives' bodies had never been identified, found the site especially meaningful and many imagined the unknown soldier to be in fact their own son, husband, or brother.[13]

The Imperial War Museum also opened in 1920 as a national memorial to the Great War and an archive of war-related materials. The museum had been proposed early in 1917 by Sir Alfred Mond, the First Commissioner of Works. The War Cabinet approved the idea on 5 March 1917 with a grant of £3000 to begin collecting artifacts. The original plans to build a massive complex on an 11-acre site in Hyde Park were radically scaled back in the postwar climate of austerity. The museum was first installed in the old Crystal Palace at Sydenham, and in 1936 it moved to its current home at the former Bedlam insane asylum.[14] Budgetary constraints caused the downfall of many other grand memorial schemes, the most famous of which was Charles Fawley's plan for rebuilding portions of the City of Westminster in central London as an Empire War Memorial. The central feature of this proposal was the creation of a new 120-foot wide Empire Avenue stretching from the Embankment to Victoria Station. The Avenue would incorporate three plazas as sites for monuments and would lead to a new War Memorial Bridge replacing Lambeth Bridge, decorated with bronze statues of war heroes.[15]

The vast majority of British war memorials were small, inexpensive monuments erected by localities and funded by popular subscription. In villages, towns, and cities across the British Isles, people followed the example of the London Cenotaph by constructing monuments to the dead in the absence of actual graves. Exhibitions on memorial designs were held at the Victoria and Albert (V & A) Museum and National Academy in 1919 and 1920. The V&A also published a pamphlet, *Inscriptions Suggested for War Memorials* (1919), in an attempt to guide local decisions and ensure that 'appropriate' wording would prevail nationwide. Most of the suggestions were from the Bible or the 'classics' of British literature, reflecting the general traditionalism of most postwar memorial art. Local monuments in particular were sponsored by conservative social elites who looked to the past for their aesthetic and moral inspiration. In the years immediately following the war, most Britons sought to honor the sacrifices of their friends and relations and, in doing so, to transcend the horrors of war. George Mosse argues that the monument movement enabled people to create an emotionally comforting cult to the 'glorious dead' and to transform the grim reality of the war into a meaningful and sacred event.[16]

The overwhelming majority of war memorials followed the conventions of the genre – obelisks, figures of a weeping female, winged Victory, St George, and the idealized soldier. A cross was by far the most common local memorial, usually placed on the village green or in the churchyard and inscribed with the names of the local men who had died in the war. The Christian ideal of self-sacrifice figured in many memorials – a favorite inscription was Christ's words from St John's Gospel: 'Greater love hath no man than this, that a man lay down his life for his friends' (15:13). The spirit of patriotism and triumphalism was also frequently present, as in Goscombe John's massive monument in Newcastle, 'The Response, 1914', commemorating the raising of local regiments. It consists of a procession of life-size bronze figures being led by a figure of winged Victory. The men of Newcastle are shown bidding farewell to their wives and children as they march off to war. John, who was born in 1860, continued to work in the Victorian aesthetic tradition as well as to present the past century's heroic image of war. Derwent Wood's Machine Gun Corps Memorial in Hyde Park is another famous example of the persistence of the victorious tradition in war monuments. A bronze nude in the classical style depicts David holding up the sword of Goliath. The inscription on the base proclaims triumphantly: 'Saul hath slain his thousands, but David his tens of thousands.'[17]

While most memorials respected traditional values and reiterated the righteousness of Britain's cause, some monuments sought to celebrate the achievement of peace rather than that of victory over the enemy. At Leeds, for example, the war memorial took the form of an allegorical figure of peace, holding a dove. A few locales even produced socialist war memorials which emphasized the 'blood of sacrifice' of working people for a better world. At St Mark's Church in Leicester, for instance, the memorial window showed a black man supplicating for freedom and a woman clutching the Charter of the League of Nations. By commissioning this window, the parishioners and their 'red' vicar made clear their conviction that the war must bring to pass certain 'aspects of the Kingdom of God on earth,' such as self-determination of the native races, education of the poor, and greater freedom for the worker. Eric Gill's war memorial at the University of Leeds blamed the rich for the war through its use of the device of Christ driving the moneychangers out of the temple. Gill emphasized his allegory by depicting the figures in modern dress.[18]

Some argued over the design or symbolism of memorials, while others rejected the likes of obelisks, cenotaphs, and winged Victories altogether, preferring something more practical or beneficial to the living. Robert Jones, a prominent surgeon, felt that the best memorial to the war dead would be a stronger commitment to social welfare: 'Are our memorials to be spiritual or material, living and permanent, or dead and cold: For my part I have no hesitation in saying that marble or brass has no re-echoing voice in me. My feeling is, that the heroic spirit that sent our beloved dead to their end should be reflected in an equally heroic effort on our part to make and keep the nation efficient.' People like Jones favored hospitals and scholarships over the more usual 'marble or brass.' Disputes over the nature of a local memorial frequently coalesced along class lines, with the elite advocating a cross, statue, or plaque, and many working people preferring something 'useful' like a social hall, recreational field, or an endowed cottage. The workers' view was expressed by a returned soldier in Cambridge, who wrote to the local paper: 'As a discharged and disabled soldier I should like to be allowed to suggest that a much better and more substantial form of memorial would be the erection of a number of semi- or self-contained cottages to accommodate a number of disabled heroes, who now very often find it difficult to get cottages within reasonable distance of a town and in the fresh country air.' If the local elite were footing the bill, they may have favored crosses over cottages as the thrifty alternative, but also as the one more in keeping with their sense of what was 'fitting.'[19]

In cities, with their larger resources, it was possible to divide funds between monuments and charitable projects, and memorials often took the form of hospitals, museums, or churches. Darlington, for example, built a Memorial Hospital, while Ipswich added a memorial wing on to its hospital, and Portsmouth gave £10 000 for the improvement of its town hospital. Stockport and Aberdeen constructed memorial art galleries. In Liverpool, it was decided that the northeast transept of the city's new cathedral would serve as a war memorial. A marble cenotaph served as an altar, flanked by statues of a soldier and sailor. Schools also frequently built libraries, classrooms, chapels, or assembly halls as war memorials. These additions usually contained a plaque with the names of former students who had died in the war.[20]

Many locales also produced commemorative books to honor their war dead. In 1920, through the gift of a wealthy industrialist, all the young men of Keighley, Yorkshire, who had served in the war, or the families of those killed, were presented with a copy of *Local Heroes of the Great War*. The cover was embossed with the flags of Britain and its allies, and the title printed in large, gilt letters. The book contained pictures and vital statistics of the hundreds of local men who had died in the war.[21] Regiments and schools often published similar commemorative volumes, as did the nation's colonies and dominions. Almost every household in Australia and New Zealand had a copy of the *Anzac Album*, proudly displayed next to the family Bible. Like most local memorials or battlefield monuments, the most important feature of commemorative books was the names of the war dead – which were invested with an almost transcendent importance. The very act of cataloging the dead may have helped survivors accept the reality of their death.

While the British venerated their own nation's war dead, they frequently neglected the graves of imperial soldiers, especially in Africa and the Middle East. Military cemeteries in Africa contained a central memorial stone, but not individual headstones, as colonial authorities argued that Africans had not yet reached 'the stage of civilization' at which individual graves would be appreciated. Over the years the cemeteries were often abandoned and allowed to revert to nature. The Basra memorial in Iraq, commemorating the imperial soldiers who died in the Mesopotamian campaign, listed the names of all 8000 British war dead, but only the names of 665 Indian officers. The names of more than 33 000 Indian soldiers who died were not inscribed on the memorial.[22]

In India, however, the imperial government sponsored an elaborate All-India War Memorial in Delhi, hoping thereby to strengthen Indian ties to Britain at the very time when Gandhian nationalism was working to sever them. The memorial, built during the 1920s, was a massive stone arch designed by Edwin Lutyens and inscribed with the names of 13 617 Indian soldiers who had died in the war. Its inauguration in 1931 was intended to shore up imperial ties, and at the unveiling ceremony, General Fabian Ware spoke of India 'standing freely shoulder to shoulder with other nations of the Empire on the side of right and freedom.' After independence in 1947 the memorial was renamed India Gate and was appropriated as a symbol of the Indian nationalist movement. It was transformed from a site of mourning to a site of festivity.[23]

The Irish Free State, like independent India, downplayed the memorialization of its war dead, hoping to forget Irish support for the British war effort which nationalists now found embarrassing. The Irish National War Memorial, originally planned for central Dublin, was eventually built in a park far outside the city and was not completed until 1938. Due to nationalist opposition, the memorial was never 'officially' dedicated and it fell into decay and disrepair. In marked contrast to this neglect, Protestants in Northern Ireland, who remained part of the United Kingdom after 1922, proudly commemorated their community's participation in the war. Conflicting memories of the First World War continue to divide the two Irelands.[24]

* * *

A highly elaborated ritual of remembrance developed in the years following the war, centered on Armistice Day, 11 November. A defining feature of this commemoration was the public observance of two minutes' silence at 11 a.m. – the eleventh hour of the eleventh day of the eleventh month – marking the moment when the war ended. The two minutes' silence had been the idea of Sir Percy Fitzpatrick, a politician from South Africa, where a silence had been observed every noon during the war as a reminder of the distant conflict. The silence was observed for the first time in Britain on Armistice Day, 1919. It was intended not only to honor the war dead, but to unite a country caught up in postwar political and economic turmoil. According to an editorial in the *Daily Express*: 'It is our duty to see that they did not die in vain, and for the accomplishment of that duty all classes must combine as they did to win the war, unselfishly and harmoniously. There must be a truce in domestic quarrels, an end to industrial strife. We must all pull together lest the rewards of victory be thrown away.'[25] The silence could hardly end social conflict, but for a moment it swept the nation up in collective emotion and solidarity. When clocks chimed 11, all activity stopped. Even the most cynical individuals reported being struck by the irresistible force of the silence. People, gathered together in public or at their places of work, wept openly as they remembered their dead friends and relatives. Some of this mood is captured in John Freeman's poem, 'Armistice Day':

> Earth's pulse still was beating,
> The bright stars circling;
> Only our tongues were hushing.
> While Time ticked silent on, men drew
> A deeper breath than passion knew.[26]

Throughout the years that led to the Second World War, on Armistice Day, in towns across Britain, people would assemble near the local war memorial at 11 a.m. to observe the silence. This was usually followed by the singing of hymns and the national anthem, the laying of wreaths, and the sounding of the 'last post' by a bugler. Civic and Church leaders participated in the ceremonies, as did veterans, schoolchildren, and youth organizations like the Boy Scouts. Certain literary texts and symbols became associated with honoring the war dead. Laurence Binyon's poem, 'For the Fallen,' was frequently recited at public commemorations:

> They shall grow not old, as we that are left grow old:
> Age shall not weary them, nor the years condemn.
> At the going down of the sun and in the morning
> We will remember them.[27]

Poppies became the most common emblem of remembrance, inspired by John McCrae's popular poem 'In Flanders Fields':

> In Flanders fields the poppies blow
> Between the crosses, row on row,

That mark our place, and in the sky
The larks, still bravely singing, fly
Unheard amid the guns below . . .[28]

In 1921, the British Legion began selling paper poppies to be worn on Armistice Day as a way of honoring the dead and as a fund-raising effort. By the 1930s, over 20 million poppies were being sold each year, raising more than half a million pounds.[29]

In his history of postwar commemoration, *Fallen Soldiers*, George Mosse argues that the nation's image-makers made saints of dead soldiers and shrines of their graves and monuments, which helped perpetuate heroic myths about the war and maintain the old social order. Memorialization of the war, however, provoked anger in some, especially ex-servicemen. Siegfried Sassoon criticized war memorials as politically motivated attempts to glorify the war. In his poem, 'On Passing the New Menin Gate', he declares:

Well might the Dead who struggled in the slime
Rise and deride this sepulchre of crime.[30]

Visiting war memorials in Flanders, Vera Brittain also repudiated them as 'a cheating and a camouflage', since they continued to suggest that the war had been noble and glorious.[31] Some maintained that the politicians who erected the monuments were the very men who sent off the young to die in 1914 and who, in the postwar world, did little to assist veterans. During the labor unrest and strikes of the 1920s, war memorials often served as rallying places for workers, many of whom were war veterans. In 1921, there were protests at a number of Armistice Day ceremonies. In London, unemployed veterans marched to the Cenotaph wearing pawn-shop tickets instead of medals. In Liverpool, a group of out-of-work soldiers shouted 'what we need is food not prayers.'[32]

As the decade progressed, more critical evaluations of the war emerged, challenging the triumphalist rhetoric expressed in many memorials and Armistice Day ceremonies. In his speech unveiling Dundee's War Memorial in 1925, Sir Ian Hamilton criticized the government's neglect of unemployed servicemen and reflected harshly on the war's destructiveness: 'There is no reason it [the memorial] should not endure till the scientists who invented poison gas carry out their principles to a logical conclusion and explode their own planet.' Some later war memorials rejected the dominant chivalric and romantic traditions. For example, the 1925 Royal Artillery Memorial at Hyde Park Corner included a number of realistic bronze soldiers by Charles Sargeant Jagger that stood in stark contrast to the idealized classical figures found on most memorials. At the time, Jagger was harshly criticized for the 'gruesomeness' of his depiction of a dead soldier at the north end of the monument. One critic condemned Jagger for using the 'war memorial as a means of forcing home on the minds of the public the horror and terror of war.' Jagger had served as a soldier at Gallipoli and the Western Front and his work reflected the more nuanced attitude toward the war that was developing during the 1920s.[33]

Disagreement over the war's meaning came to a head in 1925 over a campaign led by the Reverend Dick Sheppard to make Armistice Day a more solemn occasion. Sheppard and his supporters were especially critical of the Victory balls and dances which had become common the evening before 11 November. As Sheppard explained in a letter to *The Times*: 'a fancy dress ball on a grand scale as a tribute to the Great Deliverance which followed on the unspeakable agony of 1914–18 seems to me not so much irreligious as indecent.'[34] Conservatives like Lord Curzon defended the balls. They wanted to emphasize the celebration of victory and imperial glory, and resisted the notions that the war had been 'an unspeakable agony' and that Armistice Day should be a day of national mourning. There was considerable debate in the press during the Fall of 1925, but the advocates of a new solemnity generally prevailed, as many cities refused dance licenses that year for 10 and 11 November.[35]

* * *

The critical rethinking of the war's meaning culminated in the late 1920s with the publication of numerous bleak and angry war novels and memoirs. The public response of many of the war's participants, especially soldiers, had been delayed. At first, those who had been through the war felt that their experience could not or should not be communicated. Many veterans struggled to suppress their memories, and others believed that language itself was inadequate to the task of conveying the horrors of the war. In the years immediately afterwards, silence was the frequent response of many. Only with the passage of years were veterans able to revisit their war memories. Blunden, Graves, and Aldington had all attempted to describe their wartime experiences shortly afterwards, but had given up. Wartime traumas needed to be observed from a distance before they could be recounted. The need to inform a new generation about the reality of war also seemed more urgent as another war appeared increasingly likely.[36]

The years from 1928 to 1933 saw a tremendous resurgence of popular interest in the war, and there was an explosion of novels and memoirs on the subject, many of them written by former soldiers. Among the best known of these works are Ford Madox Ford, *Last Post* (1928), Siegfried Sassoon, *Memoirs of a Fox-Hunting Man* (1928), Richard Aldington, *Death of a Hero* (1929), Robert Graves, *Good-Bye to All That* (1929), Mary Borden, *The Forbidden Zone* (1929), Henry Williamson, *The Wet Flanders Plain* (1929), Edmund Blunden, *Undertones of War* (1930), Frederick Manning, *Her Privates, We* (1930), and Vera Brittain, *Testament of Youth* (1933). These books utterly rejected earlier romanticized depictions of the war, instead portraying it as a brutal slaughter and tragedy. In so doing, they radically reshaped the public attitude toward the war, and they continue to dominate the historical imagination today.[37]

The new war books often depicted the war as a futile slaughter engineered by power-hungry politicians and incompetent generals. They also exposed the chivalric language of propaganda as a lie and a mockery – in Aldington's words, 'the supreme and tragic climax of Victorian cant.'[38] The authors, many of whom had served as soldiers and nurses, contradicted patriotic propaganda and exposed the public to the gruesome details of trench warfare and the mortal consequences of military blunders.

Like the earlier anti-war poetry of Sassoon, Owen, and Rosenberg, the war books of Graves, Aldington, Williamson, and others depicted the squalor of the trenches and the horrors of frontline experience. They savagely debunked the popular romantic images of warfare. In *Good-Bye to All That*, Graves recalled:

> I saw a group bending over a man lying at the bottom of the trench. He was making a snoring noise mixed with animal groans. At my feet lay the cap he had worn, splashed with his brains. I had never seen human brain before; I somehow regarded them as a poetical figment. One can joke with a badly-wounded man and congratulate him on being out of it. One can disregard a dead man. But even a miner can't make a joke that sounds like a joke over a man who takes three hours to die, after the top part of his head has been taken off by a bullet fired at twenty yards' range.[39]

Death was not pretty, and Graves and his fellow soldier-authors had no intention of making it seem so.

In these accounts, soldiers had no illusions about the war and they make no pretense about chivalry. They swear, drink, fornicate, and generally give in to the dark forces within. According to Manning: 'Men had reverted to a more primitive stage in their development, and had become nocturnal beasts of prey, hunting each other in packs: this was the uniformity, quite distinct from the effect of military discipline, which their own nature had imposed on them.'[40] In one of the darkest depictions of the war, from James Hanley's novella, *The German Prisoner* (1930), two British soldiers take refuge in a shell hole where they encounter a frightened German soldier. They kick him to death and then dance on his corpse until a shell blows them all to pieces. Such graphic retellings of the war's brutality contributed to a new anti-heroic understanding of warfare which was dramatically at odds with a thousand years of western literary tradition.

Perhaps the most enduring legacy of the anti-war literature is the idea of a 'lost generation.' For some, this referred to the nearly million British and colonial soldiers killed in the war, and the many others seriously incapacitated. As Vera Brittain maintained in *Testament of Youth* (1933), 'the finest flowers of English manhood had been plucked from a whole generation.'[41] The war dead represented one in seven of those who served and one in ten of those of military age. Ten years after the Armistice, another two-and-a-half million men were receiving pensions for war disabilities and 48 mental hospitals were still tending 65 000 shell-shock victims. The public presence of blind and limbless ex-servicemen were constant reminders of the human costs of the war.[42] These dead and injured soldiers constituted the 'lost generation', whom Brittain and others came to see as the missing political and cultural leaders of the postwar years and the cause of their nation's decline. As late as 1962, J. B. Priestley still maintained that 'nobody, nothing will shift me from the belief which I shall take to the grave that the generation to which I belonged, destroyed between 1914 and 1918, was a great generation, marvelous in its promise.'[43]

For others the 'lost generation' referred to the survivors, young men and women whose lives had been scarred by the war, who lacked a sense of belonging, and who felt doomed to drift through life. This sense of alienation was expressed by Sassoon, who saw himself forever separated from those who had not been in the war, since he 'had experienced something that they couldn't share or imagine.'[44] Much of the literature of disillusionment expressed the difficulty of living with the memory of the war. The narrator of Aldington's novel *Death of a Hero* (1929) cannot rid himself of his survivor's guilt: 'What right have I to live? Is it five million, is it ten million, is it twenty million? What does the exact count matter? There they are and we are responsible. Tortures of hell, we are responsible. When I meet an unmaimed man of my generation, I want to shout at him: "How did you escape?" . . . It is dreadful to have outlived your life, to have shirked your fate, to have overspent your welcome.'[45] Ruth Holland expresses feelings similar to Aldington's in *The*

Lost Generation (1932), as does May Wedderburn Cannan in *The Lonely Generation* (1934). The heroine of Cannan's novel was a VAD whose life after the war is lonely and purposeless. She can find no place for herself in the 'dance mad' Britain of the 1920s.

Some felt permanently trapped inside their war experiences, unable to put them aside. Charles Carrington recalled in the 1960s that 'the 1916 fixation had caught me and stunted any mental growth, so that even ten years later I was retarded and adolescent. I could not escape from the comradeship of the trenches which had become a mental internment camp.'[46] Ivor Gurney, the poet and composer, died in a mental hospital in 1937, 20 years after he had been gassed in France. He continued writing about the war convinced that it had never ended.[47] Less pathologically, though no less relentlessly, Siegfried Sassoon, Vera Brittain, and Henry Williamson made their war experiences the centerpiece of their writing for the rest of their lives. Edmund Blunden likewise continually returned to the war in his poetry. Shortly before his death in 1974, he wrote: 'My experiences in the First World War have haunted me all my life and for many days I have, it seemed, lived in that world rather than this.'[48]

The disjuncture between the pessimistic war books of the late 1920s and earlier more optimistic narratives calls for some explanation, and recent scholarship has complicated our understanding of the books' composition and intent. Leonard Smith in *The Embattled Self* (2007) and Janet Watson in *Fighting Different Wars* (2004) make clear that many of the authors of popular anti-war books, like Robert Graves and Vera Brittain, had depicted the war more positively in their earlier wartime letters and diaries, endorsing the conflict with Germany as necessary and just. Many testimonies written during the war were also chaotic and incoherent, as soldiers and frontline war workers often felt overwhelmed by the war's destructiveness and rapid transformation of their lives. Years of reflection were necessary to secure a more critical distance and to compose narratives that would make sense of the war to readers.[49]

In the meantime many Britons were becoming disillusioned with postwar society. The war had not made the world more secure nor had it ended hostility between nations. The League of Nations proved ineffective in promoting peaceful conflict resolution, and by the 1930s another war appeared increasingly likely. An economic downturn in the 1920s and a worldwide depression in the 1930s meant that many people who had struggled through the Great War in the hopes of a better future were now experiencing serious hardships. Disillusionment with the troubled postwar world led some Britons to begin re-evaluating the war itself as well as the state's wartime role in molding public opinion. The popular and spontaneous support for the war was forgotten or suppressed in

favor of the belief that the government had lied to people and manipulated them through propaganda. Since the war had not produced a lasting peace or a more prosperous and harmonious society, some people
began to question the necessity of so many lost lives. What had the war
really been for? Who had benefited from it?

The war books of 1928–33 expressed a growing cynicism in postwar
culture, but they were not as uniformly anti-war as many people now
imagine. As Brian Bond points out in *The Unquiet Western Front* (2002),
few writers at the time suggested that Britain should not have fought the
war or that it was not worth winning.[50] The ex-soldiers who wrote most
of the books expressed considerable ambivalence about the war. They
decried the brutality and waste, but remembered fondly the comradeship, the adventure, and the higher purpose of working for the good
of others. Despite the miserable conditions of trench warfare and the
mass death, a number of soldier memoirists still remembered the war
as an exhilarating experience. Some works represented the war as *both*
terrible and worthwhile. Most famous in this regard is war veteran R. C.
Sherriff's hit play, *Journey's End,* which ran for a record 593 performances
in 1928–29. The play candidly portrayed the horrors of war, but differed
from many of the war books of 1929 in that its soldier protagonists were
celebrated for their dedication, endurance and dogged adherence to
public school values.[51]

While a new generation of postwar writers and intellectuals was
haunted by the war and treated aspects of it in a harsher light, this did
not preclude other, more patriotic and celebratory, views. As Samuel
Hynes argues in *A War Imagined* (1991), alongside the interwar counter-
culture that rejected the war and its values, was 'a conservative culture
that clung to and asserted traditional values... Each culture had its art, its
literature, and its monuments, and each denied the other.'[52] Many British
authors continued to uphold the heroic literary tradition of war writing,
and many British readers rejected 'the defeatist novels and fiercely petu-
lant journals' of the late 1920s and early 1930s.[53] The Conservative journalist Douglas Jerrold, for one, published a pamphlet in 1930, *The Lie About
the War,* in which he attacked the spate of anti-war books then current. He
represented the viewpoint of those who still saw the war as both necessary
and meaningful. Some people continued to write idealistic and romantic
novels of the war, and they still found a readership. C. S. Forester's *Brown
on Resolution* (1929) and Leslie Roberts's *When the Gods Laughed* (1930)
presented the war as a field for adventure and a means for individuals to
prove their worth.[54]

The press remained essentially conservative, royalist, and imperial in
outlook, as did school textbooks, teaching manuals, and much of popular

culture. Robert Kee remembered from his schooldays in the 1930s that the war was bathed in the 'glare of national self-congratulation and piety.' Children were taught that 'we had beaten the Germans. The retreat from Mons had been a wonderful thing. Angels had appeared for us there. We had won the Battle of the Somme. Sir Douglas Haig was a great hero.'[55] Widely read commemorative histories of the war still chronicled it in the old pious manner. Mythic and heroic representations of the war still dominated in adventure stories, juvenile fiction, and cinema.[56]

At the very time when thousands read Graves's and Aldington's unromantic anti-war narratives, millions saw popular films like *Wings* (1927), *Hell's Angels* (1930), and *The Dawn Patrol* (1930) which celebrated the heroic adventures of First World War aviators. Throughout the 1920s, British Instructional Films produced a whole series of films based on First World War battles, in which the engagements were depicted as glorious British victories 'in the tradition of Blenheim and Waterloo.' Fictional films about the war might depict the mud and misery of the trenches, but they also imagined it as a great adventure in which soldiers redeemed themselves through acts of bravery and self-sacrifice. In *Poppies of Flanders* (1927), for example, the war is dramatized as a noble venture, in which the protagonist, Jim Brown, is transformed from a pitiable drunkard into a courageous hero.[57]

The anti-war sentiments of some ex-soldiers, like Sassoon and Graves, were far from representative of all veterans. Hundreds of thousands of veterans joined the British Legion, an organization of ex-servicemen that assisted disabled and unemployed veterans and honored the memory of the war dead. The Legion sponsored the annual 'Poppy Day,' which raised money for veterans in need, and the organization upheld a patriotic view of the war. Most Legion members remained proud of their service and refused to buy into the notion that the war had been unnecessary or mistaken in its aims.[58]

* * *

Disagreement over the war's meaning continued into the 1930s. The recognition by some people of the horrors of war led them to a new desire to avoid future conflict, and commemoration of the Great War's dead became intertwined with the peace movement. Pacifist organizations like the Peace Pledge Union and the Quakers held public meetings on Armistice Day and distributed anti-war literature. In 1930 the Peace Committee of the Society of Friends handed out a pamphlet by J. B. Priestley, *The Lost Generation*, which argued that the human costs of war can never be justified: 'Most of the men who were boys when I was a boy cannot sit and drink with me. Loos and Gallipoli and the Somme did for them. They went and saved something and never came back. What it was they saved I cannot exactly tell, but I do know that I have never seen anything since 1918 that was worth their sacrifice.'[59] In 1933, the Women's Cooperative Guild began selling white 'peace' poppies on Armistice Day. This new emblem was later taken up by the Peace Pledge Union and the wearing of white poppies became part of an alternative Armistice Day observance.[60]

Pacifists challenged conventional interpretations of the war by re-imagining the memorialization of the war dead. Rather than honoring 'heroes' who had died for a glorious cause, they emphasized the 'martyrdom' of soldiers who had been sacrificed to the greed of capitalists and the hollow ambitions of politicians and generals. Patriotic symbols were contested and imaginatively reworked. For example, Nurse Edith Cavell, whose death at the hands of a German firing squad had long been used by conservative propagandists as a symbol of the enemy's barbarism, was given another meaning by those in the peace movement. Her final words – 'I realize that patriotism is not enough. I must have no hatred or bitterness towards anyone' – were seen by pacifists as reaching out to a larger loyalty than a narrow devotion to the state. Shaw protested that by omitting her last words from her memorial in London, jingoists were using her as an instrument of pro-war propaganda. In 1929, the Labour government added the inscription 'patriotism is not enough' to her statue's pedestal.[61]

The patriotic lexicon of 1914 had lost much of its persuasive force by the time of the Second World War. No one cheered when war broke out in 1939, and no one imagined it would be a great adventure. The experience of this war only confirmed the grim lessons of the Great War. The technology of warfare had grown more destructive and further transgressive of the boundaries between combatants and civilians. Fewer British soldiers died in the Second World War, but the bombing of British cities was far more devastating. The German 'blitz' damaged four million homes and killed some 60 000 people. Nonetheless, Britons never doubted the moral purpose of the fight against Hitler and Fascism, which only underscored the supposed pointlessness of the First World War. Prussianism now seemed almost benign when compared to Nazism. In June 1946, it was agreed that the Sunday preceding 11 November would be observed as Remembrance Sunday, in honor of those killed in both wars and that the inscription '1939–1945' would be added beneath 'The Glorious Dead 1919' on the Whitehall Cenotaph. Most towns did not build a separate memorial to the dead of the Second World War, but added their names (usually considerably fewer) to those inscribed on their memorials to the Great War.[62]

* * *

During the 1950s, memories of the First World War had apparently been eclipsed by the experience of the Second, but there was a resurgence of interest in the earlier conflict during the 1960s. This time proved to be a decade of protest and the questioning of traditional values and beliefs. Not surprisingly this interest was reflected in a reflowering of the literature of disillusionment and in cynical, anti-heroic representations of the Great War. Popular histories of the war, such as Alan Clark's *The Donkeys* (1961), Barbara Tuchman's *The Guns of August* (1962), and A. J. P. Taylor's *The First World War* (1963), reinforced the negative images of the First World War as a cruel and futile slaughter. Anthony Burgess's dystopic novel, *The Wanting Seed* (1962), imagined a future genocide in which the First World War served as a blueprint for mass slaughter. Joan Littlewood's irreverent stage play, 'Oh! What a Lovely War' (1963), mocked the pretensions of Britain's wartime politicians and generals in the spirit of 1960s anti-authoritarianism. The popular film *King and Country* (1964) was a sympathetic telling of the story of a First World War private shot for desertion, while *Lawrence of Arabia* (1962) highlighted the duplicity of British diplomats, who exploit the Arab revolt for their own imperialist agenda. By the end of the decade the war was firmly understood as a tragedy and the soldiers who fought in it as victims. Earlier, positive, representations of the war were forgotten or else firmly rejected as being the result of deceptive propaganda.[63]

The British reading public rediscovered the postwar literature of disillusionment and there was a resurgence of war memoirs and novels in the 1960s and 1970s. New editions of Aldington's *Death of a Hero* and Brittain's *Testament of Youth* were published. Charles Carrington, who had published his war memoirs, *A Subaltern's War*, in 1929 under the pseudonym Charles Edmonds, revisited this material in his 1965 book, *Soldier from the Wars Returning*. Frederic Manning's anti-war novel, *Her Privates, We* (1930), was finally published in its unexpurgated version (including much profanity) in 1977 as *The Middle Parts of Fortune*. A whole new series of war memoirs also appeared, including George Coppard's *With a Machine Gun to Cambrai* (1969), Eric Hiscock's *The Bells of Hell Go Ting-a-Ling-a-Ling* (1976), H. E. L. Mellersh's *Schoolboy into War* (1978), and P. J. Campbell's *In The Cannon's Mouth* (1979). These works were very much in the tradition of Graves and Sassoon, and reinforced the pessimistic view of the First World War.

Modern perceptions of the war, especially, have been shaped by the anti-war poets, Blunden, Owen, Sassoon, and Rosenberg, whose work has steadily grown in influence over the years. Benjamin Britten's 1962 *War Requiem* featured poems by Owen and Sassoon recited to musical accompaniment. In 1963, C. Day Lewis edited a new edition of Owen's poetry and in 1965, Bernard Bergonzi published *Heroes' Twilight*, a ground-breaking study of war poetry that brought new critical attention to the genre. The continued teaching of the war poets' work in schools has ensured that the wartime literature of disillusionment has become part of the standard literary canon and national heritage. Long after the more voluminous patriotic literature of the war years has been forgotten, the poems of Owen, Sassoon, and Rosenberg continue to exert tremendous influence on popular perceptions of the First World War. On 11 November 1993, the 75th anniversary of the Armistice, the front page of the *Guardian* featured Owen's 'Anthem for Doomed Youth' as the definitive summary of the war's meaning.

Contemporary attitudes toward the First World War emphasize its tragic and oppressive themes: mass death, xenophobia, deceptive propaganda, and technological savagery. As Gary Sheffield notes, 'a reference to the First World War is often used as a shorthand for stupidity, blind obedience, failures of leadership, and deadlock.'[64] This popular image of the war has completely supplanted earlier heroic and idealized versions, and finds continual expression in textbooks, movies, novels, and television. Fictional best-sellers like Sebastian Faulk's *Birdsong* (1993) and Pat Barker's critically acclaimed war trilogy, *Regeneration* (1991), *The Eye in the Door* (1993), and *The Ghost Road* (1995), movingly convey the traumatic war experiences of British soldiers as they struggle with shell-shock. With somewhat broader strokes, the 1989 BBC comedy series *Blackadder Goes Forth* also crystallizes the negative image of the war: soldiers living in squalid trenches are blithely sent to their deaths by stupid commanders. The First World War remains etched in the popular imagination as a futile and pointless conflict which achieved little and cost the nation dearly.

Long after it ended, many Britons continue to express strong opinions about how the war should be remembered. In 1998, on the 80th anniversary of the armistice, the *Daily Express* suggested that Douglas Haig's statue in Whitehall should be torn down. Around the same time, the minister of St Mary's Church near Crewe demonstrated a similar spirit of iconoclasm when he removed a print of Clark's *The Great Sacrifice* from the sanctuary. The once popular painting from 1914, which equated a soldier's death to that of Christ, now struck the vicar as an especially egregious example of manipulative propaganda.[65]

People still react to the war in a visceral and emotional way. In 2002, viewers responded angrily to a British television reality series, *The Trench*, in which 25 young men were filmed living in a specially constructed trench to recreate a sense of wartime experience. In her discussion of the controversy, the critic Emma Hanna suggests that viewer anger was due to a contemporary belief that 'the war was a sacrosanct historical event and should be treated as such: it was seen as morally wrong to reproduce trench life.'[66]

The continuing ability of the First World War to generate controversy is especially demonstrated by the recent campaign to exonerate the 361 British and Commonwealth soldiers shot for cowardice and desertion during the war. Advocates for the executed soldiers argued that military justice was too harsh and that the Army code did not take account of psychological trauma, as many of those shot were now assumed to be suffering from shell-shock. The campaign succeeded in 2006 with an official pardon for the executed soldiers. To those who took part in the pardon campaign, the executions were yet another shameful legacy of a shameful war.[67]

The popular view of the First World War as a brutal and senseless slaughter is so deeply held that it appears impervious to historical revisionism. An early attempt to counter the pessimistic understanding of the war, Correlli Barnett and John Terraine's reappraisal of the British High Command in the 1964 BBC documentary *The Great War,* was rejected by viewers who instead interpreted the program as a confirmation of the catastrophic nature of the war. More recently, a group of largely military historians, including Brian Bond and Gary Sheffield, has vigorously disputed the long-held view of the war as tragic and futile. They instead argue that it was an important British victory and a triumph of liberal democracy over German militarism and expansionism. Whether this interpretation can replace the more negative view of the war that has predominated since the 1960s is unclear, but in the run-up to the centennial of the Great War, some Conservative politicians have adopted the revisionist view. Recent suggestions, however, that the war should be celebrated as a notable British victory and triumph of democratic values, brought forth an intense rebuke from Labour politicians and their allies in the press.

In an editorial in the *Guardian* in October 2012, Seumas Milne accused Prime Minister David Cameron of trying to 'hijack' the commemorations of the war's centennial for narrow partisan ends. Milne rejected any suggestion that the centennial should be 'a focus of national pride,' as the war was nothing more than 'a vast depraved undertaking of unprecedented savagery, in which the ruling classes of Europe dispatched their people to a senseless slaughter in the struggle for imperial supremacy.' In January 2014 the Conservative Education Secretary Michael Gove condemned 'left-wing academics' for peddling unpatriotic 'myths' about the war, including the idea that 'an out-of-touch elite' cavalierly sent British soldiers to their deaths. Gove insisted that the war was in defense of democratic values and that 'good historians' had vindicated the strategies of British generals. Gove's comments were condemned by Labour's shadow education spokesman, Tristram Hunt, himself a historian, as a 'shocking' attempt at political point-scoring. Historians were not slow to enter the fray. Richard Evans characterized Gove's approach to history as 'narrow tub-thumping jingoism.' Gary Sheffield, whose revisionist work Gove had cited with approval, took the Education Secretary to task for politicizing historical debates.[68]

Not since the 1920s has there been such strong and heated public disagreements over the meaning of the First World War. The recent intemperate exchanges between politicians and journalists underscore the difficulty of having honest, intellectual disagreements about the war in a calm and dispassionate manner. Both sides accuse the other of using the war for selfish, political ends, and both sides claim the moral high ground, insisting that their opponents' views of the war constitute an insult to those who served and died.

As in so many historical debates, the different positions about the war are not mutually exclusive. Even if, as some argue, the war was necessary and defensible from a British perspective, it can still be seen as tragic. Indeed, it is difficult to view the deaths of millions of young men otherwise. Viewing Britain's victory in the war as a positive achievement does not negate also seeing life in the trenches as an overwhelmingly negative experience. As Stephen Heathorn sensibly suggests in a recent essay, any historical understanding of the war can surely 'encompass multiple perspectives.'[69]

Notes

Introduction

1. Samuel Hynes, *A War Imagined: The First World War and English Culture* (New York: Atheneum, 1991), xi.
2. Brian Bond, *The Unquiet Western Front* (Cambridge: Cambridge University Press, 2002), and Gary Sheffield, *Forgotten Victory: The First World War, Myths and Realities* (London: Headline, 2001).
3. Jay Winter and Antoine Prost, *The Great War in History: Debates and Controversies* (Cambridge: Cambridge University Press, 2005).
4. For example, Keith Robbins's *The First World War* (Oxford: Oxford University Press, 1984) includes virtually nothing about British culture, while the recent survey edited by Stephen Constantine and others, *The First World War in British History* (London: Edward Arnold, 1995), has a single chapter entitled 'The War and British Culture.' More recent surveys by Adrian Gregory and Alan Simmonds do a better job of discussing cultural topics, but the cultural history of the war is not their central concern. Adrian Gregory, *The Last Great War: British Society and the First World War* (Cambridge: Cambridge University Press, 2008), and Alan Simmonds, *Britain and World War I* (New York: Routledge, 2012).
5. Other works which emphasize the war as a catalyst for cultural change include, Hynes, *A War Imagined*, and Modris Eksteins, *Rites of Spring: The Great War and the Birth of the Modern Age* (New York: Doubleday, 1989).
6. Gerard DeGroot, *Blighty: British Society in the Era of the Great War* (London: Longman, 1996), 311. Other works which emphasize the cultural conservatism of the war include Trevor Wilson, *The Myriad Faces of War: Britain and the Great War, 1914–1918* (Cambridge: Polity Press, 1986), and Jay Winter, *Sites of Memory, Sites of Mourning: The Great War in European Cultural History* (Cambridge: Cambridge University Press, 1995).

7. See Susan Kingsley Kent's review essay, 'Remembering the Great War', *Journal of British Studies* 37 (January 1998), 105–10.

8. Quoted in Stuart Wallace, *War and the Image of Germany: British Academics* (Edinburgh: John Donald, 1988), 73.

1 The Realities of Modern Warfare

1. G. Hartcup, *The War of Invention: Scientific Developments, 1914–1918* (London: Brassey's, 1988), 1.

2. Peter Dewey, 'The New Warfare and Economic Mobilization', in John Turner, ed., *Britain and the First World War* (London: Unwin Hyman, 1988), 71–5.

3. Sir William Osler, *Science and War* (Oxford: Clarendon Press, 1915), 15.

4. Trevor Wilson, *The Myriad Faces of War: Britain and the Great War, 1914–1918* (Cambridge: Polity Press, 1986), 217, A. J. Hoover, *God, Germany and Britain in the Great War* (New York: Praeger, 1989), 2, J. Ellis, *The Social History of the Machine Gun* (London: Croom Helm, 1975), 111–45, and Jeremy Black, *The Great War and the Making of the Modern World* (London: Continuum, 2011), 61.

5. Wilson, *Myriad Faces of War*, 99, and Stephen Kern, *The Culture of Time and Space* (Cambridge, MA: Harvard University Press, 1983), 300.

6. Gerard DeGroot, *Blighty: British Society in the Era of the Great War* (London: Longman, 1996), 20–1.

7. Tim Travers, *The Killing Ground* (London: Allen and Unwin, 1987), 4–5, Ellis, *Social History of the Machine Gun*, 128–9, and Gary Sheffield, *Forgotten Victory: The First World War, Myths and Realities* (London: Headline, 2001), 131.

8. Travers, *Killing Ground*, 49–51.

9. Quoted in Ellis, *Social History of the Machine Gun*, 135, Travers, *Killing Ground*, 87–8, and Keith Robbins, *The First World War* (New York: Oxford University Press, 1984), 55–6.

10. Jay Winter and Antoine Prost, *The Great War in History: Debates and Controversies, 1914 to the Present* (Cambridge: Cambridge University Press, 2005), 55–6.

11. Peter Englund, *The Beauty and the Sorrow: An Intimate History of the First World War* (New York: Knopf, 2011), 371.

12. Robbins, *The First World War*, 155–6, and Travers, *Killing Ground*, 77.

13. See Conclusion in Tim Travers, *How the War Was Won: Command and Technology in the British Army on the Western Front, 1917–1918* (London: Routledge, 1992), and Black, *The Great War and the Making of the Modern World*, 70.

14. Winter and Prost, *Great War in History*, 59–60.

15. See E. B. Poulton, 'Eugenic Problems After the Great War', *Eugenics Review* 8 (April 1916), 34–49.

16. Wilson, *Myriad Faces of War*, 641, Hartcup, *War of Invention*, 181–2, and Roy MacLeod, 'The Chemists Go to War: The Mobilization of Civilian Chemists and the British War Effort, 1914–1918', *Annals of Science* 50 (1993), 459.

17. Maurice Pearton, *The Knowledgeable State: Diplomacy, War and Technology Since 1830* (London: Burnett Books, 1982), 156–60.

18. Michael Pattison, 'Scientists, Inventors, and the Military in Britain, 1915–1919: The Munitions Inventions Department', *Social Studies of Science* 13 (1983), 527.

19. Alan Simmonds, *Britain and World War I* (New York: Routledge, 2012), 76.

20. MacLeod, 'Chemists Go to War', 464–7, and Dewey, 'The New Warfare', 79.

21. Keith Vernon, 'Science and Technology', in Stephen Constantine, *et al.*, eds, *The First World War in British History* (London: Edward Arnold, 1995), 92–3.

22. Simmonds, *Britain and World War I*, 208.

23. John Terraine, *White Heat: The New Warfare, 1914–18* (London: Sidgwick and Jackson, 1982), 25–6, and DeGroot, *Blighty*, 84–5.

24. Andrew J. Hull, 'Food for Thought?: The Relations between the Royal Society Food Committees and Government, 1915–19', *Annals of Science* 59 (July 2002), 263–98.

25. Hartcup, *War of Invention*, 6–10, 190, MacLeod, 'Chemists Go to War', 461–4, Pattison, 'Scientists, Inventors and the Military', 522–7, and Vernon, 'Science and Technology', 97–101.

26. Hartcup, *War of Invention*, 44–52.

27. MacLeod, 'Chemists Go to War', 478, and Wilson, *Myriad Faces of War*, 235.

28. Seth Koven, 'Remembering and Dismemberment: Crippled Children, Wounded Soldiers, and the Great War in Great Britain', *American Historical Review* 99 (October 1994), 1186–7, Roger Cooter, 'War and Modern Medicine', in W. F. Bynum and Roy Porter, eds, *Companion Encyclopedia of the History of Medicine* (London: Routledge, 1993), 1541, Hartcup, *War of Invention*, 170, and Leo Van Bergen, "Military Medicine," in Jay Winter, ed., *The Cambridge History of the First World War* (Cambridge: Cambridge University Press, 2014), vol. 3, 288.

29. Hartcup, *War of Invention*, 168–9, and Cooter, 'War and Modern Medicine', 1543.

30. Cooter, 'War and Modern Medicine', 1546, and Hartcup, *War of Invention*, 167–8.

31. Joanna Bourke, *Dismembering the Male: Men's Bodies, Britain and the Great War* (Chicago: University of Chicago Press, 1996), 35–75, and Adrian Gregory, *The Last Great War* (Cambridge: Cambridge University Press, 2008), 266.

32. Quoted in Daniel Pick, *War Machine: The Rationalization of Slaughter in the Modern Age* (New Haven: Yale University Press, 1993), 145.

33. Albert Marrin, *The Last Crusade: The Church of England in the First World War* (Durham, NC: Duke University Press, 1974), 170, Robbins, *The First World War*, 87–8, and Wilson, *Myriad Faces of War*, 255.

34. Hartcup, *War of Invention*, 94–115, MacLeod, 'Chemists Go to War', 466, and L. F. Haber, *The Poisonous Cloud: Chemical Warfare in the First World War* (Oxford: Clarendon Press, 1986), 182–7. See also Albert Palazzo, *Seeking Victory on the Western Front: The British Army and Chemical Warfare in World War I* (Lincoln: University of Nebraska Press, 2000).

35. Wilfred Owen, 'Dulce Et Decorum Est', in Jon Silkin, *The Penguin Book of First World War Poetry* (London: Penguin, 1979), 193.

36. Robbins, *The First World War*, 88, Haber, *Poisonous Cloud*, 229, and Terraine, *White Heat*, 160.

37. Hartcup, *War of Invention*, 82–91, and Wilson, *Myriad Faces of War*, 340–4.

38. Wilson, *Myriad Faces of War*, 345, and Barbara Jones and Bill Howell, *Popular Arts of the First World War* (New York: McGraw-Hill, 1972), 70–1.

39. Wilson, *Myriad Faces of War*, 81, and Bryan Ranft, 'The Royal Navy and the War at Sea', in John Turner, ed., *Britain and the First World War* (London: Unwin Hyman, 1988), 53–5.

40. Terraine, *White Heat*, 35, Wilson, *Myriad Faces of War*, 429, and Simmonds, *Britain and World War I*, 112.

41. Wilson, *Myriad Faces of War*, 435, Hartcup, *War of Invention*, 130, Simmonds, *Britain and World War I*, 113, and Robbins, *The First World War*, 96.

42. Wilson, *Myriad Faces of War*, 87.

43. Ibid., 156–7, 391.

44. Hartcup, *War of Invention*, and Terraine, *White Heat*, 266–70.

45. *Times*, 26 December 1917, Marrin, *Last Crusade*, 169, and Kern, *Culture of Time and Space*, 311.

46. Robbins, *The First World War*, 98–101.

47. Terraine, *White Heat*, 197–201, and Pearton, *Knowledgeable State*, 172.

48. Pearton, *Knowledgeable State*, 169, Paul Virilio, *War and Cinema* (London: Verso, 1989), 1–10, and Arthur Marwick, *The Deluge: British Society and the First World War* (1965), 2nd Edition (London: Macmillan Press – now Palgrave Macmillan, 1991), 273–4.

49. Quoted in Bernard Bergonzi, *Heroes' Twilight: A Study of the Literature of the Great War* (London: Constable, 1965), 168.

50. Robbins, *The First World War*, 102. See also Dominick A. Pisano, *Legend, Memory and the Great War in the Air* (Seattle: University of Washington Press, 1992), and Robert Wohl, *A Passion for Wings: Aviation and the Western Imagination, 1908–1918* (New Haven: Yale University Press, 1994).

51. Kern, *Culture of Time and Space*, 308.

52. Wyndham Lewis, 'The French Poodle', in Trudi Tate, ed., *Women, Men and the Great War: An Anthology of Stories* (Manchester: Manchester University Press, 1995), 169.

53. Jones and Howell, *Popular Arts*, 74–5.

54. Eric Leed, *No Man's Land: Combat and Identity in World War I* (Cambridge: Cambridge University Press, 1979), 127–8, Peter Liddle, *Voices of War* (London: Leo Cooper, 1988), 176–85, Paul Fussell, *The Great War and Modern Memory* (New York: Oxford University Press, 1975), 124, and Jones and Howell, *Popular Arts*, 56.

55. Tracey Loughran, 'Shell Shock, Trauma, and the First World War: The Making of a Diagnosis and Its Histories,' *Journal of the History of Medicine and Allied* Sciences 67 (January 2012), 94–119, Ted Bogacz, 'War Neurosis and Cultural Change', *Journal of Contemporary History* 24 (1989), 233–5, Elaine

Showalter, *The Female Malady: Women, Madness and English Culture, 1830–1980* (New York: Pantheon, 1985), 167–8, and John Brophy and Eric Partridge, *The Long Trail: Soldiers' Songs and Slang, 1914–18* (London: Sphere Books, 1965), 118.

56. Bogacz, 'War Neurosis and Cultural Change', 232, 239, Showalter, *Female Malady*, 178, and Leed, *No Man's Land*, 164.

57. Showalter, *Female Malady*, 176–7.

58. Bogacz, 'War Neurosis and Cultural Change', 236–46. See also Eric Dean, 'War and Psychiatry', *History of Psychiatry* 4 (1993), 61–82, Peter Leese, 'Problems Returning Home: The British Psychological Casualties of the Great War', *Historical Journal* 40 (1997), 1055–67, and Peter Barham, *Forgotten Lunatics of the Great War* (New Haven: Yale University Press, 2004), 189.

59. Corelli Barnett, *The Swordbearers: Supreme Command in the First World War* (New York: Signet Books, 1963), John Terraine, *Douglas Haig: The Educated Soldier* (London: Hutchinson, 1963), Peter Simkins, *Kitchener's Army: The Raising of the New Armies, 1914–1916* (Manchester: Manchester University Press, 1988), and Brian Bond, ed., *The First World War and British Military History* (Oxford: Oxford University Press, 1991. See also Gary Sheffield and Geoffrey Till, eds., *The Challenge of High Command: The British Experience* (Basingstoke: Palgrave Macmillan, 2003).

60. Black, *The Great War and the Making of the Modern World*, 99, 197–9, Sheffield, *Forgotten Victory*, 129, 204, 240, and David Stevenson, *Cataclysm: The First World War as Political Tragedy* (New York: Basic Books, 361–4.

61. Stephen Broadberry and Mark Harrison, "The Economics of World War I: An Overview," in Broadberry and Harrison, eds., *The Economics of World War I* (Cambridge: Cambridge University Press, 2005), 3–40, and Roger Chickering, *Imperial Germany and the Great War, 1914–1918*, 2nd edition (Cambridge: Cambridge University Press, 2004), 92–3, 172, 176–7.

62. Marwick, *Deluge*, 175, 276–7.

63. Brophy and Partridge, *Long Trail*, 102–3.

64. W. Heath Robinson, *Hunlikely!* (London: Duckworth, 1916).

65. D. S. L. Cardwell, 'Science in World War I', *Proceedings of the Royal Society of London* (1975), 452, and DeGroot, *Blighty*, 219.

66. Claire Tylee, *The Great War and Women's Consciousness* (Iowa City: University of Iowa Press, 1990), 39, and A. J. Hoover, *God, Germany and Britain in the Great War* (New York: Praeger, 1989), 5.

67. Quoted in Pick, *War Machine*, 194.

68. MacLeod, 'Chemists Go to War', 481, and Alex King, *Memorials of the Great War in Britain* (Oxford: Berg, 1998), 222.

69. G. S. Street, *At Home in the War* (London: Heinemann, 1918), 113–14.

70. Christopher Coker, *War and the 20th Century: A Study of War and Modern Consciousness* (London: Brassey's, 1994), 104–9, and Sue Malvern, 'War As It Is', *Art History* 9 (1986), 490.

71. George Otte, 'Mrs Humphry Ward, the Great War and the Historical Loom', *Clio* 19 (1990), 278–9.

2 Class, Labor, and State Control

1. Leo Chiozza Money, *Riches and Poverty* (London: Methuen and Co., 1905), 1, 72, and Harold Perkin, *The Rise of Professional Society: England Since 1880* (London: Routledge, 1989), 191.

2. See esp. Arthur Marwick, *The Deluge: British Society and the First World War* (1965), 2nd edition (London: Macmillan Press – now Palgrave Macmillan, 1991), 96–127. See also Perkin, *Rise of Professional Society*, 171–286.

3. Among revisionist works, see esp. G. D. DeGroot, *Blighty: British Society in the Era of the Great War* (London: Longman, 1996), and Bernard Waites, *A Class Society at War: England 1914–1918* (Leamington Spa: Berg, 1987).

4. Robert Roberts, *The Classic Slum: Salford Life in the First Quarter of the Century* (London: Penguin, 1971), 186.

5. Perkin, *Rise of Professional Society*, 174–5, and Alan Simmonds, *Britain and World War I* (New York: Routledge, 2012), 197.

6. W. T. Rodgers and Bernard Donoughue, *The People into Parliament* (London: Thames and Hudson, 1966), 71–2.

7. Quoted in Albert Marrin, *The Last Crusade: The Church of England in the First World War* (Durham, NC: Duke University Press, 1974), 250.

8. Perkin, *Rise of Professional Society*, 187, Rodgers and Donoughue, *People into Parliament*, 73, and Martin Ceadel, 'Pacifism', in Jay Winter, ed., *The Cambridge History of the First World War* (Cambridge: Cambridge University Press, 2014), vol. 2, 598.

9. Ian Dewhirst, *The Story of a Nobody: A Working-Class Life, 1880–1939* (London: Mills and Boon, 1989), 39. For a more general discussion of working-class alienation from national politics, see Standish Meacham, *A Life Apart: The English Working Class, 1890–1914* (Cambridge, MA: Harvard University Press, 1977), 194–220.

10. Roberts, *Classic Slum*, 186.

11. Catriona Pennell, *A Kingdom United: Popular Responses to the Outbreak of the First World War in Britain and Ireland* (Oxford: Oxford University Press, 2012), 30–5.

12. Waites, *Class Society at War*, 187.

13. Pennell, *A Kingdom United*, 150–2.

14. Sylvia Pankhurst, *The Home Front* (1932), reprint (London: The Cresset Library, 1987), 26.

15. J. M. Bourne, *Britain and the Great War* (London: Edward Arnold, 1989), 201. Traditional naval policy had been predicated on the notion that maritime supremacy would limit high casualties in wartime and preserve food supplies for the working-class diet, reduction of which, it was feared, would bring about the collapse of civilian morale.

16. J. M. Winter, *The Great War and the British People* (London: Macmillan Press – now Palgrave Macmillan, 1985), 35.

17. Pankhurst, *Home Front*, 16.

18. David Silbey, *The British Working Class and Enthusiasm for War, 1914–1916* (New York: Frank Cass, 2005), 104–28.

19. DeGroot, *Blighty*, 48–9, and Pennell, *A Kingdom United*, 64–5.
20. Dewhirst, *Story of a Nobody*, 39–40.
21. Roberts, *Classic Slum*, 189.
22. David Cannadine, *The Decline and Fall of the British Aristocracy* (New Haven: Yale University Press, 1990), 72–6.
23. M. Girouard, *Return to Camelot: Chivalry and the English Gentleman* (New Haven: Yale University Press, 1981), 287–8.
24. Quoted in DeGroot, *Blighty*, 227.
25. Cyril Anthony Bertram, *The Sword Falls* (London: George Allen and Unwin, 1929), and Winter, *Great War and British People*, 33.
26. Peter Grant argues that widespread support for the war can be measured through the public's substantial contributions to numerous voluntary and charitable organizations. Peter Grant, 'An Infinity of Personal Sacrifice: The Scale and Nature of Charitable Work in Britain during the First World War', *War and Society* 27 (October 2008), 67–88.
27. Quoted in Roberts, *Classic Slum*, 187.
28. George Dangerfield, *The Strange Death of Liberal England* (1935), reprint (New York: Capricorn Books, 1961), 402–25.
29. Quoted in Nick Mansfield, 'Class Conflict and Village War Memorials', *Rural History* 6 (1995), 73.
30. Ian Beckett, *Home Front, 1914–1918* (London: National Archives, 2006), 45, and David Bilton, *The Home Front in the Great War* (Barnsley: Pen and Sword, 2004), 35.
31. Ibid., 155–6, 228.
32. Perkin, *Rise of Professional Society*, 202.
33. Pankhurst, *Home Front*, 129–30, and J. Boswell and B. Johns, 'Patriots or Profiteers?: British Businessmen and the First World War', *Journal of European Economic History* 11 (1982), 423–45.
34. J. McDermott, '"A Needless Sacrifice": British Businessmen and Business as Usual in the First World War', *Albion* 21 (1989), 263–82, and DeGroot, *Blighty*, 54–73.
35. Perkin, *Rise of Professional Society*, 196–7.
36. Ibid., 193–6.
37. Ibid., 197–8.
38. Trevor Wilson, *The Myriad Faces of War: Britain and the Great War, 1914–1918* (Cambridge: Polity Press, 1986), 221, and Adrian Gregory, *The Last Great War* (Cambridge: Cambridge University Press, 2008), 288.
39. Keith Middlemas, *Politics in Industrial Society: The Experience of the British System since 1911* (London: Deutsch, 1980).
40. Perkin, *Rise of Professional Society*, 171–86.
41. Wilson, *Myriad Faces of War*, 410.
42. Marwick, *Deluge*, 56–85.
43. Perkin, *Rise of Professional Society*, 226–8, and Simmonds, *Britain and World War I*, 120, 297.
44. Sidney Webb and Arnold Freeman, *Great Britain After the War* (London: George Allen and Unwin, 1916), 8.

45. Susan Pedersen, 'Gender, Welfare and Citizenship in Britain during the Great War', *American Historical Review* 95 (1990), 983–1006.

46. Quoted in Bernard Waites, 'The Effect of the First World War on Class and Status in England, 1910–20', *Journal of Contemporary History* 11 (1976), 39.

47. Perkin, *Rise of Professional Society*, 201.

48. Winter, *Great War and the British People*, 52, Perkin, *Rise of Professional Society*, 238, and David Silbey, 'Bodies and Cultures Collide: Enlistment, the Medical Exam, and the British Working Class, 1914–1916', *Social History of Medicine* 17 (April 2004), 61–76. The incapacity of many Boer War recruits had led to a Parliamentary Investigation. See Committee on Physical Deterioration, Report and Minutes, *Parliamentary Papers*, 1904, vol. 32.

49. Leonard Darwin, 'Eugenics During and After the War', *Eugenics Review* 7 (July 1914), 91–2.

50. J. M. Winter, 'The Impact of the First World War on Civilian Health in Britain', *Economic History Review* 30 (1977), 498.

51. Richard A. Soloway, 'Eugenics and Pronatalism in Wartime Britain', in Richard Wall and Jay Winter, eds, *The Upheaval of War: Family, Work and Welfare in Europe, 1914–18* (Cambridge: Cambridge University Press, 1988), 379.

52. Wilson, *Myriad Faces of War*, 151–3, and Peter Dewey, 'Nutrition and Living Standards in Wartime Britain', in Wall and Winter, *Upheaval of War*.

53. John Stevenson, *British Society, 1914–45* (London: Penguin, 1984), 81.

54. Simmonds, *Britain and World War I*, 197.

55. John Burnett, *Plenty and Want: A Social History of Food in Britain from 1815 to the Present Day* (London: Routledge, 1989), 244–5.

56. Dewhirst, *Story of a Nobody*, 69–70.

57. Pankhurst, *Home Front*, 209.

58. Quoted in Wilson, *Myriad Faces of War*, 405, and Pankhurst, *Home Front*, 143.

59. Burnett, *Plenty and Want*, 244–5, and Gregory, *The Last Great War*, 214.

60. Waites, *Class Society at War*, 224–5, and Karen Hunt, 'The Politics of Food and Women's Neighborhood Activism in First World War Britain', *International Labor and Working-Class History* 77 (Spring 2010), 18.

61. Burnett, *Plenty and Want*, 243, 246–8.

62. Wilson, *Myriad Faces of War*, 540, and Gary Sheffield, *Forgotten Victory: The First World War, Myths and Realities* (London: Headline, 2001), 58.

63. Noel Whiteside, 'The British Population at War', in John Turner, ed., *Britain and the First World War* (London: Unwin Hyman, 1988), 86.

64. Winter, *Great War and the British People*, 105, and Winter, 'Impact of the First World War on Civilian Health', 489–95. Winter's conclusions have been challenged by Linda Bryder who argues that he under represents the poorest segments of the community whose living standards may have deteriorated. L. Bryder, 'The First World War: Healthy or Hungry?', *History Workshop Journal* 24 (1987), 141–57.

65. Winter, *Great War and British People*, 188–214.

66. Waites, 'Effect of the First World War on Class and Status', 35.

67. Roberts, *Classic Slum*, 199.

68. G. D. Sheffield, 'The Effect of the Great War on Class Relations in Britain: The Career of Major Christopher Stone, DSO, MC', *War and Society* 7 (1989), 88.

69. Wilson, *Myriad Faces of War*, 245, and DeGroot, *Blighty*, 32. For the fullest discussion of the public schools and the war, see Peter Parker, *The Old Lie: The Great War and the Public School Ethos* (London: Constable, 1987).

70. DeGroot, *Blighty*, 164–5.

71. Eric Leed, *No Man's Land: Combat and Identity in World War I* (Cambridge: Cambridge University Press, 1979), 84.

72. Bourne, *Britain and the Great War*, 221, and Parker, *The Old Lie*, 164.

73. Robert Graves, *Goodbye to All That* (1929), reprint (New York: Doubleday, 1957), 97.

74. Quoted in Sheffield, 'Effect of the Great War on Class Relations', 101.

75. Quoted in Wilson, *Myriad Faces of War*, 41.

76. John Keegan, *The Face of Battle* (London: Cape, 1976), 221.

77. Quoted in Sheffield, 'The Effect of the Great War on Class Relations', 101.

78. Ibid., 93–102.

79. M. Petter, '"Temporary Gentlemen" in the Aftermath of the Great War: Rank, Status and the Ex-Officer Problem', *Historical Journal* 37 (1994), 127–52.

80. Quoted in DeGroot, *Blighty*, 298.

81. Charles Carrington, *Soldier from the Wars Returning* (London: Hutchinson, 1965), 161.

82. G. S. Street, *At Home in the War* (London: Heinemann, 1918), 26.

83. Cannadine, *Decline and Fall of the British Aristocracy*, 76–8.

84. C. F. G. Masterman, *England After War* (1922), reprint (New York: Garland, 1985), 33.

85. Cannadine, *Decline and Fall of the British Aristocracy*, 83.

86. Winter, *Great War and the British People*, 83–92.

87. Perkin, *Rise of Professional Society*, 226.

88. F. M. L. Thompson, *English Landed Society in the 19th Century* (London: Routledge and Kegan Paul, 1963), 329–32.

89. The expression is Stanley Baldwin's, referring to the new Conservative MPs from business backgrounds in the 1918 Parliament.

90. Waites, *Class Society at War*, 58, 74, 103, and Christine Grandy, 'Avarice and Evil Doers: Profiteers, Politicians, and Popular Fiction in the 1920s', *Journal of British Studies* 50 (July 2011), 667–89.

91. Ibid., 49–51, 116–17, and DeGroot, *Blighty*, 292.

92. Masterman, 'The Plight of the Middle Class', *England After War*, 49–83, and Waites, *Class Society at War*, 51.

93. See, for example, W. R. Inge, 'The Future of the English Race', *Outspoken Essays* (London: Longmans, Green and Company, 1919).

94. Roberts, *Classic Slum*, 200, and Waites, *Class Society at War*, 279. Wage and price statistics from Simmonds, *Britain and World War I*, 175.

95. Quoted in Julia Bush, *Behind the Lines: East London Labour, 1914–1919* (London: Merlin Press, 1984), 195.

96. Roberts, *Classic Slum*, 210.

97. Quoted in Mansfield, 'Class Conflict and Village War Memorials', 73–4.

98. Keith Robbins, *The First World War* (New York: Oxford University Press, 1984), 134.

99. Martin Pugh, 'Domestic Politics', in Stephen Constantine, *et al.*, eds, *The First World War in British History* (London: Edward Arnold, 1995), 22–5.

100. Perkin, *Rise of Professional Society*, 204. See also Alastair Reid, 'The Impact of the First World War on British Workers', in Wall and Winter, *Upheaval of War.*

101. Rodgers and Donoughue, *People into Parliament*, 78–80. For a history of the wartime influence of socialist ideas on the Labour Party, see J. M. Winter, *Socialism and the Challenge of War: Ideas and Politics in Britain* (London: Routledge and Kegan Paul, 1974).

102. Pugh, 'Domestic Politics', 22.

103. Ross McKibbin, *The Evolution of the Labor Party, 1910–24* (Oxford: Oxford University Press, 1974), and Julia Bush, *Behind the Lines: East London Labor, 1914–1919* (London: Merlin Press, 1984).

104. Quoted in Perkin, *Rise of Professional Society*, 192.

105. Roberts, *Classic Slum*, 238, Waites, *Class Society at War*, 178, and Wilson, *Myriad Faces of War*, 822–5.

106. Waites, *Class Society at War*, 27–8, 265–9, and DeGroot, *Blighty*, 303.

107. P. B. Johnson, *Land Fit for Heroes* (Chicago: University of Chicago Press, 1968), and Wilson, *Myriad Faces of War*, 812.

108. DeGroot, *Blighty*, 328.

109. Peter H. Liddle, *Voices of War: Front Line and Home Front* (London: Leo Cooper, 1988), 249.

110. Waites, *Class Society at War*, 98.

111. Masterman, *England After War*, 101, and Kevin Morgan, *Ramsay MacDonald* (London: Haus, 2006).

112. Perkin, *Rise of Professional Society*, 204–15.

113. Ibid., 217.

3 Gender, Sex, and Sexuality

1. Arthur Marwick, *The Deluge* (1965), 2nd edition (London: Macmillan Press – now Palgrave Macmillan, 1991), 133–4.

2. See, for example, Susan Kingsley Kent, *Making Peace: The Reconstruction of Gender in Interwar Britain* (Princeton: Princeton University Press, 1993), Susan Grayzel, *Women's Identities at War: Gender, Motherhood, and Politics in Britain and France during the First World War* (Chapel Hill: University of North Carolina Press, 1999), and Nicoletta Gullace, 'White Feathers and Wounded Men: Female Patriotism and the Memory of the Great War', in *Journal of British Studies* 36 (April 1997), 178–206.

3. Kent, *Making Peace*, 9.

4. Gerard DeGroot, *Blighty: British Society in the Era of the Great War* (London: Longman, 1996), 38–9.

5. H. G. Wells, *Mr Britling Sees It Through* (New York: Macmillan, 1916), 182.

6. Quoted in Bernard Bergonzi, *Heroes' Twilight: A Study of the Literature of the Great War* (London: Constable, 1965), 32.

7. Quoted in Claire M. Tylee, *The Great War and Women's Consciousness: Images of Militarism and Womanhood in Women's Writings, 1914–64* (Iowa City: University of Iowa Press, 1990), 36. See also M. Adams, *The Great Adventure: Male Desire and the Coming of World War I* (Bloomington: University of Indiana Press, 1990).

8. Joanna Bourke, *Dismembering the Male: Men's Bodies, Britain and the Great War* (Chicago: University of Chicago Press, 1996), 76–123.

9. Richard Aldington, *Death of a Hero* (New York: Covici-Friede, 1929), 264.

10. Peter Parker, *The Old Lie: The Great War and the Public School Ethos* (London: Constable, 1987), 192.

11. Ian Dewhirst, *The Story of a Nobody: A Working-Class Life, 1880–1939* (London: Mills and Boon, 1980), 41–2.

12. Maurice Rickards and Michael Moody, *The First World War: Ephemera, Mementoes, Documents* (London: Jupiter, 1975), 19–20, and Gullace, 'White Feathers and Wounded Men', 178–206.

13. Alan Wilkinson, *The Church of England and the First World War* (London: SPCK, 1978), 96.

14. Quoted in Albert Marrin, *The Last Crusade: The Church of England in the First World War* (Durham, NC: Duke University Press, 1974), 185.

15. Christabel Pankhurst, *The War* (London: WSPU, 1914), 11.

16. Diana Condell and Jean Liddiard, *Working for Victory?: Images of Women in the First World War, 1914–18* (London: Routledge, 1987), 7.

17. Pankhurst, *The War*, 7, 16, 18.

18. Jo Vellacott, 'Feminist Consciousness and the First World War', *History Workshop* 23 (Spring 1987), 94–5, and Johanna Alberti, *Beyond Suffrage: Feminists in War and Peace* (London: Macmillan Press – now Palgrave Macmillan, 1989), 55.

19. Sharon Ouditt, *Fighting Forces, Writing Women: Identity and Ideology in the First World War* (London: Routledge, 1994), 142.

20. Alberti, *Beyond Suffrage*, 71, and Grayzel, *Women's Identities at War*, 157.

21. Laura E. Nym Mayhall, *The Militant Suffrage Movement* (Oxford: Oxford University Press, 2004), 118, 127–30.

22. Trevor Wilson, *The Myriad Faces of War: Britain and the Great War, 1914–1918* (Cambridge: Polity Press, 1986), 708.

23. Quoted in Janet Watson, 'Khaki Girls, VADs and Tommy's Sisters: Gender and Class in First World War Britain', *International History Review* 19 (1997), 49. See also Carol Acton, 'Best Boys and Aching Hearts: The Rhetoric of Romance as Social Control in Wartime Magazines for Young Women,' in Jessica Meyer, ed., *British Popular Culture and the First World War* (Leiden: Brill, 2008), 173–93.

24. Vera Brittain, *Testament of Youth* (1933), reprint (London: Wideview Books, 1978), 100–1.

25. Arthur Marwick, *Women at War* (London: Fontana, 1977), 54, and Deborah Thom, 'Women and Work in Wartime Britain', in Richard Wall and Jay Winter, eds, *The Upheaval of War: Family, Work and Welfare in Europe, 1914–18* (Cambridge: Cambridge University Press, 1988), 303.

26. Angela Woollacott, *On Her Their Lives Depend: Munitions Workers in the Great War* (Berkeley: University of California Press, 1994), 17–19, Thom, 'Women and Work in Wartime Britain', 308, and Antoine Prost, 'Workers', in Jay Winter, ed., *The Cambridge History of the First World War* (Cambridge: Cambridge University Press, 2014), vol. 2, 334.

27. Marwick, *Women at War*, 83–4, and Ouditt, *Fighting Forces, Writing Women*, 15–27.

28. Deirdre Beddoe, *Back to Home and Duty* (London: Pandora, 1989), 12.

29. Rickards and Moody, *World War I Ephemera*, 229, and Condell and Liddiard, *Working for Victory?*, 20–31.

30. Brittain, *Testament of Youth*, 213, and Condell and Liddiard, *Working for Victory?*, 46–51.

31. Thom, 'Women and Work in Wartime Britain', 302–3, DeGroot, *Blighty*, 127–8, and Alan Simmonds, *Britain and World War I* (New York: Routledge, 2012), 136.

32. Qtd. in Amy Bell, 'Women's Politics, Poetry, and the Feminist Historiography of the Great War', *Canadian Journal of History* 42 (Winter 2007), 425.

33. Ouditt, *Fighting Forces, Writing Women*, 54–5.

34. Gail Braybon and Penny Summerfield, *Out of the Cage: Women's Experiences in Two World Wars* (London: Pandora, 1987), 35, and Marwick, *Women at War*, 56.

35. Braybon and Summerfield, *Out of the Cage*, 73, and Simmonds, *Britain and World War I*, 137.

36. Woollacott, *On Her Their Lives Depend*, 81–3, and Ian Beckett, *Home Front, 1914–1918* (London: National Archives, 2006), 88.

37. Braybon and Summerfield, *Out of the Cage*, 62, and Claire Culleton, *Working-Class Culture, Women, and Britain, 1914–1921* (New York: St Martin's Press – now Palgrave Macmillan, 1999), 152–68.

38. Cate Haste, *Rules of Desire: Sex in Britain, World War I to the Present* (London: Chatto & Windus, 1992), 42.

39. Cynthia Enloe, *Does Khaki Become You? The Militarization of Women's Lives* (London: Pluto, 1983), 179.

40. *Times*, 18 May 1916, and Sylvia Pankhurst, *The Homefront* (1932), reprint (London: The Cresset Library, 1987), 207.

41. Woollacott, *On Her Their Lives Depend*, 167–87, DeGroot, *Blighty*, 129.

42. DeGroot, *Blighty*, 97.

43. Condell and Liddiard, *Working for Victory?*, 53–63, and Krisztina Robert, 'Gender, Class and Patriotism: Women's Paramilitary Units in First World War Britain', *International History Review* 19 (1997), 52–3.

44. Robert, 'Gender, Class and Patriotism', 53–65, J. Gould, 'Women's Military Service in First World War Britain', in Margaret Higonnet, *et al.*, eds, *Behind the Lines: Gender and the Two World Wars* (New Haven: Yale University Press, 1987), and Doron Lamm, 'Emily Goes to War: Explaining the Recruitment to the Women's Army Auxiliary Corps in World War I', in Billie Melman, ed., *Borderlines: Gender and Identities in War and Peace, 1870–1930* (New York: Routledge, 1998).

45. Magnus Hirschfeld, *The Sexual History of the World War* (New York: Cadillac Publishing, 1941), 101. See also Julie Wheelwright, *Amazons and Military Maids* (London: Pandora, 1989), 40–1.

46. Gould, 'Women's Military Service', 118.

47. Quoted in Culleton, *Working-Class Culture, Women and Britain*, 52.

48. Watson, 'Khaki Girls, VADs and Tommy's Sisters', 38–44, and Lucy Noakes, '"Playing at Being Soldiers"?: British Women and Military Uniforms in the First World War', in Meyer, *British Popular Culture*, 143.

49. Simmonds, *Britain and World War I*, 285.

50. Sandra Gilbert, 'Soldier's Heart: Literary Men, Literary Women, and the Great War', *Signs* 8 (Spring 1983), 422–50.

51. Elaine Showalter, *The Female Malady: Women, Madness and English Culture, 1830–1980* (New York: Pantheon, 1985), 167–71.

52. Ana Carden-Coyne, 'Gendering the Politics of War Wounds', in Carden-Coyne, ed., *Gender and Conflict Since 1914* (Basingstoke: Palgrave MacMillan, 2012), 83–97, and Julie Anderson, *War, Disability and Rehabilitation in Britain* (Manchester: Manchester University Press, 2011), 42–71.

53. Ana Carden-Coyne, *Reconstructing the Body: Classicism, Modernism, and the First World War* (Oxford: Oxford University Press, 2009), 160–212.

54. Sandra Gilbert and Susan Gubar, *No Man's Land: The Place of the Woman Writer in the Twentieth Century*, vol. 2 (New Haven: Yale University Press, 1989), and Kent, *Making Peace*, 44.

55. Siegfried Sassoon, 'Glory of Women', in Jon Silkin, ed., *The Penguin Book of First World War Poetry* (London: Penguin, 1979), 132.

56. Kent, *Making Peace*, 14, and Wilfred Owen, 'Disabled', in Silkin, *Penguin Book of First World War Poetry*, 194.

57. Gullace, 'White Feathers and Wounded Men', 205.

58. Trudi Tate, ed., *Women, Men and the Great War: An Anthology of Stories* (Manchester: Manchester University Press, 1995), 85.

59. Gilbert and Gubar, *No Man's Land*, vol. 2, 293, and Ouditt, *Fighting Forces, Writing Women*, 8.

60. Quoted in James Longenbach, 'The Women and Men of 1914', in Helen Cooper, ed., *Arms and the Woman: War, Gender, and Literary Representation* (Chapel Hill: University of North Carolina Press, 1989), 111.

61. Helen Zenna Smith [Evadne Price], *Not So Quiet: Stepdaughters of War* (1930), reprint (New York: The Feminist Press, 1989), 92–3. See also the memoirs of nurse Lesley Smith, *Four Years Out of Life* (1931).

62. Vera Brittain, *Lady into Woman: A History of Women from Victoria to Elizabeth II* (London: Andrew Dakers, 1953), 186.

63. Smith, *Not So Quiet*, 126.

64. Haste, *Rules of Desire*, 35, 51–3, and Rickards and Moody, *First World War Ephemera*, 22.

65. Angela Woollacott, '"Khaki Fever" and Its Control: Gender, Class, Age and Sexual Morality on the British Homefront in the First World War', *Journal of Contemporary History* 29 (April 1994), 325–47, Philippa Levine '"Walking the

Streets in the Way No Decent Woman Should": Women Police in World War I', *Journal of Modern History* 66 (March 1994), 34–78, and Rickards and Moody, *First World War Ephemera*, 22.

66. Levine, 'Walking the Streets', 43–5, Condell and Liddiard, *Working for Victory?*, 65–7, and Lucy Bland, 'In the Name of Protection: The Policing of Women in the First World War', in Julia Brophy and Carol Smart, eds, *Women in Law: Explorations in Law, Family and Sexuality* (London: Routledge, 1985).

67. Marwick, *Deluge*, 83.

68. Pankhurst, *Homefront*, 98, and Haste, *Rules of Desire*, 41–2.

69. Susan Grayzel, '"The Mothers of Our Soldiers' Children": Motherhood, Immorality and the War Baby Scandal, 1914–18', in Claudia Nelson and Anne Sumner Holmes, eds, *Maternal Instincts: Visions of Motherhood and Sexuality in Britain, 1875–1925* (New York: St Martin's Press – now Palgrave Macmillan, 1997), 127.

70. Havelock Ellis, 'Eugenics in Relation to the War', *The Philosophy of Conflict and Other Essays in War Time* (New York: Houghton Mifflin, 1919), 127, Marie Stopes, *The Race* (London: A. C. Fifield, 1918), 70, and Grayzel, 'The Mothers of Our Soldiers' Children', 132.

71. Charles Carrington, *Soldier from the Wars Returning* (London: Hutchinson, 1965), 163–5.

72. John Ivelaw-Chapman, *The Riddles of Wipers: An Appreciation of the Wipers Times, A Journal of the Trenches* (London: Leo Cooper, 1997), 54.

73. John Laffin, *World War I in Postcards* (Gloucester: A. Sutton, 1988), 12, 71–83.

74. Ivelaw-Chapman, *Riddles of Wipers*, 52–9, J. G. Fuller, *Troop Morale and Popular Culture in the British and Dominion Armies, 1914–1918* (Oxford: Oxford University Press, 1990), 105–6, and David A. Boxwell, 'The Follies of War: Cross-Dressing and Popular Theatre on the British Front Lines, 1914–18', *Modernism/Modernity* 9 (2002), 1–20.

75. Fuller, *Troop Morale*, 75, and Haste, *Rules of Desire*, 48–9.

76. Ivelaw-Chapman, *Riddles of Wipers*, 52, and Mark Harrison, 'The British Army and the Problem of Venereal Disease', *Medical History* 39 (1995), 138.

77. Haste, *Rules of Desire*, 50, and Harrison, 'The British Army and the Problem of Venereal Disease', 139–48.

78. *Times*, 6 February 1917, and Philip Hoare, *Oscar Wilde's Last Stand* (New York: Arcade, 1997), 92.

79. Quoted in Julie Wheelwright, *The Fatal Lover: Mata Hari and the Myth of Women in Espionage* (London: Collins and Brown, 1992), 1.

80. Enloe, *Does Khaki Become You?*, 26–7, and Haste, *Rules of Desire*, 54.

81. Grayzel, *Women's Identities at War*, 147, and Harrison, 'The British Army and the Problem of Venereal Disease', 148.

82. Bourke, *Dismembering the Male*, 124–70.

83. Aldington, *Death of a Hero*, 23, and Parker, *The Old Lie*, 168–95. For an insightful analysis of soldiers' romantic friendships, see Santanu Das, '"Kiss Me, Hardy": Intimacy, Gender, and Gesture in World War I Trench Literature', *Modernism/Modernity* 9 (2002), 51–74.

84. Dean Rapp, 'Sex in the Cinema: War, Moral Panic, and the British Film Industry, 1906–1918', *Albion* 34 (Fall 2002), 439, Laura Doan, *Fashioning Sapphism: The Origins of Modern English Lesbian Culture* (New York: Columbia University Press, 2001), 2, and Hoare, *Oscar Wilde's Last Stand*, 35.

85. Jeffrey Weeks, *Coming Out: Homosexual Politics in Britain from the Nineteenth Century to the Present* (London: Quartet Books, 1977), 13, Hoare, *Oscar Wilde's Last Stand*, 28, Harrison, 'The British Army and the Problem of Venereal Disease', 149–53, A.D. Harvey, 'Homosexuality and the British Army during the First World War', *Journal of the Society for Army Historical Research* 79 (Winter 2001), 313–19, and Glenford D. Howe, 'Military–Civilian Intercourse, Prostitution and Venereal Disease among Black West Indian Soldiers during World War I', *Journal of Caribbean History* 31 (1997), 98–9.

86. Paul Fussell, *The Great War and Modern Memory* (Oxford: Oxford University Press, 1975), 270–309. See also Martin Taylor, *Lads: Love Poetry of the Trenches* (London: Constable, 1989).

87. Mark Lilly, *Gay Men's Literature in the 20th Century* (New York: New York University Press, 1993), 67, 78–9.

88. For example, Peter Liddle alluded to Fussell as 'a regrettably well-known American professor dabbling in the subject' of the war, who 'wholly misunderstands what he reads' with regard to soldiers' friendships. *Voices of War* (London: Leo Cooper, 1988), 142.

89. Rose Allatini, *Despised and Rejected* (1918) reprint (London: GMP Publishers, 1988), 348. See also Tylee, *The Great War and Women's Consciousness*, 122–3.

90. Quoted in Hoare, *Oscar Wilde's Last Stand*, 27, 89.

91. Ibid., 57–8, 152.

92. David Trotter, 'Lesbians Before Lesbianism: Sexual Identity in Early Twentieth Century British Fiction', in Melman, *Borderlines*.

93. Alison Oram and Annmarie Turnbull, eds., *The Lesbian History Sourcebook* (London: Routledge, 2001), 34–7.

94. Emily Hamer, *Britannia's Glory: A History of Twentieth-Century Lesbians* (London: Cassell, 1996), 40–65.

95. Radclyffe Hall, *The Well of Loneliness* (New York: Sun Dial Press, 1928), 311, 468.

96. Wheelwright, *Amazons and Military Maids*, 152–54, Gould, 'Women's Military Service', 121, and Weeks, *Coming Out*, 106–7.

97. Haste, *Rules of Desire*, 56, and Leslie Hall, *Hidden Anxieties: Male Sexuality, 1900–1950* (London: Polity Press, 1991), 8.

98. Marie Stopes, *Radiant Motherhood* (London: G. P. Putnam's Sons, 1920), 11.

99. DeGroot, *Blighty*, 208, and M. F. K. Fisher, *The Art of Eating* (New York: Macmillan Press – now Palgrave Macmillan, 1990), 313.

100. Grayzel, *Women's Identities at War*, 111.

101. DeGroot, *Blighty*, 214, and Pankhurst, *The War*, 13.

102. Ouditt, *Fighting Forces, Writing Women*, 20.

103. Quoted in Nicola Beauman, '"It Is Not the Place of Women to Talk of Mud": Some Responses of British Women Novelists to World War I', in Dorothy

Goldman, ed., *Women and World War I: The Written Response* (London: Macmillan Press – now Palgrave Macmillan, 1993), 135.

104. Beddoe, *Back to Home and Duty*, 12–14.

105. Culleton, *Working-Class Culture, Women and Britain*, 32, and Braybon and Summerfield, *Out of the Cage*, 2.

106. Leed, *No Man's Land*, 202–3, and Bourke, *Dismembering the Male*, 162–70.

107. Jay Winter, *The Great War and the British People* (Cambridge: Cambridge University Press, 1986), Chapter 8. See also Katherine Holden, 'Imaginery Widows: Spinsters, Marriage, and the "Lost Generation" in Britain after the Great War', *Journal of Family History* 30 (October 2005), 388–409. A recent exposition of a generation of women unable to marry is Virginia Nicholson, *Singled Out: How Two Million British Women Survived After the First World War* (Oxford: Oxford University Press, 2008).

108. Sheila Rowbotham, *Hidden from History* (London: Pluto Press, 1973), 124.

109. Haste, *Rules of Desire*, 62–77, 91–8.

110. Kent, *Making Peace*, 6–17, 114–18.

111. Radclyffe Hall, 'Miss Ogilvy Finds Herself', in Tate, *Women, Men and the Great War*, 131.

112. Alberti, *Beyond Suffrage*, 135–89.

113. Jeffrey Weeks, *Sex, Politics and Society* (London: Longman, 1981), 188, and Harold Perkin, *The Rise of Professional Society: England Since 1880* (London: Routledge, 1989), 235–6.

114. Woollacott, *On Her Their Lives Depend*, 166.

115. Quoted in Perkin, *Rise of Professional Society*, 234. See also Irene Andrews and M. A. Hobbs, *The Economic Effects of the War upon Women and Children in Great Britain* (New York: Oxford University Press, 1918).

116. Thom, 'Women and Work in Wartime Britain', 317, and Angela K. Smith, *Suffrage Discourse in Britain during the First World War* (Burlington, VT: Ashgate, 2005), 90.

4 Nation, Race, and Empire

1. Robert Roberts, *The Classic Slum* (London: Penguin Books, 1971), 190.

2. Albert Marrin, *The Last Crusade: The Church of England in the First World War* (Durham, NC: Duke University Press, 1974), 93.

3. A. H. Sayce, 'Hermann's a German: A Review of Teutonic Pretensions', *The Times*, 22 December 1914. For a wider treatment of British intellectuals' anti-German activities, see Charles Bailey, 'The British Protestant Theologians in the First World War: Germanophobia Unleashed', *Harvard Theological Review* 77 (1984), 195–221.

4. Quoted in Jan Mackay and Pat Thane, 'The Englishwoman', in Robert Colls, ed., *Englishness* (London: Croom Helm, 1986), 222.

5. Quoted in Philip E. Hager and Desmond Taylor, eds., *The Novels of World War I: An Annotated Bibliography* (New York: Garland, 1981), 20.

6. Ivan Hannaford, *Race: The History of an Idea in the West* (Baltimore: The Johns Hopkins University Press, 1996), 227–8.

7. For a discussion of Victorian and Edwardian racial theories and attitudes, see Christine Bolt, *Victorian Attitudes Towards Race* (London: Routledge and Kegan Paul, 1971), and B. Schwarz, ed., *The Expansion of England: Race, Ethnicity and Culture* (London: Routledge, 1996).

8. Marrin, *Last Crusade*, 92, and Stuart Wallace, *War and the Image of Germany: British Academics* (Edinburgh: John Donald, 1988), 182–3.

9. For the history of degenerationist thought, see Daniel Pick, *Faces of Degeneration* (Cambridge: Cambridge University Press, 1989), and J. E. Chamberlin and Sander Gilman, eds, *Degeneration: The Dark Side of Progress* (New York: Columbia University Press, 1985).

10. Quoted in John MacKenzie, *Propaganda and Empire* (Manchester: Manchester University Press, 1984), 229. For other contemporary accounts of national decline, see James Cantlie, *Degeneration amongst Londoners* (1885), Arnold White, *Efficiency and Empire* (1901), and A. J. Balfour, *Decadence* (1908).

11. Leonard Darwin, 'Eugenics During and After the War', *Eugenics Review* (7 July 1915), 94, 106.

12. Among the considerable literature on the eugenics movement, see especially G. R. Searle, *Eugenics and Politics in Britain, 1900–1914* (Leyden: Noordhoff International, 1976), Lyndsay Farrell, *The Origin and Growth of the British Eugenics Movement, 1865–1925* (New York: Garland, 1985), and Richard A. Soloway, *Demography and Degeneration: Eugenics and the Declining Birthrate in Twentieth-Century Britain* (Chapel Hill: University of North Carolina Press, 1990).

13. Mrs Belloc Lowndes, *Good Old Anna* (London: Hutchinson, 1915).

14. Panikos Panayi, 'Anti-German Riots in London during the First World War', *German History* 7 (1989), 184–203. For a more general discussion of anti-German feeling, see Arthur Marwick, *The Deluge: British Society and the First World War* (1965), 2nd Edition (Basingstoke: Macmillan Press – now Palgrave Macmillan, 1991), 71–9.

15. Panayi, 'Anti-German Riots', 185–9.

16. Panikos Panayi, *The Enemy in Our Midst* (Oxford: Oxford University Press, 1991). See also Panikos Panayi, 'An Intolerant Act by an Intolerant Society: The Internment of Germans in Britain during the First World War', *Immigrants and Minorities* 11 (1992), 53–75, and Annette Becker, 'Captive Civilians', in Jay Winter, ed., *The Cambridge History of the First World War* (Cambridge: Cambridge University Press, 2014), vol. 3, 266.

17. Quoted in Cate Haste, *Keep the Home Fires Burning: Propaganda in the First World War* (London: Allen Lane, 1977), 126.

18. The Russian Jewish community had been feared as a potential source of 'racial' contamination since the late nineteenth century. The Anthropometric Committee warned that Jews had already undermined the vigor of the Polish nation and might do the same to Britain if their population remained unchecked. Parliament passed an Aliens Act in 1905 largely designed to

restrict Jewish immigration. J. M. Winter, *The Great War and the British People* (London: Macmillan Press – now Palgrave Macmillan, 1985), 15.

19. Julia Bush, 'East London Jews and the First World War', *London Journal* 6 (1980), 147–61.

20. Ibid., 150.

21. David Cesarani, 'An Embattled Minority: The Jews in Britain during the First World War', *Immigrants and Minorities* 8 (1989), 61–81. See also Gerry Rubin, 'Race, Retailing and Wartime Regulation', *Immigrants and Minorities* 7 (1988), 184–205.

22. Bush, 'East London Jews and the First World War', 154–6, and John Stevenson, *British Society, 1914–45* (London: Penguin Books, 1984), 57.

23. Trevor Wilson, *The Myriad Faces of War: Britain and the Great War, 1914–1918* (Cambridge: Polity Press, 1986), 403.

24. Cesarani, 'An Embattled Minority', 70–2.

25. Ibid., 46. A useful discussion of what was held to constitute 'Englishness' can be found in Colls, *Englishness*.

26. John Brophy and Eric Partridge, *The Long Trail: Soldiers' Songs and Slang* (London: Sphere Books, 1965), 67, 82–3, 113.

27. A. J. Stockwell, 'The War and the British Empire', in John Turner, ed., *Britain and the First World War* (London: Unwin Hyman, 1988), 42.

28. Winter, *The Great War and the British People*, 75, and Stephen Constantine, 'Britain and the Empire', in Stephen Constantine, Maurice W. Kirby, and Mary B. Rose, eds, *The First World War in British History* (London: Edward Arnold, 1995), 260–1.

29. Laura Tabili, *'We Ask for British Justice': Workers and Racial Difference in Late Imperial Britain* (Ithaca, NY: Cornell University Press, 1994), 15–16. See also Peter Fryer, *Staying Power: The History of Black People in Britain* (London: Pluto, 1987).

30. H. G. Wells, *Mr. Britling Sees It Through* (New York: Macmillan, 1917), 201.

31. Curzon was Viceroy of India (1898–1905) and author of several books promoting British imperialism; Milner was Governor General of Cape Colony at the time of the Boer War and a key architect of the Union of South Africa; Smuts was South African Defense Minister.

32. Bernard Porter, *The Lion's Share* (London: Longman, 1984), 237–49.

33. Constantine, 'Britain and Empire', 259–60.

34. Jeremy Black, *The Great War and the Making of the Modern World* (London: Continuum, 2011), 237.

35. Quoted in Bernard Bergonzi, *Heroes' Twilight: A Study of the Literature of the Great War* (London: Constable, 1965), 47.

36. MacKenzie, *Propaganda and Empire*, 35.

37. Peter Green, *Classical Bearings* (London: Thames and Hudson, 1989), 41.

38. Quoted in Sir Harry Hamilton Johnston, *Black Man's Part in the War* (London: Simpkin, Marshall, Hamilton, Kent and Co., 1917), back cover.

39. A. J. Hoover, *God, Germany and Britain in the Great War: A Study of Clerical Nationalism* (New York: Praeger, 1989), 68, and Ian Holt, *Till the Boys Come*

Home: The Picture Postcards of the First World War (London: Macdonald and Jones, 1977), 177.

40. Basil Mathews, *Three Years' War for Peace* (London: Hodder and Stoughton, 1917), 38. See also Lewis Harcourt, *A Free Empire in War Time* (London: Victoria League, 1915).

41. J. Holland Rose, *How the War Came About* (London: The Patriotic Publishing Company, 1914), 24.

42. Quoted in Hoover, *God, Germany and Britain in the Great War*, 69.

43. MacKenzie, *Propaganda and Empire*, 35.

44. Edwyn Bevan, *Brothers All: The War and the Race Question* (London: Oxford University Press, 1914), 6, 14.

45. Quoted in Johnston, *Black Man's Part in the War*, 79.

46. See, for example, MacKenzie, *Propaganda and Empire*, 1.

47. Harold Lasswell, *Propaganda Techniques in World War I* (Boston: MIT Press, 1927), 55.

48. MacKenzie, *Propaganda and Empire*, 75, 156–7.

49. Nicholas Reeves, *Official British Film Propaganda During the First World War* (London: Croom Helm, 1986), 171.

50. For general histories of the war in the Middle East, see E. Kedourie, *Britain and the Middle East: The Vital Years, 1914–1921* (Cambridge: Bowes and Bowes, 1956), E. Monroe, *Britain's Moment in the Middle East, 1914–1956* (London: Chatto, 1963), and Briton C. Busch, *Britain, India, and the Arabs, 1914–1921* (Berkeley: University of California Press, 1971).

51. Graham Dawson, *Soldier Heroes: British Adventure, Empire and the Imagining of Masculinities* (London: Routledge, 1994), 171–88. Lawrence's own account of the Arabian campaigns, *Seven Pillars of Wisdom* (1926), did little to dispel the myth-making.

52. For the dominions at war, see P. N. S. Mansergh, *The Commonwealth Experience* (London: Weidenfeld & Nicolson, 1969), Chapter 6, and E. M. Andrews, *The Anzac Illusion: Anglo-Australian Relations during World War I* (Cambridge: Cambridge University Press, 1993).

53. Rolf Pfeiffer, 'Exercises in Loyalty and Trouble Making: Anglo-New Zealand Friction at the Time of the Great War', *Australian Journal of Politics and History* 38 (1992), 178.

54. Philip Haythornthwaite, *The World War I Sourcebook* (London: Arms and Armour Press, 1992), 131–7, 158–63, 267–70, 296–8.

55. Albert Grundlingh, *Fighting Their Own War: South African Blacks and the First World War* (Johannesburg: Raven Press, 1987), 21–3.

56. Constantine, 'Britain and the Empire', 264, and Denis Judd, *Empire: The British Imperial Experience from 1765 to the Present* (New York: Basic Books, 1996), 250.

57. Judd, *Empire*, 250.

58. Andrews, *The Anzac Illusion*, 153–4.

59. See Christopher Pugsley, *Gallipoli: The New Zealand Story* (Auckland: Hodder and Stoughton, 1984), and Andrews, *The Anzac Illusion*, 165–89.

60. Constantine, 'Britain and the Empire', 263–9.

61. Quoted in Pfeiffer, 'Exercises in Loyalty and Trouble Making', 181.
62. See essays in John Eddy and Deryck Schreuder, eds, *The Rise of Colonial Nationalism* (Sydney: Allen and Unwin, 1988).
63. Judd, *Empire*, 254.
64. Constantine, 'Britain and the Empire', 262.
65. David Killingray, 'The War in Africa', in Hew Strachan, ed., *World War I: A History* (New York: Oxford University Press, 1998), 99.
66. Johnston, *Black Man's Part in the War*, 10.
67. Stockwell, 'The War and the British Empire', 46, Keith Robbins, *The First World War* (Oxford: Oxford University Press, 1984), 135, and John H. Morrow, Jr., *The Great War: An Imperial History* (London: Routledge, 2005), 313.
68. Bhupendranath Basu, *Why India is Heart and Soul with Great Britain* (London: Macmillan Press – now Palgrave Macmillan, 1914), 1. See also Mancherjee Bhownaggree, *The Verdict of India* (London: Hodder and Stoughton, 1916).
69. Rosina Visram, 'The First World War and the Indian Soldiers', *Indo-British Review* 16 (1989), 17. For general accounts of India and the war, see also J. M. Brown, 'War, Britain and India, 1914–18', in M. R. D. Foot, ed., *War and Society* (London: Elek, 1973), and D. C. Ellenwood and S. D. Pradhan, eds, *India and World War I* (New Delhi: Manohar, 1978).
70. Although South Africa was a self-governing dominion, the position of its black population was analogous to that of people in the dependencies.
71. Grundlingh, *Fighting Their Own War*, 13–14.
72. Glenford Howe, 'West Indian Blacks and the Struggle for Participation in the First World War', *Journal of Caribbean History* 28 (1994), 30.
73. David Killingray, 'All the King's Men? Blacks in the British Army in the First World War', in Rainer Lotz and Ian Pegg, eds, *Under the Imperial Carpet: Essays in Black History* (Crawley: Rabbit, 1986), 166–7, 178–9.
74. Howe, 'West Indian Blacks', 33–49.
75. Grundlingh, *Fighting Their Own War*, 39–49. See also Tyler Stovall, 'The Color Line behind the Lines: Racial Violence in France during the Great War', *American Historical Review* 103 (June 1998), 737–69, and Michael Summerskill, *Chinese on the Western Front: Britain's Chinese Work Force in the First World War* (London: Summerskill, 1982).
76. Visram, 'The First World War and the Indian Soldiers', 17.
77. Jeffrey Greenhut, 'The Imperial Reserve: The Indian Corps on the Western Front', *Journal of Imperial and Commonwealth History* 12 (1983), 54–6.
78. Greenhut, 'The Imperial Reserve', 57–65.
79. Visram, 'The First World War and the Indian Soldiers', 25, and David Omissi, *Indian Voices of the Great War: Soldiers' Letters, 1914–18* (New York: St Martin's Press – now Palgrave Macmillan, 1999), 32.
80. Gregory Morton Jack, 'The Indian Army on the Western Front, 1914–1915: A Portrait of Collaboration', *War in History* 13 (July 2006), 329–62. For a more negative assessment of the Indian Army, see Greenhut, 'The Imperial Reserve', 65–8.
81. Greenhut, 'The Imperial Reserve', 68.

82. Peter Lennon, 'Dishonoured Legion', *Guardian Weekly*, 28 October–3 November 1999.
83. For the war in Africa, see Melvin Page, ed., *Africa and the First World War* (London: Macmillan Press – now Palgrave Macmillan, 1987), Byron Farwell, *The Great War in Africa* (New York: Norton, 1986), and P. Gifford and W. R. Louis, eds, *Britain and Germany in Africa: Imperial Rivalry and Colonial Rule* (New Haven: Yale University Press, 1967).
84. James K. Matthews, 'First World War and the Rise of African Nationalism: Nigerian Veterans as Catalysts of Change', *Journal of Modern African Studies* 20 (1982), 493–502.
85. David Killingray and James K. Matthews, 'Beasts of Burden: British West African Carriers in the First World War', *Canadian Journal of African Studies* 13 (1979), 7–22, Geoffrey Hodges, *The Carrier Corps: Military Labor in the East African Campaign of 1914 to 1918* (New York: Greenwood Press, 1986), and Killingray, 'The War in Africa', 93–9.
86. Tabili, '*We Ask for British Justice*', 27.
87. Visram, 'The First World War and the Indian Soldiers', 22.
88. Quoted in Grundlingh, *Fighting Their Own War*, 103.
89. Omissi, *Indian Voices of the Great War*, 113–14, 119, and Visram, 'The First World War and the Indian Soldiers', 21–2.
90. K. Jeffery, *An Irish Empire? Aspects of Ireland and the British Empire* (Manchester: Manchester University Press, 1996).
91. For the Irish and race, see L. P. Curtis, *Anglo-Saxons and Celts: A Study of Anti-Irish Prejudice in Victorian England* (Bridgeport, CT: Conference on British Studies, 1968), and Noel Ignatiev, *How the Irish Became White* (New York: Routledge, 1995).
92. For a history of the Home Rule crisis, see A. T. Q. Stewart, *The Ulster Crisis* (London: Faber, 1967), and Patricia Jalland, *The Liberals and Ireland: The Ulster Question in British Politics to 1914* (Brighton: Harvester Press, 1980).
93. David Fitzpatrick, ed., *Ireland and the First World War* (Dublin: Trinity History Workshop, 1986).
94. Catriona Pennell, *A Kingdom United* (Oxford: Oxford University Press, 2012), 163–97.
95. Terence Denman, 'The Catholic Irish Soldier in the First World War: The Racial Environment', *Irish Historical Studies* 27 (1991), 354.
96. For the Easter Rising, see Charles Townshend, *Easter 1916: The Irish Rebellion* (London: Penguin, 2005), and Alan J. Ward, *The Easter Rising: Revolution and Irish Nationalism* (Arlington Heights: Harlan Davidson, 1980).
97. Charles Townshend, *The British Campaign in Ireland, 1919–21: The Development of Political and Military Policies* (Oxford: Oxford University Press, 1975), and D. W. Harkness, *The Restless Dominion: The Irish Free State and the British Commonwealth of Nations, 1921–31* (London: Macmillan Press – now Palgrave Macmillan, 1969).
98. Andrews, *The Anzac Illusion*, 126–7.
99. 'Colouring the map red' was standard parlance for imperial expansion, as world maps customarily used red to designate British possessions.

100. Porter, *The Lion's Share*, 249. See also W. Roger Louis, *Great Britain and Germany's Lost Colonies, 1914–1919* (Oxford: Clarendon Press, 1967).
101. Ruth Henig, 'Foreign Policy', in Constantine, *The First World War in British History*, 205.
102. Grundlingh, *Fighting Their Own War*, 15.
103. Visram, 'The First World War and the Indian Soldiers', 23.
104. Melvin Page, 'Black Men in a White Men's War', in Page, *Africa and the First World War*, 4.
105. Grundlingh, *Fighting Their Own War*, 124.
106. Tabili, *'We Ask for British Justice'*, 23.
107. Ibid., 15.
108. Jacqueline Jenkinson, 'The 1919 Race Riots in Britain: A Survey', in Lotz and Pegg, *Under the Imperial Carpet*, 180–203.
109. Ibid., 195.
110. Pat Thane, 'The British Imperial State and the Construction of National Identities', in Billie Melman, ed., *Borderlines: Genders and Identities in War and Peace, 1870–1930* (London: Routledge, 1998), 43.
111. Howe, 'West Indian Blacks and the Struggle for Participation', 55, and Lennon, 'Dishonoured Legion', 20.
112. Quoted in Albert Grundlingh, 'The Impact of the First World War on South African Blacks', in Page, *Africa and the First World War*, 61.
113. A Southern racist, Woodrow Wilson only supported national self-determination for European peoples like Czechs and Poles. He did not believe that colonized peoples in Africa and Asia were capable of self-government. See Erez Manela, *The Wilsonian Moment: Self-Determination and the International Origins of Anticolonial Nationalism* (Oxford: Oxford University Press, 2007), 24–30.
114. Porter, *The Lion's Share*, 239–42.
115. Morrow, *The Great War: An Imperial History*, 313. For Amritsar and its aftermath, see R. Furneaux, *Massacre at Amritsar* (London: Allen and Unwin, 1963), and R. Kumar, ed., *Essays on Gandhian Politics: The Rowlett Satyagraha* (Oxford: Clarendon Press, 1977).
116. Pfeiffer, 'Exercises in Loyalty and Trouble Making', 188.

5 Propaganda and Censorship

1. Quoted in Michael Sanders and Philip M. Taylor, *British Propaganda during the First World War, 1914–18* (London: Macmillan Press – now Palgrave Macmillan, 1982), 255.
2. Jay Winter, 'Popular Culture in Wartime Britain', in Aviel Roshwald and Richard Stites, eds., *European Culture in the Great War: The Arts, Entertainment, and Propaganda, 1914–1918* (Cambridge: Cambridge University Press, 1999), 330, 347–8.
3. Harold Lasswell, *Propaganda Techniques in World War I* (Boston, MA: MIT Press, 1927), 10.

4. Gary S. Messinger, *British Propaganda and the State in the First World War* (Manchester: Manchester University Press, 1992), 5, and Sanders and Taylor, *British Propaganda*, 38–42.

5. Arthur Marwick, *The Deluge* (1965), 2nd edition (London: Macmillan Press – now Palgrave Macmillan, 1991), 85.

6. Sanders and Taylor, *British Propaganda*, 40, 107–8.

7. Mrs Humphry Ward, *England's Effort: Letters to an American Friend* (New York: Scribner's, 1916), and Messinger, *British Propaganda and the State*, 57–69.

8. Sanders and Taylor, *British Propaganda*, 52–3, 109.

9. Cate Haste, *Keep the Home Fires Burning: Propaganda in the First World War* (London: Allen Lane, 1977), 22–3.

10. Albert Marrin, *The Last Crusade: The Church of England in the First World War* (Durham, NC: Duke University Press, 1974), 130.

11. Nicoletta Gullace, 'Sexual Violence and Family Honor: British Propaganda and International Law during the First World War', *American Historical Review* 102 (June 1997), 721.

12. Stuart Wallace, *War and the Image of Germany: British Academics* (Edinburgh: John Donald, 1988), 60, and Marrin, *Last Crusade*, 101–2.

13. Arnold Bennett, *Liberty: A Statement of the British Case* (London: Hodder and Stoughton, 1914), 22, 58.

14. *Punch*, 15 September 1915, and Marrin, *Last Crusade*, 126.

15. John Horne and Alan Kramer, *German Atrocities, 1914: A History of Denial* (New Haven: Yale University Press, 2001), 9–86. See also Jeff Lipkes, *Rehearsals: The German Army in Belgium, August 1914* (Leuven, 2007).

16. 'Torture of a Canadian Officer', *Times*, 10 May 1915, 7.

17. Haste, *Keep the Home Fires Burning*, 102, and Trevor Wilson, *The Myriad Faces of War: Britain and the Great War, 1914–1918* (Cambridge: Polity Press, 1986), 156.

18. Horne and Kramer, *German Atrocities*, 196–204.

19. Wilson, *Myriad Faces of War*, 183–90.

20. Messinger, *British Propaganda and the State*, 30.

21. Quoted in Claire Tylee, *The Great War and Women's Consciousness: Images of Militarism and Womanhood in Women's Writings, 1914–64* (Iowa City: University of Iowa Press, 1990), 94–5.

22. Examples of wartime propaganda cartoons include Edmund Sullivan, *The Kaiser's Garland* (London: Heinemann, 1915), Alfred Leete, *The Bosch Book* (London: Duckworth, 1916), Arthur Moreland, *The History of the Hun* (London: Palmer and Hayward, 1917), and J. Murray Allison, ed., *Raemaekers' Cartoon History of the War* (New York: Century, 1918). See also E. Demm, 'Propaganda and Caricature in the First World War', *Journal of Contemporary History* 28 (1993), 163–92, and Roy Douglas, *The Great War, 1914–1918: The Cartoonists' Vision* (London: Routledge, 1995).

23. Gullace, 'Sexual Violence and Family Honor', 743, Wilson, *Myriad Faces of War*, 740, and Kevin Brownlow, *The War, the West and the Wilderness* (New York: Knopf, 1979), 7, 153.

24. John Stevenson, *British Society, 1914–45* (London: Penguin, 1984), 75.

25. Julie Wheelwright, *The Fatal Lover: Mata Hari and the Myth of Women in Espionage* (London: Collins and Brown, 1992), 120–2. Examples of propaganda books which exploited Cavell's execution include Charles Sarolea, *The Murder of Nurse Cavell* (London: G. Allen and Unwin, 1915), and William S. Murphy, *In Memoriam: Edith Cavell* (London: Stoneham, 1916).

26. Shane Barney, 'The Mythic Matters of Edith Cavell: Propaganda, Legend, Myth, and Memory', *Historical Reflections* 31 (Summer 2005), 217–33.

27. Sanders and Taylor, *British Propaganda*, 16–17, 103.

28. H. Rider Haggard, *A Call to Arms* (London: R. Clay, 1914), 4, Arthur Conan Doyle, *To Arms!* (London: Hodder and Stoughton, 1914), 1, and Horatio Bottomley, *Bottomley's Battle Cry* (London: Oldhams, 1914), 10–12.

29. Haste, *Keep the Home Fires Burning*, 55.

30. Maurice Rickards, *Posters of the First World War* (London: Evelyn, Adams and Mackay, 1968), 8, and Messinger, *British Propaganda and the State*, 214–24.

31. Maurice Rickards and Michael Moody, *The First World War: Ephemera, Mementoes, Documents* (London: Jupiter, 1975), 9, Joseph Darracott, *The First World War in Posters* (New York: Dover, 1974), 25, and Philip Dutton, 'Moving Images?: The Parliamentary Recruiting Committee's Poster Campaign, 1914–16', *Imperial War Museum Review* 4 (1989), 43–57.

32. Dutton, 'Moving Images?', 51, and Rickards, *Posters of the First World War*, 11, 34.

33. Darracott, *First World War in Posters*, frontispiece, and Rickards, *Posters of the First World War*, 47–9.

34. Stevenson, *British Society, 1914–45*, 62, Felicity Goodall, *A Question of Conscience* (London: Sutton, 1997), 8, and Nicholas Hiley, '"The British Army Film", "You!" and "For the Empire": Reconstructed Propaganda Films', *Historical Journal of Films, Radio and TV* 5 (1985), 165–82.

35. For examples, see Darracott, *First World War in Posters*, 3–39.

36. Haste, *Keep the Home Fires Burning*, 6, L. J. Collins, *Theatre at War, 1914–1918* (London: Macmillan Press – now Palgrave Macmillan, 1998), 43–50, and Wilson, *Myriad Faces of War*, 647.

37. Nicholas Reeves, *Official British Film Propaganda during the First World War* (London: Croom Helm, 1986), 210–11.

38. Sanders and Taylor, *British Propaganda*, 9–19.

39. DeGroot, *Blighty: British Society in the Era of the Great War* (London: Longman, 1996), 183, and Sanders and Taylor, *British Propaganda*, 19–24.

40. *London Opinion*, 17 October 1914.

41. Sanders and Taylor, *British Propaganda*, 27, and Colin Lovelace, 'British Press Censorship during the First World War', in G. Boyce, ed., *Newspaper History from the 17th Century to the Present Day* (London: Constable, 1978), 314–15.

42. Marwick, *Deluge*, 113, Sanders and Taylor, *British Propaganda*, 32, and Deian Hopkin, 'Domestic Censorship in the First World War', *Journal of Contemporary History* 5 (1970), 157–60.

43. Robert Roberts, *The Classic Slum* (London: Penguin, 1971), 202.

44. Sanders and Taylor, *British Propaganda*, 33.

45. Peter Putnis, 'Share 99: British Government Control of Reuters during World War I', *Media History* 14 (August 2008), 141–65.

46. John McEwen, 'The National Press during the First World War: Ownership and Circulation', *Journal of Contemporary History* 17 (1982), 459–86.

47. Particularly negative depictions of the wartime press can be found in Philip Knightly, *The First Casualty* (New York: Harcourt, 1975), and Niall Ferguson, *The Pity of War* (New York: Basic Books, 1999).

48. J. M. Bourne, *Britain and the Great War* (London: Edward Arnold, 1989), 206.

49. Lovelace, 'British Press Censorship', 318.

50. Bourne, *Britain and the Great War*, 207–9.

51. Ian Dewhirst, *The Story of a Nobody: A Working-Class Life, 1880–1939* (London: Mills and Boon, 1980), 64–5.

52. Qtd. in Jeremy Black, *The Great War and the Making of the Modern World* (London: Continuum, 2011), 100.

53. Paul Fussell, *The Great War and Modern Memory* (New York: Oxford University Press, 1975), 21–2.

54. Robert Wohl, *The Generation of 1914* (Cambridge: Harvard University Press, 1979), 93, and Pennell, *A Kingdom United*, 64–5. See also Allen J. Frantzen, *Bloody Good: Chivalry, Sacrifice, and the Great War* (Chicago: University of Chicago Press, 2004).

55. Charles Bailey, 'The British Protestant Theologians in the First World War: Germanophobia Unleashed', *Harvard Theological Review* 77 (1984), 203, and Marrin, *Last Crusade*, 139.

56. Marrin, *Last Crusade*, 92–7, and A. J. Hoover, *God, Germany and Britain in the Great War: A Study in Clerical Nationalism* (New York: Praeger, 1989), 31. Hundreds of prophetic and apocalyptic writings were published during the war. See, for example, Katherine Julius, *Awake! O Isles of the Sea* (London: R. Scott, 1917), Marr Murray, *Bible Prophecies and the Plain Man* (London: Hodder and Stoughton, 1915), and Henry Sulley, *Is It Armageddon?* (London: Simpkin, Marshall, Hamilton, Kent, 1915).

57. Marrin, *Last Crusade*, 215–16.

58. Keith Robbins, *The First World War* (New York: Oxford University Press, 1984), 157–8.

59. Alan Wilkinson, *The Church of England and the First World War* (London: SPCK, 1978), 180, and Peter Parker, *The Old Lie: The Great War and the Public School Ethos* (London: Constable, 1987), 192.

60. Marrin, *Last Crusade*, 153, 175, Marwick, *Deluge*, 172, and Joseph Dawson, *Christ and the Sword* (London: C. H. Kelly, 1916), 101.

61. Wilson, *Myriad Faces of War*, 178.

62. Sylvia Pankhurst, *The Homefront* (1932), reprint (London: The Cresset Library, 1987), 368, and Vellacott, *Bertrand Russell and the Pacifists*, 210–15.

63. Brock Milman, 'HMG and the War Against Dissent, 1914–18', *Journal of Contemporary History* 40 (July 2005), 413–40, and Pennell, *A Kingdom United*, 106.

64. Brock Milman, *Managing Domestic Dissent in First World War Britain* (London: Frank Cass, 2000), 30–8, 63, 75–81.

65. Marvin Swartz, *The Union of Democratic Control in British Politics during the First World War* (Oxford: Clarendon Press, 1971), 42–66, and Sue Malvern, 'War As It Is', *Art History* 9 (1986), 498.

66. Adrian Gregory, *The Last Great War* (Cambridge: Cambridge University Press, 2008), 101–6.

67. James McDermott, 'Conscience and Military Service Tribunals during the First World War', *War in* History 17 (January 2010), 60–85, and Felicity Goudall, *A Question of Conscience* (London: Sutton, 1997), 1–27, 53–72. See also Martin Ceadel, *Pacifism in Britain, 1914–1945* (Oxford: Oxford University Press, 1980).

68. Messinger, *British Propaganda and the State*, 49–50, and Sanders and Taylor, *British Propaganda*, 63–4.

69. Sanders and Taylor, *British Propaganda*, 146, and Stevenson, *British Society, 1914–45*, 75–6.

70. Sanders and Taylor, *British Propaganda*, 67, and David Stevenson, *Cataclysm: The First World War as a Political Tragedy* (New York: Basic Books, 2004), 374.

71. Haste, *Keep the Home Fires Burning*, 41, and Alan Simmonds, *Britain and World War I* (New York: Routledge, 2012), 246.

72. Hopkin, 'Domestic Censorship', 163–4, and Haste, *Keep the Home Fires Burning*, 171–2, and Milman, *Managing Domestic Dissent*, 177–83.

73. Messinger, *British Propaganda and the State*, 123–61.

74. Reeves, *Official British Film Propaganda*, 15, and Sanders and Taylor, *British Propaganda*, 120–41.

75. Jane Carmichael, *First World War Photographers* (London: Routledge, 1989), and Jorge Lewinski, *The Camera at War* (New York: Simon and Schuster, 1978).

76. Brownlow, *The War, the West and the Wilderness*, 3, and Nicholas Hiley, 'The British Cinema Auditorium', in Karel Dibbets and Bert Hogenkamp, eds, *Film and the First World War* (Amsterdam: Amsterdam University Press, 1995), 161–2.

77. Nicholas Reeves, 'Official British Film Propaganda', in Michael Paris, ed., *The First World War and Popular Cinema* (New Brunswick: Rutgers University Press, 2000), 29, and Tim Travers, 'Canadian Film and the First World War', in Paris, *First World War and Popular Cinema*, 96.

78. Rachael Low, *The History of British Film*, vol. 3: *1914–1918* (1950), reprint (London: Routledge, 1997), 152, and Reeves, *Official British Film Propaganda*, 46–61, 158–60.

79. Alastair H. Fraser, Andrew Robertshaw and Steve Roberts, *Ghosts of the Somme: Filming the Battle, June–July 1916* (Barnsley: Pen and Sword, 2009), 170, and Reeves, 'Official British Film Propaganda', in Paris, *First World War and Popular Cinema*, 40.

80. Reeves, *Official British Film Propaganda*, 26, 65–8, 118, 191–205.

81. Arthur Lennig, 'Hearts of the World', *Film History* 23 (December 2011), 436–8.

82. Russell Merritt, 'D. W. Griffith Directs the Great War', *Quarterly Review of Film Studies* 6 (Winter 1981), 45–65, Reeves, *Official British Film Propaganda*, 121–4, and Lennig, 'Hearts of the World', 456, note 35.

83. Reeves, *Official British Film Propaganda*, 127–31, 193–4.

84. Messinger, *British Propaganda and the State*, 223.

85. Dutton, 'Moving Images?', 54, Marwick, *Deluge*, 92, Haste, *Keep the Home Fires Burning*, 158, Claire Culleton, *Working-Class Culture, Women, and Britain, 1914–1921* (New York: St Martin's Press – now Palgrave Macmillan, 1999), 41, and Pennell, *A Kingdom United*, 190–3.

86. Nicholas Hiley, '"Kitchener Wants You" and "Daddy What Did YOU Do in the Great War?": The Myth of British Recruiting Posters', *Imperial War Museum Review* 11 (1997), 40–58.

87. Ian Beckett, *Home Front, 1914–1918* (London: National Archives, 2006), 175.

88. J. G. Fuller, *Troop Morale and Popular Culture in the British and Dominion Armies, 1914–1918* (Oxford: Oxford University Press, 1990), 150–1, and Culleton, *Working-Class Culture, Women, and Britain*, 65.

89. Robert Graves, *Good-Bye to All That* (1929), reprint (New York: Doubleday, 1957), 228–32.

90. Bernard Waites, *A Class Society at War: England, 1914–1918* (Leamington Spa: Berg, 1987), 203, Joanna Bourke, *Dismembering the Male: Men's Bodies, Britain and the Great War* (Chicago: University of Chicago Press, 1996), 22, and David Monger, 'Soldiers, Propaganda and Ideas of Home and Community in First World War Britain', *Cultural and Social History* 8 (2011), 331–54.

91. Michael Roper, 'Maternal Relations: Moral Manliness and Emotional Survival in Letters Home during the First World War', in Stefan Dudink, Karen Hagemann and John Tosh, eds., *Masculinities in Politics and War* (Manchester: Manchester University Press, 2004), 297, 305, Daniel Todman, *The Great War: Myth and Memory* (London: Continuum, 2005), 2, and Pennell, *A Kingdom United*, 121.

92. Quoted in Tylee, *The Great War and Women's Consciousness*, 39.

93. Quoted in Marwick, *Deluge*, 81.

94. Richard Aldington, 'The Case of Lieutenant Hall', in Trudi Tate, ed., *Women, Men and the Great War: An Anthology of Stories* (Manchester: Manchester University Press, 1995), 88.

6 Art and Literature

1. Paul Fussell, *The Great War and Modern Memory* (New York: Oxford University Press, 1975), and Modris Eksteins, *Rites of Spring: The Great War and the Birth of the Modern Age* (New York: Anchor Books, 1989).

2. Ted Bogacz, '"A Tyranny of Words": Language, Poetry and Antimodernism in England in the First World War', *Journal of Modern History* 58 (1986), 643–68, and Rosa Bracco, *Merchants of Hope: Middlebrow Writers in the First World War* (Oxford: Berg, 1993).

3. Rupert Brooke, 'Peace', in *The Collected Poems of Rupert Brooke* (New York: Dodd, Mead and Company, 1931), 111.

4. Quoted in Samuel Hynes, *A War Imagined: The First World War and English Culture* (New York: Atheneum, 1991), 12.

5. H. D. Rawnsley, 'Louvain', in Albert Marrin, *The Last Crusade: The Church of England in the First World War* (Durham, NC: Duke University Press, 1974), 89. See also Hynes, *A War Imagined*, 67–75, and John Cowper Powys, *The Menace of German Culture* (London: W. Rider and Son, 1915).

6. Alec Ellis, *Public Libraries and the First World War* (Upton: Ffynnon Press, 1975), 1–20, and Fred Askew, *Shakespeare Tercenary Souvenir* (Lowestoft: Flood, 1916).

7. Bogacz, 'Tyranny of Words', 655, and Maurice Rickards, *Posters of the First World War* (London: Evelyn, Adams and Mackay, 1968), 12.

8. Richard Cork, *A Bitter Truth: Avant-Garde Art and the Great War* (New Haven: Yale University Press, 1994), 29, and James Longenbach, 'The Women and Men of 1914', in Helen M. Cooper, ed., *Arms and the Woman: War, Gender, and Literary Representation* (Chapel Hill: University of North Carolina Press, 1989), 97–8.

9. Gary S. Messenger, *British Propaganda and the State in the First World War* (Manchester: Manchester University Press, 1992), 34, and Hynes, *A War Imagined*, 26.

10. Messinger, *British Propaganda and the State*, 39.

11. G. B. Shaw, *Common Sense About the War* (London: Statesman Publishing Company, 1914), 3, 5.

12. Thomas Hardy, 'And There Was A Great Calm', in Candace Ward, ed., *World War I British Poets* (New York: Dover, 1997), 58.

13. Quoted in Hynes, *A War Imagined*, 83–4.

14. See Paul Delany, *D. H. Lawrence's Nightmare: The Writer and His Circle in the Years of the Great War* (New York: Basic Books, 1979).

15. Hynes, *A War Imagined*, 36–8, and Keith Robbins, *The First World War* (New York: Oxford University Press, 1984), 156.

16. John Ferguson, *The Arts in Britain in World War I* (London: Stainer and Bell, 1980), 23–4, and Harold Lasswell, *Propaganda Techniques in World War I* (Boston, MA: MIT Press, 1927), 75.

17. L. J. Collins, *Theatre at War, 1914–1918* (London: Macmillan Press – now Palgrave Macmillan, 1998), 1–42, and John MacKenzie, *Propaganda and Empire* (Manchester: Manchester University Press, 1984), 50.

18. Collins, *Theatre at War*, 185, and G. S. Street, *At Home in the War* (London: Heinemann, 1918), 104–12. On the widespread demonization of the Kaiser, see Lothar Reinermann, 'Fleet Street and the Kaiser: British Public Opinion and Wilhelm II', *German History* 26 (2008), 469–85.

19. G. B. Shaw, *Heartbreak House and Playlets of the War* (New York: Brentano's, 1919), Preface, xliv, and James Bishop, ed., *The Illustrated London News Social History of the First World War* (London: Angus and Robertson, 1982), 117.

20. Collins, *Theatre at War*, 34–46, and Cate Haste, *Rules of Desire: Sex in Britain, World War I to the Present* (London: Chatto & Windus, 1992), 51.

21. Trevor Wilson, *The Myriad Faces of War: Britain and the Great War, 1914–1918* (Cambridge: Polity Press, 1986), 390, and Maurice Rickards and Michael Moody, *The First World War: Ephemera, Mementoes, Documents* (London: Jupiter, 1975), 21.

22. Collins, *Theatre at War*, 185–201, and Shaw, *Heartbreak House and Playlets of the War*, 247–72.

23. Shaw, *Heartbreak House and Playlets of the War*, Preface, liv.
24. Allan Monkhouse, 'Shamed Life', in *War Plays* (London: Constable and Company, 1916), 20, and *The Conquering Hero* (London: E. Benn, 1923).
25. James Fox, 'Traitor Painters: Artists and Espionage in the First World War, 1914–1918', *British Art Journal* 9 (Spring 2009), 62–8.
26. Shaw, *Heartbreak House*, xx. See also Cork, *Bitter Truth*, 138, and Hynes, *A War Imagined*, 102, and James Fox, 'Fiddling While Rome Is Burning: Hostility to Art during the First World War, 1914–1918', *Visual Culture in Britain* 11 (March 2010), 49–65.
27. Peter Harrington, 'Early Paintings of the Great War', *Imperial War Museum Review* 7 (1992), 47, Cork, *Bitter Truth*, 72–3, and John Laffin, *World War I in Postcards* (Gloucester: Alan Sutton, 1988), 85–97.
28. Quoted in Clair Tylee, *The Great War and Women's Consciousness* (Iowa City: University of Iowa Press, 1990), 23. See also, Stuart Sillars, *Art and Survival in First World War Britain* (London: Macmillan Press – now Palgrave Macmillan, 1987), 17.
29. Peter Harrington, 'Religious and Spiritual Themes in British Academic Art during the Great War,' *First World War Studies* 2 (October 2011), 145–64, and Joanna Bourke, *Dismembering the Male: Men's Bodies, Britain, and the Great War* (Chicago: University of Chicago Press, 1996), 213.
30. Laffin, *World War I in Postcards*, 90–1, and Harrington, 'Early Paintings of the Great War', 46–54.
31. Cork, *Bitter Truth*, 129–37.
32. J. M. Winter, *The Experience of World War I* (London: Macmillan Press – now Palgrave Macmillan, 1988), 235, and Michael Sanders and Philip M. Taylor, *British Propaganda during the First World War, 1914–18* (London: Macmillan Press – now Palgrave Macmillan, 1982), 122–3.
33. Sue Malvern, '"War As It Is": The Art of Muirhead Bone, C. R. W. Nevinson and Paul Nash, 1916–17', *Art History* 9 (December 1986), 487–515, Charles Doherty, 'The War Art of C. R. W. Nevinson', *Imperial War Museum Review* 8 (1993), 48–62, and David Boyd Haycock, *A Crisis of Brilliance* (London: Old Street, 2009), 260–1.
34. Meirion and Susie Harries, *The War Artists: British Official War Art of the 20th Century* (London: Michael Joseph, 1983), 44–51.
35. Quoted in Cork, *Bitter Truth*, 198.
36. Ibid., 220. See also, Harries, *War Artists*, 86–9, 99.
37. Robert Upstone, *William Orpen: Politics, Sex and Death* (London: Imperial War Museum, 2005), 37–46.
38. Michael Walsh, 'C.R.W. Nevinson: Conflict, Contrast and Controversy in Paintings of War', *War in History* 12 (April 2005), 182.
39. Hynes, *A War Imagined*, 195, and Harries and Harries, *War Artists*, 88.
40. Stephen Kern, *The Culture of Time and Space, 1880–1918* (Cambridge, MA: Harvard University Press, 1983), 303–4, and E. L. Kahn, *The Neglected Majority: 'Les camoufleurs'*, *Art History and World War I* (New York: University Press of America, 1984), 97–140.
41. Harries and Harries, *War Artists*, 59, 152.

42. Tylee, *Great War and Women's Consciousness*, 79.

43. Rudyard Kipling, 'For All We Have and Are', in Ward, *World War I British Poets*, 63–4.

44. Coulson Kernahan, 'To "Little" Belgium', in *Songs and Sonnets for England in War Time* (London: John Lane, 1914), 21.

45. 'Victory Day', in John Oxenham, *'All's Well!': Some Helpful Verse for These Dark Days of War* (London: Methuen, 1915), 64.

46. Robert Bridges, 'Lord Kitchener', in Marcus Clapham, ed., *First World War Poetry* (Ware, Hertfordshire: Wordsworth Poetry Library, 1995), 14.

47. Janet Montefiore, '"Shining Pins and Wailing Shells": Women Poets and the Great War', in Dorothy Goldman, ed., *Women and World War I: The Written Response* (London: Macmillan Press – now Palgrave Macmillan, 1993), 62–3.

48. Brooke, 'The Soldier', in *Collected Poems*, 115.

49. Bernard Bergonzi, *Heroes' Twilight: A Study of the Literature of the Great War* (London: Constable, 1965), 36, and Tim Cross, ed., *The Lost Voices of World War I* (London: Bloomsbury, 1988), 54.

50. Julian Grenfell, 'Into Battle', in Jon Silkin, ed., *The Penguin Book of First World War Poetry* (London: Penguin, 1979), 83.

51. John Ivelaw-Chapman, *The Riddles of Wipers: An Appreciation of the Wipers Times, A Journal of the Trenches* (London: Leo Cooper, 1997), 35.

52. Charles Hamilton Sorley, 'To Germany', in Ward, *World War I British Poets*, 5.

53. Cross, *Lost Voices*, 69–70.

54. Gilbert Frankau, 'The Other Side', in *The Other Side and Other Poems* (New York: Knopf, 1918), 8.

55. Isaac Rosenberg, 'Dead Man's Dump', in Silkin, *Penguin Book of First World War Poetry*, 221.

56. Siegfried Sassoon, 'They', in Ward, *World War I British Poets*, 34.

57. Robert Graves, *Good-Bye to All That* (1929), reprint (New York: Doubleday, 1957), 260.

58. Muriel Stuart, 'Forgotten Dead, I Salute You', in Montefiore, 'Shining Pins and Wailing Shells', 68.

59. Jessie Pope, 'The Call', in Catherine Reilly, ed., *Scars Upon My Heart: Women's Poetry and Verse of the First World War* (London: Virago, 1981), 88.

60. Siegfried Sassoon, 'Suicide in the Trenches', in Clapham, *First World War Poetry*, 102.

61. Wilfred Owen, 'Dulce Et Decorum Est', in Silkin, *Penguin Book of First World War Poetry*, 193.

62. Helen Hamilton, 'The Ghouls', in Reilly, *Scars Upon My Heart*, 47.

63. Mary Borden, 'Unidentified', in Montefiore, 'Shining Pins and Wailing Shells', 66.

64. Street, *At Home In the War*, 92.

65. Quoted in Philip E. Hager and Desmond Taylor, *The Novels of World War I: An Annotated Bibliography* (New York: Garland, 1981), 87.

66. Rudyard Kipling, 'Mary Postgate', in Trudi Tate, ed., *Women, Men and the Great War: An Anthology of Stories* (Manchester: Manchester University Press, 1995), 256, 267.

67. May Sinclair, 'Red Tape', in Tate, *Women, Men and the Great War*, 202, 209.

68. Laura Stempel Mumford, 'May Sinclair's *Tree of Heaven*: The Vortex of Feminism, the Community of War', in Cooper, *Arms and the Woman*.

69. Ezra Pound, 'Hugh Selwyn Mauberley', in *Selected Poems* (London: Faber and Gwyer, 1928), 160.

70. Fussell, *Great War and Modern Memory*, 325–6.

71. Hynes, *A War Imagined*, 348. See also Trudi Tate, *Modernism, History and the First World War* (Manchester: Manchester University Press, 1998).

72. Jay Winter, *Sites of Memory, Sites of Mourning: The Great War in European Cultural History* (Cambridge: Cambridge University Press, 1995).

7 *Popular Culture*

1. Claire Tylee, *The Great War and Women's Consciousness* (Iowa City: University of Iowa Press, 1990), 107.

2. Helen Small, 'Mrs Humphry Ward and the First Casualty of War', in Suzanne Raitt and Trudi Tait, eds, *Women's Fiction and the Great War* (Oxford: Clarendon Press, 1997), 20.

3. T. W. Koch, *Books in Camp, Trench and Hospital* (London: J. M. Dent and Sons, 1917), 13.

4. S. Nevile Foster, *Plain Tales from the War* (London: Collins, 1914), 3. For other examples, see *Deeds That Thrill the Empire* (London: Hutchinson, 1916), and Percy Westerman, *Deeds of Pluck and Daring in the Great War* (London: Blackie and Son, 1917).

5. Ian Hay, *The First Hundred Thousand* (New York: Houghton Mifflin, 1915), 84.

6. William LeQueux, *German Spies in England: An Exposure* (London, 1915), 72.

7. C. S. Peel, *How We Lived Then, 1914–1918* (London: John Lane, 1929), 39–40, and Julie Wheelwright, *The Fatal Lover: Mata Hari and the Myth of Women in Espionage* (London: Collins and Brown), 42.

8. 'Sapper', [H. C. McNeile], 'Spud Trevor of the Red Hussars', in Trudi Tate, ed., *Women, Men and the Great War: An Anthology of Stories* (Manchester: Manchester University Press, 1995), 247.

9. John MacKenzie, *Propaganda and Empire* (Manchester: Manchester University Press, 1984), 76.

10. Tylee, *The Great War and Women's Consciousness*, 71.

11. Jane Potter, '"A Great Purifier": The Great War in Women's Romances and Memoirs, 1914–18', in Raitt and Tait, *Women's Fiction and the Great War*.

12. Jane Potter, *Boys in Khaki, Girls in Print: Women's Literary Responses to the Great War* (Oxford: Oxford University Press, 2008), 8.

13. Trevor Wilson, *The Myriad Faces of War: Britain and the Great War, 1914–1918* (Cambridge: Cambridge University Press, 1986), 706, and Peter H. Liddle, *Voices of War: Front Line and Home Front* (London: Leo Cooper, 1988), 81.

14. Quoted in J. G. Fuller, *Troop Morale and Popular Culture in the British and Dominion Armies, 1914–1918* (Oxford: Oxford University Press, 1990), 37.

15. Gerard DeGroot, *Blighty: British Society in the Era of the Great War* (London: Longman, 1996), 242.

16. Siegfried Sassoon, 'Blighters', in Candace Ward, ed., *World War I British Poets* (New York: Dover, 1997), 33–4.

17. Dorothea York, ed., *Mud and Stars: An Anthology of World War Songs and Poetry* (New York: Holt, 1931), 200–20, and L. J. Collins, *Theatre at War, 1914–1918* (London: Macmillan Press – now Palgrave Macmillan, 1998), 12.

18. DeGroot, *Blighty*, 239.

19. Jay Winter, 'Popular Culture in Wartime Britain', in Aviel Roshwald and Richard Stites, eds., *European Culture in the Great War* (Cambridge: Cambridge University Press, 1999), 333–5.

20. John Stevenson, *British Society, 1914–45* (London: Penguin, 1984), 382, and Fuller, *Troop Morale and Popular Culture*, 111–12.

21. Rachael Low, *The History of British Film*, vol. 3: *1914–1918* (1950), reprint (London: Routledge, 1997), 178–89, and Arthur Lennig, 'Hearts of the World', *Film History* 23 (December 2011), 448.

22. Kevin Brownlow, *The War, the West and the Wilderness* (New York: Knopf, 1979), 26–43.

23. James Walvin, *Leisure and Society, 1830–1950* (London: Longman, 1978), 129, Cate Haste, *Keep the Home Fires Burning: Propaganda in the First World War* (London: Allen Lane, 1977), 59, and Ian Dewhirst, *The Story of a Nobody: A Working-Class Life, 1880–1939* (London: Mills and Boon, 1980), 39.

24. Fuller, *Troop Morale and Popular Culture*, 86–7.

25. DeGroot, *Blighty*, 230, Wilson, *Myriad Faces of War*, 164, and John Osborne, 'To Keep the Life of the Nation on the Old Line', *Journal of Sport History* 14 (1987), 143–4.

26. Colin Veitch, 'Play Up! Play Up! And Win the War!: Football, the Nation and the First World War', *Journal of Contemporary History* 20 (1985), 363–74, Malcolm Brown, *Tommy Goes to War* (Stroud: Tempus, 1999), 104, and Albert Marrin, *The Last Crusade: The Church of England in the First World War* (Durham, NC: Duke University Press, 1974), 164.

27. Arthur Marwick, *The Deluge: British Society and the First World War* (1965), 2nd edition (London: Macmillan Press – now Palgrave Macmillan, 1991), 102–8, and Bernard Waites, *A Class Society at War: England 1914–1918* (Leamington Spa: Berg, 1987), 121–2.

28. Maurice Rickards and Michael Moody, *The First World War: Ephemera, Mementoes, Documents* (London: Jupiter, 1975), 12, and John Walton, 'Leisure Towns in Wartime: The Impact of the First World War in Blackpool and San Sebastian', *Journal of Contemporary History* 31 (1996), 603–18.

29. W. J. Claydon, 'Picture Postcards, 1914–1918, Were the Antithesis of the War in the Trenches', *British History Illustrated* 5 (1978–79), 57–8, and John

Laffin, *World War I in Postcards* (Gloucester: Alan Sutton, 1988), 1–8. See also I. Holt, *Till the Boys Come Home: The Picture Postcards of the First World War* (London: Macdonald and Jones, 1977).

30. Laffin, *World War I in Postcards*, 15–30.

31. Rickards and Moody, *First World War Ephemera*, 66.

32. J. M. Bourne, *Britain and the Great War* (London: Edward Arnold, 1989), 206, J. M. Winter, *The Experience of World War I* (London: Macmillan Press – now Palgrave Macmillan, 1988), 188–9, and Claire Culleton, *Working-Class Culture, Women, and Britain, 1914–1921* (New York: St Martin's Press – now Palgrave Macmillan, 1999), 82.

33. Liddle, *Voices of War*, 72–4, and Rickards and Moody, *First World War Ephemera*, 17, 99.

34. James Bishop, *The Illustrated London News' Social History of the First World War* (London: Angus and Robertson, 1982), 106.

35. DeGroot, *Blighty*, 107–8.

36. Angela Woollacott, *On Her Their Lives Depend: Munitions Workers in the Great War* (Berkeley: University of California Press, 1994), 82, Rickards and Moody, *First World War Ephemera*, 25, and Wilson, *Myriad Faces of War*, 172.

37. Rickards and Moody, *First World War Ephemera*, 23, 100, Wilson, *Myriad Faces of War*, 172, and Haste, *Keep the Home Fires Burning*, 115–16.

38. George Mosse, *Fallen Soldiers: Reshaping the Memory of the World Wars* (Oxford: Oxford University Press, 1990), 126–56.

39. Barbara Jones and Bill Howell, *Popular Arts of the First World War* (New York: McGraw-Hill, 1972), 70–1, and John Ivelaw-Chapman, *The Riddles of Wipers: An Appreciation of the Wipers Times, A Journal of the Trenches* (London: Leo Cooper, 1997), 88.

40. DeGroot, *Blighty*, 220–1, Dewhirst, *Story of a Nobody*, 68, Joanna Bourke, *Dismembering the Male: Men's Bodies, Britain, and the Great War* (Chicago: University of Chicago Press, 1996), 182, and David Bilton, *The Home Front in the Great War* (Barnsley: Pen and Sword, 2004), 153.

41. Richard Cork, *A Bitter Truth: Avant-Garde Art and the Great War* (New Haven: Yale University Press, 1994), 169, MacKenzie, *Propaganda and Empire*, 246, Bourke, *Dismembering the Male*, 141–2, and Bilton, *Home Front*, 189.

42. Jones and Howell, *Popular Arts*, 142–7, MacKenzie, *Propaganda and Empire*, 216–17, Rickards and Moody, *First World War Ephemera*, 95, and Peter Parker, *The Old Lie: The Great War and the Public School Ethos* (London: Constable, 1987), 192.

43. Geoffrey Arundel Whitworth, *The Child's ABC of the War* (G. Allen and Unwin, 1914), Nina MacDonald, *Wartime Nursery Rhymes* (London: Routledge, 1918), 13, 24, and DeGroot, *Blighty*, 217.

44. James Yoxall, *Why Britain Went to War* (London: Cassell and Company, 1914), 5, 8. See also J. Holland Rose, *How the War Came About: Explained to the Young People of All English-Speaking Countries* (London: The Patriotic Publishing Company, 1914), and Frank Johnson, *The King's Call: Why Britain Went to War* (London: Pilgrim Press, 1914).

45. Rev. John Henry Buckeley, *Four Plays for School Children* (London: Routledge, 1917), and Gary S. Messinger, *British Propaganda and the State in the First World War* (Manchester: Manchester University Press, 1992), 92–3.

46. Stuart Sillars, *Art and Survival in First World War Britain* (London: Macmillan Press – now Palgrave Macmillan, 1987), 39–47. See also Thomas Joseph Kehoe, *The Fighting Mascot: The True Story of a Boy Soldier* (New York: Dodd, Mead and Company, 1918), and Frederick Haydn Dimmock, *The Scouts' Book of Heroes* (London: C. A. Pearson, 1919).

47. Philip E. Hager and Desmond Taylor, *The Novels of World War I: An Annotated Bibliography* (New York: Garland, 1981), 339, and Tylee, *Great War and Women's Consciousness*, 33.

48. Paul Fussell, *The Great War and Modern Memory* (New York: Oxford University Press, 1975), 86, and Winter, 'Popular Culture in Wartime Britain,' 336–7.

49. Fuller, *Troop Morale and Popular Culture*, 57, 81–113.

50. Gareth Stedman Jones, 'Working-Class Culture and Working-Class Politics in London, 1879–1900', *Journal of Social History* 7 (1974), 478–9.

51. Fuller, *Troop Morale and Popular Culture*, 95–101, York, *Mud and Stars*, 228.

52. Sylvia Pankhurst, *The Homefront* (1932), reprint (London: Cresset, 1987), 121, and John Brophy and Eric Partridge, *The Long Trail: Soldiers' Songs and Slang, 1914–18* (London: Sphere Books, 1965), 35.

53. Parker, *The Old Lie*, 180, and Fuller, *Troop Morale and Popular Culture*, 38–9.

54. Brophy and Partridge, *The Long Trail*, 15–29, York, *Mud and Stars*, 214, and Charles Carrington, *Soldier from the Wars Returning* (London: Hutchinson, 1965), 148–54. See also Colin Walsh, ed., *Mud, Songs and Blighty: A Scrapbook of the First World War* (London: Hutchinson, 1975).

55. Brown, *Tommy Goes to War*, 63, Brophy and Partridge, *The Long Trail*, 78, and Ivelaw-Chapman, *Riddles of Wipers*, 28–9.

56. Susan Grayzel, *Women's Identities at War* (Chapel Hill: University of North Carolina Press, 1999), 126–7, Brophy and Partridge, *The Long Trail*, 102, 122, and Ivelaw-Chapman, *Riddles of Wipers*, 42–3.

57. Ivelaw-Chapman, *Riddles of Wipers*, 112, Jones and Howell, *Popular Arts*, 64, and Carrington, *Soldier from the Wars Returning*, 97–8. For examples of Bruce Bairnsfather's cartoons, see T. and V. Holt, eds, *The Best Fragments from France* (Cheltenham: Phin Publishing, 1978).

58. Martin Taylor, '*The Open Exhaust* and Some Other Trench Journals of the First World War', *Imperial War Museum Review* 5 (1990), 18–27, and Fuller, *Troop Morale and Popular Culture*, 3–13.

59. Ivelaw-Chapman, *Riddles of Wipers*, 3–10, 48–51, and Malcolm Brown, ed., *The Imperial War Museum Book of the First World War* (London: Sidgwick and Jackson, 1991), 263–71.

60. Ivelaw-Chapman, *Riddles of Wipers*, 101–12, and J. M. Winter, *The Great War and the British People* (London: Macmillan Press – now Palgrave Macmillan, 1985), 286–7.

61. Wilson, *Myriad Faces of War*, 756, and Fuller, *Troop Morale*, 18.

62. Brophy and Partridge, *The Long Trail*, 32, Ivelaw-Chapman, *Riddles of Wipers*, 39, and Fuller, *Troop Morale and Popular Culture*, 137–8.

63. Jay Winter, 'Popular Culture in Wartime Britain,' 330, 346.

8 Remembering and Memorializing the War

1. Paul Fussell, *The Great War and Modern Memory* (New York: Oxford University Press, 1975), and George Mosse, *Fallen Soldiers: Reshaping the Memory of the World Wars* (Oxford: Oxford University Press, 1990).

2. Nick Mansfield, 'Class Conflict and Village War Memorials, 1914–24', *Rural History* 6 (1995), 75, Alan Wilkinson, *The Church of England and the First World War* (London: SPCK, 1978), 170, and Penelope Curtis, 'The Whitehall Cenotaph: An Accidental Monument', *Imperial War Museum Review* 9 (1994), 41.

3. Philip Dutton, 'The Dead Man's Penny: A History of the Next of Kin Memorial Plaque', *Imperial War Museum Review* 3 (1988), 60–8.

4. Peter Liddle, *Voices of War* (London: Leo Cooper, 1988), 207, and John Laffin, *World War I in Postcards* (Gloucester: A. Sutton, 1988), 95.

5. Joanna Bourke, *Dismembering the Male: Men's Bodies, Britain, and the Great War* (Chicago: University of Chicago Press, 1996), 213–20, and Wilkinson, *Church of England and the First World War*, 176.

6. Jay Winter, *Sites of Memory, Sites of Mourning: The Great War in European Cultural History* (Cambridge: Cambridge University Press, 1995), 62–77, and David Cannadine, 'War and Death, Grief and Mourning in Modern Britain', in J. Whaley, ed., *Mirrors of Mortality: Studies in the Social History of Death* (London: Europa, 1981), 228–9.

7. Alan Borg, *War Memorials from Antiquity to the Present* (London: Leo Cooper, 1991), 72–5, and Thomas Laqueur, 'Memory and Naming in the Great War', in John Gillis, ed., *Commemorations: The Politics of National Identity* (Princeton: Princeton University Press, 1994), 153.

8. Mosse, *Fallen Soldiers*, 81–4.

9. Borg, *War Memorials*, 73, and Wilkinson, *Church of England in the First World War*, 302.

10. Laqueur, 'Memory and Naming', 154–9, Borg, *War Memorials*, 128, and Daniel Sherman, 'Bodies and Names: The Emergence of Commemoration in Interwar France', *American Historical Review* 103 (April 1998), 444.

11. Bob Bushaway, 'Name Upon Name: The Great War and Remembrance', in Roy Porter, ed., *Myths of the English* (Cambridge: Polity Press, 1992), 150–1, Cannadine, 'War and Death', 231, and Mosse, *Fallen Soldiers*, 152.

12. Borg, *War Memorials*, 74, Winter, *Sites of Memory, Sites of Mourning*, 98, and Alex King, *Memorials of the Great War in Britain* (Oxford: Berg, 1998), 25.

13. Bourke, *Dismembering the Male*, 236–7.

14. Gaynor Kavanagh, 'Museum as Memorial: The Origins of the Imperial War Museum', *Journal of Contemporary History* 23 (1988), 77–97.

15. Borg, *War Memorials*, 140.

16. Mosse, *Fallen Soldiers*, Introduction, and Geoff Dyer, *The Missing of the Somme* (London: Penguin, 1994), 65.

17. Derek Boorman, *At the Going Down of the Sun: British First World War Memorials* (York: Sessions, 1988), 34–49, King, *Memorials of the Great War*, 176, and Catherine Moriarty, 'Christian Iconography and First World War Memorials', *Imperial War Museum Review* 6 (1991), 69.

18. Richard Cork, *A Bitter Truth: Avant-Garde Art and the Great War* (New Haven: Yale University Press, 1994), 265–6, Mansfield, 'Class Conflict and Village War Memorials', 74, and King, *Memorials of the Great War*, 179.

19. Seth Koven, 'Remembering and Dismemberment: Crippled Children, Wounded Soldiers and the Great War in Great Britain', *American Historical Review* 99 (October 1994), 1185, and Mansfield, 'Class Conflict and Village War Memorials', 77. For veterans' preference for practical memorial projects over monuments, see Douglas Higbee, 'Practical Memory: Organized Veterans and the Politics of Commemoration', in Jessica Meyer, ed., *British Popular Culture and the First World War* (Leiden: Brill, 2008), 197–216.

20. Boorman, *At the Going Down of the Sun*, 115–20, Wilkinson, *Church of England in the First World War*, 296, and Borg, *War Memorials*, 138.

21. Ian Dewhirst, *The Story of a Nobody* (London: Mills and Boon, 1980), 76.

22. Michele Barrett, 'Death and the Afterlife: Britain's Colonies and Dominions', in Santanu Das, ed., *Race, Empire and First World War Writing* (Cambridge: Cambridge University Press, 2011), 302–3, 309–10, 315.

23. David A. Johnson and Nicole F. Gilbertson, 'Commemorations of Imperial Sacrifice at Home and Abroad: British Memorials of the Great War', *The History Teacher* 43 (August 2010), 577–9, 582.

24. Keith Jeffery, *Ireland and the Great War* (Cambridge: Cambridge University Press, 2000), 109–23.

25. Adrian Gregory, *The Silence of Memory: Armistice Day, 1919–1946* (Oxford: Berg, 1994), 11, and Wilkinson, *Church of England in the First World War*, 298.

26. Marcus Clapham, ed., *First World War Poetry* (Ware, Hertfordshire: Wordsworth, 1995), 24.

27. Ibid., iii.

28. Ibid., 48.

29. Gregory, *Silence of Memory*, 29–30, 99–108.

30. Siegfried Sassoon, 'On Passing the New Menin Gate', in Clapham, *First World War Poetry*, 104.

31. Claire Tylee, *The Great War and Women's Consciousness* (Iowa City: University of Iowa Press, 1990), 222.

32. Mansfield, 'Class Conflict and Village War Memorials', 77, and Gregory, *Silence of Memory*, 57.

33. Boorman, *At the Going Down of the Sun*, 33–4, 151, and Dutton, 'Dead Man's Penny', 68.

34. *Times*, 20 October 1925.

35. King, *Memorials of the Great War*, 216–17, and Gregory, *Silence of Memory*, 67–72. See also Janet Watson, *Fighting Different Wars* (Cambridge: Cambridge University Press, 2004), 292–6.

36. Eric Leed, *No Man's Land: Combat and Identity in World War I* (Cambridge: Cambridge University Press, 1979), 191–2, and Samuel Hynes, *A War Imagined: The First World War and English Culture* (New York: Atheneum, 1991), 425.

37. Other anti-war books include: Peregrine Acland, *All Else is Folly* (1929), George Blake, *The Path of Glory* (1929), George Godwin, *Why Stand We Here?* (1930), Terence Mahon, *Cold Feet* (1929), Liam O'Flaherty, *Return of the Brute* (1929), H. M. Tomlinson, *All Our Yesterdays* (1930), Henry Williamson, *The Patriot's Progress* (1930), Ronald Gurner, *Pass Guard at Ypres* (1930), Vernon Bartlett, *No Man's Land* (1930), and Helen Zenna Smith, *Not So Quiet* (1930).

38. Richard Aldington, *Death of a Hero* (New York: Covici-Friede, 1929), 230.

39. Graves, *Good-Bye to All That*, 114.

40. Frederic Manning, *Her Privates, We* (London: P. Davies, 1930), 72.

41. Vera Brittain, *Testament of Youth* (1933), reprint (London: Wideview, 1978), 610.

42. John Stevenson, *British Society, 1914–45* (London: Penguin, 1984), 94.

43. J. B. Priestley, *Margin Released* (London:Heinemann, 1962), 136.

44. Siegfried Sassoon, *Memoirs of an Infantry Officer* (London: Faber and Faber, 1930), 126.

45. Richard Aldington, *Death of a Hero* (New York: Covici-Friede, 1929), 207.

46. Charles Carrington, *Soldier from the Wars Returning* (London: Hutchinson, 1965), 252.

47. Martin Taylor, 'Ivor Gurney: "Only the Wanderer"', *Imperial War Museum Review* 2 (1987), 98–105.

48. Fussell, *Great War and Modern Memory*, 256.

49. Janet Watson, *Fighting Different Wars: Experience, Memory, and the First World War in Britain* (Cambridge: Cambridge University Press, 2004), 185–218, and Leonard V. Smith, *The Embattled Self: French Soldiers' Testimony of the Great War* (Ithaca: Cornell University Press, 2007), 151–64.

50. Bond, *Unquiet Western Front*, 28.

51. Bracco, *Merchants of Hope*, 145–99, and Bergonzi, *Heroes' Twilight*, 195–7.

52. Samuel Hynes, *A War Imagined: The First World War and English Culture* (New York: Atheneum, 1991), 283.

53. Cyril Falls, *War Books: A Critical Guide* (London: P. Davies, 1930), 93.

54. Other books that rejected postwar disillusionment and continued to present the war in a positive light include: Arthur Beverly Baxter, *The Parts Men Play* (1920), Hugh Kimber, *San Fairy Ann* (1927), Ernest Raymond, *The Jesting Army* (1930), Elliot White Spring, *War Birds and Lady Birds* (1931), and C. S. Forester, *The African Queen* (1935).

55. Gregory, *Silence of Memory*, 37.

56. Michael Paris, 'Boys' Books and the Great War', *History Today* (November 2000), 44–9.

57. Michael Paris, 'Enduring Heroes: British Feature Films and the First World War, 1919–1997', in Michael Paris, ed., *The First World War and Popular Cinema* (New Brunswick: Rutgers University Press, 2000), 51–73, and Michael Hammond and Michael Williams, 'Goodbye to All That or Business as Usual?: History and Memory of the Great War in British Cinema', in Hammond and

Williams, eds, *British Silent Cinema and the Great War* (Basingstoke: Palgrave Macmillan, 2011), 1–18.

58. Niall Barr, *The Lion and the Poppy: British Veterans, Politics and Society, 1921–1939* (Westport, CT: Praeger, 2005).

59. J. B. Priestley, *The Lost Generation* (London: Society of Friends, 1930).

60. Gregory, *Silence of Memory*, 152–3, King, *Memorials of the Great War*, 201–4.

61. Wilkinson, *The Church of England in the First World War*, 223.

62. Curtis, 'The Whitechapel Cenotaph', 40.

63. G. D. Sheffield, '"Oh! What a Futile War!": Representations of the Western Front in Modern British Media and Popular Culture', in Ian Stewart and Susan Carruthers, eds, *War, Culture and the Media: Representations of the Military in 20th Century Britain* (Trowbridge: Flicks Books, 1996), 66.

64. Ibid., 55.

65. Gary Sheffield, *Forgotten Victory: The First World War, Myths and Realities* (London: Headline, 2001), 23, and Peter Harrington, 'Religious and Spiritual Themes in British Academic Art during the Great War', *First World War Studies* 2 (October 2011), 150.

66. Emma Hannah, *The Great War on the Small Screen: Representing the First World War in Contemporary Britain* (Edinburgh: Edinburgh University Press, 2009), 148.

67. Jeremy Black, *The Great War and the Making of the Modern World* (London: Continuum, 2011), 227–8, and Douglas Peifer, 'The Past in the Present: Passion, Politics, and the Historical Profession in the German and British Pardon Campaigns', *Journal of Military History* 71 (October 2007), 1107–32.

68. Seumas Milne, 'The First World War: The Real Lessons of This Savage Imperial Bloodbath', *The Guardian*, 16 October 2012, and Toby Helm, Vanessa Thorpe and Philip Oltermann, 'Labour Condemns Michael Gove's "Crass" Comments on First World War', *The Observer*, 4 January 2014.

69. Stephen Heathorn, 'The Mnemonic Turn in the Cultural Historiography of Britain's Great War', *Historical Journal* 48 (December 2005), 1120.

Further Reading

Primary sources

Beckett, I. F. W., *The First World War: The Essential Guide to Sources in the UK National Archives* (Richmond: Public Record Office, 2002).

Brophy, John and Eric Partridge, *The Long Trail: Soldiers' Songs and Slang, 1914–18* (London: Sphere Books, 1965).

Clark, Nicholas, *Memories of the Front: Primary Source Material from the Great War* (Carlton: Erran, 1995).

Darracott, Joseph, *The First World War in Posters* (New York: Dover, 1974).

Gosling, Lucinda, *Brushes and Bayonets: Cartoons, Sketches and Paintings of World War I* (Oxford: Osprey, 2008).

Hamilton, Ian. *500 of the Best Cockney War Stories* (Stroud: Amberley, 2009).

Holt, Ian, *Till the Boys Come Home: The Picture Postcards of the First World War* (London: Macdonald and Jones, 1977).

Imperial War Museum, *Lives of the First World War*. Online site devoted to experience of soldiers and civilians: www.iwm.org.uk/centenary/lives-of-the-first-world-war.

Laffin, John, *World War I in Postcards* (Gloucester: Alan Sutton, 1988).

Liddle, Peter, *Voices of War: Front Line and Home Front* (London: Leo Cooper, 1988).

MacArthur, Brian, *For King and Country: Voices from the First World War* (London: Little, Brown, 2008).

Omissi, David, ed., *Indian Voices of the Great War: Soldiers' Letters, 1914–18* (New York: St Martin's Press – now Palgrave Macmillan, 1999).

Reilly, Catherine, ed., *Scars Upon My Heart: Women's Poetry and Verse of the First World War* (London: Virago, 1981).

Rickards, Maurice and Michael Moody, *The First World War: Ephemera, Mementoes, Documents* (London: Jupiter, 1975).

Rickards, Maurice, *Posters of the First World War* (London: Evelyn, Adams and Mackay, 1968).

Sadler, John and Rosie Serdiville, *Tommy at War: 1914–1918, the Soldiers' Own Stories* (London: Robson Press, 2013).

Silkin, Jon, ed., *The Penguin Book of First World War Poetry* (London: Penguin, 1979).

Tate, Trudi, ed., *Women, Men and the Great War: An Anthology of Stories* (Manchester: Manchester University Press, 1995).

Wainwright, Martin, *Wartime Country Diaries* (London: Guardian Books, 2007).

Ward, Chris, *Living on the Western Front: Annals and Stories, 1914–1919* (London: Bloomsbury, 2013).

York, Dorothea, ed., *Mud and Stars: An Anthology of World War Songs and Poetry* (New York: Holt, 1931).

General and theoretical

Black, Jeremy. *The Great War and the Making of the Modern World* (London: Continuum, 2011).

Bourne, J. M., *Britain and the Great War* (London: Edward Arnold, 1989).

Coker, Christopher, *War and the 20th Century: A Study of War and Modern Consciousness* (London: Brassey's, 1994).

Constantine, Stephen, Maurice W. Kirby, and Mary B. Rose, eds, *The First World War in British History* (London: Edward Arnold, 1995).

DeGroot, Gerard, *Blighty: British Society in the Era of the Great War* (London: Longman, 1996).

Ferguson, Niall, *The Pity of War* (New York: Basic Books, 1999).

Gregory, Adrian. *The Last Great War: British Society and the First World War* (Cambridge: Cambridge University Press, 2008).

Keegan, John, *The Face of Battle* (London: Cape, 1976).

Kern, Stephen, *The Culture of Time and Space, 1880–1918* (Cambridge, MA: Harvard University Press, 1983).

Leed, Eric J., *No Man's Land: Combat and Identity in World War I* (Cambridge: Cambridge University Press, 1979).

Marwick, Arthur, *The Deluge: British Society and the First World War* (1965), 2nd Edition (London: Macmillan Press – now Palgrave Macmillan, 1991).

Robbins, Keith, *The First World War* (New York: Oxford University Press, 1984).

Simmonds, Alan, *Britain and World War I* (New York: Routledge, 2012).

Stevenson, David, *Cataclysm: The First World War as Political Tragedy* (New York: Basic Books, 2004).

Stevenson, John, *British Society, 1914–45* (London: Penguin, 1984).

Strachan, Hew, *The First World War*, revised edition (London: Simon and Schuster, 2014).

Turner, John, ed., *Britain and the First World War* (London: Unwin Hyman, 1988).

Wilson, Trevor, *The Myriad Faces of War: Britain and the Great War, 1914–1918* (Cambridge: Polity Press, 1986).

Winter, Jay, ed., *The Cambridge History of the First World War*, 3 vols (Cambridge: Cambridge University Press, 2014).

Wohl, Robert, *The Generation of 1914* (Cambridge, MA.: Harvard University Press, 1979).

Nationalism and imperialism

Andrews, E. M., *The Anzac Illusion* (Cambridge: Cambridge University Press, 1993).

Cesarani, David, 'An Embattled Minority: The Jews in Britain during the First World War', *Immigrants and Minorities* 8 (1989), 61–81.

Constantine, Stephen, 'Britain and the Empire', in Constantine, *et al.*, eds, *The First World War in British History* (London: Edward Arnold, 1995).

Das, Santanu, *Race, Empire and First World War Writing* (Cambridge: Cambridge University Press, 2011).

Ellenwood, D. C. and S. D. Pradhan, eds, *India and World War I* (New Delhi: Manohar, 1978).

Fitzpatrick, David, ed., *Ireland and the First World War* (Dublin: Trinity History Workshop, 1986).

Grundlingh, Albert, *Fighting Their Own War: South African Blacks and the First World War* (Johannesburg: Raven Press, 1987).

Hodges, Geoffrey, *The Carrier Corps: Military Labor in the East African Campaign of 1914 to 1918* (New York: Greenwood Press, 1986).

Howe, Glenford, 'West Indian Blacks and the Struggle for Participation in the First World War', *Journal of Caribbean History* 28 (1994), 27–62.

Jack, George Morton, 'The Indian Army on the Western Front, 1914–1915: A Portrait of Collaboration,' *War in History* 13 (July 2006).

Jeffery, Keith, *Ireland and the Great War* (Cambridge: Cambridge University Press, 2000).

Jenkinson, Jacqueline, 'The 1919 Race Riots in Britain: A Survey', in Rainer Lotz and Ian Pegg, eds, *Under the Imperial Carpet: Essays in Black History* (Crawley: Rabbit, 1986).

Killingray, David, 'All the King's Men?: Blacks in the British Army in the First World War', in Lotz and Pegg, *Under the Imperial Carpet.*

Levine, Philippa, 'Battle Colors: Race, Sex, and Colonial Soldiery in World War I', *Journal of Women's History* 9 (1998), 104–30.

Lloyd, Anne, 'Between Integration and Separation: Jews and Military Service in World War I Britain,' *Jewish Culture and History* 12 (Summer/Autumn 2011), 41–60.

Matthews, James K., 'World War I and the Rise of African Nationalism: Nigerian Veterans as Catalysts of Change', *Journal of Modern African Studies* 20 (1982), 493–502.

Morrow, John H., *The Great War: An Imperial History* (New York: Routledge, 2004).

Nasson, Bill, 'Why They Fought: Black Cape Colonists and Imperial Wars, 1899–1918,' *International Journal of African Historical Studies* 37 (2004), 55–70.

Panayi, Panikos, *The Enemy in Our Midst* (Oxford: Oxford University Press, 1991).

Page, Melvin, ed., *Africa and the First World War* (London: Macmillan Press – now Palgrave Macmillan, 1987).

Pugsley, Christopher, *Gallipoli: The New Zealand Story* (Auckland: Hodder and Stoughton, 1984).

Stockwell, A. J., 'The War and the British Empire', in John Turner, ed., *Britain and the First World War* (London: Unwin Hyman, 1988).

Tabili, Laura, *'We Ask for British Justice': Workers and Racial Difference in Late Imperial Britain* (Ithaca, NY: Cornell University Press, 1994).

Sex and gender

Adams, M., *The Great Adventure: Male Desire and the Coming of World War I* (Bloomington: Indiana University Press, 1990).

Alberti, Johanna, *Beyond Suffrage: Feminists in War and Peace* (London: Macmillan Press – now Palgrave Macmillan, 1989).

Anderson, Julie, *War, Disability, and Rehabilitation in Britain* (Manchester: Manchester University Press, 2011).

Beddoe, Deirdre, *Back to Home and Duty* (London: Pandora, 1989).

Bourke, Joanna, *Dismembering the Male: Men's Bodies, Britain, and the Great War* (Chicago: University of Chicago Press, 1996).

Boxwell, David A., 'The Follies of War: Cross-Dressing and Popular Theatre on the British Front Lines, 1914–1918,' *Modernism/Modernity* 9 (January 2002), 1–20.

Braybon, Gail and Penny Summerfield, *Out of the Cage: Women's Experiences in Two World Wars* (London: Pandora, 1987).

Carden-Coyne, Ana, *Reconstructing the Body: Classicism, Modernism, and the First World War* (Oxford: Oxford University Press, 2009).

Cohler, Deborah, *Citizen, Invert, Queer: Lesbianism and War in Early 20th-Century Britain* (Minneapolis: University of Minnesota Press, 2010).

Culleton, Claire, *Working Class Culture, Women, and Britain, 1914–1921* (London: St. Martin's Press – now Palgrave Macmillan, 1999).

Dawson, Graham, *Soldier Heroes: British Adventure, Empire and the Imagining of Masculinities* (London: Routledge, 1994).

Gilbert, Sandra, 'Soldier's Heart: Literary Men, Literary Women, and the Great War', *Signs* 8 (Spring 1983), 422–50.

Gould, Jenny, 'Women's Military Service in First World War Britain', in Margaret Higonnet, *et al.*, eds, *Behind the Lines: Gender and the Two World Wars* (New Haven: Yale University Press, 1987).

Grayzell, Susan, *Women's Identities at War: Gender, Motherhood, and Politics in Britain and France during the First World War* (Chapel Hill: University of North Carolina Press, 1999).

———, *Women and the First World War* (Harlow: Pearson, 2002).

Gullace, Nicoletta, 'White Feathers and Wounded Men: Female Patriotism and the Memory of the Great War', *Journal of British Studies* 36 (April 1997), 178–206.

Higonnet, Margaret, Jane Jenson, Sonya Michel, and Margaret Collins Weitz, eds, *Behind the Lines: Gender and the Two World Wars* (New Haven: Yale University Press, 1987).

Kent, Susan Kingsley, *Making Peace: The Reconstruction of Gender in Interwar Britain* (Princeton: Princeton University Press, 1993).

Lee, Janet, *War Girls: The First Aid Nursing Yeomanry in the First World War* (Manchester: Manchester University Press, 2005).

Levine, Philippa, '"Walking the Streets in the Way No Decent Woman Should": Women Police in World War I', *Journal of Modern History* 66 (March 1994), 34–78.

Melman, Billie, ed., *Borderlines: Genders and Identities in War and Peace, 1870–1930* (New York: Routledge, 1998).

Meyer, Jessica, *Men of War: Masculinity and the First World War* (Basingstoke: Palgrave Macmillan, 2012).

Noakes, Lucy, *Women in the British Army: War and the Gentle Sex, 1907–1948* (London: Routledge, 2006).

Ouditt, Sharon, *Fighting Forces, Writing Women: Identity and Ideology in the First World War* (London: Routledge, 1994).

Robert, Krisztina, 'Gender, Class, and Patriotism: Women's Paramilitary Units in First World War Britain', *International History Review* 19 (1997), 52–65.

Smith, Angela K., *Suffrage Discourse in Britain during the First World War* (Aldershot: Ashgate, 2005).

Tylee, Claire M., *The Great War and Women's Consciousness: Images of Militarism and Womanhood in Women's Writings, 1914–64* (Iowa City: University of Iowa Press, 1990).

Vellacott, Jo, 'Feminist Consciousness and the First World War', *History Workshop* 23 (Spring 1987), 81–101.

Watson, Janet, 'Khaki Girls, VADs and Tommy's Sisters: Gender and Class in First World War Britain', *International History Review* 19 (1997), 32–51.

Woollacott, Angela, 'Khaki Fever and Its Control: Gender, Class, Age and Sexual Morality on the British Homefront in the First World War', *Journal of Contemporary History* 29 (April 1994), 325–47.

———, *On Her Their Lives Depend: Munitions Workers in the Great War* (Berkeley: University of California Press, 1994).

Social class and war socialism

Barr, Niall, *The Lion and the Poppy: British Veterans, Politics and Society, 1921–1939* (London: Praeger, 2005).

Bilton, David, *The Home Front in the Great War* (Barnsley: Pen and Sword, 2004).

Boswell, Jonathon and Bruce Johns, 'Patriots or Profiteers?: British Businessmen and the First World War', *Journal of European Economic History* 11 (1982), 423–45.

Bryder, Linda, 'The First World War: Healthy or Hungry?', *History Workshop Journal* 24 (1987), 141–57.

Bush, Julia, *Behind the Lines: East London Labour, 1914–1919* (London: Merlin Press, 1984).

Cannadine, David, *The Decline and Fall of the British Aristocracy* (New Haven: Yale University Press, 1990).

Dewey, Peter, 'Nutrition and Living Standards', in Wall and Winter, *The Upheaval of War*.

Gazeley, Ian and Andrew Newall, 'The First World War and Workin-Class Food Consumption in Britain,' *European Review of Economic History* 17 (2013), 71–94.

Lobell, Steven, 'The Political Economy of War Mobilization: From Britain's Limited Liability to Continental Commitment,' *International Politics* 43 (July 2006), 283–304.

Middlemas, Keith, *Politics in Industrial Society: The Experience of the British System since 1911* (London: Deutsch, 1980).

Pedersen, Susan, 'Gender, Welfare and Citizenship in Britain during the Great War', *American Historical Review* 95 (1990), 983–1006.

Pennell, Catriona, *A Kingdom United: Popular Responses to the Outbreak of the First World War in Britain and Ireland* (Oxford: Oxford University Press, 2012).

Perkin, Harold, *The Rise of Professional Society: England Since 1880* (London: Routledge, 1989).

Reid, Alastair, 'The Impact of the First World War on British Workers', in Wall and Winter, *The Upheaval of War.*

Sheffield, G. D., 'The Effect of the Great War on Class Relations in Britain', *War and Society* 7 (1989), 87–105.

Silbey, David, *The British Working Class and Enthusiasm for War, 1914–1916* (London: Frank Cass, 2005).

Soloway, Richard A., 'Eugenics and Pronatalism in Wartime Britain', in Wall and Winter, *The Upheaval of War.*

Waites, Bernard, *A Class Society at War: England, 1914–1918* (Leamington Spa: Berg, 1987).

Wall, Richard and Jay Winter, eds, *The Upheaval of War: Family, Work and Welfare in Europe, 1914–18* (Cambridge: Cambridge University Press, 1988).

Winter, J. M., *The Great War and the British People* (London: Macmillan Press – now Palgrave Macmillan, 1985).

———, 'The Impact of the First World War on Civilian Health in Britain', *Economic History Review* 30 (1977), 487–507.

Propaganda, censorship, and dissent

Bailey, Charles, 'British Protestant Theologians in the First World War: Germanophobia Unleashed', *Harvard Theological Review* 77 (1984), 195–221.

Demm, E., 'Propaganda and Caricature in the First World War', *Journal of Contemporary History* 28 (1993), 163–92.

Dutton, Philip, 'Moving Images?: The Parliamentary Recruiting Committee's Poster Campaign, 1914–16', *Imperial War Museum Review* 4 (1989), 43–58.

Fraser, Alastair H., Andrew Robertshaw, and Steve Roberts, *Ghosts of the Somme: Filming the Battle, June–July 1916* (Barnsley: Pen and Sword, 2009).

Goudall, Felicity, *A Question of Conscience* (London: Sutton, 1997).

Gullace, Nicoletta, 'Sexual Violence and Family Honor: British Propaganda and International Law during the First World War', *American Historical Review* 102 (June 1997), 714–47.

Haste, Cate, *Keep the Home Fires Burning: Propaganda in the First World War* (London: Allen Lane, 1977).

Hiley, Nicholas, '"The British Army Film," "You!," and "For the Empire": Reconstructed Propaganda Films', *Historical Journal of Films, Radio and TV* 5 (1985), 165–82.

———, ' "Kitchener Wants You," and "Daddy What Did YOU Do In The Great War?": The Myth of British Recruiting Posters,' *Imperial War Museum Review* 11 (1997), 40–58.

Hoover, A. J., *God, Germany and Britain in the Great War: A Study in Clerical Nationalism* (New York: Praeger, 1989).

Horne, John and Alan Kramer, *German Atrocities, 1914: A History of Denial* (London: Yale University Press, 2001).

Lennig, Arthur, 'Hearts of the World,' *Film History* 23 (December 2011), 428–58.

Lipkes, Jeff, *Rehearsals: The German Army in Belgium, August 1914* (Leuven: Leuven University Press, 2007).

Lovelace, Colin, 'British Press Censorship during the First World War', in G. Boyce, ed., *Newspaper History from the 17th Century to the Present Day* (London: Constable, 1978).

Marrin, Albert, *The Last Crusade: The Church of England in the First World War* (Durham, NC: Duke University Press, 1974).

McDermott, James, 'Conscience and the Military Service Tribunals during the First World War,' *War in History* 17 (January 2010), 60–85.

McEwen, John, 'The National Press during the First World War: Ownership and Circulation', *Journal of Contemporary History* 17 (1982), 459–86.

Messinger, Gary S., *British Propaganda and the State in the First World War* (Manchester: Manchester University Press, 1992).

Millman, Brock, *Managing Domestic Dissent in First World War Britain* (London: Frank Cass, 2000).

Monger, David, 'Soldiers, Propaganda and Ideas of Home and Community in First World War Britain,' *Cultural and Social History* 8 (2011), 331–54.

Parker, Peter, *The Old Lie: The Great War and the Public School Ethos* (London: Constable, 1987).

Reeves, Nicholas, *Official British Film Propaganda during the First World War* (London: Croom Helm, 1986).

Sanders, Michael and Philip M. Taylor, *British Propaganda during the First World War, 1914–18* (London: Macmillan Press – now Palgrave Macmillan, 1981).

Wallace, Stuart, *War and the Image of Germany: British Academics* (Edinburgh: John Donald, 1988).

Art and literature

Bergonzi, Bernard, *Heroes' Twilight: A Study of the Literature of the Great War* (London: Constable, 1965).

Bogacz, Ted, '"A Tyranny of Words": Language, Poetry and Antimodernism in England in the First World War', *Journal of Modern History* 58 (1986), 643–68.

Buitenhuis, Peter, *The Great War of Words: British, American, and Canadian Propaganda and Fiction, 1914–1933* (Vancouver: University of British Columbia Press, 1987).

Cecil, Hugh, *The Flower of Battle: How Britain Wrote the Great War* (Steerforth, 1996).

Collins, L. J., *Theatre at War* (London: Macmillan Press – now Palgrave Macmillan, 1994).

Cork, Richard, *A Bitter Truth: Avant-Garde Art and the Great War* (New Haven: Yale University Press, 1994).

Doherty, Charles, 'The War Art of C. R. W. Nevinson', *Imperial War Museum Review* 8 (1993), 48–62.

Eksteins, Modris, *Rites of Spring: The Great War and the Birth of the Modern Age* (New York: Anchor Books, 1989).

Fox, James, 'Fiddling While Rome is Burning: Hostility to Art during the First World War, 1914–1918,' *Visual Culture in Britain* 11 (March 2010), 49–65.

———, 'Traitor Painters: Artists and Espionage in the First World War, 1914–18,' *British Art Journal* 9 (Spring 2009), 62–8.

Fussell, Paul, *The Great War and Modern Memory* (New York: Oxford University Press, 1975).

Goldman, Dorothy, ed., *Women and First World War: The Written Response* (London: Macmillan Press – now Palgrave Macmillan, 1993).

Gough, Paul, *'A Terrible Beauty': British Artists and the First World War* (Bristol: Samson and Co., 2010).

Hager, Philip E. and Desmond Taylor, eds, *The Novels of World War I: An Annotated Bibliography* (New York: Garland, 1981).

Harries, Meirion and Susie, *The War Artists: British Official War Art of the 20th Century* (London: Michael Joseph, 1983).

Harrington, Peter, 'Religious and Spiritual Themes in British Academic Art during the Great War,' *First World War Studies* 2 (October 2011), 145–64.

Haycock, David Boyd, *A Crisis of Brilliance: Five Young British Artists and the Great War* (London: Old Street Publishing, 2009).

Hynes, Samuel, *A War Imagined: The First World War and English Culture* (New York: Atheneum, 1991).

Malvern, Sue, 'War As It Is: The Art of Muirhead Bone, C. R. W. Nevinson, and Paul Nash, 1916–17', *Art History* 9 (1986), 487–515.

Montefiore, Janet, '"Shining Pins and Wailing Shells": Women Poets and the Great War', in Goldman, *Women and World War I*.

Parfitt, George, *Fiction of the First World War* (London: Faber, 1988).

Peters, David, ed., *Wyndham Lewis and the Art of Modern War* (Cambridge: Cambridge University Press, 1998).

Raitt, Suzanne and Trudi Tate, eds, *Women's Fiction and the Great War* (Oxford: Clarendon Press, 1997).

Sillars, Stuart, *Art and Survival in First World War Britain* (London: Macmillan, 1987).

Tate, Trudi, *Modernism, History and the First World War* (Manchester: Manchester University Press, 1998).

Upstone, Robert, *William Orpen: Politics, Sex and Death* (London: Imperial War Museum, 2005).

Viney, Nigel, *Images of Wartime* (Newton Abbot: David and Charles, 1991).

Walsh, Michael, 'C.R.W. Nevinson: Conflict, Contrast and Controversy in Paintings of War,' *War in History* 12 (April 2005), 178–207.

Watkins, Glenn, *Proof through the Night: Music and the Great War* (Berkeley: University of California Press, 2003).

Popular culture

Bracco, Rosa, *Merchants of Hope: Middlebrow Writers in the First World War* (Oxford: Berg, 1993).

Brownlow, Kevin, *The War, the West and the Wilderness* (New York: Knopf, 1979).

Douglas, Roy, *The Great War, 1914–1918: The Cartoonists' Vision* (London: Routledge, 1995).

Fuller, J. G., *Troop Morale and Popular Culture in the British and Dominion Armies, 1914–1918* (Oxford: Oxford University Press, 1990).

Hiley, Nicholas, 'Ploughboys and Soldiers: The Folk Song and the Gramophone in the British Expeditionary Force, 1914–1918', *Media History* 4 (1998), 61–76.

Ivelaw-Chapman, John, *The Riddles of Wipers: An Appreciation of the Wipers Times, A Journal of the Trenches* (London: Leo Cooper, 1997).

Jones, Barbara and Bill Howell, *Popular Arts of the First World War* (New York: McGraw-Hill, 1972).

Low, Rachael, *The History of British Film*, vol. 3: *1914–1918* (1950), reprint (London: Routledge, 1997).

Meyer, Jessica, ed., *British Popular Culture and the First World War* (Leiden: Brill, 2008).

Osborne, John, 'To Keep the Life of the Nation on the Old Line', *Journal of Sport History* 14 (1987), 137–50.

Paris, Michael, *The First World War and Popular Cinema* (New Brunswick: Rutgers University Press, 2000).

Potter, Jane, *Boys in Khaki, Girls in Print: Women's Literary Responses to the Great War* (Oxford: Oxford University Press, 2008).

Roshwald, Aviel and Richard Stites, eds., *European Culture in the Great War: The Arts, Entertainment, and Propaganda, 1914–1918* (Cambridge: Cambridge University Press, 1999).

Saunders, Nicholas, *Matters of Conflict: Material Culture, Memory and the First World War* (London: Routledge, 2004).

Taylor, Martin, '*The Open Exhaust* and Some Other Trench Journals of the First World War', *Imperial War Museum Review* 5 (1990), 18–27.

Veitch, Colin, 'Play Up! Play Up! And Win the War!: Football, the Nation and the First World War', *Journal of Contemporary History* 20 (1985), 363–78.

Science and technology

Barham, Peter, *Forgotten Lunatics of the Great War* (New Haven: Yale University Press, 2004).

Bogacz, Ted, 'War Neurosis and Cultural Change', *Journal of Contemporary History* 24 (1989), 227–56.

Cooter, Roger, 'War and Modern Medicine', in W. F. Bynum, ed., *Companion Encyclopedia of the History of Medicine* (London: Routledge, 1993).

Dean, Eric, 'War and Psychiatry', *History of Psychiatry* 4 (1993), 61–82.

Dewey, Peter, 'The New Warfare and Economic Mobilization', in John Turner, ed., *Britain and the First World War* (London: Unwin Hyman, 1988).

Ellis, J., *The Social History of the Machine Gun* (London: Croom Helm, 1975).

Girard, Marion, *A Strange and Formidable Weapon: British Responses to World War I Poison Gas* (Lincoln: University of Nebraska Press, 2008).

Haber, L. F., *The Poisonous Cloud: Chemical Warfare in the First World War* (Oxford: Clarendon Press, 1986).

Harrison, Mark, *The Medical War: British Military Medicine in the First World War* Oxford: Oxford University Press, 2010).

Hartcup, G., *The War of Invention: Scientific Developments, 1914–1918* (London: Brassey's, 1988).

Koven, Seth, 'Remembering and Dismemberment: Crippled Children, Wounded Soldiers and the Great War in Great Britain', *American Historical Review* 99 (October 1994), 1167–1202.

Leese, Peter, *Shell Shock, Traumatic Neurosis and the British Soldiers of the First World War* (New York: Palgrave Macmillan, 2002).

Loughran, Tracey, 'Shell Shock, Trauma and the First World War: The Making of a Diagnosis and Its Histories,' *Journal of the History of Medicine and Allied Sciences* 67 (January 2012), 94–119.

MacLeod, Roy, 'The Chemists Go to War', *Annals of Science* 50 (1993), 455–81.

Mayhew, Emily, *Wounded: A New History of the Western Front in World War I* (Oxford: Oxford University Press, 2013).

Palazzo, Albert, *Seeking Victory on the Western Front: The British Army and Chemical Warfare in World War I* (Lincoln: University of Nebraska Press, 2000).

Pattison, Michael, 'Scientists, Inventors, and the Military in Britain, 1915–19: The Munitions Inventions Department', *Social Studies of Science* 13 (1983), 521–68.

Pearton, Maurice, *The Knowledgeable State: Diplomacy, War and Technology Since 1830* (London: Burnett Books, 1982).

Pick, Daniel, *War Machine: The Rationalization of Slaughter in the Modern Age* (New Haven: Yale University Press, 1993).

Pisano, Dominick, *Legend, Memory and the Great War in the Air* (Seattle: University of Washington Press, 1992).

Ranft, Bryan, 'The Royal Navy and the War at Sea', in Turner, *Britain and the First World War*.

Terraine, John, *White Heat: The New Warfare, 1914–1918* (London: Sidgwick and Jackson, 1982).

Travers, Tim, *How the War Was Won: Command and Technology in the British Army on the Western Front, 1917–18* (London: Routledge, 1992).
——, *The Killing Ground* (London: Allen and Unwin, 1987).
Vernon, Keith, 'Science and Technology', in Stephen Constantine, ed., *The First World War in British History* (London: Edward Arnold, 1995).
Wohl, Robert, *A Passion for Wings: Aviation and the Western Imagination, 1908–1918* (New Haven: Yale University Press, 1994).

Memory and memorialization

Bond, Brian, *The Unquiet Western Front: Britain's Role in Literature and History* (Cambridge: Cambridge University Press, 2002).
Boorman, Derek, *At the Going Down of the Sun: British First World War Memorials* (York: Sessions, 1988).
Borg, Alan, *War Memorials from Antiquity to the Present* (London: Leo Cooper, 1991).
Bushaway, Bob, 'Name Upon Name: The Great War and Remembrance', in Roy Porter, ed., *Myths of the English* (Cambridge: Polity Press, 1992).
Curtis, Penelope, 'The Whitehall Cenotaph: An Accidental Monument', *Imperial War Museum Review* 9 (1994), 31–41.
Dutton, Philip, 'The Dead Man's Penny: A History of the Next of Kin Memorial Plaque', *Imperial War Museum Review* 3 (1988), 60–8.
Dyer, Geoff, *The Missing of the Somme* (London: Penguin, 1994).
Garfield, John, *The Fallen: A Photographic Journey Through the War Cemetaries and Memorials of the Great War, 1914–1918* (London: Leo Cooper, 1990).
Gregory, Adrian, *The Silence of Memory: Armistice Day, 1919–1946* (Oxford: Berg, 1994).
Heathorn, Stephen, 'Historiographical Review: The Mnemonic Turn in Cultural Historiography of Britain's Great War,' *Historical Journal* 48 (December 2005), 1103–24.
Jalland, Pat, *Death in War and Peace: A History of Loss and Grief in England, 1914–1970* (Oxford: Oxford University Press, 2010).
Kavanagh, Gaynor, 'Museum as Memorial: The Origins of the Imperial War Museum', *Journal of Contemporary History* 23 (1988), 77–97.
King, Alex, *Memorials of the Great War in Britain* (Oxford: Berg, 1998).
Laqueur, Thomas, 'Memory and Naming in the Great War', in John Gillis, ed., *Commemorations: The Politics of National Identity* (Princeton: Princeton University Press, 1994).
Mansfield, Nick, 'Class Conflict and Village War Memorials, 1914–24', *Rural History* 6 (1995), 67–87.
Moriarty, Catherine, 'The Material Culture of Great War Remembrance', *Journal of Contemporary History* 34 (1999), 653–62.
Mosse, George, *Fallen Soldiers: Reshaping the Memory of the World Wars* (Oxford: Oxford University Press, 1990).

Peifer, Douglas, 'The Past in the Present: Passion, Politics, and the Historical Profession in the German and British Pardon Campaigns,' *Journal of Military History* 71 (October 2007), 1107–32.

Sheffield, Gary, *Forgotten Victory: The First World War, Myths and Realities* (London: Headline, 2001).

Todman, Daniel, *The Great War: Myth and Memory* (London: Continuum, 2005).

Watson, Janet, *Fighting Different Wars: Experience, Memory, and the First World War in Britain* (Cambridge: Cambridge University Press, 2004).

Whittingham, Clare, 'Mnemonics for War: Trench Art and the Reconciliation of Public and Private Memory,' *Past Imperfect* 14 (2008), 86–119.

Williams, David, *Media, Memory and the First World War* (Montreal: McGill University Press, 2009).

Winter, Jay, *Sites of Memory, Sites of Mourning: The Great War in European Cultural History* (Cambridge: Cambridge University Press, 1995).

Winter, Jay and Antoine Prost, *The Great War in History: Debates and Controversies* (Cambridge: Cambridge University Press, 2005).

Index

advertisements, 79, 89, 193–5, 204
Africa, 100–3, 107–9, 111–12, 115, 216
agriculture, 13, 67–8
Air Force, 21–3
airplanes, 19, 22–3, 143
alcohol, *see* drink
Aldington, Richard (1892–1962), 74, 172, 219
   Death of a Hero, 60, 82, 153, 220, 221, 226
Allan, Maud (1873–1956), 85
Allatini, Rose (1890–1980)
   Despised and Rejected, 84, 178–9
Anderson, Julie, 73
anti-German violence, 97–8
anti-Semitism, 25, 98, 99
anti-war literature, 140, 151–2, 161, 172–5,
   178–9, 219–22
aristocratic attitudes to the war, 34–5
Armistice Day, 216–19, 224–5
Army, 8–11, 26, 47–9, 70–2, 78–80, 83, 100,
   109–11, 184
Asquith, Herbert Henry (1852–1928),
   Prime Minister (1908–16), 12, 40–1,
   45, 121
atrocity stories, 62, 95, 123–6, 143, 145
attrition, 26–7
Australia, 97, 100–1, 104, 114, 215
avant-garde art, *see* modernism

Baby Week, 43
Bairnsfather, Bruce (1888–1959), 203–4
Barker, Pat, 2, 227
Barham, Peter, 26
Barnett, Corelli, 26, 228
Barrie, James (1860–1937), 147, 156, 179
Basu, Bhupendranath (1856–1924), 108
Beaverbrook, William Maxwell Aitken, Lord
   (1879–1964), 119, 135, 143–4, 167

Belgian refugees, 61, 64, 98–9, 124, 131
Belgium, 32, 34, 59, 62, 96, 99, 101,
   121–2, 123
Belloc, Hilaire (1870–1953), 204
Bennett, Arnold (1867–1931), 35, 120, 123,
   156, 179
Besant, Annie (1847–1933), 108
Billing, Noel Pemberton (1881–1948), 84–5
birth control, 87, 90, 91–2
Blomfield, Reginald (1856–1942), 210–11
Blunden, Edmund (1896–1974), 219, 222
   Undertones of War, 220
Boer War (1899–1902), 9, 12, 16, 31, 43, 96,
   105
Bonar Law, Andrew (1858–1923), 41, 109
Bond, Brian, 2, 5, 26, 223, 228
Bone, Muirhead (1876–1953), 165
Borden, Mary (1886–1968), 175, 220
Botha, Louis (1862–1919), South African
   Prime Minister (1910–19), 105
Bottomley, Horatio (1860–1933), 98, 127,
   136, 204
Boy Scouts, 59, 196, 198, 217
Bridges, Robert (1844–1930), Poet Laureate
   (1913–30), 137, 171
British Army Medical Service (BAMS), 15, 80
British Empire, 99–118
   see also, dominions; Africa; India;
   Middle East
British Empire Union, 102–3, 120, 185
British Instructional Films, 224
British Legion, 218, 224
British National Workers League, 141
Brittain, Vera (1893–1970), 65, 75, 218, 222
   Testament of Youth, 220–1, 226
Brooke, Rupert (1887–1915), 61–2, 155, 170–2
Browne, Stella (1880–1955), 76, 89

Bryce Report, 124–5
Buchan, John (1875–1940), 102, 143, 157, 185, 197
    Greenmantle, 84, 186
Butler, Lady Elizabeth (1846–1933), 162–3

Caine, Hall (1853–1931), 69, 147, 157
Canada, 13, 81, 97, 105–6
Cannadine, David, 34, 50
Carden-Coyne, Ana, 73
Carrington, Charles (1897–1990), 49, 78, 222, 226
cartoons, 17, 24, 27, 37, 46, 72, 121, 123, 125, 134, 193, 203
Cavell, Edith (1865–1915), 61–2, 125–6, 145, 148, 195, 225
cemeteries, 209, 210–12
    see also memorials
Cenotaph, 212, 213, 218, 225
censorship, 76, 90, 110, 133–5, 144, 145, 160–1, 166, 178–9
Central Committee for National Patriotic Organizations (CCNPO), 120
Chamberlain, Austen (1863–1937), 144
Chamberlain, Neville (1869–1940), 160
Chaplin, Charlie (1889–1977), 190
Chesterton, G. K. (1874–1936), 156–7
children, 21, 37, 43, 55, 77, 124, 126, 182, 196–9, 224
Church of England, 90, 137–8, 209
Churchill, Winston (1874–1965), 19, 29, 171, 211
cinema, 65, 103, 125, 133, 145–8, 189–90, 224
Clark, James (1858–1943), 163, 227
class conflict, 31–40, 69–70
Clyde Workers Committee (CWC), 38–9
coalition government, 40–1, 44, 54
Cole, G. D. H. (1889–1959), 53
communications, battlefield, 10
conscientious objectors, 41, 136, 140, 141–2, 162
Cornwell, John (1900–1916), 198
court martials, 83, 111, 228
Crimean War (1853–6), 16
Curzon, George, Lord (1859–1925), 41, 100, 219

Dane, Clemence [Winifred Ashton] (1888–1965), 184
Darwin, Leonard (1850–1943), 43, 96
Dawson, Margaret Damer (1875–1920), 77, 86
Defense of the Realm Act (DORA), 39, 45, 76, 81, 84, 133–4, 144
degeneration, 12, 78, 96
DeGroot, Gerard, 4, 34, 47

Delafield, E. M. (1890–1943)
    The War Workers, 87
Department of Information, 142–4, 146, 165
Department of Scientific and Industrial Research (DSIR), 14
Devonport, Lord (1856–1934), 45
Dicey, A. V. (1835–1922), 6
disabled soldiers, 16, 73–4
disillusionment, 28–9, 56, 91, 152–3, 179, 219–23
dissent, 36–7, 63–4, 105–6, 140–2, 148–9, 157–8, 160–1, 163–5, 178, 218–19
    see also conscientious objectors; pacifism
domesticity, 64–5, 87–90
dominions, 104–7, 114
    see also Australia; Canada; New Zealand; South Africa
dominion soldiers, 81, 83, 100, 105, 106
Doyle, Arthur Conan (1859–1930), 22, 80, 120, 127, 156–7, 185, 210
drink, 37, 44, 192

Easter Rising, 113–14
Eden, Anthony (1897–1977), 49
education, 28, 55, 196
Elgar, Sir Edward (1857–1934), 158
Eliot, T. S. (1888–1965), 179, 180
Ellis, H. Havelock (1859–1939), 76, 78
espionage, 28, 81, 97, 184–6
eugenics, 43, 78, 96, 114
Evans, Richard, 229

Fawcett, Millicent Garrett (1847–1929), 62–3, 67, 88, 92
film, *see* cinema
food, 44–6, 67, 88
    see also drink
Ford, Ford Maddox (1873–1939), 220
France, 10, 34, 78
Frankau, Gilbert (1884–1952), 172
Freud, Sigmund (1856–1939), 25, 28
Fussell, Paul, 3, 5, 83–4, 175, 180, 199

Gallipoli, Battle of, 105–7, 136, 219
Galsworthy, John (1869–1933), 120, 156, 179
Gandhi, Mohandas (1869–1948), 108, 118
George V (1865–1936), King (1910–36), 17, 54–5, 109, 192, 199, 211
Germany, 10–12, 17, 19, 20, 27, 38, 46, 96, 100–1, 122
Gertler, Mark (1891–1939), 165
Gilbert, Sandra, 73, 75
Gosse, Edmund (1849–1928), 155, 157–8
Gould, Nat (1857–1919), 183
Gove, Michael, 229

gramophones, 189, 194
Graves, Robert (1895–1985), 48, 150, 154, 172, 219
  Good-Bye to All That, 153, 220
Grenfell, Julian (1888–1915), 101, 171–2
Griffith, D. W. (1880–1948), 147
  Hearts of the World, 125
Gurney, Ivor (1890–1937), 222

Haggard, H. Rider (1856–1925), 73, 127, 157
Hague Convention, 123
Haig, Sir Douglas (1861–1928), 9, 18, 19, 227
Hall, Radclyffe (1886–1943), 91
  The Well of Loneliness, 86, 90
Hamilton, Mary (1884–1966)
  Dead Yesterday, 178
Hardie, Keir (1856–1915), 31, 32, 36, 37
Hardy, Thomas (1840–1928), 156–7, 159, 174
Haverfield, Evelina (1867–1920), 70, 86
Hawkins, Anthony Hope (1863–1933), 157
Hay, Ian [John Hay Beith] (1876–1952), 48, 183
  The First Hundred Thousand, 184, 186
Heathorn, Stephen, 229
Henderson, Arthur (1863–1935), 32, 41, 54
Henty, G. A. (1832–1902), 59, 73, 198
Hiley, Nicholas, 149
historiography of the war, 1–5, 26, 30, 58–9, 73–5, 84, 92, 180, 220, 228
homosexuality, 59, 81–7
  see also lesbianism
Horne, John, 123
housing, 55–6
Hughes, William (1864–1952), Australian Prime Minister (1915–23), 118
humor, 190, 200–4
  see also cartoons
Hunt, Tristram, 229
Hunt, Violet (1866–1942), 75
Hynes, Samuel, 1, 169, 223

illegitimacy, 77–8
Imperial War Museum, 213
India, 100, 107, 216
India War Memorial, 216
Indian National Congress, 107, 108, 118
Indian soldiers, 101, 108–9, 110–11, 112, 116
industrial production, 11–15
  see also munitions workers
infant mortality, 43–4, 46
internment of enemy aliens, 97
Ireland, 101, 113–15, 123, 149, 216
Irish National War Memorial, 216

Jagger, Charles Sargeant (1885–1934), 218–19
Jones, David (1895–1974), 180

Kaiser, *see* William II
Kaye-Smith, Sheila (1887–1956)
  Little England, 176
Keegan, John, 3, 48
Kemp-Welch, Lucy (1869–1958), 128, 162
Kennington, Eric (1888–1960), 165–6
Kent, Susan Kingsley, 73–4, 91
Kernahan, Coulson (1858–1943), 170
khaki fever, 76–7
Kipling, Rudyard (1865–1936), 17, 59, 73, 156–8, 170, 176–7, 183, 195, 211
  The Eyes of Asia, 103
Kirchner, Raphael (1876–1917), 79
Kitchener, Horatio, Lord (1850–1916), War Minister (1914–16), 9, 17, 18, 80, 96, 100, 128, 134, 148, 195
Kramer, Alan, 123

Labour Party, 31, 32, 37, 43, 54, 142
Lasswell, Harold, 103, 120
Lauder, Harry (1870–1950), 131, 188
Lawrence, D. H. (1885–1930), 74, 179
  The Rainbow, 76, 85, 158
Lawrence, T. E. (1888–1935), 84, 104
League of Nations, 115, 118, 142, 214, 222
Leed, Eric, 24, 47
LeQueux, William (1864–1927), 124, 183, 184–5
lesbianism, 85–7
Lewis, Percy Wyndham (1882–1957), 24, 156, 169, 179
Lloyd George, David (1863–1945), Minister of Munitions (1915–16), Prime Minister (1916–22), 13, 18, 37, 38, 40–1, 53, 54, 56, 65, 106, 118, 135, 143, 144, 148
Lodge, Sir Oliver (1851–1940), 210
logistics, 10
Londonderry, Edith, Marchioness of (1879–1959), 71–2
lost generation, 50–1, 221–2
Lusitania, HMS, 20, 34, 97, 124, 125–6, 148, 190
Lutyens, Edwin (1869–1944), 210, 212, 216

Macaulay, Rose (1881–1958), 68
  Non-Combatants and Others, 178
MacDonald, Ramsay (1866–1937), 32, 36, 56–7
Machen, Arthur (1863–1947), 178
McCrae, John (1872–1918), 217–18
McDermott, James, 142

McNeile, Cyril 'Sapper' (1888–1937), 183–4, 186
Manners, Lady Diana (1892–1954), 50
Manning, Frederic (1882–1935), 226
  Her Privates, We, 220
Marwick, Arthur, 3, 4, 58–9
masculinity, 59–61, 73–5, 128, 184
Masefield, John (1878–1967), 121, 151
Massey, William (1856–1925), New Zealand Prime Minister (1912–25), 81
Masterman, C. F. G. (1874–1927), 50, 52, 56, 120–1, 143, 156, 197
Mata Hari [Margaretha Zelle] (1876–1917), 81, 185
maternity, 43–4, 88–90
medicine, 15–16, 80
memorials, 107, 208, 212–16
Middle East, 103–4, 111, 115, 216
Middleton, Jim (1878–1962), 43
Milner, Alfred, Lord (1854–1925), 41, 100, 143
Ministry of Food, 45, 146
Ministry of Information, 102, 144–5, 148, 167, 169
Ministry of Munitions, 13, 14, 40–1, 68
Ministry of Pensions, 25, 42
modernism, 154, 156, 168–9, 179–80
Money, Leo Chiozza (1870–1944), 30
Monkhouse, Allan (1858–1936), 161
Montagu, Edwin (1879–1924), Secretary of State for India (1917–22), 117–18
Mosse, George, 213, 218
Munitions Inventions Department (MID), 14, 15, 27
munitions workers, 68–70
Murray, Gilbert (1866–1957), 122, 156
museums, 161–2, 213
music, 158–9, 187–9, 200–2
music halls, 187–8
mutinies, 108, 111

Nash, Paul (1889–1946), 154, 165–6, 169, 179
National Union of Women's Suffrage Societies (NUWSS), 62
National War Aims Committee (NWAC), 143–4, 145
nationalism, 93–5, 97, 106, 113, 118
Navy, 19–21, 71, 103, 133, 188
Nevinson, C. R. W. (1889–1946), 165–6, 179
New Zealand, 81, 100, 104, 215
Newbolt, Sir Henry (1862–1938), 158, 198
newspapers, 97–8, 134–7, 140, 144
Nietzsche, Friedrich (1844–1900), 155
Northcliffe, Alfred Harmsworth, Lord (1865–1922), 135, 143, 144

novels, 28, 60–1
  adventure novels, 103, 183–6, 198–9
  homefront novels, 175–8
  romance novels, 61, 66, 67, 186–7
  see also anti-war literature
nurses, 61, 66–7, 75, 106, 112, 125, 126, 151, 187, 193, 197

Oppenheim, E. Phillips (1866–1946), 184
Orczy, Emma, Baroness (1865–1947), 60
Orpen, William (1878–1931), 168
Osler, Sir William (1849–1919), 8
Ottoman Empire, 101, 125, *see also* Middle East
Owen, Wilfred (1893–1918), 2, 4, 18, 25, 74, 172–5, 204, 208, 227
Oxenham, John [William Arthur Dunkerley] (1852–1941), 4, 170–1, 175

pacifism, 63–4, 141–2, 178, 224–5
painting, 18, 156, 161–9, 227
Pankhurst, Christabel (1880–1958), 62–3, 71, 88
Pankhurst, Emmeline (1858–1928), 62–3, 65
Pankhurst, Sylvia (1882–1962), 36, 45, 63, 70, 77, 173, 201
  The Home Front, 33, 75
Parker, Sir Gilbert (1862–1932), 121
Parliament, 36, 53–4, 56, 74, 86, 91, 113, 121, 141, 144, 169
Parliamentary Recruiting Committee (PRC), 126–31, 149
Patch, Harry, 1
Pennell, Catriona, 34, 114, 137
Pethick-Lawrence, Emmeline (1867–1954), 63, 70
photography, 23, 47, 66, 123, 126, 145
poetry, 18, 35, 56, 69, 79, 124, 157, 169–75, 202–5, 217, 227
poison gas, 17–18, 125, 168
Ponsonby, Arthur (1871–1946), 141, 152
Pope, Jessie (1868–1941), 4, 174–5
postcards, 60, 79, 101, 163, 192–3, 209
posters, 34, 44, 60, 69, 88, 101, 122, 126, 127–31, 148–9, 190
Pound, Ezra (1885–1972), 156, 179
Press Bureau, 134
Priestley, J. B. (1894–1984), 59, 221, 224–5
propaganda, 33, 62, 89, 94, 101, 103–4, 119–53, 162, 165, 189, 220, 227
prostitution, 76, 78, 79–80, 81, 98
psychiatry, 25–6

race riots, 117
racism, 95–6, 98, 101, 110–12, 116–18

Raemaekers, Louis (1869–1956), 125, 131
rationing, 45–6
recruitment, 34, 60, 126–31
religion, 24, 76, 102, 122, 137–40, 163, 174
Reuters News Agency, 135
Rhondda, David Thomas, Lord (1856–1918),
    45–6
Rivers, W. H. R. (1864–1922), 25
Roberts, Robert, 32, 34, 47, 53
Robinson, William Heath (1872–1944), 27–8
Rosenberg, Isaac (1890–1918), 172–3
Rowntree, Seebohm (1871–1954), 42
Royal Academy, 162
royal family, 97, 163, 208, *see also* George V
Royal Society, 14, 17
Royal Society of British Artists, 162
Ruck, Berta (1878–1978), 85
    The Girls at His Billet, 187
    The Land Girl's Love Story, 4, 67–8
rural society, 33, 114
Russell, Bertrand (1872–1970), 140
Russia, 10, 123
Russian Revolution, 39, 45, 53, 71, 142, 144

Salisbury, James Cecil, Marquess of
    (1861–1947), 80
Sandes, Flora (1876–1956), 71, 186
Sargent, John Singer (1856–1925), 18, 167–8
Sassoon, Siegfried (1886–1967), 4, 25, 74,
    140, 170, 172–5, 204, 218, 220, 222
Sayce, A. H. (1845–1933), 95
Scharlieb, Mary (1845–1930), 81
scientists, 14–15, 27–8
Second World War, 90, 152, 225
sexual attitudes, 58, 72, 75–81, 83, 86–7
sexual violence, 62, 124–5
Shakespeare, William, 155–6, 159
Shaw, George Bernard (1856–1950), 29, 159,
    162, 165, 225
    Augustus Does His Bit, 161
    Common Sense about the War, 140, 157
    Heartbreak House, 161
Sheffield, Gary, 2, 5, 227, 228, 229
shell-shock, 24–6, 73, 173, 180, 221,
    227, 228
Sheppard, Richard (1880–1937), 219
Sherriff, R. C. (1896–1975)
    Journey's End, 223
Silbey, David, 33, 34
Simkins, Peter, 26
Singapore, 108
Sinclair, May (1863–1946), 157, 177
    The Tree of Heaven, 178
Sinn Fein, 114, 115, 149
Smith, F. E. (1872–1930), 134

Smith, Helen Zenna [Evadne Price]
    (1896–1985)
    Not So Quiet, 75, 76
Smith, Leonard, 222
Smith-Dorrien, Sir Horace (1858–1930), 160
Smuts, Jan (1870–1950), 22, 100, 105, 106
social purity campaigns, 76–7, 81, 84–5, 160
social welfare policies, 42–7, 54–6
Soldiers' and Sailors' Families Association
    (SSFA), 42
Somme, Battle of the, 10, 18–19, 27, 135–6,
    146, 151, 162–3, 191, 211
Sorley, Charles Hamilton (1895–1915), 172
South Africa, 105, 109, 112, 143, 216–17
South African Native Labor Contingent
    (SANLC), 109–10, 112, 116
South African Native National Congress
    (SANNC), 108
Spencer, Stanley (1891–1959), 169, 179
spies and spy literature, *see* espionage
spiritualism, 210, *see also* superstition
sports, 34, 73, 183, 189, 190–1
Stone, Christopher Reynolds (1882–1965), 49
Stopes, Marie (1880–1958), 78
    Married Love, 87, 91
Street, G. S. (1867–1936), 29, 175
strikes, 31, 38–9, 45, 53, 57
Studdert-Kennedy, G. A. (1883–1929), 94,
    138–9
submarines, *see* u-boats
suffrage, 53–4, 72, 91
Suffragettes, 33, 62, 63, 65, 74
superstition, 24
Sutherland, Millicent, Duchess of
    (1867–1955), 70

tanks, 9, 18–19
Tawney, R. H. (1880–1962), 149
Terraine, John, 26, 228
theater, 159–61, 200–1
Thomas, Hugh Owen (1834–1891), 15
Tomb of the Unknown Warrior, 212
Tomlinson, H. M. (1873–1958)
    Waiting for Daylight, 48
trade unions, 31, 37, 54, 68
Trades Union Congress (TUC), 32, 54
trench warfare, 8–9, 11, 26, 73, 150–1,
    220, 228
troop journals, 149, 172, 201, 203–5

u-boats, 20–1, 45, 97, 146
Union for Democratic Control (UDC), 141
United States of America, 13, 20, 27, 114, 115,
    121, 190
universities, 15–16, 88, 91, 122, 140, 214

venereal disease, 79–81
Versailles Peace Conference, 107, 117
Vietnam War, 208
Voluntary Aid Detachment (VAD), 66–7, 70

Wadsworth, Edward (1889–1949), 156, 169
Walpole, Hugh (1884–1941), 151
war artists, 165–9
war babies, 77
War Graves Commission, 210–11
War Memorials Committee, 167
Ward, Mrs. Humphry (1851–1920), 29, 121,
    157, 177, 179, 183
Watson, Janet, 222
Webb, Sidney (1859–1947), 41, 54
Weizmann, Chaim (1874–1952), 15
Wellington House (Propaganda Bureau),
    120–1, 123, 135, 156, 165
    see also Department of Information,
    Ministry of Information
Wells, H.G. (1866–1946), 12, 14, 27, 29, 148, 156
    Mr. Britling Sees It Through, 4, 59, 100, 177
    The War that Will End War, 122, 157
West, Arthur Graeme (1891–1917), 172
West Indian soldiers, 83, 109, 111, 117
white feather campaign, 60, 64, 74
Wilde, Oscar (1854–1900), 59, 84–5
William II (1859–1941), German Emperor
    (1888–1918), 17, 37, 127, 138, 157, 159,
    188, 198

Williamson, Henry (1895–1977), 222
    The Wet Flanders Plain, 220
Wilson, Trevor, 20, 40
Wilson, Woodrow (1856–1924),
    United States President (1913–21),
    117, 142, 144
Winnington-Ingram, Arthur (1858–1946),
    Bishop of London (1901–39), 43,
    138–9
Winter, Jay, 90, 180
Wohl, Robert, 137
Women's Freedom League, 64
Women's International League for Peace and
    Freedom, 63, 141
Women's Land Army, 66, 67–8
women's military auxiliaries, 70–2, 86, 148
Women's Peace Conference, 63
women police, 77, 86
Women's Social and Political Union
    (WSPU), 63
women war workers, 65–70, 89–90, 92
Woodville, R. Caton (1856–1927), 162, 163
Woolf, Virginia (1882–1941), 158, 179, 180
working-class attitudes to the war, 32–4

Yealland, Lewis (1885–1954), 25
Ypres, Battle of, 12, 211

Zangwill, Israel (1864–1926), 156
Zeppelins, 21, 28, 145, 160